The book is simply the reference as no other book was published on this subject.

Amadou Soumano, *Deputy Director & Lead Counsel, Africa Finance Corporation*

For any project finance professional working in Africa this is a very useful book that provides a comprehensive overview with many examples of projects closed on the continent.

Nivaldo Pignot, *General Counsel, AMEA Power*

This is a must read for anyone conducting or acting on the African project finance market.

Guy Stéphane Gbla, *Vice Président, Ecobank Capital*

Legal and Financial Aspects of Project Finance in Africa is a groundbreaking and indispensable resource for anyone involved in the development and financing of infrastructure projects on the continent. As the only book dedicated to this critical subject, it fills a significant gap in the literature by providing comprehensive examples of projects and practical advice from the initial development stages through to financing.

Fatmi Squalli, *Group Head of Structured and Project Finance, Attijaiwafabank*

Clear, practical, and profoundly insightful, this book sets the standard for understanding and succeeding in project finance across Africa. A definitive resource for investors, policymakers, practitioners and anyone involved in infrastructure projects on the continent.

Me Gorgon Feliho, *Avocat (France) and Solicitor (England & Wales), Chief Legal Counsel at the African Development Bank*

Legal and Financial Aspects of Project Finance in Africa is the definitive guide in its field, offering readers the tools and knowledge they need to successfully manage and finance infrastructure projects in one of the world's most dynamic and challenging environments.

Mylène Junius, *General Counsel, Eranove*

Legal and Financial Aspects of Project Finance in Africa

This book offers a comprehensive analysis of the specifics of project financing in Africa and suggests how to structure and operate those projects in an emerging continent.

Infrastructure development in Africa is essential to meet the needs of the population and is a major lever for economic and social development. Financing solutions exist to offset the limited investment capacity of African sovereign States, particularly through involving the private sector and project financing. In view of the challenges and specific features of the African continent, this book looks at the ways in which project financing is used in the region. Describing the structuring of infrastructure projects from inception to development and financing and then construction, the book offers insights into African legal frameworks and drafting of financing contracts, and preparation of financial models. It also covers management of disputes and the principles of bankability. Offering a global yet harmonised view of applicable regulatory frameworks, the book is a practical and comprehensive guide to project finance and business law in Africa.

This book will be of interest to practitioners, researchers and students in the field of finance law, business and banking law and law in Africa.

Boris Martor, a graduate of the DJCE and Panthéon-Sorbonne University, is a Bird&Bird partner and has worked in the infrastructure sector in Europe and Africa for over 25 years. He teaches at the Universities of Paris Assas and Sorbonne Paris Nord and as part of training courses at the École des Mines Paris Tech.

Ousmane Diawara, a graduate of the École des Mines de Nancy, has been working for over 15 years with public and private players in the development and financing of infrastructure projects, particularly in Africa. He gives numerous training courses on this subject.

Routledge Studies on Law in Africa Studies

Social and Economic Rights in Africa
International and Public Law Perspectives
Nsongurua Udombana

Financial Inclusion Regulatory Practices in SADC
Addressing prospects and challenges in the 21st Century
Edited by Howard Chitimira and Tapiwa Victor Warikandwa

The African Continental Free Trade Area Agreement
The Development of a Rules-Based Trading Order
Kofi Kufuor

Corporate Governance in Africa
Victor Ediagbonya

Legal and Financial Aspects of Project Finance in Africa
Boris Martor and Ousmane Diawara

For more information about this series, please visit: www.routledge.com/Routledge-Studies-on-Law-in-Africa/book-series/RSOLIA

Legal and Financial Aspects of Project Finance in Africa

Boris Martor and Ousmane Diawara

Routledge
Taylor & Francis Group
LONDON AND NEW YORK

First published 2026
by Routledge
4 Park Square, Milton Park, Abingdon, Oxon OX14 4RN

and by Routledge
605 Third Avenue, New York, NY 10158

Routledge is an imprint of the Taylor & Francis Group, an informa business

British Library Cataloguing-in-Publication Data
A catalogue record for this book is available from the British Library

ISBN: 978-1-041-01903-9 (hbk)
ISBN: 978-1-041-01905-3 (pbk)
ISBN: 978-1-003-61689-4 (ebk)

DOI: 10.4324/9781003616894

Typeset in Times New Roman
by Apex CoVantage, LLC

Contents

Preface

It would have taken some courage, or temerity, to tackle the task of writing a book on project finance in Africa, given the vast and heterogeneous nature of the subject, the sometimes-elusive rules and the diversity of projects that make it impossible to have a perfectly clear vision. In other words, the uncertain scope of "project finance", combined with its shifting content and subject matter, made the challenge of systematising it particularly daunting.

Boris Martor and Ousmane Diawara were courageous enough to take up the challenge, and it's fair to say that they have risen to the challenge.

This is a fine, clear and rigorous book on the development, financing and monitoring of infrastructure projects in Africa. The book is aimed at a wide audience of legal practitioners, bankers, developers, academics and students. As the first book on the subject to focus exclusively on Africa and based on the authors' long experience in the field, it hits its target perfectly.

Project financing and public-private partnerships represent, on the African continent and in all their diversity, a major vector for development and an essential contribution to Africa's economic growth. They are a key phenomenon in business life and a cornerstone of local geostrategy.

Given this importance, it is crucial that projects are designed, structured and then implemented under the best possible conditions of legal and financial security.

Securing this requires in-depth, global knowledge of the sector, its environment and its prerequisites. Faced with this need, the role of academics and practitioners is to compile, collate, systematise and explain data. There are very few, if any, French-language works devoted specifically to the subject covered in this book. Some of them are no longer up to date with a subject that is constantly evolving, given the economic, legal and, now, health context in which it is evolving.

With almost 25 years' experience in this field, Boris Martor and Ousmane Diawara offer the reader a wealth of knowledge and points of reference, illuminated by a sharp operational vision that is particularly valuable.

The subject is dealt with comprehensively but with great intellectual rigor by the authors, who do not fail to defend their legal convictions or innovative ideas with finesse and humility.

Boris Martor and Ousmane Diawara's clear, didactic plan takes the reader on a long journey through project financing, from its conceptual aspects to its economic and financial dimensions, via institutional and legal requirements.

The authors have produced an exemplary work which, through a resolutely practical, concrete and technical approach, provides food for thought. It will undoubtedly stimulate doctrine on this subject, at a time when it is essential to anticipate and capture developments, and when it is crucial to bring thinking to the intersection of operational and professional concerns on the one hand, and conceptual reflections on the other.

Boris Martor and Ousmane Diawara's book, which in a way revisits the traditional dialogue between theory and practice, law and economics, standards and figures, is therefore to be welcomed. I wish it all the success it deserves. It is an important contribution to our knowledge of the contemporary dynamics of public-private partnerships around the world.

Stéphane BRACONNIER
Chairman, Paris-Panthéon-Assas University

Foreword

Why a book on project financing in Africa?

Infrastructure development is vital for the African continent. Not only is it necessary to meet the essential needs of the population, but it is also a lever for growth and economic and social development for every country on the continent.

Infrastructure development must remain a priority for African governments, as well as for all the donors already present on the continent. These countries have invested a great deal in the sector in recent years but not enough to make up for the structural deficit in infrastructure, while at the same time needs are increasing very rapidly. In 2020, the AfDB estimated annual needs at between USD 137 and 177 billion.[1] This deficit is the result of an accumulation of investment shortfalls over a number of years, and it will continue to grow as long as investment falls short of requirements. The continent's population is set to double between now and 2050, and it will be concentrated in cities, which are expected to be home to up to 1.3 billion people, compared with 472 million today. The growing urbanisation of Africa's population is a real challenge for existing and future infrastructures. All infrastructure sectors need massive support, whether energy, transport, water and sanitation, ICTs or social infrastructure. Infrastructure financing solutions exist to make up this shortfall, but they need to be deployed more widely across the continent, otherwise demographic suffocation and limited economic development will result.[2]

At the same time, infrastructure development must take account of the increasingly pressing imperatives of climate change and the growing need to build and develop living environments that are highly resilient and sustainably respectful of the environment. These imperatives have become even more acute since the onset of the Covid-19 global health crisis, with a significant drop in foreign investment in Africa.[3] Economic growth models in both developed and developing economies

1 ICA c/o AfDB, "Trends in infrastructure financing in Africa – 2019–2020", *ICA Report*, 2022, p. 29.

2 For more perspectives, see also L. Bergala, "Prospective 2021, Rétrospective 2020 l'Afrique a besoin de financer ses infrastructures", *Revue Banque*, no. 851, January 2021.

3 See the UNCTAD World Investment Report 2021 and https://unctad.org/fr/news/les-flux-dinvestissement-vers-lafrique-significativement-affectes-par-la-pandemie.

need to be thoroughly rethought. The coronavirus crisis has highlighted the continent's unexpected capacities in terms of digital transition (with the digitisation of government services proceeding apace), but it has also highlighted the limits of current growth drivers and the need to re-examine current public policies and public infrastructure development programmes in the years ahead.

Although African governments are still the main investors, their investment capacity is limited by their budgets, which cannot cover all their needs. It is therefore necessary to mobilise all sources of funding, including the private sector, which has an important role to play on the continent. Private investors have been financing the ICT sector in Africa for a long time. Other sectors, notably energy projects, are receiving more and more private funding. This trend needs to be endorsed, encouraged and strengthened so that private investors can play a greater part in filling the gap. This will necessarily involve the liberalisation of certain sectors and the willingness of governments to open up to private investment. But it also means that infrastructure projects must meet their requirements in terms of business model, structuring, security and financial profitability.

Investment in infrastructure should also serve as an opportunity to develop a low-carbon economic and social model. In the face of climate change, Africa can play a decisive role, firstly because of its potential for producing low-carbon energy, such as solar, wind and hydro power, and secondly because the continent is the most exposed to the consequences of climate change. Indeed, Africa is particularly vulnerable to the proliferation of these problems: of the ten cities most exposed to extreme climatic events, eight are located in Africa.[4] The infrastructure choices made by governments and financial institutions will determine the continent's ability to combat climate change and to build resilience and adaptation. They will also have an impact on the climate challenges faced by the planet, as Africa will be one of the last regions to industrialise.

Faced with these issues and challenges, structuring projects using project finance is undoubtedly a preferred way of mobilising the capacities of investors and private sector players to finance and build the infrastructure that is lacking and sustainable on the continent. Project finance is a technique known throughout the world for developing infrastructure by mobilising private capital. Given the difficulties facing the African continent, its use, while desirable, is still too low in terms of volume and number of projects.

This book attempts to take account of the key issues involved in financing infrastructure projects in Africa and to address the legal, financial and operational problems that need to be considered when setting up these projects. It aims to provide solutions for practitioners and to serve as a tool for building the capacity of national players in the field. It also fills a gap by being one of the few books dedicated to the financing of infrastructure projects in Africa written in English.

4 Report by Verisk Maplecroft, "Climate change vulnerability index", 2018.

Acknowledgements

The authors would like to thank Esther Amega, Gael Tanguy, Jalal El Ahdab, Mohinder Nagra and Manale El Idrissi for all their help and support in the preparation of this book.

Abbreviations

AfDB	African Development Bank
AfreximBank	African Export-Import Bank
ALSF	African Legal Support Facility
AREI	Africa Renewable Energy Initiative
AU	African Union
BOAD	West African Development Bank
BOOT	Build Own Operate Transfer
BOT	Build Operate Transfer
CCJA	Common Court of Justice and Arbitration
CEMAC	Central African Economic and Monetary Community
COD	Commercial Operation Date
CTF	Clean Technology Fund
DBFO	Design Build Finance Operate
DBSA	Development Bank of Southern Africa
DFI	Development Finance Institution
DSCR	Debt Service Coverage Ratio
EAAIF	Emerging Africa and Asia Infrastructure Fund
EBRD	European Bank for Reconstruction and Development
ECA	Export Credit Agencies
ECOWAS	Economic Community of West African States
EGR	Effective Global Rate
EIB	European Investment Bank
EPC	Engineering Procurement Construction
ESG	Environmental Social and Governance
EU	European Union
GDP	Gross Domestic Product
GEEREF	Global Energy Efficiency and Renewable Energy Fund
ICA	Infrastructure Consortium for Africa
ICT	Information and Communication Technologies
IFC	International Finance Corporation
IFI	International Financial Institutions
IFRS	International Financial Reporting Standards
IPP	Independent Power Producer

IPPF	Infrastructure Project Preparation Facility
IRR	Internal Rate of Return
JBA	Joint Bidding Agreement
JDA	Joint Development Agreement
kWh	kilowatt-hour
MASEN	Moroccan Agency for Solar Energy
MCC	Millennium Challenge Corporation
MMR	Major Maintenance Renewal
MoU	Memorandum of Understanding
NEPAD	New Partnership for Africa's Development
NPV	Net Present Value
NREP	National Rural Electrification Programme
O&M	Operation and Maintenance
OECD	Organisation for Economic Cooperation and Development
OHADA	Organisation for the Harmonisation of Business Law in Africa
PCG	Partial Credit Guarantee
PIDA	Programme for Infrastructure Development in Africa
PIDG	Private Infrastructure Development Group
PPA	Power Purchase Agreement
PPF	Project Preparation Facilities
PPFN	Project Preparation Facilities Network
PPIAF	Public-Private Infrastructure Advisory Facility
PPP	Public-Private Partnerships
PRG	Partial Risk Guarantee
RCCM	Trade and Personal Property Credit Register
SADC	Southern African Development Community
SPV	Special Purpose Vehicle or Project Company
TAF	Technical Assistance Facility
TDB	Trade and Development Bank
UAOC	OHADA Uniform Act on organisation of collective procedures for the settlement of liabilities
USD	United States Dollar
USAID	United States Agency for International Development
VAT	Value Added Tax
VfM	Value for Money
WAEMU	West African Economic and Monetary Union
WB	World Bank
WPA	Water Purchase Agreement

Introduction

1 Outsourcing. – Africa needs heavy investment in public infrastructure. Traditionally, it is the public sector that initiates projects, finances them and awards contracts to build these infrastructures. However, the public sector's financial difficulties, as well as those associated with awarding and managing major investment projects, have led to greater development of privately financed projects, with increased outsourcing of responses to essential infrastructure needs. As a result, project finance techniques have emerged in Africa, as in other regions of the world. Initially limited in Africa to projects in the natural resources sector, project finance techniques have developed in all sectors, including telecommunications, transport, energy and waste management. The African continent is following the trend observed in other regions towards outsourcing a range of global services to the private sector: the design, construction, financing and operation of infrastructure being accomplished on behalf of the public sector.

2 Definition. – Project *finance* is a long-established technique for repaying the construction, operating and financing costs of a project using the revenues generated by its operation. It is the revenues (or *cash flows*) generated that make the project bankable and, depending on their level of security and the commitments of the project developers and the public sector, provide sufficient guarantees to lenders to finance the project. This technique involves the developers creating a project company (SPV), or dedicated company, whose main asset is the right to operate and manage the infrastructure it has financed and built. Basically, the project company makes a profit from the operation of the infrastructure which shall enable it to repay the lenders and generate dividends for its shareholders. In return, the public party pays rent (or the project company receives income from users of the infrastructure) and mobilises resources to manage and monitor the project. In this way, it benefits from the infrastructure over the long term. In some cases, where the project is entirely financed by users, the project company pays no fees, and the operator receives the revenues. There are two main types of public-private partnerships (PPP) projects: public-pay projects, where the public sector pays the project company directly, as in the case of the construction and operation of a public building; and user-pay projects, such as toll motorways. It is important to emphasise the distinction between raising the finance (which, in this case, is raised from the private sector) and the cost

DOI: 10.4324/9781003616894-1

of the infrastructure. While the search for and raising of finance (debt and equity) is delegated to the private sector, the cost of the infrastructure *ultimately* remains the responsibility of the public sector, particularly for infrastructure where no revenue is generated by users. The rents invoiced by the project company to the public party take into account all the costs incurred by the latter (construction costs, operating costs, transaction costs, bank financing costs, shareholder remuneration). It is therefore necessary to demystify the all-too-common belief that PPP is a solution for reducing the State budget or that it is a way for the State and taxpayers to develop infrastructure without having to bear the cost. If users do not cover all the costs of the project, there will necessarily be a direct impact on public finances. The long-term costs to the public purse therefore need to be analysed in detail, through an analysis of the budgetary sustainability of the various projects, in order to ensure the social and economic relevance of each of them. So the use of PPPs, and by extension project financing, cannot be based solely on budgetary considerations. It can be justified by the overriding benefits (availability of infrastructure in a shorter time-frame, better cost control than public project management, better quality of service, assurance of quality maintenance over the long term, impact on the economic and social development of the country or region concerned), given the higher associated costs (more complex transactions requiring greater external support, higher financing costs, remuneration of private shareholders).

3 Distinction from other debt financing techniques. – Project finance is one of a number of debt financing methods that need to be distinguished. Other debt financing instruments including bank loans, the most traditional form of debt financing, have the advantage that the only cost is the interest rate. However, they are not accessible to all investors. Emerging companies are finding it difficult to obtain such loans, and to provide guarantees and security. Tougher banking regulations have also restricted access to this type of financing. Similarly, although mandatory financing has developed as bank loan financing has become less accessible, it remains reserved for the strongest and highest-rated companies. This technique allows the issuer to tailor the securities to its needs, whether in terms of maturity, yield or the option between conversion and redemption in shares.

It is still difficult to put a figure on the proportion of international export credits. These consist of contributions made by the home country of the private operator to encourage it to operate in a given country, despite the local risks.

Factoring is characterised by the transfer of receivables by the company to a specialised institution (factoring company or “factor”). This financing technique can be used to meet a company’s cash flow requirements. However, companies cannot use this method of financing on a permanent basis. It is reserved for companies that carry out business-to-business activities.

Finally, mezzanine debt is a hybrid financing technique, combining debt and equity. This type of financing assumes that the senior debt is repaid before the final loan is taken out. Highly risky for the lender, this type of debt financing nonetheless offers a higher return than senior debt and allows the lender to convert its debt into equity if it is not repaid on time.

4 Distinction with PPPs. – The concepts of project finance and PPP are commonly associated. Project finance is a financing technique that focuses on building the project's financial model on the basis of the revenue it generates, excluding any recourse on principle to developers or sponsors, since only the project company will be responsible for repaying the debts incurred. Project financing involves structuring a method of recourse to the private sector that focuses on the dedicated structure formed by its shareholders. PPPs are a family of public contracts that take many forms, with legal systems that have many similarities across African countries. In civil law countries and French-speaking areas, we have been talking for several centuries about concessive techniques, which form the oldest model of PPPs. These are the forms most commonly found in the French-speaking countries of Africa. Over the last 20 years, the majority of these countries have adopted laws on PPPs,[1] making it possible to unify the PPP regime in each country. In English-speaking African countries, reference is made to schemes known by the acronym BOOT, *Build Own Operate Transfer*. These make it possible to carry out the same type of operation in the form of a PPP, mainly using the project finance technique. In practice, there may be PPPs without private project financing, where no private sector financing will be mobilised, or where infrastructure management is simply delegated, with no significant investment, i.e. no construction or renovation of works. However, in the case of PPPs comprising a series of services (design, construction, financing and operation), there will be almost systematic recourse to the project financing technique. This is because the project's developer shareholders wish to isolate their risks within this dedicated company using project finance, and all the more so in Africa, given certain more salient risks.

5 Distinction from IPPs. – In the energy sector, where PPPs and the use of project finance are very common in Africa, reference is often made to the acronym IPP (*Independent Power Producer*), which will be used in this book. It is important to distinguish this from other concepts. IPP is a way of naming players in the energy production sector who are independent of national energy production companies. It refers to independent private producers who design, develop, finance and operate power plants. These plants are very often built using project financing techniques, with the main contract linking them to the public sector often being a PPP-type contract.

6 Private project financing. – In addition, it should be noted that the project finance technique can be used for purely private projects, not involving the public sector. We are not going to cover this technique in such detail in this book. It is possible, for example, for a manufacturer to develop a project on its site, by creating a dedicated company which takes on debt without recourse to its parent company. This company will generate income from the sale of goods or services rendered by this new autonomous installation, which will be used to repay the debt and remunerate the shareholding parent company.

1 See Appendix 4, African tour of PPP texts for structuring project finance with the public sector.

7 Terms used. – The idea of this book is to provide a practical and structured insight into the use of project finance techniques in Africa to address the continent's public infrastructure deficit. It covers many sectors and areas of the continent and will often refer to the term concession or PPP to illustrate the points made. PPP is defined by the WB as "a long-term contract between a private party and a government entity for a public service for which the private party bears significant risk and management responsibility. Remuneration is linked to performance". These terms are used generically to designate the main contract, which is the pivot and key asset of the project company in the context of its activity. This term is intended to cover all types of PPP, concession or BOT-type operating contracts that enable a project company to operate an infrastructure and structure and finance its project for the needs of the public sector. In practice, a different contract name may exist in each country. But this will have little impact on the rest of the discussion as described in this book, which seeks to provide a continental view of African project finance, supported by examples drawn from practice in different countries. The term "State contracts" is sometimes used[2] to refer to large-scale infrastructure investments requiring a complex contractual package with specific risks and strategic implications for the public parties.

8 Practical experience. – This book is the fruit of our reflections and consultancy activities during our various mandates carried out on the African continent since the end of the 1990s. We would be delighted to receive any criticism or comments from readers that would help to improve its content, accuracy and use by practitioners, researchers and students. As project finance touches on a wide range of disciplines and specialties, this book does not claim to deal in depth with all the facets of each of the areas of expertise that can be mobilised. It focuses more on the legal and financial aspects and outlines the infrastructure financing activity that Africa sorely needs. Some of the projects in which we have been involved, or players with whom we have collaborated, are cited by way of illustration to provide a broader perspective.

9 Project chronology. – We wanted to build this book more or less following the chronology of project financing: the development, financing and management of infrastructure projects during their operation. This seemed to us to give a practical representation of how projects are structured and financed. The book is therefore divided into three parts on the development, financing and monitoring of project financing. With regard to project development, we set out to describe the prerequisites for setting up a project, the environment and the issues and challenges associated with project financing in Africa. We also felt that it would be useful to shed some light on the different types of projects in the different sectors. In this first part, we describe the players involved, the structuring stages and the different project contracts.

2 On the concept of State contracts, see in particular M. Audit, S. Bollée and P. Callé, *Droit du commerce international et des investissements étrangers*, 2nd ed, LGDJ, 2016, p. 208 et seq.

In the second part we present an overview of the players in this phase and their respective roles in project financing. In this same section we present the principles of bankability of financing contracts, elements for understanding the role of the project's financial model and its construction, as well as a grid for reading and apprehending risks.

In the third and final part, the book describes how project-financed infrastructure projects should be executed once they have been financed. In particular, it deals with the procedures for monitoring implementation, managing contractual difficulties and disputes, and the procedures or impacts associated with refinancing projects during the contractual implementation period.

Several appendices provide practical information. We hope that this first edition will prove useful to our readers. We hope to have the opportunity to talk to as many of them as possible. We hope that it will make a further contribution to the construction and financing of many future projects on the African continent.

Part 1

Project development

1 The environment and prerequisites

Section 1. Current situation, specific features and challenges

10 Infrastructure, a vector for growth. – Infrastructure is an essential link in the chain of economic growth and social development, particularly on the African continent. Governments and their agencies have traditionally been responsible for providing this infrastructure, financed by their tax revenues. On the African continent, countries suffer from severe infrastructure backlogs, not only in the creation of new infrastructure but also in the renovation and rehabilitation of existing infrastructure.[1] Investment is growing but is not enough to close the gap. Despite the growth in investment, needs continue to grow faster, *ultimately* leading to a growing infrastructure deficit. One of the major challenges for Africa's economic growth and social progress therefore lies in the more rapid development of its infrastructure, and models are being sought to facilitate the standardisation and acceleration of projects, given the immense needs. In fact, in 2017, the United Nations Economic Commission for Europe (UNECE) launched a programme to draft a Model Law to provide a framework for infrastructure projects financed by the private sector. The final version was endorsed by the 16th session of the Committee on Innovation, Competitiveness and Public-Private Partnerships (31 May–2 June 2023).[2] Similarly, many observers would like to facilitate access to financing, in particular by making it possible to aggregate multiple infrastructure projects through the introduction of standardised documentation that would be available free of charge and accepted by all parties (purchasers, governments, lenders, operators, developers, etc.), and would reduce the cost of appraising applications by adapting the requirements of lenders to the size of projects.[3]

1 Johann Lübbe Pr Eng, "Project finance as driver of economic growth in Africa", *Civil Engineering*, October 2016, p. 56.

2 ECE/CECI/WP/PPP/2022/5.

3 Antoine Huard and Benjamin Fremaux, *Solar Energy in Africa: A Bright Future*, Institut Montaigne, 2019, p. 59.

DOI: 10.4324/9781003616894-3

§ 1. The current state of infrastructure financing in Africa

A. Overall trends and constraints

11 Reduction of investments. – The global health crisis linked to the Covid-19 pandemic has had a major impact on all economies worldwide, particularly those on the continent from March 2020, and has led to a reduction in financial commitments for infrastructure funding. The continent went into recession in 2020, with African GDP shrinking by 1.9%, the worst result on record. This recession has resulted in an estimated additional financing requirement of 285 billion dollars between 2021 and 2025.[4] The pandemic has also led to a 5% drop in financial commitments for infrastructure financing between 2019 and 2020, from USD 85 billion to USD 81 billion.[5] The medium- and long-term impact of the Covid-19 crisis on African infrastructure financing is still difficult to assess in its entirety, as the last large-scale report was published by the ICA in 2022 and only covered the period 2019–2020. The report scheduled for the end of 2024 covering the period 2021–2022 will provide a better understanding of the effects of the crisis.

12 Economic and geographical constraints. – Infrastructure development in Africa today is still hampered by the region's economic geography. Specifically, Africa has more landlocked countries (16 in total) than any other continent, and more sparsely populated countries than any other emerging region on the planet. The average population density is 44 people per km^2, which is slightly lower than the density observed in other low- and middle-income countries in the rest of the world.[6]

13 Reduction in commitments to finance infrastructure projects in Africa. – According to the ICA, total infrastructure commitments in 2020 amounted to USD 81 billion, down almost 20% from the peak in 2018 (USD 100.8 billion). The ICA explains this sharp fall by the impact of Covid-19 to a large extent, with national and bilateral spending reallocated to emergency interventions linked to the pandemic (health spending, social issues, economic recovery). This decline is particularly marked for bilateral and multilateral institutions (−67% between 2018 and 2020) and relatively smaller for national governments (−11% over the period). This slowdown can also be explained by the significant reduction in Chinese investment in infrastructure, from USD 25.7 billion in 2018 to USD 6.5 billion in 2020, a reduction of 75%. The infrastructure financing gap on the continent is estimated at between USD 59 billion and USD 96 billion in 2020, an increase of more than 10% since 2018.[7] These figures illustrate how little use

4 International Monetary Fund, "Background note for the international financing summit for Africa high-level event", 12 May 2021.

5 ICA, Infrastructure Consortium for Africa, "Trends in infrastructure finance in Africa – 2019–2020", *ICA Report*, 2022.

6 Mthuli Ncube, Charles Leyeka Lufumpa and George Kararach, "Infrastructure, political economy and Africa's transformational agenda", *in* Mthuli Ncube and Charles Leyeka Lufumpa, *Infrastructures in Africa, Lessons for Future Development*, Bristol University Press, 2017, pp. 654–646.

7 ICA, Infrastructure Consortium for Africa, "Trends in infrastructure financing in Africa – 2019–2020", *op. cit.*

is being made of project finance for African infrastructure, despite the continent's great needs. However, many countries are encouraging the private sector to pursue an investment policy in Africa by using PPP, which are now well identified on the continent as a means of fostering the emergence of missing infrastructure. Nevertheless, the role of the private sector in financing infrastructure in Africa is becoming increasingly important. Despite the pandemic, private sector financing of infrastructure has increased considerably, rising from USD 12 billion to USD 19 billion between 2018 and 2020.[8]

14 A historic fall in Chinese investment and loans. – Chinese loans have fallen drastically in 2022 and are at their lowest levels since 2004. At its peak in 2016, China had disbursed USD 28.5 billion in loans, compared with just USD 1 billion in 2022. In particular, China was heavily involved in financing energy infrastructure, lending USD 17.7 billion in 2016, even though it will not have disbursed any loans in this sector in 2022.[9] There are two reasons for this drop: firstly, the economic difficulties faced by China, which has had to support domestic consumption and reduce domestic debt levels since the Covid-19 crisis; and secondly, the problems of over-indebtedness of African economies, leading to a risk of default that worries China, which has become the leading creditor of the African continent.[10]

15 A deterioration in the public finances of African economies. – The problem of over-indebtedness among African nations is one of the main obstacles to the development of infrastructure financing, with some African governments experiencing extremely high debt-to-GDP ratios, such as Eritrea (175%), Cape Verde (160%), Mozambique (133%) and Angola (103%).[11] The average debt ratio in sub-Saharan Africa rose significantly between 2013 and 2022, increasing from 30% to 60% of GDP according to the IMF, which also entails significant debt repayment costs. The 2023 UNCTAD report estimates that eight African countries are in debt distress and 13 are at high risk of debt distress.[12] However, it is important to note that the infrastructure default rate in Africa is the lowest in the world, at just 2.1%, compared with 10% for Eastern Europe and 8% for Asia in 2021.[13]

16 A massive urbanisation phenomenon coupled with a demographic explosion, reinforcing the need to finance appropriate urban infrastructure. – According to the IMF, the African continent is expected to have 2.5 billion inhabitants in 2050, compared with 1.4 billion today, and the urban population is set to

8 *Ibid.*

9 Boston University Global Development Policy Center, Chinese Loans to Africa Database, https://www.bu.edu/gdp/chinese-loans-to-africa-database/.

10 IMF, "Sub-Saharan Africa and China: Economic relations at a crossroads", *Regional Economic Outlook for Sub-Saharan Africa*, October 2023.

11 Jerry HAAR, "Modernizing infrastructure vital to fulfilling Africa's promise", *Wilson Center*, 26 April 2023.

12 UNCTAD, "Trade and development report update", April 2023.

13 Kevin KELHOFFER, "Examining infrastructure as an asset class", *Moody's Analytics Report*, September 2021.

almost triple to 1.5 billion by 2050.[14] For example, the city of Lagos will have 32 times more inhabitants in 2035 than in 1960. Two-thirds of this urban growth is due to births in the city, and the remainder to an influx of rural populations in search of better economic opportunities. The AfDB highlights the lack of coordination between the players involved, as well as the low level of participation by cities in the financing, development and planning of infrastructure projects.[15]

17 The African continent is one of the areas most affected by the consequences of global warming. – Urban areas in Africa are likely to suffer disproportionately from the consequences of climate change, as the continent as a whole is warming 1.5 times faster than the global average and these regions are becoming increasingly vulnerable to the impacts of climate change (droughts, increased rainfall, rising sea levels, etc.).[16] The infrastructure deficit in Africa presents an excellent opportunity to develop green infrastructure:[17] more resistant to climate change and a vector for a better quality of urban life, public health and better economic opportunities for local populations. The development of green infrastructure relies in particular on increased recourse to PPP and makes it possible to attract groups of specialised institutional investors or green funds.[18] Numerous multilateral institutions and initiatives have already been set up. For example, the Alliance for Green Infrastructure in Africa (AGIA), developed in collaboration with the AfDB, Africa50 and the AU, aims to mobilise $10 billion in financing for green infrastructure projects (green hydrogen, ecological urban transport systems, electric vehicles, renewable energies, etc.).[19] At COP28 in Dubai at the end of 2023, international institutions, foundations and governments have already pledged USD 175 million to the AGIA.[20]

18 Significant dynamism in the extractive sectors, particularly mining. – The exponential demand for strategic minerals, coupled with the difficulty of exploiting certain ores, means that dedicated infrastructures need to be developed as part of mega-projects, which can be inter-company or even transnational. Demand for strategic minerals, which include critical minerals such as bauxite, cobalt, copper, graphite, lithium, manganese and nickel, as well as other minerals useful for the

14 Andrew Stanley, "The African century", *IMF Finance & Development Report*, September 2023.

15 Astrid R. N. Haas, Anton Cartwright, Aweng Garang and Vera Songwe, "From millions to billions: Financing the development of African cities", *African Development Bank Report*, 8 November 2023.

16 WWF, "The case for investment in green infrastructure in African cities", *WWF Report*, March 2020.

17 Dr. Akinwumi Adesina, "Opening speech by Dr. Akinwumi A. Adesina president, African development bank group chairman, Africa50 boards of directors at the Africa50 InfraForum and general shareholders meeting Lomé, Togo", 3 July 2023.

18 WWF, "The case for investment in green infrastructure in African cities", *op. cit.*

19 Dr. Akinwumi Adesina, "Opening speech by Dr. Akinwumi A. Adesina president, African development bank group chairman, Africa50 boards of directors at the Africa50 infraForum and general shareholders meeting Lomé, Togo", *op. cit.*

20 "COP28: $175M pledged for African green infrastructure", *Ecofin Agency*, 3 December 2023.

energy transition (rare earths, platinum, iron and zinc), is exploding worldwide due to their key role in the manufacture of batteries, for example, and therefore electric vehicles, an essential component of the transition. Demand for critical minerals is expected to more than double by 2030.[21] More than 450 projects are currently under study or development across the continent.[22] Africa plays a key role in the development of these minerals, holding 85% of manganese reserves, 80% of platinum and chromium reserves, 47% of cobalt reserves and 21% of graphite reserves.[23] This dynamism, coupled with the difficulty of accessing the mines, is illustrated by the need to resort to mega projects with significant infrastructure components. For example, the Simandou iron ore mining project in Guinea involves the construction of 552 km of rail track and a port at a total cost of USD 20 billion.[24] Transnational projects are also needed to export ore from landlocked countries, as illustrated by the Lobito Corridor, a 600 km trans-regional rail infrastructure construction project linking the south of the Democratic Republic of Congo (DRC) and the north-west of Zambia to global markets via the port of Lobito in Angola.[25]

B. Analysis by sector

19 Transport. – The transport sector is the one with the largest share of financial commitments in both 2019 and 2020, when it amounted to $34 billion (42% of total commitments). Despite a financing gap that widened slightly between 2019 and 2020, transport was the only sector to see its financial commitments increase over this period (+1.7%).[26]

20 Water and sanitation. – The commitment gap in the water and sanitation sector remains by far the largest: it is 4 to 12 times higher than that of transport and 3 to 12 times higher than that of energy. In 2018, commitments amounted to USD 13.3 billion and decreased to USD 8.1 billion in 2020, thereby widening the commitment gap for financing water and sanitation infrastructure.[27]

21 Energy. – The energy sector continues to account for around a quarter of total infrastructure financing commitments, amounting to USD 23.5 billion in 2020. Despite this, the energy infrastructure financing gap has widened between 2019 and 2020 by 17%.[28]

21 *Ibid.*

22 Africa Business+ & EY, "Critical minerals: The pivotal outlook", December 2023. https://www.africabusinessplus.com/en/817802/critical-minerals-the-pivotal-outlook/

23 Gracelin Baskaran, "Prospects for U.S. minerals engagement with Africa", *Report by the Center for Strategic & International Studies*, 29 August 2023.

24 Tom Wilson, "World's biggest mining project to start after 27 years of setbacks and scandals", *Financial Times*, 7 January 2024.

25 Ben Payton, "Rail attracts lust", *New African*, 8 September 2023.

26 ICA, "Trends in infrastructure financing in Africa – 2019–2020", *op. cit.*

27 *Ibid.*

28 *Ibid.*

22 ICT. – Although there was a slight drop in 2020 due to the pandemic, funding for ICT infrastructure is still on an upward trend – investment more than tripled between 2017 and 2018, with telecoms companies upgrading their equipment, in particular to move to 4G and eventually 5G.[29]

23 The global chessboard. – Despite its efforts, Africa remains the world's least infrastructure-endowed region, partly because of its low overall GDP.[30] The water and sanitation sector remains the most underfunded, with population growth outstripping increases in coverage. Around 340 million Africans have no access to drinking water. The deficit in this sector is estimated between USD 40 and 50 billion, representing half of the overall infrastructure deficit. In the transport sector, the deficit remains significant, ranging from USD 4 to 16 billion annually.[31] The Economic Commission for Africa has set out guidelines for the energy sector and sustainable infrastructure in Africa in the post-Covid-19 period[32] with a view to providing support in several directions: revision of energy sector frameworks, investment in energy pools, development of the FTAA zone, digitisation of transport infrastructure, rail and intelligent transport connectivity and a single African air market. In addition to the priority given to infrastructure, the commission is encouraging the stimulation of economies through the use of PPPs and the financing of infrastructure projects by the private sector.

C. *Analysis by region*

24 Geograhical data. – Of the USD 81 billion in commitments to the continent in 2020, West Africa received USD 22.3 billion (27%), North Africa USD 16.8 billion (21%), East Africa USD 14.8 billion (18%), Southern Africa USD 10.1 billion (12%), the Republic of South Africa USD 9.5 billion (12%) and Central Africa USD 5.3 billion (7%). There is a decrease in commitments between 2019 and 2020 in all regions, with the exception of North Africa (+1.7 billion USD) and, to a lesser extent, Central Africa (+300 million USD). Conversely, the Republic of South Africa saw the biggest drop, from USD 12 billion in 2019 to USD 9.5 billion in 2020, even though it had a peak in commitments in 2018 of USD 18 billion.[33]

The trend in infrastructure financing in North Africa is upwards, with an average of USD 16 billion in 2019–2020 compared with USD 13.7 billion over the period 2015–2017, despite a cyclical downturn in 2019. Financial commitments

29 *Ibid.*

30 ICA, Infrastructure Consortium for Africa, "Infrastructure finance trends in Africa – 2018", *ICA Report*, 2018.

31 ICA, "Trends in infrastructure financing in Africa – 2019–2020", *op. cit.*

32 United Nations, Economic and Social Council, Economic Commission for Africa, Committee on Private Sector Development, Regional Integration, Trade, Infrastructure, Industry and Technology, "Prospects for sustainable energy and infrastructure in Africa in the post-Covid-19 period", 9–10 December 2021, second meeting Addis Ababa.

33 *Ibid.*

from the private sector have more than tripled between 2019 and 2020, representing more than 40% of total commitments in 2020. Commitments in West Africa have increased slightly in terms of amount but remain relatively similar to previous years in terms of share of total commitments on the African continent. East Africa saw its commitments fall by 9% between 2019 and 2020, although they remain more modest than in 2018. In Central and Southern Africa, commitments fell considerably over the period 2019–2020 compared with 2018, with a drop of 24% and 21% respectively between 2018 and 2019, which can be explained in part by the reduction in Chinese commitments in the region. Lastly, the Republic of South Africa saw a sharp fall in its commitments between 2018 and 2020 (−89%), illustrated in particular by the sharp drop in private sector commitments, which fell from 7.7 billion in 2018 to 1.7 billion in 2020.

Africa is often the subject of generalities when commenting on its situation in terms of infrastructure, project financing or the rule of law. It is essential to remember Africa's diversity, as we will see in Part 3 in relation to languages, cultures and the rule of law. The disparity that exists in different States can create real differences for infrastructure investors. Countries differ widely in terms of legal traditions, regulatory environment, levels of political stability, human capacity, maturity of the financial sector, historical background, cultures, languages, natural resources, climate, geography and so on. The resulting complex mix of variables can significantly affect a country's attractiveness to private investors.

25 Country by country analysis. – However, it is possible to assess the attractiveness of investment in infrastructure projects in each sub-Saharan country based on indicators of the favourable environment and economic opportunities.[34] For example, South Africa is well ahead of the other countries in terms of the regulatory environment, the availability of finance, precedents and the ability of the public and private sectors to conclude agreements. Rwanda, Botswana and Mauritius have a strong regulatory environment for infrastructure investment but are relatively small markets. Nigeria, Tanzania and Ethiopia have sufficient regulatory environments and economic opportunities to attract investors. Nigeria, the largest country in economic and demographic terms, has a mixed record when it comes to private investment in infrastructure. Only South Africa has completed more infrastructure PPPs in the last 25 years than Nigeria. But Nigeria's regulatory environment still has room for improvement: government capacity, political will and associated demonstration policies, as well as macroeconomic stability, are issues, and the number of highly successful deals remains limited.[35] Zambia, Ghana and Kenya have a good balance of enabling environments and economic opportunities and therefore fall somewhere in the middle. These countries offer great opportunities, have an improving regulatory environment and growing public and private capacity, but successful investment in these countries may still

34 BCG & AFC, "Infrastructure financing in Sub-Saharan Africa, best practices from ten years in the field", 2017.

35 *Ibid.*

require a great deal of effort. Côte d'Ivoire, Cape Verde, Gabon, Cameroon and Gambia have benefited from a flow of projects, and their governments have been relatively attractive partners on a case-by-case basis, but they do not always have strong enabling environments or significant economic opportunities. Other countries such as Comoros, Equatorial Guinea, Lesotho, Mauritania, Niger and South Sudan do not currently have a regulatory framework that is conducive to private investment in transport and electricity infrastructure. The Democratic Republic of Congo does not have a highly structured and attractive regulatory framework for private investment in infrastructure, but sector ministries negotiate ad hoc agreements using their own guidelines, particularly in the mining, electricity and cement sectors. A study by Proximo explored project finance infrastructure by region in late 2024. The data were used to examine the number of lenders that participated in at least one tranche of a project financing in each region from 2019 to the present. Several regions were combined into larger super-regions for easier comparison. The resulting analysis divided the number of lenders by population and by the number of deals closed in each region. It shows project finance lenders per million inhabitants and per deal. The findings reveal that Asia, and to a lesser extent the Middle East and Africa, are relatively underserved by project finance lenders in relation to their population, while North America is well served. However, when measuring banks per closed deal, Asia, the Middle East and Africa perform better.[36]

The diagram in Figure 1.1 distinguishes between the most traditional methods of infrastructure financing, with public sector financing, which carries the investment and the debt if it has recourse to borrowing, private sector financing, known as "corporate" financing, and project financing with the addition of a project company or SPV.

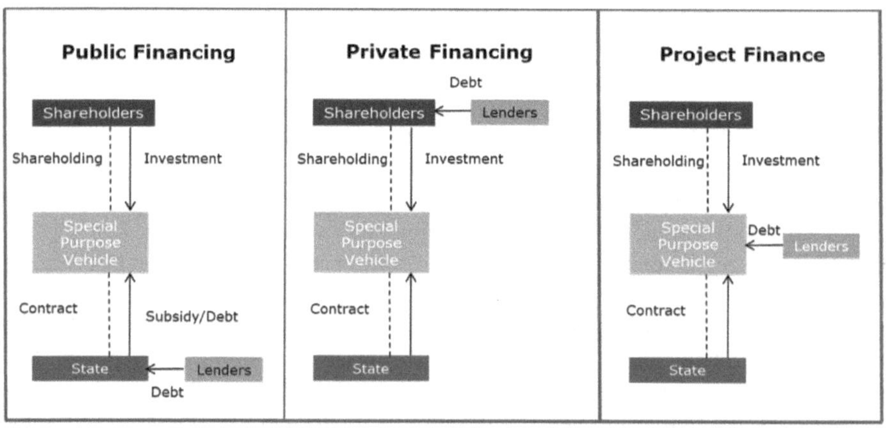

Figure 1.1 Distinguishing project financing from other forms of infrastructure financing

36 https://www.linkedin.com/posts/proximo–infra_infrastructurefinance-asiapacific-projectfinance-activity-7274429780932853760-RI7a?utm_source=share&utm_medium=member_desktop

§ 2. *Specific features of infrastructure financing in Africa*

A. *Pre-eminence of African public funds*

26 Public sector financing. – Public sector budgets continue to dominate as the primary source of funding for infrastructure in Africa.[37] Public funds are particularly important in sub-Saharan Africa, where a number of countries devote 5–6% of GDP to infrastructure investment.[38] Although commitments to infrastructure finance in Africa declined in 2019 and 2020 after peaking at USD 100.8 billion in 2018, the share of African public funds increased. In 2019 and 2020, African governments accounted for 41% of commitments, up from 37% in 2018. African government commitments continue to rise, reaching USD 33.4 billion in 2020, up from USD 24 billion in 2015 (+39%). In 2020, the transport sector accounted for more than half (56%) of African governments' total infrastructure commitments, followed by the water and sanitation sector (19%).[39]

27 Financial constraints. – To sustain and increase this pace, African countries must continue to increase their tax revenues and improve domestic resource mobilisation in order to bridge the infrastructure gap. Domestic resource mobilisation efforts and results vary from country to country.[40] Many African governments are facing a rising debt-to-GDP ratio, which is likely to limit their infrastructure spending in the coming years. The average debt ratio in sub-Saharan Africa almost doubled between 2013 and 2022, rising from 30% to 60% of GDP according to the IMF, with significant debt repayment costs. In particular, debt levels have increased recently with the combined shocks of the pandemic and the repercussions of the war in Ukraine. The median debt ratio rose to almost 10% of GDP in 2020 in sub-Saharan Africa.[41] The number of African nations classified by the International Monetary Fund (IMF) as over-indebted has risen from six in 2021 to eight in 2023.[42] However, this increase needs to be qualified, as the number of African countries classified by the IMF as being at high risk of debt distress has decreased from 15 in 2021 to 13 in 2023.[43] China has become the continent's main creditor, and the debt of African countries is at its highest level in 20 years.[44]

37 ICA, "Trends in infrastructure financing in Africa – 2019–2020", *op. cit.*

38 Kannan Lakmeeharan, Qaizer Manji, Ronald and Harald Poeltner, "Solving Africa's infrastructure paradox", *McKinsey & Company*, 6 March 2020.

39 ICA, "Trends in infrastructure financing in Africa – 2019–2020", *op. cit.*

40 George Kararach, "Innovative financing for infrastructure: Africa50 fund issues", *in* Mthuli Ncube and Charles Leyeka Lufumpa (eds.), *Infrastructures in Africa, Lessons for Future Development*, Bristol University Press, 2017, p. 624.

41 World Bank Group, "Understanding public spending trends for infrastructure in developing countries", January 2022.

42 UNCTAD, "Trade and development report 2023", October 2023.

43 Direction Générale du Trésor – République française, "L'endettement de l'Afrique subsaharienne", January 2022.

44 *Africa Risk Reward Index Control Risks and Oxford Economics* quoted by *Les Echos*, Yves Bourdillon, 21 September 2021.

28 Impact of Chinese investments. – A question always arises as to the actual effect of Chinese investments on Africa value chain as China is said to only have interest in Africa's resources.[45] The countries involved in infrastructure projects in Africa will often be bound by agreements with the IMF, which may require them to respect certain limits on their financial commitments as part of the financial assistance provided by the IMF. Thus, as we shall see, arrangements relating to sovereign guarantees or guarantees granted on behalf of governments or national companies may need to be declared to, or authorised by, the IMF in order to be put in place. While we do not necessarily agree on the legal nature and scope of the commitments entered into by States with the IMF, in practice it will be necessary to take this into account during the implementation of countries by studying for each country the possible investment restrictions imposed by this institution.[46]

B. The fundamental role of the DFIs[47]

29 DFI strategic role. – As we shall see in Chapter 3, which is devoted to project financing stakeholders, although they are sometimes criticised for the lengthy appraisal process for financing projects, multilateral or bilateral financing institutions known as development finance institutions or DFIs[48] play a fundamental role in developing a favourable environment for identifying, developing and financing projects, particularly by private partners.[49]

They have unique characteristics in the provision of finance linked to the design and implementation of structural reforms and institution-building programmes. Their participation is often conditional on the commitment of governments to reform their public policies and change their practices. This is where they differ from private lenders.[50] They are also involved in coordinating and monitoring infrastructure financing.[51]

30 Capacity building. – For the most part, public players in Africa lack the experience and capacity to set up and finance infrastructure projects in association with private parties.[52] For many years, bilateral and multilateral DFIs have been stepping in to

45 Review of world economics, 2024-11 Vito Amendolagine, Andrea F Presbitero, Roberta Rabellotti, Chinese infrastructure lending in Africa and participation in global value chains | Review of World Economics.

46 M. Audit, S. Bollée and P. Callé, *Droit du commerce international et des investissements étrangers*, *op. cit.*, no. 251.

47 Multilateral development banks and development finance institutions, respectively.

48 e.g., UK's CDC Group, US's OPIC.

49 Mthuli Ncube, "Infrastructure deficit and financing needs in Africa", *in* Mthuli Ncube and Charles Leyeka Lufumpa, *Infrastructures in Africa, Lessons for Future Development*, Bristol University Press, 2017, p. 597.

50 Rabah Arezki and Amadou Sy, "Financing Africa's infrastructure deficit: From development banking to long-term investing", *Journal of African Economies*, 2016, vol. 25, AERC supplement 2, p. ii61.

51 George Kararach, *op. cit.*, p. 636.

52 *Ibid.*, p. 634.

fill the funding gap by investing in the necessary technical capacity.[53] They are also helping to train governments in transaction monitoring, planning and risk allocation.[54] The collaboration of governments and their agencies with these institutions is therefore essential.

Their involvement has a multiplier effect on private capital insofar as it ensures that serious assessments are carried out and that a prudent approach is adopted.[55] They have the expertise and flexibility in terms of investment objectives and contractual negotiations. Their involvement can therefore pave the way for a viable commitment from institutional and private investors.[56]

31 Risk Guarantee. – In addition, these institutions can strengthen their support for risk management, by granting special cover such as PRGs, PCGs or political risk insurances.[57] PRGs have been shown to generate up to 10 times the value of the guarantee in terms of additional financing. Political risk management instruments encourage governments to implement reforms. These guarantees improve borrowers' access to financial markets by sharing credit risk with lenders and guarantors.[58] They are fundamental to the structuring of project finance involving public parties in Africa.

C. *Crucial issues in terms of environmental development for the planet*

32 Africa's potential. – According to the United Nations, the African continent will have a population of 2.5 billion by 2050. Africa has the largest reserves of renewable energy on the planet. In fact, 17 of the world's 35 most resource-rich countries are African.[59] Africa, therefore, has the potential to commit to the development of low-carbon infrastructures and to unlock financing from specialised funds. These are fundamental to reducing the costs and risks of such investments. For example, the CTF[60] can raise 5 times its value in clean energy solutions.[61]

33 Important energy needs. – In addition to the imperative need for energy to support the continent's growth, the Covid-19 pandemic has reminded us that without energy it is not possible to provide certain vital care, or to ensure the continuity of the education system, or to telework. Above all, this crisis should be a wake-up call to the more than 600 million Africans for whom electricity is still inaccessible. The energies of the future will have to be resilient and affordable, in Africa more than anywhere else. Only renewable energies can meet these challenges. Their decentralised nature means that as

53 *Ibid.*

54 Kannan Lakmeeharan, Qaizer Manji, Ronald and Harald Poeltner, *op. cit.*

55 *Ibid.*

56 Rabah Arezki, Amadou Sy, *op. cit.*, p. ii61.

57 See paragraph 347 below.

58 Mthuli Ncube, *op. cit.*, p. 609.

59 *Ibid.*, p. 621.

60 The Clean Technology Fund, administered by the World Bank, helps developing countries catalyse the private investment needed to combat climate change by deploying low-carbon technologies.

61 *Ibid.*

many people as possible can benefit from them. Their operation, less affected by the disruption of supply systems in times of crisis, provides greater resilience.[62]

34 DFIs' role. – To this end, the AfDB is leading the mobilisation of resources under the Green Fund for Africa, which will provide direct financing for eligible projects on the continent.[63]

Multilateral development institutions can also strengthen their role in setting standards for the economic and social appraisal of investments and for environmental sustainability.[64] In this sense, they are essential for the financing of infrastructure projects.

Focus: the development of renewable energy projects: the case of the hybrid solar power plant at the Essakane mine in Burkina Faso

Mining operators are now looking to reduce their energy supply costs and cut their carbon footprint. Against this backdrop, a number of infrastructure development projects involving renewable energies have been launched in Africa. One example is the project to develop a hybrid solar power station to supply the Essakane gold mine in Burkina Faso.

A solar project developed in response to the mine's growing energy needs

The Essakane mine, located in the far north of the country in the Sahel region of Burkina Faso, is not connected to SONABEL. Its energy needs were estimated at 312 GWh per year, previously supplied exclusively by a thermal power station running on heavy fuel oil and capable of generating up to 57 MW. Since 2009, the mine has been managed by IAMGOLD Essakane SA (IAMGOLD), a Canadian company. IAMGOLD owns 90% of the mine's capital, with the remaining 10% held by the government of Burkina Faso. IAMGOLD began commercial production in July 2010 and initially had a mine life plan of at least eight years. Given the good exploration results obtained, in 2010 IAMGOLD continued to explore the Essakane lands (1,300 km²) with a view to extending the mine life to at least 15 years. This has led to an increase in monthly energy requirements, which rose from 14 GWh to 26 GWh in 2015,[65] mainly as a result of "hard rock processing".

62 Group opinion piece, "The energy of the future must be green, resilient and affordable, in Africa more than anywhere else", co-edited by Ousmane Diawara.

63 *Ibid.*

64 George Kararach, *op. cit.*, p. 636.

65 Energies-media, "Burkina Faso: la mine d'or Essakane se dotte d'une centrale solaire de 15 MW", 2018.

A project to increase energy production capacity was therefore studied and took the form of a 15 MW hybrid thermal-solar power plant project, which was inaugurated on 16 March 2018 after ten months of work to build it. This plant will reduce CO_2 emissions by 18,500 tonnes/year. The 130,000 photovoltaic panels scattered over 22 hectares will enable the mine to reduce its fuel consumption by around 6 million litres of fuel oil per year. The solar power plant will provide the Essakane gold mine with low-cost, low-carbon electricity.

A project developed autonomously by private players with the help of an IPP

As the mine is located in an area of Burkina Faso not served by the national grid (SONABEL), IAMGOLD was able to develop a self-consumption production project without having to issue an official call for tenders in accordance with the energy sector law in force at the time in Burkina Faso. The project was carried out through a partnership between various private players: the mining company IAMGOLD, the French group Total Eren, the project sponsor, African Energy Management Platform (AEMP), an independent electricity producer, and Wärtsilä, the builder of the power plant.

An IPP, Total Eren, was selected for a 15-year PPA following a restricted tender process. The IPP has undertaken to (i) develop, finance, build and operate the solar power plant; and (ii) manage the SCADA system between the solar power plant and the oil-fired power plant. The PPA will be paid in CFA francs, partly indexed to changes in the USD/FCFA exchange rate. This is a "Take or Pay" type PPA between IPP and IAMGOLD. Solar production is favoured over use of the HFO plant in order to minimise the use of fuel oil and reduce production costs. IAMGOLD sends a daily forecast of its electricity requirements to the IPP, which is then able to better manage production from the PV plant and the HFO plant. Essakane Solar SAS sells the electricity produced by the solar power plant to IAMGOLD for the duration of the purchase agreement.

It should be noted that the mining group had a time constraint that did not allow project financing to be put in place prior to construction. The project was therefore initially financed by equity. Project financing was then put in place after construction. The IPP signed a credit agreement for around FCFA 9.2 billion (around USD 16.5 million) with the Banque Internationale pour le Commerce, l'Industrie et l'Artisanat du Burkina (BICIAB), the Burkina Faso subsidiary of the BNP Paribas Group. The innovative nature of the project turned away a number of traditional lenders. The project involved creating the world's largest hybrid solar power plant, and the buyer was a mine with no government support.

Structure of the Essakane solar power plant project

In January 2014, IAMGOLD and SONABEL signed a partnership agreement to use surplus production from the heavy fuel oil power plant. The aim of the agreement is to provide electricity to the village of Essakane Site. This initiative is part of the PRIELER project to strengthen electrical infrastructure and rural electrification. The total cost of the work is estimated at nearly USD 1 million. As part of this partnership, SONABEL has undertaken to carry out the work of supplying electricity to the village (purchase of equipment, execution and supervision of the work). IAMGOLD has undertaken to finance the work (purchase of equipment, construction of the urban MV/LV network) to the tune of around USD 500,000 and to authorise the installation and maintenance of the lines within its operating perimeter.

D. Developing new methods and sources of financing

35 Infrastructure gap. – In terms of infrastructure financing in Africa, given the lag in infrastructure development on the continent, players are trying to develop new solutions aimed at attracting private capital, mostly local, and catalysing financing.

The United Nations Economic Commission for Africa and NEPAD are calling for the development of a local bond market in the infrastructure sector. *Infrastructure bonds* are bond instruments issued on the market to raise long-term financing for infrastructure development. A number of countries have already issued these instruments, including Ethiopia, Kenya, Nigeria and South Africa.[66] *Diaspora bonds* are also issued by governments to raise funds from their diaspora abroad. Ethiopia issued two in 2008 and 2021, with mixed success. Nigeria, Rwanda and Zimbabwe have also shown interest in this new source of financing.[67]

36 Sovereign funds. – Sovereign wealth funds and institutional investors have also become involved. This allows them to diversify their portfolios while helping them to achieve their return objectives.[68] Sovereign wealth funds may not have the same investment horizons or the same investment policies as other types of funds. Sovereign wealth funds are still making a relatively minor contribution in Africa, although Singapore and the United Arab Emirates have invested in Africa.[69] This can be explained by the fact that the construction risk inherent in infrastructure projects can dissuade these investors, who are relatively risk averse. In addition, they often lack in-house skills specific to African infrastructure.[70] African sovereign wealth funds are emerging, with a few examples in Morocco, Senegal and Gabon, but their role in project financing is still relatively small on a continental scale.

66 UN and NEPAD, *16 Infrastructure Projects for African Integration*, 2016, p. 67.
67 *Ibid.*
68 Rabah Arezki, Amadou Sy, *op. cit.*, p. ii60.
69 *Ibid.*
70 *Ibid.*

These funds will certainly have a more important role to play as institutional investors in the future on the continent. They can play a role in planning and facilitating the refinancing of assets once they are operational.[71] Risks are then considerably reduced, as those associated with the construction and commissioning phases are eliminated.[72] It is possible to envisage refinancing on an asset-by-asset basis or by securitising multiple assets. The latter option could attract institutional investors by bundling existing projects into a tradable instrument. The funds raised by issuing these securities could then be allocated to new projects which, on their own, would not be able to attract such financing.[73]

§ 3. Challenges specific to the African continent

A. Commercial viability, bankability, deal flow and project selection

37 Infrastructure development dilemna. – The African infrastructure market highlights a paradoxical situation: abundant funds and a willingness to invest exists and a large number of projects are underway, but the funds *ultimately* disbursed remain low compared to the needs of harmonious economic and social development in Africa. The problem is not structural but rather stems from shortcomings expressed at the project design stage, with the selection of low-impact projects, the weakness of feasibility studies and business plans, and the inability to agree on the distribution of risks.[74]

However, the private sector will only get involved in predictable projects that offer an adequate return on risk, with stable revenues that can be used to repay the debt and guarantee the profitability required by shareholders.[75] These factors are key to the success of project financing.

38 Unlocking private finance. – To unlock private finance, Africa needs to increase the number of *bankable* projects. Unfortunately, there are inadequate or obsolete procedures for awarding public contracts, a lack of rules for managing unsolicited projects (unsolicited bids) and a lack of mechanisms for issuing competitive invitations to tender.[76] The selection and development of projects have a significant influence on their bankability and, *de facto,* on the funding required to bring them to fruition. A survey of the private sector in terms of financing can enable more effective decisions to be made within the framework of the project in the selection phase.[77] Better project design, feasibility studies and project selection processes can save African governments huge sums of money in these sectors.[78]

71 ICA c/o ADB, pp. 21–22.
72 *Ibid.*
73 *Ibid.*
74 Kannan Lakmeeharan, Qaizer Manji, Ronald and Harald Poeltner, *op. cit.*
75 *Ibid.*
76 Mthuli Ncube, *op. cit.*, p. 597.
77 George Kararach, *op. cit.*, p. 630.
78 ICA c/o ADB, *op. cit.*, p. 4.

This mismatch between investment demand and financing in the sector is due to the lack of well-structured projects.[79] These projects require complex financial and legal arrangements in order to achieve effective and efficient closings.[80] Most infrastructure projects fail to reach financial close: less than 10% reach this stage, and 80% of projects fail at the feasibility and business plan stage.[81]

39 Private sector. – Private sector investors need to invest time and money to establish themselves in a country and will only do so if there are prospects for significant and predictable transactions.[82] In the absence of a large and high-quality pipeline of projects, the costs can easily outweigh the potential benefits of investing in infrastructure compared to other less complex asset classes. Similarly, a consistent and reliable legal framework for infrastructure projects is required. In some African countries, such frameworks either do not exist or are extremely weak.[83]

B. Political risk, regulatory risk and counterparty risk

40 Political Risk. – Political risk is one of the biggest concerns for private investors and lenders in Africa. Arbitrary political influence can take many forms, particularly on the African continent as in other emerging zones: expropriation, coup d'état, sudden caps on the prices that private infrastructure operators are allowed to charge, new regulations or unilateral renegotiation of existing contracts by new governments.[84]

In Africa, political risk stems mainly from political uncertainty and the unpredictability of decision-makers, as well as recurring national and regional conflicts on the continent.[85] For example, investors and lenders currently avoid projects located in certain regions such as the Central African Republic, Somalia and Sudan.[86]

41 Risk mitigation. – Solutions exist to mitigate this risk, such as political risk insurance, partial guarantees offered by DFIs, State guarantees and the drafting of security contractual stipulations.[87] However, when it comes to project finance investments, measuring the political risk perceived by the investor will be key to assessing each project finance.[88] Furthermore, it should be borne in mind that building good practices and institutions takes time, but their development can contribute to huge efficiency gains and enable governments to successfully undertake many more projects.[89]

One or more solvent counterparties (from the public sector or users, depending on whether the PPP is public-pay or non-public-pay) are essential to guarantee revenues that will ensure repayment of the debt. In project financing involving

79 George KARARACH, *op. cit.*, p. 629.
80 *Ibid.*
81 Kannan LAKMEEHARAN, Qaizer MANJI, Ronald and Harald POELTNER, *op. cit.*
82 *Ibid.*
83 George KARARACH, *op. cit.*, p. 629.
84 *Ibid.*
85 ICA c/o ADB, *op. cit.*, p. 18.
86 George KARARACH, *op. cit.*, p. 633.
87 ICA c/o ADB, *op. cit.*, p. 18.
88 Kannan LAKMEEHARAN, Qaizer MANJI, Ronald and Harald POELTNER, *op. cit.*
89 George KARARACH, *op. cit.*, p. 629.

payment of the SPV by the public sector, the low creditworthiness of local African public entities may raise questions because of the delicate reliability of this type of counterparty. The issue is also critical for project financing where revenues are generated directly from users. Particular attention needs to be paid to tariff setting and collection issues for these projects.

These risks, which are most often identified during the structuring and auditing of African projects, are real but do not generally lead to a higher risk of default. On the contrary, the default rate for infrastructure-related debt in Africa is lower than for the same debt in North America, and lower than in other emerging regions such as Latin America and the Caribbean.[90]

C. Lack of capacity, bureaucracy, red tape, corruption

42 Local deficiencies. – In Africa, weak administrative capacity and the ensuing slowness translate into higher transaction costs for investors.[91]

To promote a programme of major projects in Africa, governments need to find the political will to take a number of important decisions quickly and transparently. This challenge is most often compounded by the lack of experience and capacity gaps of the public officials responsible for advising policymakers and implementing projects.[92] The need for Africa to invest in the culture of project governance is therefore of great importance[93] in order to succeed in project financing.

The dominant focus at the moment is about closing the funding gap and moving projects from the design phase to implementation. However, quality control of project implementation should not be overlooked. Weaknesses in the implementation of funding have a significant impact on the quality of infrastructure. African countries and multilateral organisations must also focus on downstream issues relating to the management and implementation of contracts.[94] Their actions are sometimes in competition and not always sufficiently convergent.

D. National planning and sectoral governance

43 Project planning. – The funding shortfall in the main sectors concerned is explained in particular by the need to reform national planning in order to improve project design and feasibility analysis. In some African countries, it is impossible to obtain long-term visibility: there is often a structural deficit in national public companies, political uncertainty accentuated by decisions that sometimes lack rationality and chronic financial difficulties on the part of the State, which is therefore unable to provide a guarantee as a last resort.[95]

90 *Ibid.*, p. 19.
91 *Ibid.*, p. 18.
92 George Kararach, *op. cit.*, p. 634.
93 *Ibid.*
94 *Ibid.*, p. 635.
95 Antoine Huard and Benjamin Fremaux, *Solar Energy in Africa: A Bright Future*, Institut Montaigne, 2019, p. 55.

44 Long term monitoring. – In the financing of infrastructure projects, the assets in question have a long lifespan and the decisions taken regarding the selection of projects have lasting effects on the cost and quality of services.[96] The maintenance and monitoring of infrastructure projects is as important as new investment, as we shall see in the third part of this book. Stricter routine maintenance regimes can free up valuable resources for other investments.[97] This means strengthening sector governance to ensure better maintenance of existing infrastructure, improving pricing policies and practices, and improving the quality of services. Addressing these issues could result in substantial savings for African economies. Resolving the infrastructure deficit is therefore not just a matter of building new infrastructure[98] but also of thinking about how it should be monitored. Part 3 of this book deals with these issues.

E. Limited availability of local funding

45 Limited domestic players. – Due to the poor development of local capital markets, local banks are often unable to provide long-term loans. Africa is therefore limited by low domestic revenues and must tap foreign sources of finance. Attracting funds from the private sector, particularly from abroad, is a major challenge in bridging Africa's structural financing gap. With the exception of the ICT sector, the private sector provides only a small share of financing, which is only allocated to projects that are heavily protected by State guarantees or multilateral donors.

Today, innovative regional players such as AfreximBank, Trade and Development Bank (TDB) and DBSA[99] are emerging. Some countries, such as Morocco and South Africa, have been particularly active in project finance for over a decade. Banks in these countries have set up dedicated teams capable of arranging this type of financing. The robustness of their financial institutions and the diversity of their refinancing sources enable them to offer borrowers financing terms comparable to those offered by DFIs for an ever-increasing number of projects. These same institutions are increasingly interested in other countries on the continent. However, the amounts of local financing are often insufficient and not widely mobilised.[100] In a report, NEPAD proposed innovative solutions for developing local financing.[101] These, along with the question of financing involving local African banks, will be discussed in greater detail in the second part of this book.

96 ICA c/o ADB, *op. cit.*, p. 3.

97 *Ibid.*, p. 4.

98 George KARARACH, *op. cit.*, p. 635.

99 *Development Bank of Southern Africa.*

100 *Ibid.*, p. 625.

101 In particular, an African infrastructure development fund, an Africa Credit Guarantee Facility, the promotion of Africa-Owned Equity Funds, the development of the bond market, the securitisation of funds transferred by the diaspora, the establishment of strategic sovereign development funds, the mobilisation of sovereign pension funds, the establishment of regional capital markets and the promotion of new PPP models. UN and NEPAD, *16 Infrastructure Projects for African Integration*, 2016, p. 41.

Example of project financing by local banks: container terminal 3 at the Port of Tanger Med II

Tanger Alliance is a company set up by Marsa Maroc to operate container terminal 3 (TC3) at the port of Tanger Med II under a concession contract signed with the Tanger Med Special Agency (TMSA). Eurogate International (Germany), Contship Italia (Italy) and Hapag Lloyd have acquired a stake in Tanger Alliance to strengthen the project's implementation capacity.

Investments in the project included the acquisition of equipment, the construction of superstructures and studies worth 175 million euros. In view of the timing constraints for the start of commercial operations, Tanger Alliance initially arranged a bridging loan from its shareholders to cover financing needs before arranging bank financing to cover construction needs (construction costs, pre-operating costs and financing costs) and repayment of the shareholders' bridging loan.

Following a competitive bidding process involving most European commercial banks, DFIs and local banks, a banking pool including Moroccan banks was selected to provide the debt financing. 133 million was provided by a consortium of Moroccan banks comprising the Banque Centrale Populaire Group as mandated arranger, the Attijariwafa Bank Group as co-arranger, the Bank Of Africa Group and CIH Bank. This pool was able to offer competitive terms with a 16-year maturity and financing in euros that matched the needs identified for the project.

F. Energy transition and climate finance

46 The African continent has enormous potential in terms of energy transition. – It has 60% of the world's solar potential and 40% of strategic minerals for decarbonisation but requires very substantial financial resources to finance these investments and deal with the consequences of climate change.[102]

The continent's needs in terms of climate finance are immense and investment flows are still insufficient

According to the think tank Climate Policy Initiative, Africa will need USD 2.8 trillion between 2020 and 2030 to implement its NDCs (Nationally Determined Contributions), the national climate action plans agreed under the Paris Agreement in 2015. The annual need to achieve these NDCs is USD

102 Perrine Mouterde, "Le continent africain un potentiel incroyable en matière d'énergies renouvelables", *Le Monde*, 5 December 2023.

277 billion, while annual flows of climate finance to Africa stand at USD 29.5 billion, 9 times less than the estimated needs.[103]

The gap between climate investment needs and flows varies across countries, although all sub-regions receive significantly less than their estimated needs. The largest gap is in Central Africa and East Africa, which average 26% and 23% of GDP respectively. North African countries have the smallest climate investment gap (3% of GDP). These differences can be explained in particular by differences between countries relating to socio-political and economic instability, the country's regulations and governance, microeconomic conditions such as the lack of bankable projects, and the lack of technical capacity to attract international financing.[104]

Customer financing needs and flows in Africa (USD billion, annual average)[105]

86% of climate investments in Africa are financed by public institutions

Of the USD 29.5 billion of climate investment in Africa, USD 25.3 billion came from public funds (86%) on average over the period 2019–2020. Multilateral DFIs represent the largest source of climate investment in Africa (USD 11.6 billion), followed by governments (USD 6.4 billion) and bilateral DFIs (USD 5.3 billion).

Private investors account for only 14% of total funds and are mainly made up of private companies (USD 1.6 billion) and commercial banks (USD 1.1 billion). The share of private sector climate investment in Africa (14%) is much lower than in other regions such as Latin America and the Caribbean (49%), East Asia and the Pacific (39%) and South Asia (37%).

Multilateral climate funds invested USD 1 billion, or 3.5% of total climate investments. The main funds are the Green Climate Fund (43%), the Global Environment Facility (27%), the CTF (13%), the Least Developed Countries Fund (9%) and the Adaptation Fund (4%).[106]

32% of climate investments are concentrated in the energy sector

Of the USD 29.5 billion in annual investment between 2019 and 2020, the energy sector is the biggest beneficiary of climate investments on the

103 Chavi Meattle, Rajashree Padmanabhi, Pedro de Aragão Fernandes, Anna Balm, Githungo Wakaba, Daniela Chiriac, Bella Tonkonogy and Dharshan Wignarajah, "Landscape of climate finance in Africa", Climate Policy Initiative, September 2022.

104 *Ibid.*

105 Flows are annual averages for 2019 and 2020; needs are annual averages for the period 2020–2030. Source: CPI, "Landscape of climate finance in Africa", op. cit.

106 *Ibid.*

continent (32%), followed by agriculture and forestry (16%), transport (9%), water (9%) and construction & infrastructure (4%). The energy sector in particular attracted the majority of private investment, as energy projects generally have a more stable risk-return profile.[107]

New initiatives to promote the growth of climate finance emerged, notably at COP28 in Dubai

At COP28, held in the United Arab Emirates (UAE) in December 2023, the UAE announced the creation of a USD 30 billion climate fund with the aim of attracting USD 250 billion in investment for the countries of the South.[108] In addition, the Green Climate Fund reached a record level of financing at COP28, with an additional commitment of USD 3.5 billion (including USD 3 billion from the United States), bringing the total amount committed to USD 12.8 billion.[109]

G. The US strategy for project financing in Africa

47 US-Africa initiatives. – Structured around a differentiated intervention method, the United States' strategy in Africa has recently evolved, reflecting a desire to increase American investment on the African continent. This new American positioning in Africa is taking place against a backdrop of increased competition with China. It aims to strengthen coordination with regional players, combat climate change and promote economic development.

Updated in 2022, the United States' strategy in Africa is based on three priorities: closer ties and greater coordination with African regional institutions; increased cooperation to combat climate change and promote a just energy transition; and increased funding for economic projects that are a priority for African countries, including the mobilisation of private capital.[110] To achieve its objectives and finance projects developed on the African continent, the United States relies on various organisations. Firstly, there are its development agencies: the USAID, created in 1961, and the Millennium Challenge Corporation (MCC), created in 2004. These agencies make their interventions conditional on compliance with the objectives set out in the US strategy and provide grants and time-limited technical assistance to the countries in which they operate. The United States also has the US Development Finance Corporation (DFC), which

107 *Ibid.*

108 William James, "UAE president announces $30 bln fund to bridge climate finance gap", *Reuters*, 1 December 2023.

109 Green Climate Fund, "COP28: Green climate fund reaches record funding level", 3 December 2023.

110 US Department of State, "Fact sheet: US strategy for Sub-Saharan Africa", 8 August 2022.

works with the private sector to propose financing solutions. Launched in 2020, this institution was created by merging the activities of USAID's Overseas Private Investment Corporation (OPIC) and the Development Credit Authority (DCA).[111] With the DFC, the United States wanted to bring the agencies closer to their investments. OPIC's main constraint was the exclusive use of debt, which forced private equity investors to create specialised vehicles and various specific arrangements to obtain financing from the US institution. This prevented OPIC from taking part in joint operations with its European counterparts such as France's Proparco, Germany's DEG and Belgium's BIO.[112] Finally, the US Export-Import Bank (US EXIM) plays a role in facilitating trade and strengthening economic ties with Africa, in particular by supporting exports from US companies to the continent.

48 Specific methods of intervention by American development agencies: the case of MCC compacts. – The intervention method used by the United States differs from that used by most bilateral development agencies, as can be seen from the MCC's "compact" programmes. With these programmes, the US development agency does not limit itself to funding, but extends its scope of intervention to project management, in coordination with the partner government, by creating structures to implement the projects financed. For example, the second compact signed between the government of Benin and the MCC gave rise to the Millennium Challenge Account Benin II (MCA II). This structure was responsible for implementing the programme financed to the tune of USD 391 million by the MCC over a period of six years (2017 to 2023) to improve the quantity and quality of electricity supply in Benin. The government of Benin also contributed USD 32 million to the financing of the programme. The main activities and components of the project to achieve the objective were: (i) support for policy, regulatory and institutional reform; (ii) capacity building for the Société Béninoise d'Energie Electrique (SBEE); and (iii) public information and education on reforms and energy efficiency.[113] The creation of an entity such as MCA II is not a common practice among development agencies, which are generally content to fund the ministries concerned by their project.

Between 2004 and 2021, the MCC will have approved almost $14 billion in grants through its "Compacts" and "Threshold Programmes". Threshold programmes, which last between one and two years, help countries to improve their governance and their eligibility score for Compacts. The improvement in country governance is seen by some observers as the "MCC effect". Indeed, the large amounts of the grants (on average $350 million) encourage future beneficiaries to undertake major reforms in order to be eligible. These reforms mainly concern the fight against corruption, the traceability of public spending, the transparency of contract award procedures and access to healthcare for children. Côte d'Ivoire

111 https://www.dfc.gov/.

112 Joël Té-Léssia Assoko, "USA-Afrique: une nouvelle agence américaine pour l'investissement", *Jeune Afrique*, 19 August 2019.

113 MCA-Bénin II, "Rapport d'achèvement du programme", September 2023.

improved its performance on MCC indicators from 5 to 14 (out of 20) between 2011 and 2016, culminating in the approval of its first Compact programme.[114]

Such reforms are key to favour the emergence of PPP projects financed in the health sector. For example, in 2015 in Kenya, General Electric (GE) secured a $230 million PPP contract to supply diagnostic equipment such as ultrasound and electrocardiograph machines to 98 hospitals and to equip 11 intensive care units. The contract obliges GE to keep the machines in working order at least 95% of the time.[115]

49 An announced increase in US investment in the continent after years of decline. – With the new 2022 strategy, the United States is aiming to significantly increase investment in Africa by devoting USD 55 billion over three years to the continent.[116] This contrasts with the decline that occurred in previous years as a result of a less proactive policy under the Trump administration, as can be seen from the evolution of USAID funding in Africa over this period. In 2020, the United States committed USD 243 million in the form of grants awarded by USAID, compared with USD 297 million in 2018, a drop of 18%. The two sectors in which the United States invested the most in 2020 were the water and sanitation sector, which accounted for 74% of total commitments (USD 180 million), and the energy sector, with 25% of total commitments (USD 60 million). Egypt in particular has benefited from investments in the water and sanitation sector, with USD 11 million invested to improve access to water and sanitation in underserved rural communities in Upper Egypt. Also in 2020, a USD 1.9 million grant was awarded to Nigeria as part of USAID's Power Africa initiative to, among other things, contribute to the development of a national electricity metering policy.[117]

50 Investment targeting strategic infrastructure in a context of competition with China. – The new American strategy in Africa is very clear on the issue of competition with China. This competition is illustrated by investments in strategic infrastructure, particularly in the transport and energy sectors, where China already has a strong presence on the African continent (see focus on ChinAfrica). The Global Infrastructure and Investment Partnership (GIIP) initiative, worth USD 600 billion over five years and designed to bridge the global infrastructure gap, was launched by the G7 in 2023 at the instigation of the United States.

Within this framework, the United States plans to invest in infrastructure projects related to transport, digital access, agriculture and clean energy.[118] It has announced a USD 250 million investment in a railway line between the port of

114 Joël Té-Léssia Assoko, "États-Unis – Afrique: cinq questions pour comprendre l'influence de la MCC", *Jeune Afrique*, 25 October 2022.

115 Africa's Business Revolution, "How to succeed in the worlds' next big growth market", *Harvard Business Review Press*, p. 66, 2018.

116 Piotr Smolar, "Au sommet États-Unis-Afrique, Joe Biden, partenaire séducteur des pays africains", *Le Monde*, 15 December 2022.

117 ICA c/o AfDB, "Trends in infrastructure financing in Africa – 2019–2020", *op. cit.*

118 US Department of State, "Accelerating the US-Africa partnership after the 2022 US-Africa leaders summit", 13 December 2023.

Lobito in Angola and the copper-rich mining area of the DRC and Zambia (the Lobito corridor). Washington will also provide USD 900 million for two solar farm projects in Angola and invest USD 300 million in data centres in Ghana.[119]

Section 2. Prerequisites

51 Contents. – The development of infrastructures requires prerequisites such as the creation of an environment favourable to PPPs (§ 1), the creation of units dedicated to major infrastructure projects within the relevant ministries (§ 2) and the use of external expertise (§ 3).

§ 1. Favourable legal environment

52 Enabling environment. – Given the scale of the investment required, the private sector plays a crucial role in the economic development of the African continent[120] as a complement to public infrastructure funding. However, in Africa, the private sector can often be confronted with a legal and institutional environment that is unsuitable for investment due to its instability, immaturity or obsolescence. Governments therefore need to implement national policies that are favourable to private sector investment in infrastructure (simplified procedures, easier ways of organising structures and securing assets or protecting property), and they also need to introduce appropriate legal frameworks[121] on certain points, such as clear, modern texts governing PPPs. It is commonly said that "(p)olicies that improve the quality of projects at entry, address currency risk, relax capital controls, and enable cost recovery pricing can unlock private sector participation in infrastructure financing".[122] Similarly, governments need to ensure that infrastructure-related sectors are effectively regulated by structured independent authorities.

§ 2. PPP units

53 Capacity building. – PPP projects are often poorly structured due to a lack of skills or experience within the relevant ministries in Africa.[123] Although the trend is for governments to take ownership of the project finance model, given the number

119 Solveig Godeluck, "Washington advocates a collective response", *Les Echos*, 19 October 2023.

120 Sénégal, "Projet de loi relatif aux contrats de partenariat: Exposé des motifs", 2021, p. 1, [Online], consulted on 8 October 2021. https://library.pppknowledgelab.org/Government%20of%20Senegal/documents/2797/download

121 African Development Bank, "African economic outlook", *Chapter 3 – Africa's Infrastructure: Considerable Potential But Limited Impact on Equitable Growth*, p. 84, 2018 [Online], accessed 8 Oct. 2021. https://www.afdb.org/fileadmin/uploads/afdb/Documents/Publications/2018AEO/Perspectives_Economiques_en_Afrique_2018_-_fr_Chapitre3.pdf

122 Global policy, 2024-05, Vol. 15 (2), pp. 465–474, Joseph Mawejje, Private sector participation in infrastructure in emerging market and developing economies: Evolution, constraints, and policies – Mawejje – 2024 – Global Policy – Wiley Online Library.

123 *Ibid.*, p. 85.

of projects already deployed, there is still a significant need for skills development. Because PPP projects are particularly complex, governments need to design institutional architectures that are organised and equipped to develop this type of project.[124] Within this architecture, units dedicated to PPPs will play a central role in structuring and setting up projects. It is vital that they have the skills and resources needed to carry out the technical and legal assistance tasks.[125]

§ 3. External expertise

54 Advisers. – The use of external expertise is essential for the various parties involved in financing infrastructure projects, and even more so in Africa, where the choice of people with knowledge of the specific nature of these projects is essential. Although public parties are increasingly experienced in developing infrastructure projects, they are still not sufficiently experienced to manage, develop and complete infrastructure projects. External experts may include legal advisers, financial experts,[126] tax experts, environmental experts or insurance specialists. Their assistance at various stages or throughout the project is an effective way of avoiding the materialisation of certain risks that can be damaging to the contracting parties, including lenders.[127]

It should be remembered that financial institutions often require the opinion of technical experts before disbursing loans. These may include construction and completion audits or environmental compliance checks. As for insurers, they provide advice to the project company and lenders to cover certain project-related risks, such as property damage, delays in starting up operations or operating losses.[128]

124 ALSF and NRF, "Projet de partenariats public-privé (PPP), Dans le secteur des infrastructures", pp. 50 and 51, [Online], published online in June 2020, consulted on 8 October 2021. https://alsf.academy/sites/default/files/2020-06/PPP%20Handbook%20-%20FR_0.pdf

125 See paragraph 389.

126 Association of Chartered Certified Accountants & Chartered Professional Accountants, "Bridging Africa's infrastructure gap: Putting the accountant at the heart of decision-making", June 2019 [Online], accessed 8 Oct. 2021.

127 Géry Deffontaines, "Les consultants dans les PPP: entre expertise au service du client public et intermédiation pour protéger le 'marché'", *Politiques et management public* [Online], Vol. 29/1.2012, online since 26 June 2014, accessed 8 Oct. 2021. https://journals.openedition.org/pmp/4640

128 ALSF and NRF, "Projet de partenariats public-privé (PPP), Dans le secteur des i", p. 81 [Online], uploaded June 2020, accessed 8 Oct. 2021. https://alsf.academy/sites/default/files/2020-06/PPP%20Handbook%20-%20FR_0.pdf

2 The different forms of infrastructure projects

Section 1. The importance of understanding the economic model of the underlying infrastructure project

55 Families of PPPs. – As explained in the introduction, there are two main families of projects delegated in the form of PPPs which make it possible to structure project financing: those involving public payment, i.e. where the public sector pays the project company directly, for example in the case of the construction and operation of a public building; and projects involving payment by users, such as toll motorways. These families are described in more detail later in this chapter. It is important to emphasise the distinction between the raising of finance (which in this case comes from the private sector) and the cost of the infrastructure *in the end*. If the search for and raising of finance (debt and equity) are delegated to the private sector, the cost of the infrastructure will *ultimately* be borne by the public sector, particularly for infrastructure where no revenue is generated by users. The rents charged by the project company to the public party take into account all the costs incurred by the latter (construction costs, operating costs, transaction costs, bank financing costs, shareholder remuneration). PPPs are therefore not a solution for reducing the State's budget. If users do not cover the entire costs of the project, there will necessarily be an impact on public finances.

56 Overall long-term costs. – The long-term costs for the public sector or users must therefore be analysed in detail, by analysing the budgetary sustainability of the various projects, to ensure the social and economic relevance of each of them. The use of PPPs, and by extension project financing, can therefore only be justified on budgetary, accounting or financial grounds. This recourse can only be justified by the preponderance of the benefits induced (availability of the infrastructure within a shorter timeframe, better cost control than under public contracting, better quality of service, assurance of quality maintenance over the long term, impact on the economic development of the country or region concerned) compared with the associated costs, which are necessarily greater (transactions that are more complex to carry out and therefore require greater external support, higher financing costs, remuneration of private shareholders).

DOI: 10.4324/9781003616894-4

57 Public payment or user payment. – The two main types of contractual arrangements that can be envisaged for the implementation of infrastructure projects (with initial investment to be borne by the private partner) can be summarised as follows:

- A global contract with public payment: the private partner is remunerated through rent payments from the public party, possibly reduced by revenues from users and other ancillary revenues (if the project generates revenues); the private partner is responsible for the design, financing of all or part of the project, construction, maintenance and operation of the infrastructure. This type of arrangement is possible whether or not the project generates revenue from users. This type of project will only be feasible in African countries with a high level of creditworthiness.
- This approach is often described as concessionary, in which the private partner bears the investment and the risk related to the use of the infrastructure. It is responsible for the design, financing of all or part of the infrastructure, construction, maintenance and operation. This type of arrangement tends to be reserved for projects that generate revenue from users, where ridership is sufficiently predictable for the private partner to bear the risk. In this case, if it turns out that the revenue from users is not sufficient to ensure the economic equilibrium of the operation, several mechanisms could be considered: (i) the collection of ancillary revenue and (ii) the payment of a subsidy by the public party.

Section 2. Project business model and impact on public debt

§ 1. Debt sustainability

58 Economic viability. – While infrastructure development is crucial to economic growth, debt sustainability for each African State is a major component of national macroeconomic stability. These two concepts are linked directly or indirectly in several ways and will influence the ability of public parties to arrange the financing of infrastructure projects.

- If the public authorities bear the cost of the debt, public financing (via public finance as described above) has a clear and direct increasing impact on the level of public debt.
- Doubts about the ability of public authorities to meet their financial and contractual obligations will increase the cost of capital, as investors demand a higher return to compensate for the increased risk. Public authorities will therefore have to provide guarantees or other forms of credit support, which may put direct or indirect pressure on the government's balance sheet (as debt or contingent liabilities).
- Infrastructure projects, particularly those in the public and social interest, can have a low profitability profile. Investments with low or even negative economic rates of return can then lead to unsustainable levels of debt, triggering a downward spiral in sovereign ratings and an increase in the State's debt servicing commitments.

59 Debt/GDP ratio. – In order to maintain a debt/GDP ratio at a sustainable level (and in line with local regulatory requirements), two options are therefore possible: increase GDP or reduce public debt, in which case the question of how to deal with the financial commitments linked to the PPP is crucial. These parameters are decisive in the development of projects, as they confirm or invalidate their feasibility.

§ 2. Off-balance sheet PPP assets and liabilities

60 Definition. – Project financing is often carried out through PPP, which are "long-term contracts between two units, under which one unit acquires or builds an asset or set of assets, operates it for a certain period, and then hands the asset over to a second unit" (World Bank, 2014). PPPs thus draw on private finance and expertise by creating a special purpose vehicle (SPV), a legal entity responsible for designing, building, operating and financing a specific infrastructure project.

61 Statistical treatment. – The question of the statistical treatment of PPP assets and liabilities in the national accounts is crucial for governments, which have to account for and report – in different ways – their financial commitments, including those made under PPP contracts. Depending on the treatment adopted, the State's PPP commitments may or may not increase public debt.

62 Heterogeneity of accounting standards for commitments given by the public sector. – There is no harmonised accounting and tax framework for PPPs[1] yet. However, African governments must comply with certain local and international accounting and financial reporting standards. They often capture and report financial information in three related frameworks:

- **Public finance statistics**, as a summary of national government finances; this may follow regional or international standards such as those issued by Eurostat (for European countries) or the IMF.
- **Government financial statements** may follow International Public Sector Accounting Standards (IPSAS), which differ from IFRS insofar as they relate to the public sector.
- **Budget documentation and financial execution**, which are part of budget preparation; they are not subject to international standards.

To remember

Maintaining off-balance sheet debt does not reduce the State's actual liabilities and may simply disguise the State's liabilities, thereby reducing the effectiveness of public debt control mechanisms. As a matter of general policy, the use of off-balance sheet debt should be carefully considered before initiating project financing, and safeguards implemented accordingly.

1 https://www.imf.org/external/np/fad/2004/pifp/eng/031204.pdf

§ 3. Project accounting

63 Accounting method. – The main problem in accounting for PPP assets and liabilities is determining to which party these assets and the associated debt should be allocated. However, the decision to record PPP assets and liabilities on the balance sheet of the State or the private company carrying out the project is complex.

64 Economic ownership concept. – While it is not possible to lay down prescriptive rules given the variety of PPPs, the concept of economic ownership is central to determining the allocation of ownership of the assets and liabilities associated with the PPP to the public or private party. Economic ownership is itself defined either on the basis of a "risks and rewards" approach, or on the basis of a "control" approach. In the context of PPPs, the "risk and reward" approach, determined by identifying the stakeholder who bears the majority of the risk and the stakeholder who is expected to receive the majority of the reward linked to the asset, seems to be the most commonly adopted. The IMF and Eurostat use this approach, as do credit rating agencies, which often follow the IMF/Eurostat methodology for reporting PPPs in European countries.

65 IMF *Government Finance Statistics Manual.* – For African governments, the main source of guidance for the statistical reporting format is the IMF *Government Finance Statistics Manual* (*GFSM*, 2014). This manual provides guidelines for public authorities to strengthen their capacity to formulate fiscal policy, and thus classify PPP assets and liabilities. As there is still no global agreement among statisticians on the treatment of PPPs, the *GFSM* is non-prescriptive. The *Manual* does, however, follow a risk/reward approach, with assets and liabilities considered off-balance sheet if there is an adequate transfer of risks and rewards from the State to the private partner, and directly on the State's balance sheet if not.

66 Determining the economic ownership of PPP assets. – According to the IMF's *GFSM*, the factors to be considered include the risks associated with the acquisition of the asset and those associated with its operation, namely:

- **government responsibility**: the degree to which the government controls the design, quality, size and maintenance of the asset;
- **construction risk:** the party responsible for bearing the construction risks, including the risk of additional costs resulting from late delivery or failure to comply with technical and environmental specifications;
- **supply-side risks:** the extent to which the government is able to control the services provided and the associated price;
- **demand risks:** the risk that demand will be weaker than expected;
- **residual value and obsolescence risk:** the risk that the value of the asset will differ from the agreed price at the end of the contractual period;
- **availability risk:** the risk of additional costs or penalties due to the volume and/or quality of services.

The relative importance of each factor may vary depending on the contractual specifics of each PPP.

67 Statistical treatment. – If the State is considered to be the economic owner of the assets during the period of the contract but does not make any explicit payment at the start of the contract, a transaction must be imputed to cover the acquisition of the assets. If the private company is deemed to be the economic owner of the assets during the contract period, then any debt associated with the acquisition of the assets should be attributed to the private company.[2]

68 Off-balance sheet accounting by exception. – Governments may be allowed to keep project assets and liabilities off-balance sheet (as they would appear on the balance sheet of the private sector). This would allow them – to a certain extent – to use the debt for other investments and maintain a sustainable debt level.

69 Accounting for direct and indirect public commitments. – The question of the statistical treatment of PPPs in public debt is therefore essential for all stakeholders, who follow accounting and statistical frameworks. These standards provide guidelines for identifying to which units (private or public) PPP assets and associated liabilities should be attributed.

70 Sovereign guarantees. – In the case of PPPs, governments may hold significant stakes through ownership of assets, equity participation, debt financing or risk sharing, including sovereign guarantees and other credit enhancement mechanisms. These latter types of mechanisms require governments to provide one-off guarantees, which can be divided into:

- **Direct liabilities**, which cover commitments recognised by law or specified in a contractual agreement. They arise in all cases and are therefore certain. Direct liabilities include, for example, budget expenditure, sovereign debt, a grant to cover investment costs or a fixed operating subsidy.
- **Explicit contingent/conditional (or indirect) liabilities** are liabilities that depend on certain events that may or may not occur. They are explicitly described in the PPP contracts. These liabilities cover, for example, sovereign guarantees, compensation in the event of unexpected events, indemnities in the event of changes to the contract, termination indemnities and inflation indexation provisions.
- **Contingent (or indirect) implicit liabilities** are conditional commitments which are not explicitly written into the PPP contract but which are recognised once a condition or event has occurred. An example is an expenditure following a natural disaster. Implicit liabilities can therefore be considered as uncertain commitments that may result in future expenditure if specific conditions are met or if certain events occur.

71 Accounting rules for contingent liabilities: likely or unlikely to be called? – Accounting for contingent liabilities is challenging for governments, as they are

2 IMF, *Public Finance Statistics Manual*, 2014.

uncertain and sometimes difficult to quantify. As a general rule, contingent liabilities are not included in the guarantor's debt – until the realisation conditions have been met – as they are not unconditional liabilities.

72 IMF constraints. – The IMF defines contingent liabilities as "obligations that arise only if one or more specific and distinct events occur in the future". These contingencies create budgetary risks and may result from deliberate public policy or unforeseen events.

The IMF accounting framework requires contingent liabilities to be recorded as memorandum items or in the notes to the financial statements, to help users understand their nature, timing and amount.[3] However, most African States manage their accounts on a cash basis. This involves recording accounting transactions for income and expenditure only when the corresponding cash is received, or payments are made. It allows them to decide whether to disclose contingent liabilities. On the other hand, on an accrual basis, expected costs are presented in the budgetary accounts when a guarantee is granted.

73 Contingent liabilities and their macroeconomic impact. – Contingent liabilities represent significant fiscal and macroeconomic risks for African governments. A government guarantee may seem attractive in the short term, as it remains "hidden" in the financial statements, but in the long term it can be particularly costly. Given these risks, rating agencies and the IMF are paying increasing attention to these liabilities when assessing a government's creditworthiness. These liabilities have a direct impact on the amount of future loans and the attractiveness of African countries on international markets.

Section 3. The influence of the sector

The nature, distribution and quantification of risks vary depending on the sector in which project finance is structured.

§ 1. Transport

74 Project financing in the transport sector is generally very demanding in terms of initial and recurring capital expenditure. This sector necessarily mobilises a great deal of financial resources to secure land and enable passenger transport, whether for airports, railway lines or motorways. In this sector, the traffic risk is very often borne by the private partner, forcing lenders to be highly attentive to the prices set for users and to traffic forecasts. The SPV must also configure the logistical and material resources to enable the development of a safe infrastructure, given the security risks inherent in the transport sector. The risks are therefore very specific, since the sponsor of a transport project often bears not only the traffic risk but also all day-to-day operating risks for users. Similarly, the regulatory impacts can be numerous insofar as operators are subject to the uncertainties of changes in standards, rules or directives issued by

3 IMF, *Public Sector Debt Statistics: Provisions, Contingent Liabilities and Contingent Assets.*

dedicated regulatory authorities. To a certain extent, depending on the economic balance between traffic revenues and project costs, various subsidies may be negotiated contractually to ensure the bankability of projects and the sustainability of funding.

Example of motorway project financing: the Dakar – AIBD motorway

This is the first motorway PPP in sub-Saharan Africa. In 2009, the Senegalese government awarded Eiffage a 30-year contract to finance, design, build, operate and maintain the section of motorway between Dakar and Diamniadio. This 25 km motorway is the first link in the Dakar-Bamako route in Mali. The journey time between Dakar and Diamniadio has been cut from 2 hours to less than 30 minutes. In early 2014, Eiffage won the contract to extend the motorway to link Diamniadio to Blaise Diagne International Airport (AIBD) via an additional 17 km. The group is responsible for financing, design and construction, as well as operation for a period of 25 years, and handed over the entire route in October 2016. The total investment is €310m, financed by the Senegalese government and Eiffage. The financing included €60 million in senior and subordinated debt, with €36 million reinvested from operating revenues and subsidies provided by multilateral donors (AfDB, AFD) and €30 million in equity.

In summary, the project comprises 42 km of motorway for an investment of €310m for a public customer, the Republic of Senegal via APIX. The concession contracts were signed successively in July 2009 and February 2014, and commissioning took place in August 2013 (25 km) and October 2016 (17 km).[4]

On 22 December 2021, the State of Senegal and Eiffage amended the agreement relating to the Autoroute de l'Avenir concession (SECAA) to record the State's acquisition of a 25% stake in the project company. The agreement also covers the revaluation of the annual State fee, representing 2% of SECAA's annual turnover, with a minimum of 800 million FCFA per year instead of 1,000 million FCFA per year in the previous contract, as well as the readjustment of the clauses and deadlines for sharing the fruits of the concession, the freezing of tariffs indexation to inflation for five years, and the provision of lighting by the concession holder along the entire length of the current section and at the level of the diffusers. According to the details contained in a press release from the Ministry, the State has also obtained a readjustment of the concession's profit-sharing clauses and deadlines, as well as a cap on the target internal rate of return (IRR) of 17% instead of 20.1% in the supplementary contract, with a correction of the assumptions.

4 Source Eiffage.

§ 2. *Energy*

75 In the energy sector, and particularly in African IPP projects, the risk profile of the purchaser of the power generation is particularly important to consider. The risk profile of a public electricity company purchasing the energy produced is not the same in Morocco as in Guinea. The level of guarantees required by sponsors and lenders will differ. The supply of fuel, if the facility is not powered by renewable energy, is a key element to consider, as a particular supply risk may arise, in the event of a political crisis or border closure (as in the case of Mali, given the embargo in 2022). Similarly, the fate of the infrastructure at the end of the contract is another key aspect, as it may entail risks relating to environmental protection, restoration guarantees or dismantling. Furthermore, in renewable energy projects, quantifying the primary energy resource (solar, wind, hydropower) is a key point in understanding the project's economic model in order to validate its feasibility in terms of project financing. It should be emphasised that this is certainly the sector in which the most projects are carried out using this technique.

Example of IPP financing: the Azura-Edo IPP[5]

The Azura-Edo IPP is a 461 MW gas-fired open cycle power plant located on the northeastern outskirts of Benin City in Edo, Nigeria.[6] The total cost of the project amounted to approximately USD 654 million, and the plant was completed eight months ahead of schedule in May 2018. As one of the first IPPs to come online in Nigeria in over a decade, Azura-Edo has played a crucial role in addressing the country's severe power shortages.

The Azura-Edo IPP benefits from full support from the Federal Government of Nigeria, with a tripartite agreement between Azura, the Nigerian Bulk Electricity Trading PLC (NBET) and the Nigerian Ministry of Finance. Under this agreement, the Ministry of Finance backstops payments owed to Azura by NBET in the event of a termination of the PPA. Azura was one of 14 IPPs nominated by the Ministry of Finance for participation in a PRG series proposed by the World Bank. MIGA has also provided political risk insurance for the project, including breach of contract cover. The project was developed by Azura Power West Africa Limited, a Nigerian SPV incorporated specifically for this purpose.

The primary sponsor of the project is Amaya Capital, a London-based principal investment firm focused on developing energy and consumer sector projects in West Africa. Amaya's co-developers and shareholders include Aldwych International, which contributed technical expertise, the African Infrastructure Investment Fund 2 (AIIF2), and Asset and Resource Management Ltd. The Edo State government holds a 2.5% equity stake in the project

5 https://aiimafrica.com/media/case-study-detail/case-study-azura/
6 https://azurapower.com/project/azura-edo/

in exchange for the provision of land and road infrastructure and retains an option to purchase an additional 7.5% stake in cash.

The financing[7] structure for the project included a total debt tranche of approximately USD 467 million, funded through a combination of concessional loans from the FGN, senior loans from DFIs and commercial debt supported by ECAs such as Hermes, MIGA and PRG. The equity portion is primarily held by a consortium of private investors. IFC, a key financial player in the project, provided a senior loan of up to USD 125 million for its own account and co-arranged the DFI debt tranche alongside FMO (the Dutch development bank).

The plant operates under a BOOT structure, and the electricity generated is sold under a 20-year PPA with the Nigerian Bulk Electricity Trading PLC, ensuring long-term revenue stability. The Azura-Edo IPP represents a significant milestone in Nigeria's energy sector, demonstrating the successful integration of private sector involvement with government support to address the country's energy deficit and drive economic growth.

§ 3. Telecommunications

76 In the telecommunications sector, the risks of renewal and obsolescence are particularly significant due to constant and rapid technological developments. The risk of securing and making available land is also an important factor, since fibre optic and mobile network projects require many sites, either for digging trenches to lay the fibre or for installing base stations.

Each sector has its own particularities to consider. As a result, the risk allocation matrices for each party, public or private, are very different from one project to another and from one sector to another. These sectoral elements take on different significance depending on the country in which the project is developed.

For some telecommunications projects, the risks can be very specific, as illustrated by the first pan-African satellite project described next.

The orbital adventures of the first pan-African satellite

In 1992, the African States created a pan-African international organisation called RASCOM. RASCOM is a commercial intergovernmental organisation whose capital is open to the private sector and whose mission is to make available to all regions of African countries, efficient and economical means of telecommunications and to meet their sound and television broadcasting needs, using all appropriate technologies, including a regional satellite communication system suitably integrated with existing and/or planned national

7 Disclosure – Azura Edo IPP.

networks in order to foster the development of African countries. It includes 45 countries on the continent.

This organisation awarded the concession for the design, construction, financing and operation of the first pan-African satellite to RASCOMSTAR QAF, a project company registered in Mauritius in 2001.

The project company is owned by Libya Africa Investment Portfolio (63%), 45 African telephone operators (25%) and the European space manufacturer Thales Alenia Space (12%), originally Alcatel.

The overall cost of the project was USD 380 million, with debt financing provided by the AfDB, the Banque de Développement des Etats de l'Afrique Centrale (BDEAC), the Banque Ouest Africaine de Développement (BOAD) and the *Libyan Arab Foreign Bank* (LAFB).

Following its launch on 21 December 2007, a problem occurred with one of the satellite's pressure regulation sub-assemblies, causing a helium leak and delaying final orbit entry. On 8 January 2008, satellite manufacturer Thales Alenia Space began a four-week in-orbit procedure. The orbit was successfully reached, but the satellite's lifetime was reduced to two and a half years instead of 15, as a result of the helium leak. This difficulty resulted in the loss of contracts and required the insurance policies that the project company had taken out to compensate it for the losses incurred as a result of the limited lifespan of the first satellite to be called in. The insurers therefore had to compensate the project company for all the costs involved in building a new satellite and launching it, a sum estimated at around USD 230 million.

Finally, a new Rascom-QAF1R (RQ1R) satellite, identical to Rascom-QAF1, was launched on 4 August 2010 by an Ariane 5 launcher from the Guiana Space Centre. Its launch mass was approximately 3,050 kg. The Rascom-QAF1R satellite, also built by Thales Alenia Space under a turnkey contract with RascomStar-QAF, will provide telecommunications services in rural African areas, long-distance and international links, direct television services and Internet access for 18 years.

§ 4. Mines

77 The mining sector is now a strategic investment sector. In the current context of energy transition, obtaining supplies of significant quantities of critical metals has become crucial for building solar panels or high-performance batteries, which will make it possible to meet the climate challenges of decarbonisation and steer the economy towards greater sustainability. Africa, with more than 450 projects linked to critical metals identified by the end of 2024[8] and abundant and

8 Africa Business+ & EY, "Critical minerals: The pivotal outlook", *op. cit.*

diverse reserves, is emerging as a key source of these critical metals, playing a strategic role in securing global supplies and underlining the growing interdependence between Africa and other regions of the world. Other metals, such as iron, are also experiencing a strong dynamic linked to the energy transition: iron is essential to steel production, a sector that accounts for almost 8% of CO_2 emissions worldwide. It is therefore becoming necessary to decarbonise this industry, by using high quality iron ore for transformation processes that consume less energy and therefore emit less CO_2. Africa is richly endowed with such resources, such as the Simandou deposit in Guinea, whose ore has a particularly high iron content of over 65%.[9]

However, the challenges of developing and financing these projects are considerable, not least because of the lack of infrastructure, the need for long-term political and institutional dialogue and a stable legal basis.

The mining sector has been the subject of major legislative adjustments in recent years, particularly in OHADA Member States. Mali recently adopted two pieces of legislation relating to the sector on 29 August 2023: a first law on the Mining Code (Law No. 2020-040) and a second on local content in the sector (Law No. 2023-041). Within the WAEMU, a regulation on the Community Mining Code was adopted on 16 June 2023. By significantly amending the one created in 2003, it aims to create "a mining environment that is conducive to sustainable economic development and that strikes a balance between the need to put in place incentives to attract investors and the need to protect the revenue base of Member States". Several African countries are also participating in the Extractive Industries Transparency Initiative (EITI) to develop a framework conducive to investment.

The mining sector is also facing challenges related to the infrastructure needs associated with its projects. Historically, mining has focused mainly on the most accessible deposits in order to minimise infrastructure costs. As these deposits are depleted, the focus is shifting to more remote locations, presenting major logistical challenges, particularly in terms of transport and energy infrastructure. It is crucial to develop reliable and sustainable energy sources to power these remote mining operations. These developments sometimes require cooperation between States, particularly where certain landlocked countries are concerned. One example illustrating these infrastructure needs is the Lobito Corridor project, jointly developed by Zambia and the Democratic Republic of Congo, which leads to the port of Lobito in Angola.[10] Another example is COMILOG in Gabon: the world's leading manganese producer,[11] majority-owned by the French group Eramet (64%) and the Gabonese State (29%), had to build a 648 km rail network and 24 stations linking eastern and western Gabon in order to transport the ore. A subsidiary, SETRAG,

9 Tom Wilson, "World's biggest mining project to start after 27 years of setbacks and scandals", *prec.*

10 Jessica Steinberg, *Mines, Communities, and States – The Local Politics of Natural Resource Extraction in Africa*, Cambridge University Press, 2019, pp. 103–122.

11 https://comilog.eramet.com/

was set up to operate the trains used to transport the ore for export. The trains also transport passengers, goods and forestry products. To finance its transport infrastructure, COMILOG opened SETRAG's capital to the French investment fund Meridiam, which acquired a 40% stake in 2021, in particular to finance the renovation and maintenance of the Transgabonnais railway.[12] Beyond the direct link with these operations, infrastructure development is necessary for the mining sector to respond to the social risks associated with mining and to obtain the "social licence to operate". This notion was ranked as the third concern by 65% of professionals in the sector in 2023.[13]

Example: the Simandou iron ore project in Guinea

The Simandou project is the largest integrated mining and infrastructure project ever undertaken on the African continent. Located in south-east Guinea, Simandou is the world's largest untapped reserve of high-quality iron ore. The development of the project has been fraught with challenges for over 20 years, including a lack of infrastructure and licensing and regulatory issues. First production is now scheduled for late 2025. The Simandou iron ore deposits consist of four blocks, divided between the Chinese-owned company Winning Consortium Simandou (WCS), which holds blocks 1 and 2, and Simfer, owned by the Anglo-Australian group Rio Tinto and the Chinese company Chinalco, which holds blocks 3 and 4. The Guinean State owns 15% of each of the two mining companies. WCS and Simfer will be able to export up to 120 million tonnes of ore a year (60 tonnes each),[14] representing around 10% of the world market for iron ore transported by sea.[15]

The infrastructure component of the project includes the construction of port infrastructure and more than 600 km of rail track linking the mines to the port. The special feature of the project is that these infrastructures will be shared between Simfer and WCS and co-developed by the two entities, thus enabling costs to be shared. Under the co-development agreement, each entity is responsible for building part of the shared infrastructure: Simfer is responsible for building the approximately 70 km rail spur linking its mine to the main rail line, as well as a 60 mtpa transhipment port. At the same time, WCS will build the main railway line of more than 500 km, the 16 km rail spur between its mine and the main line, and a barge dock. The co-developed infrastructure and rolling stock will then be transferred to and operated by Compagnie du TransGuinéen (CTG), a *joint venture* in which Simfer and

12 https://www.meridiam.com/assets/setrag-railway/

13 Paul Mitchell, "Top ten business risks and opportunities for mining and metals", *EY*, October 2023.

14 Rio Tinto, "Simandou iron ore project update", 5 December 2023.

15 Tom Wilson, "World's biggest mining project to start after 27 years of setbacks and scandals", *prec.*

WCS each hold 42.5% of the capital, in addition to the State, which holds 15%. Ownership of the rail and port infrastructure will be transferred from CTG to the Guinean State after a 35-year operating period.

The Simandou mining and infrastructure project is financed from equity by the shareholding mining companies. For example, Simfer's capital financing requirements alone are estimated at USD 11.6 billion, including USD 5.1 billion for mine construction and USD 6.5 billion for infrastructure.[16]

One of the special features of the project is that one of the future purchasers of production is expected to take an equity stake in the companies involved in the project in order to secure its future supplies: for example, the Chinese State-owned enterprise Baowu, the world's largest steel producer, holds an 8% stake in Simfer and has entered into an agreement to acquire a 49% stake in WCS's mining and infrastructure projects. Although currently financed solely from equity, once construction is complete, parts of the project could be refinanced through project finance.

§ 5. Traditional sources of financing for the mining sector

78 Intensive Capex. – The development of mining projects involves considerable investment costs, traditionally financed from three main sources: the internal financial resources of mining companies, external borrowed funds (often in the form of long-term loans) and government financing granted to a small number of key companies in the sector.

Self-financing of mining projects by mining companies is a common practice: major mining companies use their own financial resources to finance the exploration and development phases, implying too much uncertainty about the associated revenues. Capital expenditure by the world's 30 largest mining companies rose by 6.2% in 2023, reaching around USD 109 billion, although it remains 25% below its peak of USD 146 billion in 2013.[17]

Long-term bank loans are the most commonly used financial mechanism in the mining industry. These loans generally extend over 15 years or more, depending on the project, the sector and the company concerned. Since the 1990s, bank loans have accounted for more than 50% of major mining projects. Companies wishing to use credit facilities to build or modernise a mine must provide adequate loan guarantees and alternative debt repayment guarantees. A key characteristic is that banks generally lend on the basis of the value of the underlying assets, rather than the borrower's ability to generate future cash flows. However, most banks today are wary of new mining projects, reluctant to adjust debt maturities, grant grace periods or make other concessions that borrowers need in the face of market uncertainty.

16 *Ibid.*
17 S&P Global, "Capex for 30 biggest-spending miners to rise 6.2% in 2023", 19 October 2023.

79 Critical materials. – Because of the strategic importance of mineral raw materials for the development of economies, government financing of mining projects is widely practised throughout the world. The first lever that governments or public bodies can use is to provide government guarantees, enabling companies to obtain higher loan amounts on advantageous terms (extended grace period, low interest rates). A second means of government funding for the mining industry is through tax incentives. In some countries, tax incentives are granted to mining projects for exploration periods, in order to support the growth and diversification of mineral production. For example, Madagascar passed a law in 2001 to introduce an attractive tax, legal and customs regime for mining companies in order to support investment in this sector, which is considered critical to the country's growth. Mining companies eligible for this regime were exempted from the minimum income tax. At the same time, entities processing extracted minerals and foreign service providers supplying services to eligible mining companies also benefit from reduced income tax.[18] A third lever used by public bodies concerns investment in the capital of mining companies. These interventions can be crucial for high-risk projects. In 2023, for example, the State of Quebec announced C$250 million in funding for the construction of the Nemaska lithium mine.[19] Another recent trend has seen governments set up dedicated investment funds to invest in critical minerals projects and supply chains. For example, Australia's export credit agency, Export Finance Australia, created the Critical Minerals Facility to fill gaps in private finance for critical minerals projects. In April 2022, the agency agreed to lend $1.25 billion to Australian mining company Iluka Resources to build a fully integrated rare earth separation facility in Western Australia.[20] Similarly, the US government is providing significant funding for critical minerals[21] projects: for example, the U.S. Department of Energy's Loan Programs Office made a conditional commitment of $2 billion to Redwood Materials, for the construction of a battery materials campus in the state of Nevada.[22] It also conditionally offered $700 million to US mining company Pioneer for the development of the Rhyolite Ridge lithium and boron project in Nevada,[23] and $102 million to Syrah Resources for the development of a graphite processing facility in the state of Louisiana.[24] In France, the government has invested €500 million by 2023 in a fund dedicated to critical metals, managed by InfraVia,

18 PwC, "Tax incentives for investment in Madagascar".

19 François Normand, "Québec injects another $250 million into Nemaska Lithium", *Les Affaires*, 14 June 2023.

20 Peter Ker, "Iluka shares soar on WA rare earths refinery funding", *Financial Review*, 4 April 2022.

21 See also for more general considerations on critical minerals Henry Sanderson, Volt Rush, the winners and the losers in the race go to green, One World.

22 U.S. Department of Energy, "LPO offers conditional commitment to Redwood materials to produce critical electric vehicle battery components from recycled materials", 9 February 2023.

23 Ernest Scheyder and David Shepardson, "U.S. to lend ioneer $700 million for Nevada lithium mine", *Reuters*, 13 January 2023.

24 David Shepardson, "U.S. finalizes $102.1 mln loan to Syrah Resources for Louisiana plant", *Reuters*, 27 July 2022.

which aims to help French manufacturers gain access to critical metals that are essential to the energy transition.[25] Finally, the EU has introduced measures to reduce its dependence on the main producers of critical metals, notably China. In March 2023, the European Commission proposed a Critical Raw Materials Act to encourage increased European production, recycling and refining of critical metals, and in September 2023, the European Parliament proposed the creation of a European fund for strategic raw materials.[26]

§ 6. *The rise of project finance to finance infrastructure linked to mining projects*

80 Project finance of mining infrastructure. – Easily adaptable to the uncertainties in the early phases of mining projects, project finance is proving to be a more appropriate source of financing for mine-related infrastructure, which, as we saw earlier, is booming. The infrastructure in question generally receives its revenues from the mining company, but not necessarily exclusively, thereby guaranteeing future revenue streams. These may include energy infrastructure, transport infrastructure (ports, airports, railways, roads, rolling stock) or utilities (water, waste management). These infrastructures can be developed at a later stage, once the mine has been built, which facilitates the creation of dedicated project companies. The main advantage for mining companies is the ability to secure debt financing for certain parts of a project, in particular by accessing green financing for certain assets, whereas they would not have been able to do so for their mining operations.

Example: financing of wind and solar projects in South Africa by Anglo American

Anglo American, a major mining company listed in Johannesburg and London, founded Envusa Energy in 2022, a renewable energy company jointly owned with the French company EDF Renewables.[27]

Envusa Energy has financed three wind and solar projects in South Africa in 2024, with a total electricity production capacity of 520 MW:[28] Umsobomvu (140 MW) and Hartebeesthoek (140 MW) wind projects and the Mooi Plaats (240 MW) solar project, due to come on stream in 2026.

This development will enable Anglo American to secure the energy supply to its mining sites in the country, improving its resilience to the national grid, while reducing its Scope 2 carbon emissions. The energy produced

25 InfraVia, "InfraVia launches Critical Metals Fund (CMF) with government support", 11 May 2023.

26 Lucas Miailhes and Andrew Glencross, "European law on critical metals: Less dependence, but questions still unanswered", *La Tribune*, 5 December 2023.

27 https://www.angloamerican.com/media/press-releases/2022/04-10-2022

28 Martin Creamer, "Project finance clinched for 520 MW South African wind, solar projects – Anglo", *Mining Weekly*, 2024.

will be transmitted directly to the mining sites as well as through the Eskom national grid.

Anglo American's three industrial sites in the country – Anglo American Platinum (Amplats), Kumba Iron Ore and De Beers – have signed a 20-year offtake agreement with Envusa Energy, securing future revenue streams and access to project finance.

§ 7. Alternative financing tools for the mining sector

81 The use of alternative financing tools has increased significantly over the last decade, following the decline in commodity prices in 2014,[29] with the mining sector totalling between USD 10 and 15 billion in alternative financing per year worldwide. The three most promising alternative financing options could represent around USD 800 billion of financing over the next ten years for the mining industry, constituting around 40% of the industry's estimated capital investment needs over this period.[30] The three alternative financing options are as follows:

- ***Streaming*** **and** ***net smelter returns*** **(NSRs)** involve, respectively, the sale of all or part of a mine's future production at a discounted market price, and the sale of a right to a percentage of a mine's future revenues in return for an upfront payment. Compared to traditional financing, these alternative options give the sellers more leeway because they are only committed to a percentage of future sales (not a full amount in cash). Additionally, the lender does not require any restrictions on the use of the funds obtained. In addition, *due diligence* is generally quicker than project finance (between two and six weeks) and the risks are shared with the lender.[31]
- ***Net profits interest*** **(NPI)** involves the purchase of a fixed percentage of a mine's profits in exchange for an *up-front* payment. Mainly used in the oil and gas sector, this arrangement is increasingly being used in the mining sector. NPI royalties offer the same advantages as *streaming* and *NSR*.
- **Asset monetisation –** ***tolling or joint ventures*** **(JVs):** the asset monetisation option involves selling part of the value of an existing or new asset in exchange for an income stream (toll or dividend). The main advantage of this financing arrangement is that it enables companies to raise funds without increasing their debt ratios.[32]

29 P&I, "Top global asset managers", *AUM*, 2017.
30 Sigurd Mareels, Anna Moore and Gregory Vainberg, "Alternative financing in mining", *McKinsey & Company*, 2021.
31 *Ibid.*
32 *Ibid.*

3 Project development players

Section 1. States or public parties

§ 1. The role of governments in promoting projects

82 The adoption of investment and project promotion policies and programmes. – Given the risks of market failure inherent in the African market, the role of governments is essential to the successful implementation of infrastructure development policies on the continent. Financing capacity depends on how this role is designed and implemented.[1] This involves defining policies, investment programmes and promoting infrastructure projects. For example, Côte d'Ivoire has set up a NREP, Kenya has defined a national electrification strategy and South Africa has set up a procurement programme for independent renewable energy projects. This is also the case at the supranational level. The AU has defined a PIDA that includes more than 400 projects. The main objective of the PIDA is to promote socio-economic development and poverty reduction through the implementation of integrated regional infrastructure networks. By 2023, 69 projects worth a total of USD 161 billion had reached the financing approval stage under this framework. The largest is the Abidjan-Lagos motorway project, 1,081 km long and estimated at USD 15.6 billion, linking Abidjan to Lagos via Accra, Lomé and Cotonou.[2]

83 The adoption of regulations that encourage investment in infrastructure projects. – Governments also have a role to play in putting in place clear regulations favourable to the development of and investment in major infrastructure projects.[3] This sometimes requires far-reaching reforms such as the liberalisation and restructuring of certain sectors, as in the energy sector with the end of monopolies in production and the unbundling of the various production, transport and

1 George KARARACH, *op. cit.*, p. 622.

2 Chinedu OKAFOR, "69 infrastructure projects valued at $160 billion are set to be initiated by a number of African presidents", *Business Insider Africa*, 6 February 2023.

3 Britta KLAGGE and Chigozie NWEKE-EZE, "Financing large-scale renewable-energy projects in Kenya: Investor types, international connections, and financialization", *Geografiska Annaler: Series B, Human Geography*, 2020, vol. 102, 1, p. 65.

DOI: 10.4324/9781003616894-5

distribution activities. The development of infrastructure can be a driving force behind the introduction of institutional reforms.[4]

84 The promotion of major projects by the regional economic communities. – The promotion of major projects, such as high-impact regional projects, takes place mainly within the framework of Africa's regional economic communities. There are several of these, some of which include specialised institutions, such as energy *pools* like ECOWAS and SADC. However, the NEPAD, now called AUDA-NEPAD, identifies the multiplication of these entities as a complicating factor, making the process of integrating Africa unnecessarily complex and duplicative, resulting in an inefficient use of resources.[5]

85 The involvement of African governments in project financing. – In addition to their "indirect" promotional role, African governments play a major role in infrastructure financing. They account for a significant proportion of the funds provided each year, amounting to USD 33 billion in 2020, down slightly from 2018. In 2020, the countries with the largest budget allocations are South Africa (USD 5.8 billion), Egypt (USD 3.3 billion), Tanzania (USD 3.3 billion), Ethiopia (USD 2.4 billion) and Côte d'Ivoire (USD 2.1 billion).[6] With governments facing severe budgetary constraints, some governments are tempted to reduce capital expenditure in favour of operating expenditure, while others tend to reduce maintenance costs by focusing on new construction.[7]

§ 2. *The role of governments in facilitating the conclusion of contracts*

86 Negotiating the contract with the national company. – In most infrastructure projects in Africa, the project promoters or developers have to interact with a national company, which often has a monopoly in its sector, and therefore has to negotiate and sign a contract with it. In the electricity sector, this may involve a contract for the sale of electricity to the national company by an independent private producer. In this context, the State, via its national company, has a very important role to play in ensuring that negotiations run smoothly, that the project is structured and that the interests involved are balanced so that balanced, bankable contracts can be concluded. These contracts can help to mitigate many of the risks involved, thereby facilitating financing at a lower cost.

87 The involvement of the State and its agencies. – The State and its agencies must therefore be involved in the project, preferably from the outset, whether as a regulator of the activity concerned by issuing permits and licences, or as a direct

4 Zivanemoyo Chinzara, Sébatien Dessus and Stephan Dreyhaupt, "Institutional reforms: The critical factor to attracting infrastructure investment in Sub-Saharan Africa", *Getting Infrastructure Finance Right*, 2023.

5 UN and NEPAD, "16 infrastructure projects for African integration", *op. cit.*, p. 78.

6 ICA, "Trends in infrastructure financing in Africa – 2019–2020", *op. cit.*

7 George Kararach, *op. cit.*, p. 622.

or indirect counterparty in the many contracts entered into by the project company. This requires strong national institutional and administrative capacities and that these institutions are sufficiently trained and experienced.[8] The role of the State is therefore "internal", in terms of its management, decision-making and monitoring capacity.

§ 3. The role of other public parties

88 Involvement of public sector. – Despite the predominant role played by governments in the centralised economies of Africa, and in addition to the regulatory authorities, other public players may initiate project financing.

These may be local authorities, such as the Casablanca urban community in Morocco, which has signed a delegated management contract with the Suez group Lydec for the operation of electricity, water and wastewater services.

In some countries, the government may wish to structure and appoint a dedicated agency to issue international invitations to tender and participate in the capital of project companies. This is the case of the Moroccan Agency for Solar Energy (MASEN) in Morocco.

It is certain that, over time, African markets will become increasingly structured and decentralised and that various public entities will be able to intervene more frequently outside the State itself.

Section 2. The project company

§ 1. Creation of the project company

89 Preliminary steps. – Before setting up a company, the sponsors developing the project will certainly have signed pre-contracts such as memoranda of understanding (MoU), term sheets, JDAs or consortium agreements. This documentation makes it possible to respond to a call for tenders, to propose a project or to structure and anticipate their relations, to lay the foundations for financing and decision-making procedures, prior to the creation of a dedicated company.

90 Project company. – The typical structure of a project finance package always involves the creation by the investor sponsors of a project company, which corresponds to a special purpose vehicle (SPV). This is usually set up in the form of a limited company,[9] which will be entirely dedicated to carrying out the operation. The project company is generally created *ex nihilo* in order to assure lenders that the only assets of the project company are those of the project and that the funds lent will finance only the assets of the project.[10]

8 Paris Europlace, "Marché mondial des Infrastructures, Les enjeux de la Place de Paris", *Report of the Paris Europlace Infrastructure Financing Working Group*, 9 January 2020, p. 56.

9 This will be a company where the liability of the partners is limited to their contributions.

10 David Corchia and Ivan Bénichou, *Le financement de projets*, Eska, 2000.

91 Requirement to set up a project company. – Nevertheless, the formation of the project company may be required under the laws and regulations in force in the host country of the planned project. Foreign investors may be subject to restrictions relating to the conditions of establishment and/or the choice of corporate purpose or capital structure of the vehicle that will carry out the activities required in connection with the project. For example, a foreign investor may be obliged to create and register a project company in order to carry out its activities in the host country of the project as soon as it begins its due diligence.

92 Local shareholding. – Other constraints may be imposed, such as reserving part of the project company's shareholding for national economic operators, as in Botswana or Angola, where foreign investment is prohibited or limited in certain sectors of activity and is subject to association with a local partner holding the majority of the joint company's capital.[11] The public authority may also sometimes ask the project company to involve local investors in the project in order to promote technology transfer and provide jobs and training for the local workforce.[12] This desire to involve local players is becoming increasingly common in African countries. One example is MASEN's role as a shareholder in local project companies and promoter of local development in Moroccan solar energy development projects. Many African countries have developed *local* content obligations, as is the case in Nigeria, Ghana, South Africa and Angola. It is therefore crucial to check the applicable obligations in this area as part of the project financing package.[13] In some cases, these obligations may even be combined with selection criteria based on the amount of local content proposed by the SPV when the operator is selected at the PPP award stage.[14]

93 Role of the project company. – In the context of project financing, the incorporation and registration of the project company makes it possible to limit the risk of the transaction to the project itself and thus to prohibit or limit recourse by lenders against the companies that are shareholders. This is a strategy for isolating risk by shielding the legal personality of the SPV. In fact, the operation is financed and guaranteed solely by the shareholders' contributions (known as "equity"), the loans granted by the lenders and, more rarely, the subsidies granted by the

11 Guillaume Feld, *Droit et pratique des grands projets à l'international, une perspective civiliste*, Legitech, 2020.

12 Jeffrey Delmon, *Private Sector Investment in Infrastructure, Project Finance, PPP Projects and Risk*, 2nd ed, Kluwer Law International and World Bank, PPIAF, 2009.

13 For an analysis of these obligations in the OHADA zone, see Mohamadou Fallou Mbodji, "Les obligations sociales dites de *local content* dans les législations minières et pétrolières des États membres de l'OHADA", *Revue Penant*, no. 908, July–September 2019, p. 348.

14 See, for example, in the case of Senegal, Decree no. 2021-1443 implementing Law no. 2021-23 of 2 March 2021 on public-private partnership contracts, which stipulates that at least 33% of the project company's share capital must be reserved for "local" Senegalese companies, although this may be adjusted if the preliminary assessment shows that this is necessary for optimum implementation of the project. Moreover, subcontracting is reserved "as a matter of priority" for local companies, subject to numerous exceptions.

concession-granting authority. In addition, the project company will borrow the funds needed to finance the project and will be responsible for the contracts relating to the design, construction and operation of the facility.[15] The creation of this company also fulfils a practical role in terms of contractualisation and accounting, simplifying relations between the various shareholders.

94 Normative environment of the host country. – When a company is looking to establish a long-term presence in a market, it may sometimes opt, in addition to any legal obligations, to join forces with a local partner in a joint venture that is better suited to the joint development of a business over the long term.

The creation of a project company may result from a number of considerations specific to the shareholders, in particular:

- limit their exposure to the risks of a transaction to a limited amount;
- make it easier to mobilise the necessary local resources;
- isolate the financial, accounting and administrative processing of a transaction.[16]

§ 2. Project company shareholders

A. Developers

95 Sponsors. – Developers, also known as sponsors, are typically the entities that identified the infrastructure project or led the response to a call for tenders in the case of a competitive tender.

To support these developers, various funds dedicated to development can also intervene.

96 Project Preparation Facilities. – Africa has many funding mechanisms for project preparation and development, or Project Preparation Facilities (PPFs). These are financial and technical support services, generally funded by governments or donors, most of which belong to the African PPFN.[17]

97 NEPAD-IPPF. – The NEPAD-IPPF (Infrastructure Project Preparation Facility) is a multi-donor fund hosted by the AfDB that supports African countries in the preparation of infrastructure projects. It works to make up for the lack of projects ready to receive investment. Its financial capacity is approximately $15 million per year, which, as some authors have confirmed, is still insufficient to successfully prepare projects on the continent.[18]

98 The Public-Private Infrastructure Advisory Facility (PPIAF). – The Public-Private Infrastructure Advisory Facility (PPIAF), created in 1999 by Japan and the

15 Guillaume Feld, *op. cit.*
16 Guillaume Feld, *op. cit.*
17 ICA c/o ADB, *op. cit.*, p. 19.
18 Mthuli Ncube, *op. cit.*, p. 602.

United Kingdom, is a technical assistance facility financed by 11 multilateral and bilateral donors. Hosted by the WB, it aims to increase private sector participation. AfreximBank also has a specialised project preparation unit, as does ECOWAS, which set up a project preparation and development unit in 2011.

InfraCo is also one of the IPPFs. This is a grant-funded infrastructure development company that acts as a broker to bring together financiers, the private sector and governments in low-income countries. It is involved in the early stages of development and then offers the structured project via a call for tenders. Its remuneration takes the form of a minority interest in the project company. Its capital is held by a group of development institutions from several European countries.[19]

B. *Institutional investors and investment funds*

99 An attractive source of infrastructure finance. – African and international institutional investors (in particular, pension funds, insurance companies and sovereign wealth funds) are a very attractive source of infrastructure finance because of their long-term investment and their general need to diversify risk.[20] Senegal's FONSIS and Gabon's FGIS illustrate this trend.

100 Limits on intervention by institutional investors and investment funds. – However, these players are often limited by mandate in the type of investments they can make.[21] Due to their nature, direct investments in new infrastructure projects are often ineligible for a certain category of funds (in particular pension funds and insurance companies): they do not yet have a financial history or credit rating, they do not have tradable securities as an exit, and they present a high risk.[22] A number of financial investors are not prepared to bear the construction risk associated with the initial investment in large-scale infrastructure projects and prefer to invest in a completed project that is already generating revenue. This fits well with the preferences of developers, who are often major shareholders in the construction phase and tend to sell their shares once the project is operational in order to free up capital for investment in new projects.[23]

Some critics point to the risk of perverse effects such as under-investment and excessive pricing due to the relentless pursuit of profits, restricting access to infrastructure and thereby reinforcing exclusion and inequality.[24]

101 The growing role of infrastructure investment funds. – There has been a growing number of such funds on the African continent over the past decade or so.

19 *Ibid.*, 2017, p. 598.
20 *Ibid.*, p. 21.
21 ICA c/o AfDB, "Trends in infrastructure financing in Africa – 2018", above, p. 21.
22 *Ibid.*
23 Britta Klagge and Chigozie Nweke-Eze, "Financing large-scale renewable-energy projects in Kenya: Investor types, international connections, and financialization", *Geografiska Annaler: Series B*, Human Geography, 2020, vol. 102, 1, p. 65.
24 *Ibid.*, p. 64.

Among the most active on the continent are Meridiam, Africa50, STOA, Africa Finance Corporation (AFC), African Infrastructure Investment Managers (AIIM), Emerging Africa and Asia Infrastructure Fund (EAAIF), Emerging Capital Partners (ECP), Actis and Harith. They have considerable investment capacity, and some of them are willing to take a majority stake in the development of a project and to manage its development in the same way as the developers.

There is also a growing role for private solidarity players such as mega-foundations (Ford Foundation, Bill & Melinda Gates Foundation), non-governmental organisations and corporate foundations (Google, Nike, Shell).[25]

C. *Associated industrial players*

102 The involvement of industrial players. – Other industrial players may be involved in the construction, maintenance or management of a specific technology as part of the project. Most of the time, the investments made by these private industrial players take the form of a stake in the company carrying out the infrastructure project or in the company holding the underlying construction or O&M contracts. This will also have a reassuring effect on the conceding authority when the contract is awarded and the activities carried out, and a beneficial effect on raising finance from lenders.

103 The role of the private sector. – The financial contribution, in terms of volume, of the private sector, and in particular of industrial players, remains relatively limited compared with the funds provided by African governments and bilateral or multilateral development banks and institutions. However, over time, the private sector has emerged as an entrepreneur rather than an investor in infrastructure projects.[26]

25 Vivien Foster, "The changing landscape of infrastructure in Africa, Nontraditional sources take on a growing role", *Grid Lines, PPIAF*, October 2008.

26 George Kararach, *op. cit.*, p. 622.

4 The stages of development

Here we will look at the structuring phases and the development stages to achieve project financing, which we will study in part 2 of the book.

Section 1. Main phases of project financing

104 Phases of the project. – The life of project financing can be divided into three phases:

- The development and structuring phase, followed by the financing phase: during this period, the project is designed, contracts are negotiated and signed, and capital and debt are subscribed. The end of this period is marked by the financial *closing*.
- The construction phase: during this period, financing is called in to build the project. The end of this period is generally marked by the *COD*.
- The operating phase: during this period, the project is operated and generates income (through the billing of services to users or the payment of rent by the public sector) which will be used to repay the lenders (principal and interest) and generate a return on investment for the shareholders of the project company.

105 Development and project allocation. – During the development phase, it is essential to set up a dedicated project team from each party. This includes managers and employees from each party with proven technical, legal and financial skills, as well as external advisers in various fields to ensure that the project is properly structured and managed. We will see later in this chapter that the project can be developed mainly either through an unsolicited offer from the developers to the State, or through a competitive tendering procedure initiated by the public party.

106 Financing. – Project financing requires a strategy to be put in place for all the complex tasks involved. The promoters, whether initially the person behind the call for tenders or an industrial player, carry out feasibility studies at an early stage in order to define the contours of the project. The use of project finance means that the

DOI: 10.4324/9781003616894-6

structuring aspects need to be taken into account at a very early stage, as this can influence the commercial strategy and de facto the feasibility studies.

107 Development period. – The development phase generally lasts 12 to 18 months. However, in Africa, the complexity, the lack of financial resources available to the public sector and the risks inherent in projects often extend this phase, which can last two to three years or more on average. Whether the project is put out to tender at the end of the structuring phase by the public sector or the development of the project is the result of private initiative, promoters should not underestimate the costs involved, particularly for their own staff (time spent, study or travel expenses), for external advisers, or even for setting up a local office. These costs average between 2.5% and 5% of the total cost of the project, and there is always a risk that the project will fail along the way or that the promoter will not be selected by the public party. A system for monitoring and controlling costs is therefore essential, especially as they can have a significant impact on the profitability of the project, since they will be included in the balance sheet of the project company.

The project company, for its part, is often only created at the end of this development phase and will take over the development costs incurred in order to manage the project as soon as the financial close is reached.

Section 2. Stages in the development phase of infrastructure projects

108 Main stages. – Although some of the following phases may be intertwined, or there are projects carried out by private treaty or direct agreement by exception,[1] it is possible to divide the development of infrastructure projects awarded by public tender into the following stages: the launch of the public invitation to tender by the public authority (§ 1), the identification of partners by the private operators to ensure that they put together a bid covering all the requirements of the specifications (§ 2), the due diligence and preparation of the bid by the private operators (§ 3), the submission of the bid and award of the project (§ 4), the creation of the project company (§ 5), the award of the project and finance contracts (§ 6) and, finally, the financial close (§ 7).

109 Spontaneous or unsolicited bids. – Before considering the classic award of a contract as described later, we must also consider the case of unsolicited bids submitted by operators who have identified a project and wish to propose it directly to the African public authority. Generally speaking, recent PPP laws deal with this issue.[2] Without being able to over-generalise, it is important to remember a few

1 See, for example, in the case of Senegal, Decree 2021-1443 implementing Law 2021-23 of 2 March 2021 on public-private partnership contracts, which stipulates that public authorities may use derogation procedures for awarding contracts, in particular the direct agreement procedure, which authorises direct discussions with one or more operators and their selection. This procedure is subject to prior authorisation and is provided for in limited cases (holding of exclusive rights, urgency, etc.).

2 See, for example, Law no. 032-2021 of 25 June 2021 on public-private partnerships in Burkina Faso.

principles. If an unsolicited bid is submitted, it is important to protect the intellectual property it contains. Furthermore, the submission of unsolicited bids does not exempt the public authority from checking how it should behave in this situation. Most of the time, it must examine the bid and check whether it is responsible for organising a competitive tendering process, unless it can justify an exception to the competitive tendering rules under public procurement. Lastly, the public authority must ensure that, during the call for tenders, it does not use protected elements of the unsolicited bid to put it in competition with those of other candidates. The practical difficulty in Africa remains, in the light of these principles, to find candidates to carry out certain projects while maintaining healthy competition in order to select an operator under optimum consultation conditions.

§ 1. Launch of the public invitation to tender

110 Public initiative. – In many cases, the development of the project is part of the approach of a public entity in the host country. Projects involving the provision of public sector products and services are often initially developed by a national or local government or public agency, which places the project on the market by publishing a public invitation to tender for the financing, construction of the project and operation of the infrastructure. The public tendering procedure is generally a legal requirement. It is regularly required if financing and guarantees are provided by multilateral development banks, which have the same requirements in terms of fairness, transparency and good administration. In such cases, the tendering process for the award of the contract granting the project (usually a concession or PPP contract) must follow a specific procedure.

The tendering process for a project finance PPP is normally conducted in phases: a pre-qualification phase and a tendering phase.

111 Pre-qualification phase. – A notice of invitation to tender is published in official publications and in the financial and commercial press. Interested candidates receive a summary of the project and the corresponding requirements. They are invited to submit an application demonstrating their technical and financial capacity and their experience, in particular their references in carrying out similar projects.

Following this phase, candidates who do not meet the minimum criteria are excluded from the procurement procedure and the others are invited to submit their tenders. If permitted by the applicable rules, this phase may restrict the number of bidders for the next phase to a short list. This is often preferable in order to facilitate the management of exchanges, but also because too large a number of bidders means that the chances of being selected are lower in comparison with the time and costs involved for the bidders.

112 Tender phase. – An invitation to tender is formally sent to the tenderers selected at the end of the pre-selection phase. This invitation is accompanied by a tender dossier containing information on the legal framework, the purpose of the project, the market data, the technical and/or functional scope of the project, the remuneration arrangements for the private partner, the draft contract, the criteria for evaluating the tender and the deadline for submitting tenders. These documents contain a greater or lesser number of technical specifications depending on whether the infrastructure will eventually be transferred to the contracting entity.

The tendering process must at all times respect the requirements of equal access and transparency.

§ 2. Identification of partners

113 Creation of consortia or groupings. – Following publication of the public tender notice, interested industrial players often seek to join forces with a partner, in particular to share the risks and costs of developing the project or to ensure that all the project's technical requirements are covered. This stage is carried out at the same time as the pre-qualification phase, for which the partners in a consortium who are destined to become shareholders in the project company submit a joint application.

This may take the form of the signing of various contracts, such as a JBAs and/or a JDAs which, as we have already mentioned, generally precede the signing of the project company's articles of association.

114 Development agreements. – With these contracts, the promoters ensure that a common strategy is implemented, and that roles and responsibilities are clearly divided. The JDA contract generally covers (i) the scope and structure of the project; (ii) an exclusivity agreement; (iii) management aspects and responsibilities; (iv) a programme for feasibility studies, recruitment of external advisors and negotiations with other project parties; (v) decision-making rules; (vi) arrangements for financing development costs and for capital contributions/subscriptions which are often also detailed in a subscription contract for certain projects; and (vii) project exit mechanisms and confidentiality obligations. This contract is then replaced by the shareholders' agreement, which is signed before or when the project company is created and comes into force when it is registered.

§ 3. Due diligence and preparation of the offer

115 Due diligence. – This stage assesses all aspects of the project's feasibility. Feasibility studies are generally provided by the contracting authority as part of the tender documents. The bidders (possibly accompanied by external consultants) analyse the available data and carry out market studies, profitability studies, risk studies and technical feasibility studies in order to assess the investment opportunity. At this stage, a range of different skills and expertise is required: finance, business, legal, technical, insurance, environmental and operational. This overall study is known only to the bidder and cannot differ from the analyses carried out by the banks on comparable subjects.

At the end of this stage, the bidder, made up of the members of the consortium (if applicable), decides whether or not to continue with the project by submitting a bid, and whether or not to use the project financing technique.

116 Project financing. – Financial institutions are very often involved from the earliest stages of project development, and where appropriate, from the preparation of the bid. The tender may require bidders to provide evidence that finance is available, which may take the form of a letter of intent or term sheet from the banks expressing their willingness to arrange and provide the necessary finance.[3] Tender documentation may also require financing to be at a more advanced stage. This may involve the banks carrying out their due diligence, arranging detailed financing, obtaining approvals from their credit committee, and sometimes having negotiated and signed financing documentation with the bidders. In addition, the tender for the project may be entirely separate from the financing phase. The project may be awarded and the concession or PPP contract signed before project finance is appraised and negotiated with the banks.

§ 4. Submission of the tender and award of the project

117 Content of the offer. – The bid must often contain answers on the following aspects: (i) technology envisaged, (ii) design and engineering, (iii) construction programme and details of the works, (iv) commercial viability, (v) O&M policy, (vi) cover and insurance, (vii) project costs for each phase, (viii) financial strategy and structure and (ix) proposed tariffs. It must contain all the information required by the tender documentation but, above all, it must demonstrate the bidder's understanding of the project requirements, confirm how the SPV plans to meet them and the advantages or strengths of its approach and team, as well as its tariffs.

118 Fine-tuning. – A final phase may take place in which discussions are held on the tenders and the terms of the contracts. The specifications and terms of the contracts are clarified, and a final decision is taken by the contracting entity. This last phase may not be provided for in order to comply with the requirements of equality and transparency. Alternatively, two or three bidders may be shortlisted and invited to submit their best revised final offer, taking into account the revised project specifications and documentation as discussed. In theory, contract finalisation should be rapid if model contracts were included in the tender and bidders were invited to comment on the contracts at the time of bidding. In principle, the fine-tuning should not concern substantial elements of the contract (price, duration, etc.).

119 Intangibility of tenders. – Where an award procedure subject to public procurement rules has taken place, no significant change may be made to the tender selected without the need to reopen the competitive tendering procedure.

This final negotiation phase ends with the signing of the concession contract or PPP contract, as appropriate.

3 Cf. *infra*, no. 251.

§ 5. *Creation of the project company or SPV*

120 Creation date. – A company must be newly created because in project finance, the company is supposed to have no assets or liabilities other than those relating to the project. The project company is often created at a late stage, with the exception of cases where, as we have seen, this is required in order to bid for the tender, or if in order to be awarded the project, the upstream creation of the project company is required, or possibly where authorisations or licences need to be issued directly to the project company or if the project company needs to sign project contracts directly. In most cases, the project company has no active role prior to financial close. The PPP contract and associated contracts are then signed by the successful bidder, including a set of clauses relating to the transfer of the contract to the project company to be created.

121 Shareholding. – The project company is not always directly owned by the project promoters, who sometimes use intermediate holding companies for tax reasons or to structure the management of their asset portfolio. For its part, the project company is usually registered in the country in which the project finance is being developed. Its creation involves the negotiation and signature of various legal instruments, including the company's articles of association and shareholders' agreement, as well as the subscription and payment of capital by the shareholders.

122 Exclusive purpose. – The project company is at the centre of contractual and financial relations. Its role is exclusively dedicated to carrying out the project. It may not carry out any activities other than those relating to the project. It is created and registered exclusively for this purpose. We will see in part 3 that its shareholders will also make several commitments in this respect to the lenders.

§ 6. *Awarding project and financing contracts*

123 Project documentation. – The project company may also itself be subject to requirements under local procurement rules, either under the law applicable to the company or under the rules laid down by the financing institutions involved in the project (particularly if the project has been awarded by private treaty). The project company must therefore sometimes organise tender procedures to select the various counterparties for the construction and operation of the infrastructure. The contracts concerned include the construction contract, the purchase contract, the supply contract and the O&M contract.

124 Financing documentation. – The banks carry out their own final due diligence of the project and project contracts and check the compliance of the subscriptions and the governance of the company. The banks want to ensure that the project company remains in a position to cover the servicing of the subscribed debt even in the event of downgraded scenarios. They therefore ask the private partner to carry out a series of sensitivities on the financial model[4] developed by the latter

4 See Part 2, Chapter 4 on the financial model.

as part of the project to ensure this. An audit of the financial model is generally requested in order for the banks to ensure the reliability of the results of the private partner's financial model and the associated sensitivities. The financial documentation, mainly the credit agreement, is then negotiated between the interested banks and the promoters and/or the project company. These elements are discussed in more detail in Part 2 Chapter 10.

§ 7. *Financial closing*

125 Release of conditions precedent. – This final strategic phase consists of lifting the conditions precedent set out in the financing documentation, which we will examine in the next section of the book. This is a very critical phase, as there are often a large number of conditions precedent, and there is a deadline for them to be lifted.

126 Disbursements. – Once all the conditions have been met, the project company is authorised to make the first drawdowns on the loaned funds, thereby starting the construction work (if the work has not been started using the project company's own funds even before the conditions prior to the first drawdown have been met).

5 Project contracts

127 Drafting issues. – One of the key challenges in the preparation and negotiation of contracts structuring project financing is the identification of risks. The counterpart of this challenge lies in the optimal allocation of these risks to the various stakeholders and their repercussion in the contracts that bind them together. It is not a question of assigning all the risks to the project company, which in one way or another will pass on their assumption and their costs to the project, but of verifying which party is the most appropriate to bear each of them.[1]

To remember

When allocating risk, certain key principles must be observed, as some authors have pointed out:[2]

- any risk will be borne by the party best able to assume it, in accordance with the principle of "each to his own, each to his own";
- risk must be allocated at the best cost, and any additional risk taken by a party or guarantee given by that party will have a financial impact that may be negative;
- the party taking the allocated risk must be in a position to assume it financially and operationally.

128 Risk matrix. – Although many risks can be structured, insured or identified in a risk matrix and then in the various contracts that form part of the project structuring, certain events or circumstances can affect the economic performance, stability and viability of the project. The aim is therefore either to allocate the risks to one

1 Boris Martor, *Les défis de la structuration des financements de projets d'infrastructures de production d'énergie en Afrique, Défis du droit des affaires en Afrique*, L'Harmattan, 2020.

2 V. Haubert-McGetrick and G. Ansaloni, *Financement de projet, enjeux juridiques et bancabilité d'une opération*, Revue Banque, 2011, p. 38 et seq.

DOI: 10.4324/9781003616894-7

of the parties best able to control them, who can in turn organise the means to limit these risks or their consequences, or to determine a mitigation strategy for risks that cannot be shared or allocated to one of the parties to the project or assumed by third parties.

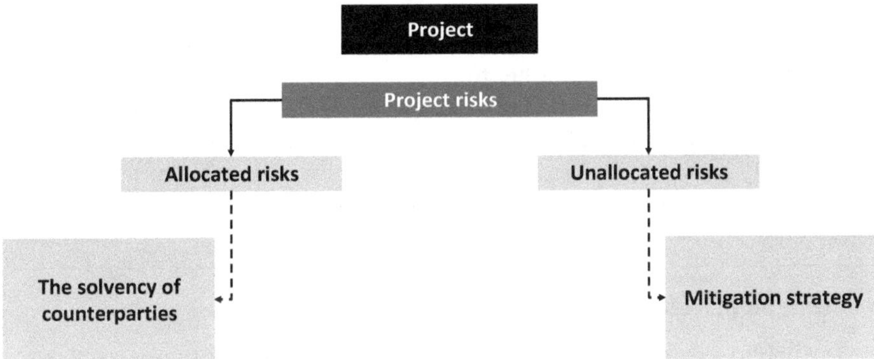

Figure 5.1 Allocation and mitigation

129 Risk assessment. – All parties to the project should carry out a detailed pre-assessment to identify all the risks likely to arise in the course of the project. This helps to understand how the risks can then be allocated between each of the parties to the project and to quantify these risks, i.e. to assess their impact on the overall cost of the project in correlation with the measured risk.

Furthermore, the willingness of lenders to finance the project depends on the certainty and reliability of the risk allocation and the solvency of the project company. The regime governing the solvency of companies is not uniform in all countries, and some African countries do not even always have a legal and regulatory regime applicable to each sector.[3]

Section 1. The main project contracts

130 Project contracts play a fundamental role in structuring the project, the shareholders' relations and the SPV's relations with third parties. The more they limit the project company's risks, the higher the value of the project and the more bankable it will be. A distinction is often made between project contracts, where the project company takes the initiative, and financing contracts, where the lenders take the initiative. The main types of project contract are the PPP contract, the purchase or sale contract (where applicable), the construction contract and the maintenance contract.

3 Julio César Bueno, *The Project and Construction Review*, 6th ed, Law Business Research, 2016.

§ 1. Concession or PPP contracts

131 Main contract. – This is a contract between a public grantor entity and the project company, under which the project is built and then transferred by the project company to the grantor authority under the terms of the contract. The awarding authority may be a national or regional government, a municipality, an agency or a national company. Infrastructure operation contracts are often used for the construction and operation of user-pay facilities such as tunnels, bridges, roads, metros, trams, ports, airports and water treatment plants.[4] As we have seen, however, there may also be projects involving public payment, i.e. payment made directly by the public client for schools, hospitals, administrative buildings, prisons, etc. These are generally known as concession contracts. In most African countries, these are known as concession contracts or PPPs.[5]

Focus on privately financed infrastructure development

The public sector will have two main options for financing its infrastructure:

- carry them out by purchasing goods and services under separate public contracts for each design, construction and operation service, financed in this case from public funds; or
- have them built and financed by the private sector, which will then bear the risks of designing, building, financing and operating the infrastructure.

There is thus a link between concessive or PPP-type global contracts insofar as project financing techniques will be associated with the implementation of projects in this form developed throughout the world as part of public service delegations or PPP contracts, but also in countries with a common law tradition in the form of BOT (Build Operate Transfer) or DBFO (Design Build Finance Operate). It should be noted that there are a multitude of cases in Africa and combinations depending on the country and the applicable legal system. Other structures, such as Build Own Operate (BOO), Build Lease Transfer (BLT), Build Transfer Operate (BTO) and Transfer of Operating Rights (TOR), are also seen as alternative options depending on the specific project and jurisdiction.

The PPP or concession contract is the central or key contract among project contracts. It is sometimes called the Implementation Agreement or the Operation Agreement in some English-speaking African countries. It is the project company's first and foremost asset, as it is this contract that will generate the revenue needed to pay for the financing of the infrastructure or service being developed. In the

4 E. R. Yescombe, *Principles of Project Finance*, Academic Press, 2002, pp. 79–103.
5 Cf. Appendix 4, African tour of PPP texts for structuring project finance with the public sector.

case of power generation projects, the main source of revenue for the SPV is a derivative contract, the PPA, usually signed with the national utility of the African country in question.

132 Structure of the contract. – This contract is usually structured as follows, with the stipulations governing the concession in particular:

- purpose;
- duration;
- property regime;
- obligations of the grantor and the licensee;
- financial and tax arrangements, including guarantees;
- control of the concession;
- modification and termination of the concession, including the consequences in terms of compensation;
- insurance;
- dispute resolution;
- final provisions; and
- annexes.[6]

Numerous points are covered, such as a description of the obligations of each party in terms of carrying out the project, issuing permits or characterising the works. Also covered are, for example, the means and consequences of expropriation if populations are located in or around the production or construction zone and guarantees regarding the security of the land.[7]

For the SPV and the lenders, the important thing is that the risk transferred to the project company by the concession contract can then be passed on to the project participants. Lenders examine contracts to determine whether the conditions, risks or burdens imposed on the project company are reasonable. The project company must pass on its obligations to the project participants, and the more demanding the terms of the concession agreement, the more expensive the underlying contracts and the less profitable the project in general.[8]

133 Signing the contract. – We have seen that project financing is structured with a project company acting as a screen for the sponsors. This is an important aspect of the system in terms of responsibility. However, the question may arise as to who submits and signs the bid (and sometimes the PPP project contract) on behalf of the sponsors when a bid is submitted in response to a call for tenders. In many cases, the project company has not yet been set up when the bids are submitted, and it is not until later that the candidates are selected. Candidates will often have to submit bids in their own name but on behalf of a company to be set up. In these circumstances, it

6 Boris Martor, *op. cit.*

7 *Ibid.*

8 Jeffrey Delmon, *op. cit.*, pp. 251–269.

is important to ensure that the contractual commitments made upstream to third parties are clearly defined, and that these commitments allow contracts to be assigned and taken over by the company when it is set up. It is also essential to sign the project contracts in their final form in the name of the borrowing project company.

134 Identity of the grantor. – The project company must also examine the identity of the granting authority to ensure that it does indeed have the rights and competence over the public sector service concerned and that it has received any necessary authorisations from its supervisory authority. It is also necessary to ensure that the project will not be jeopardised if the grantor becomes insolvent or undergoes a sectoral or other reorganisation.

Government undertakings on this subject are often required in Africa in project contracts and direct agreements.

135 Regime applicable to the main contract. – In Africa, it is useful to pay particular attention to the legal regime of the host country that will apply to the PPP contract. Some jurisdictions have adopted investment codes that allow investors to benefit from special advantages for investments made in the form of exemptions, credits or subsidies, as well as investment incentive or protection schemes. Some countries have developed specific legislation for PPP projects in order to better manage the growth of these projects. In other cases, the host country's legal system is relatively undeveloped in this area. This can lead to difficulties, as the legal basis on which the grantor commits to the concession or PPP may be unclear.[9] For example, the project company and its lenders must ensure that the granting authority has the right and competence to enter into the concession contract, and that the contract does not require specific government authorisation from a responsible minister, or empowerment of the government by Parliament, or sometimes even ratification by Parliament. In English-speaking countries, where common law has left its mark, the texts on PPPs are often less developed and the rules of administrative law implying certain principles are non-existent. Contractual freedom is therefore most often significant in English-speaking African countries structuring a PPP, DBFO or BOT.

To remember

In French-speaking Africa, project financing is always closely linked to the application of administrative law insofar as it involves public contracts and parties. The law in this region is very similar to French administrative law. For this reason, the book may refer to French law and the interpretations made by the French administrative courts. African administrative law has changed relatively little since independence, and it is often rare to find accessible and completely up-to-date case law from the administrative courts. As we shall see, African courts often even refer to French texts and decisions. It should also

9 *Ibid.*

be pointed out that, unlike in some sectors in France, African countries do not publish standard concession specifications.[10] As a result, the practice of financing African projects has developed models based on the texts adopted in each country, where applicable, but also on precedents relating to completed projects. In Anglophone countries of Africa, you would not find a similar division between administrative law and private law. In those countries, the lex corpus is usually only based on regulatory or contractual developments for PPPs even if there are more and more bills or acts passed to encourage and regulate PPPs.

A. Points to bear in mind

136 Joint interest. – Concession-granting authority has a clear interest in concluding the concession or PPP contract in order to see the development of key facilities for the country. It ensures that the elements of the contract meet its expectations. The project company, for its part, is keen to remain capable of meeting its obligations under the contract, but also to check that no obligation could conflict with the interests of the lenders or constitute a risk or an additional cost.

137 Meeting public needs. – The concession contract meets a relatively immediate infrastructure need. The completion date agreed between the parties to the concession contract is therefore a major issue for the concession-granting authority. For the project company, this date is crucial in order to avoid defaulting on its commitments to the public party, and also on its commitments under the financing contracts with its lenders. Any delay in the public projects associated with the main project (networks associated with a railway station or line, or electricity transmission lines carrying the power generated by a power station, for example) may result in the private partner being unable to bring its infrastructure into service and generate the expected level of revenue.

The difficulties of structuring and restructuring a strategic railway line, the example of Dakar-Bamako

Dakar Bamako is a strategic route created in 1924 to link the seaport of Dakar to the port of Koulikoro on the River Niger, via Bamako. It consisted of 1,287 km of rail track with 33 stations, opening up Mali and providing a livelihood for many employees and people along the route.

In 2003, the operation of the line was entrusted to the Canadian consortium Canac-Getma, which created the project company Transrail SA, whose shareholders are the State of Mali and the State of Senegal, each holding

10 On French-speaking administrative law, see for example O. Fille-Lambie, "Aspects juridiques des financements de projets appliqués aux grands services publics dans la zone OHADA", *RDAI/IBLJ*, 2001, no. 8, p. 925.

11%, private shareholders holding 22% and Transrail Investissement holding 56%. In 2006, Transrail Investissement's shareholding changed and SICF took over Canac's shares alongside Getma, which retained a 5% stake at a time when the project was already experiencing difficulties. To compensate for the withdrawal of Canac Railway, which had operating expertise, Transrail subcontracted operations to Vecturis.

In 2015, Transrail proposed a renovation plan for the line valued at €880 million, but this plan was not implemented. The transitional administration put in place in 2016, following Transrail's withdrawal, has also failed.

Since 2018, the line has been at a standstill, but a more costly project involves the construction of a new line estimated at between €2.6 billion and €3.5 billion. Another project involves renovating the line, but funding for the renovation is also estimated at almost €1 billion, which has not yet been secured.

This project illustrates the difficulties of financing and monitoring cross-border rail projects in Africa, as well as the perilous search for an economic balance in concessions for this type of investment-intensive project.

138 Performance standards. – The public authority also wishes to establish performance standards and requirements to meet its needs over the term of the concession and to inherit a compliant infrastructure at the end of the concession. These requirements cover issues such as performance, quality of service to users, consumption, operating efficiency, maintenance requirements and costs, life cycle and operating costs. In Africa, more than anywhere else, monitoring these standards is a real challenge, as we shall see in part 3.

139 Maintenance monitoring requirements. – Failure to monitor and maintain the project may result in the project losing its value and ability to operate by the time it is transferred to the public sector at the end of the contract. The grantor wants to ensure that the maintenance regime (including the replacement of parts and materials) implemented by the project company is adequate and binding to guarantee that the level of performance of the infrastructure is maintained. Indeed, the incentive to invest funds in maintenance during the final phase of the concession period may be reduced due to the imminent transfer of the project to the grantor.

140 Contribution to the public service. – Lastly, the infrastructure or project covered by the concession contract is often part of the public service. The operation of the infrastructure or project by the project company can therefore be identified as being traditionally provided by the State but delegated by exception. Its operation is therefore often conducted directly under the responsibility of the State and the relevant regulatory authorities where applicable. The acts and omissions of the delegated project company may, in some cases, be attributable in the first instance to the granting authority,[11] which

11 *Ibid.*

must then take action against the project company in the event of default. This is the case, for example, of an energy production infrastructure contributing to the public electricity production service, which will be placed under the authority of the electricity directorate and the competent regulatory authority in the sector or country concerned.

B. Distribution of risks

141 Political risk. – The risk must be borne by the party best able to manage it. This is why, in Africa in particular, the grantor generally bears most of the political risk (wars, national strikes or political instability are generally borne by the grantor). Similarly, political force majeure, which can be summed up as any act or abstention by a public party at fault, is a risk taken by the public party and liable to be compensated. The grantor must be prepared to protect the project company against any act or omission of its own authority, local governments or administrative authorities under its authority. The grantor may also argue that political risk is a risk commonly borne by the private sector in day-to-day business transactions. This is often the case in developed countries. This issue is specific to the contract and often depends on the insurance or guarantees available to the project company, which are discussed in Part 1 Chapter 5 Section 2.[12]

142 Regulatory risk. – The project company and the concession grantor undertake to comply with the main provisions of the law of the country concerned and the concession or PPP contract which form the law of the project. However, during the development of the project or its operation, the law may be subject to change. The concept of legislative change follows a regime that is negotiated within the framework of the PPP and must take account of the introduction of a new law, the amendment of existing laws and/or the modification of the interpretation thereof but also by the emergence of new legal instruments.[13] Of course, such stipulations must remain balanced and must not prevent States from developing their laws and regulations.

143 Changes in laws or regulations. – The grantor wishes the project company to bear the risk of changes in laws and regulations as a normal risk of doing business in the country. However, the project company and the lenders have an interest in the grantor or the government bearing any additional costs due to changes in laws or regulations, particularly when these changes discriminate against the project. Negotiations and discussions then take place on this point, and ceilings are set beyond which compensation will be due. These ceilings can therefore be established contractually.

144 Tax stability. – Tax stability is particularly important for the project company and the lenders. Tax changes and reforms can have a major impact on the

12 See in particular nos. 349 et seq. *below.*

13 Boris Martor, *op. cit.*

profitability of the project and its revenues, for example if a new tax is introduced or tax concessions cancelled, or if the cost of maintenance or operating operations[14] increases. Generally, tax or customs concessions are offered to the SPV for a certain period, and the public party undertakes not to change the tax and customs regime offered during the term of the contract. The parties often negotiate stability clauses in detail and provisions for reviewing the financial terms of operation if changes occur that have a significant and unfavourable impact on operations beyond certain thresholds.

145 Completion risk. – This refers to the risk of delay in the construction or handover of the facilities. This risk is generally borne entirely by the project company (except in the case of a delay caused by the concession grantor or a risk linked to the concession grantor) which, as we shall see, will be passed on to the EPC cocontractor. In certain circumstances, the grantor may have to share part of the risk. For example, the grantor may be willing to assume certain site-specific risks (site availability, soil conditions, pollution and antiquities).[15]

146 Operating risk. – This refers to the risk of revenue and expenditure relating to operations. If the revenues are collected directly by the SPV from users, the risk is that of the SPV, except in cases where it has a simple mandate to collect revenues on behalf of the public entity. In the case of public-payment infrastructure projects, such as buildings or energy production plants, the demand risk is borne by the public entity. The grantor bears that part of the operating risk relating to the responsibilities it assumes in connection with the project. In addition, where other facilities are required to operate and maintain the project (such as access road transport), this risk can be assigned to the grantor. The grantor is in the best position to manage these risks effectively. It should be noted that the operating risk, in the sense of the expenses associated with managing the infrastructure to ensure its proper O&M, remains with the SPV in a project financing arrangement.

147 Permits, licences and authorisations. – The project company is often responsible for obtaining the necessary authorisations for the construction, ownership and operation of the project, such as building permits, environmental licences and operating permits. It is also responsible for their registration, filing and other matters. However, the PPP contract in Africa often requires the State or the concession grantor to facilitate the obtaining of all these authorisations. There are also projects where the public party itself prefers to take responsibility for securing and making available the elements or authorisations relating to the land and property aspects, in order to facilitate the project and minimise the risks for the project company.

Where additional licences and permits are required, lenders will want to ensure that they are obtained prior to financial close. They will also want to ensure that the requirements for their renewal are not changed in an unreasonable or discriminatory way.

14 *Ibid.*

15 Jeffrey DELMON, *op. cit.*, pp. 251–259.

C. Duration

148 Matching the financial model. – In general, the granting authority wants a shorter concession period, while the shareholders of the SPV want a longer period to generate income for as long as possible after depreciation of the assets financed. The duration of the PPP contract should generally be limited to the period necessary to meet the requirements of the financial model for the project as a whole. This is determined by the awarding authority prior to launching the call for tenders for the PPP contract and depends on the services required from the private partner. When the private partner is responsible for building the infrastructure, the duration of the contract must allow it to amortise all the initial investments at a normal rate (as prescribed by the accounting framework in force in the country) without this duration significantly exceeding the amortisation period of the initial investments, so as not to create a situation of rent. This period must therefore correspond to the time reasonably expected by the concessionaire to amortise the investments made, with a return on equity that must be set against the volume of investment and the risk profile of the project. The maximum duration of a PPP contract is sometimes defined in legislation. If the project does not require any investment (although this would certainly not be a project finance arrangement), it is customary for the contract to run for no more than five to eight years, and more rarely for up to ten years. In the case of investments to be depreciated, it will often be between 15 and 30 years.

149 Extension of term. – Where one of the grantor's risks has materialised and the project company requires some compensation, the grantor may prefer that this compensation take the form of an extension to the term of the contract. In this way, the grantor provides the project company with more income without necessarily having to invest more funds in the project. Financing agreements may also provide for a change in debt repayment requirements when the contract term is extended due to the grantor's default. Such an extension may mean that the project company is unable to service the debt according to the schedule originally agreed.[16]

D. Guarantees

150 Guarantees given by the project company. – The grantor may require guarantees from the project company or developers, mainly when it has transferred infrastructure or other assets to the project company, but also to ensure the delivery, proper performance and return of the works at the end of the contract.

The various guarantees that can be envisaged as part of a project are as follows:

- Tender guarantee/bid security: this is a bank guarantee issued on the date of submission of tenders by all tenderers, which may be called if a tenderer withdraws or modifies its tender (during a validity period agreed in the tender regulations) or if the successful tenderer refuses to fulfil certain obligations until the concession agreement is signed;

16 Jeffrey Delmon, *op. cit.*, pp. 251–269.

- Development guarantee: this is the bank guarantee issued on the date the concession agreement is signed, replacing the bid guarantee. It guarantees the concession-granting authority in the event of default by the concessionaire before the concession agreement comes into force, particularly with regard to the fulfilment of the preconditions laid down in the concession contract;
- Completion guarantee/performance guarantee: this is the guarantee issued on the date the concession agreement comes into force, replacing the development guarantee. It may be called in whole or in part by the concession-granting authority in the event that the concessionaire fails to meet its obligations during the construction phase prior to commercial operation;
- Transfer guarantee: this is a guarantee issued at the end of the concession (two to three years before the normal expiry date of the concession) to cover any costs of works to bring the facilities up to standard or repair and environmental rehabilitation in certain cases, with a view to transferring facilities in good working order to the concession granting authority.

151 Public party guarantees. – Similarly, the project company and the lenders may wish to receive guarantees from the grantor in respect of public sector entities involved in the project whose credit risk is too high. This may be the case where the purchaser or supplier of inputs is a State-owned enterprise. However, the grantor is reluctant to provide such guarantees, as one of the reasons for entering into concessions is to avoid the project being classified as a debt for the State or public sector entity concerned. Where government guarantees are not available, some other form of credit enhancement may be required to make the project profitable.[17]

152 Exclusivity. – The public authority usually grants the project company some form of exclusivity right over the service to be provided. Where the project's revenue stream is based on actual usage by end users, this monopolistic position can be an important element in ensuring a sufficient revenue stream. For example, the project company may obtain an undertaking from the licensor that no other licence for the service in question or a related service will be granted to a third party, in a specific area or in competition with the project company, during the concession period. The validity of such exclusivities must be verified under national or regionally harmonised competition law.

153 Tax or regulatory benefits. – As we have seen previously,[18] as the project company wants to be protected against changes in regulations, it may also ask the grantor to provide certain guarantees concerning the taxation to which the project is subject. The concession contract may specify a maximum amount of taxes, duties, fees, royalties or other such charges that may be imposed on the project company. These are determined on the basis of the options offered by the investment code, the tax codes or the stipulations of the concession agreement or PPP if derogation

17 *Ibid.*
18 Cf. *supra* nº 112 et seq.

provisions or stability clauses are granted and ratified by Parliament. There are also intangibility and stabilisation clauses aimed at neutralising the impact of the State's normative power on a contractual transaction[19] or stabilisation clauses making it possible to freeze the effects of legislative amendments in certain circumstances.[20]

E. Changes to technical requirements

154 Safety requirements. – The granting authority does not generally want technical requirements to be changed by the contractor or project company without its consent. However, it is possible to provide for changes without the consent of the grantor where the changes are necessary for the safety and integrity of the project or caused by technological or operational changes. For example, in the case of an upgrade to the electricity transmission system, changes may be required to the planned connection arrangements.

155 Modifications at the request of the public entity. – For its part, the grantor generally has the right to modify the technical requirements. In such cases, the project company must at least protect its interests by requiring that such modifications do not significantly reduce the project's performance, increase the project's cost or entail a risk of non-compliance with environmental requirements.[21] Where appropriate, and ideally, the contract should provide for the economic and financial consequences of such a modification and specify how it is formalised. In particular, it must be specified whether a consultation is launched to estimate the cost of the modifications, the acceptance of the added or modified goods and the formalisation of the costs in an amendment. Modifications are discussed in more detail in section 3 below.

F. Turnaround time

156 Meeting deadlines. – The grantor may also impose penalties on the project company if construction is not completed by the agreed date. These penalties may take the form of liquidated damages and depend on the length of the delay. If completion is not achieved by a certain date, the grantor often has the right to terminate the concession contract for default. The completion date is only extended for specific reasons set out in the concession contract or by mutual agreement. These are generally breaches by the concession grantor or events that are the concession grantor's own risk, and possibly events of force majeure. The calibration and capping of these penalties must necessarily take into account the risks of bankability, to ensure that the potential burden of penalties does not prevent the project company from repaying the debt taken out with lenders.

19 D.X. Correa Angel, "La stabilité juridique dans le droit international des investissements", *Th. repr.*, 2012, pp. 228–234.

20 M. Audit, S. Bollée and P. Callé, *Droit du commerce international et des investissements étrangers, op. cit.*, no. 244.

21 *Ibid.*

G. *Restrictions on the transfer of project company shares*

157 Change of control. – Because of the importance of the identity of the shareholders, due to their financial and technical capabilities, the grantor may wish to impose certain restrictions on the transfer of shareholdings or the change of control of the project company. The grantor may wish to prohibit any transfer (direct or indirect) until sometime after completion of construction, maintain a right of approval over the identity of any transferee, and/or a guarantee from the original shareholders. These restrictions normally apply during the construction phase and may apply during part of the project's operating phase or even for its entire duration. However, given the duration of project finance contracts and the existence of a secondary market for infrastructure assets, it is imperative not to tie up shareholders in the SPV unnecessarily and to allow the asset constituted by the PPP to retain some form of liquidity on the market.

158 Substitution or *step in*. – Lenders require that the project company be able to assign its rights to the lenders and that the lenders be able to take security over the project assets. These rights are normally reinforced by the terms of the direct agreements between the lenders, the public party and the project company.

H. *Compensation in the event of termination*

159 Calculation of compensation. – The public party generally makes a payment to the project company in the event of termination of the concession agreement. In the event of default by the public party, this payment compensates the project company for the value of the project assets (which, on termination, will generally revert to the grantor) and for the loss of future revenues to be generated on the project.[22] The amount of the payment is generally equal to the total amount still owed to the lenders plus compensation for future revenue shortfalls, which may be calculated as all or part of the NPV of the expected return on equity, generally calculated by reference to the project's financial model. A less generous lump sum is usually provided for "no fault" termination, such as in the case of prolonged force majeure, and even less generous in the case of termination for fault of the project company. However, it is important to stress that the lenders must be reimbursed in such a way that the indemnity paid must always be sufficient to pay the debts incurred and not yet repaid by the project company in respect of the project finance assets.

The lenders wish to examine the possibilities of terminating the contract, and they wish to limit the grantor's ability to terminate the concession. The lenders may also require remedial rights and the right to intervene in the concession agreement to remedy any default by the project company before the grantor has the right to terminate the concession. In all cases, lenders are careful to ensure that, whatever the reason for early termination, it is totally disinterested.

22 For more details: see Part 3, Chap. 2, Section 5.

§ 2. *Contracts for the purchase of goods or services*

160 Securing supplies. – This contract is used for projects that produce a good. It allows the buyer to secure its supply and the project company to sell its product on a pre-determined basis. If a significant proportion of the financing is in the form of debt, the risks taken by the project company when selling the product must be kept to a minimum. This contract is an accessible solution for limiting these risks.[23] This is the case with the PPA for a project company operating under an IPP and selling its electricity to the national utility.

161 Market risks. – The purchase contract assigns the market risks associated with the demand for and price of the product to the purchaser. The buyer, which is often a public utility, will buy and sell the project company's production on the market, either directly to end consumers or to other buyers. This contract defines and delimits the revenue stream for the project company, and indirectly for the lenders and shareholders, over the life of the project. Although in theory the role of the buyer is limited to bearing the market risks, the buyer often plays a central role in the development of the project. Generally speaking, the buyer is one of the driving forces behind the project, and it is often the buyer who has identified the need or initiated/encouraged the presentation of the project as part of a call for tenders.[24] The terms of the purchase contract must reflect the nature of the product, the sector of activity and the relevant market. This type of contract is only appropriate for certain types of PPP. They are widely used in projects in the electricity sector, with the "PPA", and can also be used for water, with the Water Purchase Agreement (WPA), and for other industrial projects (refineries, for example). Where the granting authority benefits from the product, the elements of the purchase agreement are often included in the concession contract or any similar contract.[25]

A. Distribution of risks

162 Market risks. – Over the term of the concession, the price of the product is likely to vary. Lenders, who do not want to bear the risk of price volatility, require this risk to be externalised from the project company to the buyer. This market risk includes price, costs and demand. To reduce the risk, a market study (part of a feasibility study) may demonstrate that the project is viable.[26]

163 Take or Pay. – As far as demand is concerned, lenders do not want to leave the demand risk to the project company. When demand falls, it is mainly the buyer who bears a large part of this risk. For this reason, energy sales contracts often include "take-or-pay" mechanisms. This means that the buyer must take (buy) the product or, failing that, make a payment to the project company. He is

23 E. R. Yescombe, *op. cit.*, pp. 70–103.
24 Jeffrey Delmon, *op. cit.*, pp. 339–360.
25 *Ibid.*
26 Ronald F. Sullivan, *International Project Financing*, 3rd ed, Juris Publishing, 2009, pp. 3–1, 3–7.

therefore always obliged to make a payment based on the price agreed between the parties, whether he takes delivery of the product or not. The project company is paid as soon as it performs its obligations and, in general, is able to deliver the product.[27]

Sometimes the buyer only pays for the product delivered/purchased, based on an agreed price. However, this does not provide any long-term certainty for the project company. In other cases, the buyer agrees to purchase an agreed quantity of product, but the price paid is based on the market price at the time of purchase or on a market index. The project company therefore transfers the demand risk but retains the price risk. This type of contract is used in the mining, gas, oil and petrochemicals sectors, where the project company wants to ensure that the product will sell smoothly on international markets, but the buyer is not prepared to bear the risk associated with raw material prices. These contracts may include a floor price, in which case the result is equivalent to a take-or-pay contract at the floor price. This type of contract has seen considerable growth in the development of IPPs in Africa. However, it is sometimes called into question in certain countries, such as Ghana and Kenya, which are becoming energy surplus countries, in favour of a *take and pay* model that transfers the demand risk to the SPV.[28]

164 Operating risk. – The project company generally requires the buyer to bear all the risks associated with the operation of the project in relation to the transport system or the buyer's own acts and omissions. This allocation of risks must be reasonable and, above all, must focus on assigning to the buyer the risks that it can control.

B. Obligations of the parties

165 Most of the project company's obligations relate to operating the project in accordance with the purchaser's requirements and properly communicating the O&M programme to the purchaser. Most of these obligations are reflected in the O&M contract.

The buyer undertakes to take delivery of the product. The buyer's obligations may relate to the development of linked infrastructures, the supply of equipment or the connection with existing infrastructures. It may also provide services during operation (maintenance of its own facilities, carrying out tests, assistance, obtaining permits and licences).

C. Quantity

166 The project company generally undertakes to sell all its production, provided that a buyer has an interest and is committed to doing so. Alternatively, the project

27 E. R. Yescombe, *op. cit.*, pp. 70–103.

28 Catherine Dupuy Burin des Roziers and Carole Schertzinger, "Du *take or pay* vers du *take and pay* dans les contrats d'achat d'énergie", *La Tribune Afrique*, 9 October 2021.

company may find several buyers. For example, it may sell its electricity production both to the national electricity company and to an industrial company (mining or cement manufacturer, for example).

The buyer undertakes to order a minimum amount of products or is limited in the extent to which he can reduce his orders. This is very important for the project company, as it is often itself committed to a minimum amount of input from its supplier.

D. Technical specifications and performance

167 Technical aspects. – The purchaser wishes to define precisely the technical parameters of the operation, particularly in terms of minimum capacity and performance, or the technical characteristics of the good produced (voltage and frequency in the case of electricity, physico-chemical composition in the case of petroleum and mining products, for example). The project company undertakes to comply with these specifications, failing which it will be penalised. The buyer often requires that no changes be made to the project without its approval, or at least that no changes be made that could affect it.

E. Prices and payment

168 Purchase agreement. – The purchase contract provides the project company with its main, and often its only, income. For the project to be "bankable", the lenders must ensure that the product will be purchased at a sufficient and stable price to enable the debt to be repaid. The financial stipulations of the contract must therefore be coordinated with the financing contracts and the repayment of the debt, as well as with any other project contracts involving an expense for the project company.

169 Pricing. – The pricing mechanism should take into account inflation in the relevant market and any price changes associated with input supplies. Where the inflation risk is borne by the project company, it may use hedging mechanisms or transfer the risk to another party to the project. The pricing mechanism should also encourage the project company to maximise the efficiency of the facility. However, when pricing is entrusted to a public entity with discretionary power over pricing, the project company bears a substantial political risk and a price risk that could make the project unprofitable, unless this is strictly regulated.

A classic method of defining the amount owed by the purchaser to the project company involves a dual system that includes a payment for capacity/availability and a payment for usage/debit.[29] The capacity payment is the amount paid by the purchaser to the project company for making the infrastructure or goods produced available to it.

29 Jeffrey Delmon, *op. cit.*, pp. 339–360.

The capacity payment compensates the project company for its fixed costs associated with operating the asset it manages (construction costs, financing costs, personnel and insurance, for example). So, no matter how much product the buyer takes out, these costs will be paid. This amount can be reduced if the infrastructure delivers less than the planned capacity.

Payment to the SPV for the use of the asset is made in respect of the amount actually delivered or used by the purchaser over a certain period. This payment also covers all variable operating and maintenance costs.

The purchase contract may specify minimum levels of capacity made available by the project company to the purchaser. In the event of the project company defaulting in this respect, its liability must be transferable to the responsible project party.

§ 3. The construction contract

The construction contract is an important legal document in that it deals with construction risks relating to project financing.

170 Turnkey contract. – To complete the project and start the design, construction and operating phases, an EPC contract is generally preferred.[30] This is a construction contract that is often referred to as a "turnkey contract" because it covers the design, construction and delivery of the infrastructure. This type of contract is concluded between the EPC contractor and the project company to determine the terms and conditions for the design, engineering, supply of materials and equipment, construction and commissioning of the infrastructure. In some projects, there may be several EPCs, each with a defined role or scope. This is known as a Split EPC. The concept of the "turnkey contract" is as follows: once the project has been built and is ready to be handed over to the project company, it only needs to be operated by the latter.[31] Numerous model contracts published by FIDIC offer different forms of contractualisation, with varying degrees of development.

171 Alternatives to EPC. – In certain situations, an EPC contract may not be feasible or suitable due to factors such as project complexity, scale, the technology involved being outside the contractor's expertise, or uncertainty around costs or completion time. In such cases, alternative contract structures may be used, such as design and build contracts, convertible lump sum contracts, cost plus contracts, EPCM (Engineering, Procurement, and Construction Management) contracts or hybrid types of framework agreements.[32]

30 Understanding and Negotiating EPC Contracts, *Howard M. Steinberg*, Routledge, 2017.

31 Boris Martor, *op. cit.*

32 John Dewar, *International Project Finance – Law and Practice*, 3rd ed, Oxford University Press, p. 115.

Focus on the different types of FIDIC contracts

The FIDIC rainbow suite consists of three standard contracts:

The Red Book

- The most commonly used standard contract.
- Construction contract for all projects where the design is provided by the employer, following the traditional design procurement route. Responsibility for design rests primarily with the client.
- The contractor is paid on a measurement basis for the actual quantities of work carried out. The accepted contract amount is based on estimated quantities.

The Red Book is, of course, preferable if the employer has experience in design and wishes to have a significant role in the design process.

The **Livre rose** is a derivative of the Livre rouge for projects financed by multilateral development banks.

The Yellow Book

- Standard contract in which the design is carried out by the contractor.
- The contractor is generally paid on a flat-rate basis.

The Yellow Book is suitable for construction projects in which the contractor is in charge of most of the design.

The Silver Book

- Used for EPC/turnkey projects where the majority of the risks are attributed to the contractor.
- The design is carried out by the contractor and payment is generally on a lump-sum basis.

This model is often preferred when the project does not involve any major or unknown risks and the employer prefers to have more security in terms of price and time.

FIDIC also publishes

- the **White Paper**, which is used for international professional services contracts;

- the **Green Book**, which is a simplified model designed to facilitate the signing of contracts for relatively small projects of a repetitive nature or of short duration, with the employer providing the design (in accordance with FIDIC guidelines, USD 500,000 and six months are considered reasonable capital and duration limits for projects in which the Green Book forms are used);
- the **Golden Book**, which governs the design and build contract in which an O&M period has been added and is intended for situations where a complex range of different services continues beyond a 20-year period; and
- the **Blue Book** for contractual dredging, reclamation and ancillary construction operations for which the employer is in charge of the design.

A. Spreading risk

172 Risk transfer. – Under this type of contract, a high level of risk transfer and liability arising from the PPP contract is imposed by the project company on the contractor. There is also a limited obligation on the project sponsor to participate in the works (other than essential supervision). This allows the project company to limit its financial and legal exposure in the event of delay or default, and to be able to recover against the EPC contractor in such cases.[33] When the project company transfers the risk to a third party, for example the EPC constructor or O&M operator, this is known as "passing-through". If the project company enters into a contract with an EPC contractor, it will "pass-through" the liability for delay damages (from the PPP or concession agreement) to the EPC contractor, in an amount at least equal to the delay damages for which the project company would be liable under the concession agreement.

This type of contract should be compared with more traditional engineering or construction contracts where the risks and responsibilities (including design) are more evenly spread between the contractor and the main contractor. The latter may have a greater and more frequent involvement in decision-making and acceptance throughout the construction period.[34]

In project finance transactions, it is necessary for the project company to procure and manage all necessary insurance to safeguard the lender. By controlling and centralising insurances, the project can implement a comprehensive risk management strategy, thereby reducing overall risk. This method also minimises the likelihood of project participants needing to secure costly additional or supplementary insurance policies.[35]

33 Michel Lyonnet du Moutier, *Financement de projet et partenariats public-privé*, EMS, Management & Société, 2002.

34 *Power Projects: Development Phase*, Practical Law Energy.

35 John Dewar, *op. cit.*, p. 141.

173 Consulting engineer. – The project company sometimes calls on an engineering firm to design the project, on the basis of which a call for tenders for construction is issued. Even if the developer has the experience to manage the work under different contracts and coordinate the responsibilities of different specialist companies, this is often difficult for project finance lenders to accept. They want responsibility for construction to be isolated. They do not want the project company to find itself in the middle of numerous construction-related disputes because of a failure to manage and coordinate the work.[36]

174 Choosing a general contractor. – Another approach is to appoint an engineering company as main contractor, with responsibility for handling all aspects of the project's construction in return for payment of a fee, which may vary depending on the final construction price. This option can be economically attractive. However, the existence of variable construction costs is not necessarily acceptable to lenders because of the risk of cost overruns. Additional funds are not necessarily available within the SPV, which may make it economically difficult to operate the project. Whatever the contractual method chosen, the builders selected in Africa are often foreign or local subsidiaries of international companies.

175 Fixed price. – Under an EPC contract, the work is carried out in return for payment of a fixed price and is completed by a contractually agreed date. The EPC contract transfers significant responsibility, and therefore risk, to the contractor. This is reflected in the inclusion of a greater number of contingencies in the calculation of contract costs, and in a contract price that is higher than the final price if the work were carried out on a cost-plus basis alone.

EPC contracts are standard in the infrastructure and energy sectors. Promoters who are shareholders in the SPV and wish to take a different approach are usually required to provide completion guarantees, diluting the non-recourse nature of the transaction. Certain types of projects cannot use this type of contract. This is often the case for the extractive industries of mining and oil, or projects involving a gradual investment in a network, influenced by fluctuating demand, such as projects in the telecommunications sector.

B. *Obligations of the parties*

176 EPC obligations. – The EPC contract sets out the detailed design, technical specifications and performance criteria for the project. The contractor is responsible for building a project capable of meeting the expected performance, even if a factor may have been omitted from the initial project description. The contractor is responsible for selecting and paying all necessary sub-contractors and suppliers. The project company may have a right of supervision or even prior authorisation with regard to the main subcontractors/suppliers.[37]

36 E. R. Yescombe, *op. cit.*, pp. 105–115.
37 *Ibid.*

177 Work outside the scope. – Works outside the area made available or the subject of the contract, such as communications networks, are often excluded from the EPC contract and built by the purchaser, the concession authority or a third party. In some cases, however, they may be built on behalf of the public party and handed back. Any delay caused to the project's construction work in this respect is not the responsibility of the EPC contractor.

178 Role of the SPV. – In terms of choosing this EPC co-contractor, even if the terms of the concession or PPP contract do not necessarily require it to do so, the SPV will find it advantageous to organise a private call for tenders to select the co-contractor. Inviting bids on the basis of objective criteria that have been defined and communicated in advance will help to optimise the final cost of the construction and associated services. With the exception of the obligation to pay the contractor, the project company is only responsible for a limited number of elements, such as making the site available and providing access to it, obtaining planning permission (if this has not been entrusted to the contractor), providing access to the infrastructure needed for construction (electricity and water, for example) and ensuring that third parties perform in accordance with their contract. Additional costs caused by the discovery of pollution, hazardous waste or archaeological remains are often borne by the public party, which the project company will then claim on behalf of the builder where this has been provided for in the PPP contract.

C. *Prices and guarantees*

179 Payment due dates. – Payment is normally divided into a number of instalments based on the achievement of agreed *milestones*, such as the completion of a construction item or the delivery of a major component. These payments can be made directly by the lenders to the contractor, without passing through the accounts of the project company.

This phased payment encourages the builder to meet its obligations, and in particular to complete the project on time and at the agreed price. It also enables lenders to monitor the use of the funds disbursed. In addition to this mechanism, a percentage (between 5 and 10%) may be withheld from each payment by the project company as a guarantee for on-time completion. Part of this guarantee is paid to the contractor on completion of the project and the other part at the end of the guarantee period.[38]

To ensure that the builder has sufficient cash for the early stages of construction, such as design and site analysis, the contract generally provides for the payment of an advance shortly after work begins. In exchange, the project company may request a guarantee for the repayment of the advance. This advance is paid by the shareholders from their own funds thanks to contributions to the project company's capital.

Although the price is a fixed lump sum, the contract can sometimes put in place mechanisms that allow the contractor to increase the price. Lenders take a very

38 Jeffrey Delmon, *op. cit.*, pp. 265–320.

close look at this. This is the case when (i) the project company changes the design or performance requirements of the facility or adds new elements to the contract, (ii) a risk borne by the project company as the project owner materialises, (iii) additional costs are caused by delays due to an archaeological discovery, or (iv) a change in regulations requires a change in the design or construction of the project.

Cases of force majeure will generally be limited in this contract so as not to allow the EPC contractor to seek compensation in the slightest difficulty. In all cases, it will be usual for the EPC to be able to request an extension or compensation in this respect only insofar as the SPV would have the same right vis-à-vis the public party under the contract.

D. Completion

180 Acceptance. – The EPC contract sets out the basis on which the infrastructure is accepted and accepted by the project company. This may involve conducting tests to verify performance against agreed levels. The dates of these tests are often referred to as "Commissioning Dates".

181 Commercial Operation Date. – Completion is often subject to initial acceptance when the project meets the minimum requirements of the EPC contract, at which point the infrastructure is handed over to the project company for operation. This is known as the COD or Commercial Operation Date. Final acceptance subsequently depends on the resolution of identified issues. These points form part of the scope of work set out in the EPC contract but do not prevent the project from operating. A deadline is often included in the COD contract and can only be extended in limited circumstances.

E. Compensation and termination

182 Delay penalties. – The EPC contract provides for agreed fixed indemnities to cover the project company's losses in the event of a delay in construction or the inability of the facility to operate as stipulated. The aim is often to align these indemnities with those that the public party can claim in the event of delay under the concession/PPP contract. This is known as the "back to back" contractual technique. These predetermined amounts make it possible to avoid lengthy disputes and the resulting uncertainty. All of these indemnities are subject to a ceiling, usually equivalent to an amount that some estimate to be no more than 25–30% of the value of the contract.[39] However, there are no precise rules or recommendations, as these ceilings really have to be correlated with the project's financial model and the penalties provided for in the PPP contract.

These indemnities do not have the same role as penalties but act as fair compensation for losses incurred. With the exception of these amounts, the project

39 E. R. Yescombe, *op. cit.*, pp. 105–115.

company cannot claim lost profits or additional costs, except in the event of termination of the EPC contract. These indemnities may, however, reflect penalties provided for in the concession contract.

183 Indemnification. – These indemnities may not be sufficient to compensate the project company in the event of poor performance by the contractor. The project company therefore has the right to terminate the contract if the contractor fails to complete the project on time. Failure to meet minimum performance standards or environmental requirements also constitutes default on the part of the contractor, giving the project company a right to compensation. In certain cases, rare in practice, EPC contracts sometimes include a so-called scrap clause allowing the project company to scrap the construction, i.e. obliging the builder to compensate for any damage suffered and also to dismantle the infrastructure or construction if it does not meet certain contractually agreed standards or in the event of a defect.

184 Termination. – For its part, the contractor has the right to terminate the contract if it does not receive the scheduled payments or if other fundamental obligations are breached by the project company (such as the impossibility of access to the site). Such termination may only occur after a period of suspension of performance of the contract by the contractor.

F. Construction defects

185 Guarantee. – Once the project has been built, the operator will take possession of the facility and begin operating it. However, the builder remains liable for a certain period, at least one year, and must remedy any construction defects found. This period is known as the "warranty period". The builder's liability may include all defects in the work, or it may be limited to those defects for which the builder is responsible. In the latter case, the project company is obliged to pay the builder when it repairs a defect for which it is not responsible. This option is advantageous for the project company insofar as the builder knows the project and is able to repair the defect more efficiently. It is also in the lenders' interest for this period to last as long as possible, although an abnormally long period is likely to be reflected in the builder's price.[40]

Focus on construction guarantees in national law

The legal regime for guarantees will depend on the existence of mandatory national provisions. For example, Ivorian, Moroccan, Cameroonian and Senegalese law have a legal system applicable to the ten-year guarantee and the guarantee of perfect completion. It will therefore be useful to check how national and mandatory legal provisions can be combined in the construction contract with the contractual stipulations included in the contract.

40 Jeffrey Delmon, *op. cit.*, pp. 265–320.

186 Hidden defects. – In addition to these defects which may appear during the warranty period, there may be hidden or latent defects which only appear after the warranty period, for which the builder may remain liable. This new liability period is established by the applicable law and/or by the parties but can usefully be developed in the construction contract signed by the SPV.

§ 4. O&M contract

187 Maintenance scope. – An O&M contract covers the technical O&M obligations for the duration of the infrastructure operation. The purpose of this contract is to provide technical assistance to monitor the performance of the infrastructure deployed under the concession or PPP operating contract. It includes full maintenance of the[41] installation, including preventive and curative tasks. The comments that follow relate mainly to the practices observed in this type of contract; in practice, it does not matter which law applies. If they refer to legal points, they will mainly concern French civil law.[42]

188 Contractual standards. – These O&M contracts between the project company and the operator of the plant facilities[43] cover the preventive and corrective maintenance of the facility and generally involve mostly local staff to manage, operate and maintain a project. The role of the operator is to ensure that the project is properly operated in accordance with the contractual requirements set out in the main contract between the public authority and the project company. The precise nature of the services that the operator is required to provide varies according to the specific nature of the project and the type of products.[44] As in the case of the EPC contract, and again under the influence of the lenders who seek to ensure that the project company bears as little risk as possible, the O&M operator assumes all the risks arising from the main operating contract or PPP[45] (the so-called back to back or transparency principle) and may also benefit, in respect of its services, from the rights enjoyed by the incumbent under the main operating contract or PPP *if and insofar as* the incumbent has actually benefited from such a right (the so-called if and when principle). The indemnities or penalties relating to maintenance provided for in the concession/PPP contract are mirrored in this O&M contract between the project company and the maintenance company.

189 Experience. – The O&M contract ensures that operating and maintenance costs remain within budget and that the project will operate as planned. As the

41 Boris Martor, *op. cit.*

42 For more advice on the practice of O&M contracts, see *Operation and Maintenance (O&M) Contracts: Key Issues*, Practical Law Construction, Thomson Reuters.

43 V. *Understanding the Financing of Energy Projects*, African Development Bank Legal Support Facility.

44 Practical Law Construction, *op. cit.*

45 Boris Martor, *op. cit.*

project company has no operating history, lenders often prefer established companies with a strong track record in maintenance, with the necessary experience and financial strength, so that in the event of liability[46] they can be confident that they will deal with operating problems.

Even if the project is operated by one of the sponsors, a separate contract must be concluded. Sometimes, a single contract combines the obligations, with the EPC contractor taking responsibility for heavy maintenance over the long term, while minor maintenance is entrusted to the operator. In some cases, the maintainer may be a minority shareholder in the SPV.

A. *Services included*

190 Independence. – The scope of the services provided by the operator in charge of maintenance must be clearly defined to ensure that the division of responsibilities with the project company is clear. The project company must be able to supervise and control the operator's tasks. The functions relating to the management of the company must remain in the hands of the project company. The operator should only be responsible for maintenance and the project company for management, financing, insurance and personnel. In a standard O&M contract, the operator provides the key personnel and other staff are employed by the project company. It is important to ensure that the concession contract authorises the SPV to subcontract the O&M of the facility, and that the O&M operator itself is authorised to do so. The operator may, in fact, be responsible for recruiting subcontractors and remunerating them if this is authorised. If there is an obligation to inform or approve the project owner, it will be necessary to check whether the SPV will have to approve the subcontractors and, if so, whether the granting authority will also have to be informed.

191 Missions. – Services include planning: the maintenance operator provides input into the design of the project with regard to operational issues and maintenance operating projections and their costs. They also include the transfer of infrastructure from the contractor to the operator, who can provide assistance with commissioning and testing. Once operations begin, the operator is responsible for (i) obtaining the necessary permits and authorisations, if required for its mission; (ii) maintaining the infrastructure to industry standards and ensuring compliance with health and safety standards; (iii) drawing up the annual budget; (iv) ordering and managing inputs; (v) maintaining an up-to-date stock of spare parts and operating manuals; (vi) keeping operating costs within the annual budget; and (vii) carrying out routine and maintenance inspections as well as urgent repairs, subject to any interventions under the EPC contractor's warranties.[47]

46 E. R. Yescombe, *op. cit.*, pp. 115–117.
47 *Ibid.*

Points to watch

If the O&M contractor is not the same as the EPC contractor, it is recommended that when the contract comes into effect, a copy of the as-built documents should be provided, together with an inventory of the infrastructure and/or a handover process between the two entities during the first few months of operation. Ideally, the service provider should be aware, prior to entering into the contract, of everything that is likely to affect the performance of its assignment (e.g. technical characteristics specific to the site and the work, its location; access and working conditions; applicable laws and regulations, safety conditions in force, mobilisation of personnel and their level of competence, etc.). When the contract takes effect, it is important that these conditions have not been substantially changed.

B. Prices

192 Price structure. – The operator's remuneration may be fixed or based on a cost-plus-margin approach, the latter being the normal approach when the operator is responsible for major maintenance and renewal work. The fixed price is often indexed using an index or basket of indices reflecting the operator's cost structure. In most African countries, there are rarely reliable public indices published on a regular basis.

193 Bonus or malus. – A bonus is often paid if the performance of the infrastructure exceeds the contractually agreed standard levels. The bonus is calculated in such a way as to share the additional remuneration between the project company and the operator. Conversely, there may be a malus (penalties) if the project operates below the agreed levels, usually the guaranteed annual performance rate. These penalties are usually limited to the equivalent of one or two years' remuneration for the operator. These performance elements are very important for the SPV, but also reassuring for the lenders, who always want to be able to demand a change of O&M operator if results are not satisfactory.

In some cases, the O&M provider is responsible for the performance and maintenance of major elements of the infrastructure (e.g. the turbines in a power station) in return for payment of a fixed price over a certain period. The advantage of this mechanism is that it locks in the price of maintenance over time for certain elements, making it possible to forecast the relevant budget over the long term and incentivise performance.

To remember – penalties and transfer of risk

In an O&M contract, a number of factors may come into play in terms of penalties for both parties to the contract. The operator will be penalised if its performance is less than expected. There are a number of issues that need to be anticipated:

- Firstly, what penalties will apply if the contractual preventive/curative maintenance obligations are not fulfilled?
- Secondly, what is the consistency with the penalties that the SPV could incur for failure to maintain the concession?
- Finally, are all maintenance risks transferred to the operator by the SPV?

Section 2. Other project contracts

§ 1. Shareholders' agreement

194 Purpose. – This contract sets out the rights and obligations of the promoters with regard to their relationship within the project company. It defines how the project company will be managed, how expenditure and revenue are to be allocated, and how it will deal with the various events that occur during the concession. The shareholders' agreement is often the continuation of a development agreement initially entered into by the promoters in the early stages of the project's development.[48]

195 Development agreement. – During the development phase, the promoters enter into a development agreement governing their relationship during this period. This agreement sets out the decision-making procedures, cost sharing and equity contribution commitments of each party. In theory, the provisions of this agreement should prevent one developer from holding the consortium hostage or aggressively imposing himself on the others. This development phase represents a significant risk and investment for developers. The agreement defines how development costs will be shared and how they will be reimbursed. This may take the form of repayment through the sale of the project to the project company after financial close, or through the contribution in kind of the developed project to the project company. This type of agreement can also set out the rights and obligations of each party when the project is awarded on the basis of a call for tenders. These contracts may also be called "consortium agreements".

196 Capital of the project company. – With regard to the capital of the project company, lenders (and sometimes the concession granting authority) require a minimum level of equity: capital and shareholder loans (*equity* and *quasi-equity*). This level depends on the risk profile of the project, the country risk, the quality of the shareholder sponsors and the security already taken. Shareholders may provide subordinated debt finance to the project company. Lenders may require the capital to be injected first before the project company can draw on the loans, thus obliging the shareholders to make their contribution as soon as possible. They may agree to capital being paid in at set times during the construction phase, often at the same rate as the debt drawdown. Shareholder contributions can also take the form of contributions

48 Jeffrey DELMON, *op. cit.*, pp. 271–283.

in kind. This may be the case in emerging countries, where local shareholders do not have the cash but contribute equipment, the construction site or even raw materials.[49]

197 Sale of shares. – Shareholders wish to avoid transfers to a third party or any other unauthorised person without their prior agreement. This limit may be absolute for a given period. The shareholders' agreement may define with which type of third parties the transfer may take place or even identify third parties by name. The purpose of these restrictions is to control who can be a shareholder in the project company, taking into account criteria such as nationality, experience or financial strength. These restrictions are often reflected in the project company's articles of association. They must be thought out and reflected in line with the requirements of the invitation to tender or the contract proposed by the public party.

§ 2. Input supply contract

198 Purpose. The PPP project may require some form of input in order to operate. The project company does not want to bear the risk that the required input will not be available when it is needed. It must be available at a price that is appropriate to the project's financial model. As a result, the majority of the project company's contracts are with an input supplier to meet the project's needs, at least to the minimum level required for the project to operate.[50]

199 Commitment on terms. – This contract implies that a supplier undertakes to provide a certain quantity of inputs of a given quality at a given price. Only certain input suppliers are willing to make such a commitment for the duration of the project or concession contract. Constraints related to the relevant market or related to transport and storage may limit the interest in entering into such contracts. For example, in the case of a gas- or oil-fired IPP, it is necessary to secure the supply of oil or gas over the long term at a fixed and stable price.

Input suppliers prepared to make a long-term commitment are often protected by long-term sales agreements with other suppliers, or by a monopoly position. In the case of a local public company, the parties need to provide a solution in the event of privatisation or liberalisation to avoid the potential delays and costs of litigation.

A. Distribution of risks

200 Market risk. – The project company and lenders may not wish to bear the risk of increased input costs. Therefore, they transfer this risk to the input supplier by agreeing a fixed price (albeit usually index-linked), or to the purchaser or granting authority if it is not possible to obtain a fixed price from the input supplier. The cost of inputs includes the cost of export from the source country, import into the host country and transport to the site. The supplier is usually responsible for obtaining the necessary permits to import the input into the host country.[51]

49 *Ibid.*
50 Jeffrey Delmon, *op. cit.*, pp. 361–376.
51 *Ibid.*

The input supplier also bears the risk of supplying all the inputs required. Any failure on the part of the supplier to supply the required quantity will result in damages or a reduction in the price paid for the inputs delivered. In the event of a shortage, the input supplier will be responsible for obtaining the required quantity of inputs from other suppliers or other sources.

201 Operational risk. – The input supplier is assigned part of the project performance risk, as it is required to supply a given quantity of input at a given quality at a given time. If the input is supplied late or in insufficient quantity, the project's performance will suffer. The supplier of the input is responsible for the risk associated with this failure.

B. Main provisions

202 Quantity. – The quantity of inputs required to commission and operate the project must be carefully calculated. The input requirements for operation are based on the production demand of the project.

The project company must be able to modify the quantity of inputs to be supplied under the supply agreement according to its needs. One option is to use a "take-or-pay" system, whereby the project company pays for a given quantity of inputs per period. The project company then orders the inputs as required. In this way, it does not need to stock the inputs but rather takes delivery up to the specified quantity. This also provides the input supplier with a guaranteed minimum income. However, due to storage demands and the potential nature of the input in question, the input supplier may wish to impose a minimum and maximum quantity of inputs that the project company can order during a given period.

The parties may include a provision in the supply contract to amend the terms of the agreement in the event of a significant change in the project company's requirements, the quantity of inputs available or the market price ("*hardship clause*").

203 Source of input. – The grantor or project company may wish to impose restrictions. This may result from an interest in soliciting a specific source, for example to encourage a locally sourced contribution. It may also result from a desire to ensure consistency in the quantity and quality of the input.

204 Shipping and storage. – Responsibility for the various aspects of shipping and storage should be allocated in the input supply agreement. Specific shipping issues will largely depend on the nature of the input in question.

205 Price. – It is essential that the price of the delivered input is reasonably calculated to ensure continuity of delivery. An agreement that is fundamentally unviable from a commercial point of view is likely to result in a shortage of delivered inputs and possibly the failure of the project.[52] A base price should be set per unit, possibly depending on the quality of the input supplied. Depending on the nature of

52 *Ibid.*

the input, the parties may wish to provide for a review of the price, in which case a timetable and procedure should be established.

206 Failure to deliver. – If the input supplier does not have the quantity of inputs ordered at its disposal, it is generally required to obtain the necessary inputs on the market. The supplier is then responsible for any additional costs incurred. The project company may specify that if the input supplier fails to supply the input as contracted, then the project company may procure the missing input from other sources at the supplier's expense.

§ 3. Government support agreement

207 Purpose. – The purpose of this agreement, which is very common for many project financings in Africa, is to facilitate the completion and operation of the project by providing government support for any aspect of the project that the parties have agreed. This contract is known by a variety of names ("stability agreement", "implementation agreement", "coordination agreement", "cooperation agreement", and sometimes, confusingly, "concession agreement"). It regularly supplements the purchase agreement signed by a State entity purchasing the product from the project (e.g. PPA with a national electricity company) or a concession contract signed not by the government, but by another contracting authority. In cases where the concession contract is signed with the government, these stipulations may sometimes be included in the latter.[53]

208 Risk reduction and assumption. – A support agreement with the host State helps to reduce risks in cases where there is no clear legal framework for the project, such as for economic sectors using private finance for the first time, or where there are significant local risks, as in African countries.

The content of these agreements varies depending on the project, but some typical stipulations can be identified. This agreement generally sets out the general framework for the project and authorises the construction and operation of the project on an exclusive basis.

209 State guarantees. – A number of guarantees can be given by the State at this stage: guarantees of non-discrimination, guarantees of compensation for the project company in the event of expropriation of the project, guarantees relating to the provision of infrastructure for the project such as water, telephone lines, electricity and transport routes (road, rail).

In the same way, the government can make several commitments, in particular with regard to the availability of foreign exchange for the payment of debt and the repatriation of dividends, the issue of work permits for expatriates employed by the project company, the contractor and the operator, and the customs clearance of imported equipment.[54]

53 E. R. Yescombe, *op. cit.*, pp. 125–126.
54 *Ibid.*

Focus on exchange controls

African countries often have **exchange control mechanisms** designed to control and *ultimately* limit the outflow of foreign currency, while at the same time not restricting foreign investment. Investment codes, foreign exchange regulations and other central or regional bank regulations set out the conditions under which foreign investments can be made, with or without the possibility of subsequent outflows of dividends, capital gains and other benefits of the investment.

Depending on the country and the operation concerned, it may be necessary to make a simple declaration (prior or *retrospective*) or to obtain prior authorisation from the competent authorities. This is a major consideration when structuring project financing. The convertibility and stability of local currencies should be studied, particularly for countries that are not members of the CFA franc zone and that benefit from a fixed parity with the euro and transfer facilities with this zone.

210 Delivery of permits and authorisations. – The government plays an important role with regard to administrative permits and authorisations. It may agree to exempt the project company from the obligation to obtain permits for the import of equipment, construction and operation of the project. Alternatively, the contract may identify all necessary permits on the basis of which the government undertakes to ensure that they will be issued, subject to applications being properly submitted, and that they will not be revoked without good reason.

It may grant the project company tax benefits. The State may waive its State immunities in respect of any dispute with the SPV relating to the agreement or to difficulties encountered by the SPV.

For their part, promoters can commit to retaining their stake in the project company for a specific period.

This contract can be quite political in nature. The promoters must ensure that the procedures laid down in the host country's constitution have been followed to make the commitments effective.

§ 4. Insurance contracts

211 Existence and sizing. – The insurance requirements of project finance are significant, and so are the costs. Yet this tends to be a neglected area at the project development stage. This can lead to an underestimation of actual project costs. Indeed, all the necessary assurances may not have been taken into account during project development and budgeting. This can lead to financing being blocked, as the insurance required by lenders may not always be available or implemented.[55]

55 E. R. Yescombe, *op. cit.*, pp. 127–132.

212 Contractual insurance. – In some cases, operators are obliged to take out insurance in view of the risks they incur. This obligation may be formalised by the operating contract, by legislation or by a decision of the supervisory ministry.

In addition to the principle of the obligation to take out insurance, there are other degrees of coercion weighing on the operator. For example, the operator may be required to demonstrate its financial capacity when choosing an insurance company. In addition, the ministry responsible for mining and energy issues may, for example, set a minimum amount for which the operator must be able to present an insurance policy. Finally, certain clauses in the insurance policy may be required by law.

These obligations always apply to the private operator, who must bear the cost of the insurance contract. However, they may be extended to third parties if they are involved in the project. This is the case, for example, with sub-contractors.

For example, in Cameroon, Article 117 of the Decree of 30 June 2000 requires insurance policies to be taken out for both the operator and subcontractors of oil operations. The State must also be included as an additional insured party under the terms of these policies, and the policy must contain a clause providing for subrogation to the rights of the State. Furthermore, Article 118 of the same decree sets out a list of risks to be covered by the insurance contract.

In general, all insurance obligations will be included in the concession or PPP contract between the State or the public party and the operator, the project company.

213 Role of the broker. – From the outset of development, promoters should choose an insurance broker with experience in insuring project finance transactions and major projects in the country concerned.[56] The broker plays an important role in communicating information to the insurance company. Insurance is taken out for the first phase, construction, including commissioning and testing. It is then renewed annually during the project's operating phase.

A. *Construction phase*

214 Particulars. – The contractor can usually take out most construction risk insurance and will include the cost of this in the construction contract price. However, care must be taken to ensure that the insurance taken out by the EPC contractor is consistent with that taken out by the project finance company. This is because lenders often have numerous insurance requirements that can be difficult to meet. Lenders are keen to review all the terms and conditions for each insurance policy taken out, and to gain insight into any claims, by working with the project company, rather than leaving this to the builder. Similarly, lenders control the use of the amount paid out by the insurance through insurance indemnity delegation agreements. In fact, they ask for these delegation agreements to be put in place at the financial *closing*.

56 *Ibid.*

215 Risks covered. – The insurance required for the construction phase is relatively standard and must cover both personal injury and damage to property caused by force majeure events, as well as defects in design, materials, workmanship, on site and during transportation of the equipment. Loss of profit or additional costs that may be caused by a delay in commissioning are also covered. Insurance can cover the risk of pollution or hazardous waste being discovered on site. These insurances include professional liability cover, all-risks worksite insurance (TRC), ten-year civil liability insurance in most French-speaking countries, industrial accident and occupational illness insurance, and equipment theft and breakage insurance. All-risks site insurance is undoubtedly the most important, as it covers all damage occurring during construction, as well as equipment and materials delivered to the site. It allows the insurer to intervene outside the scope of any liability search, so that the insurer intervenes with the SPV and then calls into play the liability of any third parties who may be implicated.

B. Operating phase

216 Operational risks. – The risks specific to the construction site, the risks covered by insurance during the infrastructure's operating phase are generally the same as during the construction phase. There will therefore be several types of insurance during this phase: a multi-risk policy covering all types of damage to the SPV's assets and equipment with related business interruption insurance, a civil liability policy for all risks relating to the SPV's liability involving its fault and requiring it to repair damage, and a completed civil engineering works (OGCT) policy covering the infrastructure built against all types of climatic, safety or health events, for example. Specific insurance policies may also cover interruptions to the project company's activities.

C. Lender requirements

217 Bankers' clauses. – In addition to the delegations of insurance referred to previously, lenders have specific requirements that must be included in insurance policies to ensure that they are adequately protected. These are known as "bankers' clauses".[57]

218 Lenders' agent. – The lenders' agent will, as we shall see, be named as an additional insured (or co-insured) in the insurance policies, as may other interested parties such as the contractor, operator and purchaser. They require the insurer to undertake to inform them of any proposed cancellation or amendment of the policies, and the policies may be amended without their agreement. Similarly, the insurer undertakes to inform the lenders of any default by the project company. The lenders often have the option of paying the unpaid premiums instead of the

57 *Ibid.*

project company. Finally, the lenders' agent is often named as the sole beneficiary of the loss in the policies (with the exception of third-party injured parties). This gives them the right to take direct action against insurance companies in certain jurisdictions.

Lenders will require an audit of the insurance programme to ensure that there are no "holes in the carpet" and to understand the costs inherent in the programme.

219 Insurance program. – An insurance programme must be obtained and maintained in compliance with applicable laws. In many regions, this means using local insurers who may not have the financial strength to meet lenders' requirements. Consequently, facultative reinsurance with appropriately rated partners and mechanisms, such as reinsurance assignments, is often necessary to assure lenders that they can directly access reinsurance proceeds. Lenders usually demand that the project company secures insurance only from insurers with a specified minimum credit rating. However, this can be challenging in regions where local laws mandate the use of local insurers, especially if those insurers are unrated or have low ratings.[58]

220 Brokers' role. – An insurance broker can act as an intermediary between the insured and the insurer or, in the context of reinsurance, between the insurer and the reinsurer, to ensure that a valid contract of insurance is formed. For this, the broker writes a "broker's letter of undertaking".[59]

The contractual insurance clauses of the various contracts will also be the subject of this review to ensure that what is provided for in terms of cover is correctly reflected in the contractual clauses. The role and requirements of lenders are discussed in greater detail in Part 2 of this book, which deals with the project financing phase.

58 John Dewar, *op. cit.*, p. 146.
59 John Dewar, *op. cit.*, p. 158.

Part 2

Project financing

6 Financing players

221 Categories of players. – The development and financing of infrastructure projects require the involvement of multiple players, due to their complexity and size. In Africa, these players, whether the State, financial institutions or developers, each have a respective role that is representative of the issues and constraints weighing on the sector concerned by each project financing. During the financing phase, i.e. once the project has been developed and awarded to the SPV, the lenders will gradually and increasingly become involved in reviewing the project and will work directly with the SPV and its various boards to ensure the project is financed. More indirectly, the lenders will also be in contact with the public party, to ensure that the project is financially sustainable for the public finances or for the public entity that is the SPV's counterparty, and that the project is in line with the country's development challenges. This is often set out in a direct agreement signed between the public party and the lenders. In addition, lenders are increasingly involved upstream of the signing of project contracts, and in some cases even upstream of the launch of the call for tenders or the submission of an unsolicited bid, so that the project documentation takes account of the lenders' requirements from this stage onwards and to ensure that the contracts signed are bankable before the financing is raised.

Section 1. The role of public authorities in financing projects

§ 1. The involvement of public authorities in project financing

222 The traditional role of governments. – The State or its affiliated or deconcentrated entities are key, because first of all project financing is most often used to finance public infrastructure. In principle, however, the State or public parties are at the origin of investments relating to State-controlled sectors, where the public sector takes the initiative to satisfy the needs of its population. The State will generally have two main options, as we have indicated, to facilitate the development of its public service infrastructures: financing from its own funds, borrowing or turning to private financing, often through long-term PPP using the

DOI: 10.4324/9781003616894-9

project financing technique. Governments or their agencies have a dual interest in project financing:

- delegate to the private sector tasks for which the private sector is presumed to be more efficient in terms of management, cost control and effectiveness in carrying out tasks;
- benefit from the innovation of the private sector in implementing these projects.

Governments might sometimes use this technique as a means of de-budgeting, i.e. carrying out projects without compromising the finances of the government or its agencies, or even their ratings.[1] However, the methodologies now used by the rating agencies and the IMF focus specifically on the economics of the project and the commitments made by the State or its agencies under the PPP contracts signed. Thus, just because the debt is raised by the SPV does not mean that these financial commitments on the part of the public authorities disappear.

223 Lack of accounting standards. – As we have seen, there is as yet no harmonised accounting and fiscal framework for PPPs.[2] However, governments must comply with certain national, regional and international accounting and financial reporting standards. They often capture and report financial information in three related frameworks:

- **public finance statistics**, as a summary of government finances that can follow regional or international standards such as Eurostat or those of the IMF;
- **State financial statements**, where applicable in accordance with the regulatory requirements in force in each country; the statements may follow International Public Sector Accounting Standards (IPSAS), which differ from IFRS insofar as they relate to the public sector;
- **budget documentation and financial execution**, which are part of budget preparation; they are not subject to international standards.

To remember

Maintaining off-balance sheet debt does not reduce the State's actual liabilities and may simply disguise the State's liabilities, thereby reducing the effectiveness of public debt control mechanisms. As a matter of general policy, the use of off-balance sheet debt must be carefully considered and safeguards implemented accordingly.

1 Zine Sekfali, "Droit des financements structurés", *Revue Banque Édition*, 2004.
2 https://ppp.worldbank.org/public-private-partnership/library/public-private-partnerships-international-monetary-fund

224 Risks related to infrastructure. – In the infrastructure sector, the size of investments, the temporality of cash flows, the high initial risks due to construction time and the illiquidity of projects make purely private investments difficult and costly to structure. In many cases, they require public support, whether in the form of direct financial assistance or some form of insurance, guarantees or subsidies.[3] This includes adjustments to how non-State investors are remunerated for their involvement (e.g. through guaranteed tariffs) and instruments to mitigate the risk inherent in infrastructure projects in order to make them attractive to private and international investors.[4]

225 Direct government support. – Very often in this last context, the State, through its government, may decide to provide direct support for projects, in the form of payment guarantees, subsidies, equity investments and/or loans. These support mechanisms are particularly useful when the project cannot be bankable without them. This is often the case for projects with insufficient financial viability or subject to specific risks that investors or lenders are unable to control on their own.

226 The need for predictable cost structures. – Investors and companies prefer to have predictable cost structures.[5] This can be achieved in part *through* mechanisms put in place by the State, such as revenues paid in foreign currency or pre-determined revenues. In the renewable energy sector, many governments have introduced *feed-in tariffs*, which guarantee the purchase of electricity produced at a fixed price per kWh for a certain number of years, mitigating market risk for investors once the project has been built. Similarly, governments may have to provide guarantees to cover the counterparty risk often represented by the national *off-taker*.

Few African project finance deals are therefore viable without some form of technical or financial support from the State or its agencies. Effective project financing often involves recourse to government support, to ensure that the government bears the risks it can control more effectively than private investors, and to carry out projects that are economically viable but not financially viable.[6]

§ 2. The modalities of public sector involvement

227 Public support. – In emerging African countries, the context and constraints may require greater public support than in more developed countries. Public support usually means that the public party undertakes to support a project financially, in particular by the following means:

- direct support: in cash or in kind (for example, to cover part of the construction costs, to donate or make available land, to provide assets, to offset bid costs or to participate in major maintenance work);

3 George KARARACH, *op. cit.*, p. 621.
4 Britta KLAGGE and Chigozie NWEKE-EZE, *op. cit.*, p. 65.
5 George KARARACH, *op. cit.*, p. 631.
6 World Bank, PPPLRC, *Government Support in Financing PPPs*.

- exemption from fees, costs and other payments, that would otherwise have to be made by the project company to a public sector entity (e.g. exemption from certain taxes);
- provide financing for the project in the form of loans (including mezzanine debt) or an equity stake in the project company, or in the form of a mechanism often referred to as "viability gap funding", which corresponds to compensatory financing to guarantee the viability of the project; and
- financing through public-pay PPPs, or subsidising certain categories of users, to reduce the demand and payment risk borne by the project company.

228 Credit support. – Public bodies can also provide credit support mechanisms:

- guarantees on the repayment of the debt raised by the project company, the exchange rate, the convertibility of the local currency, the collection of tariffs, the level of authorised tariffs, the level of demand for services by users, the amount of termination indemnities and their payment, etc.;
- mechanisms to prevent default by public entities; and
- assumption of risks that insurance cannot cover.[7]

229 Public support on financing. – However, it should be noted that the lack of public support does not always seem to be an obstacle to private sector investment in infrastructure. It all depends on the risk associated with the country, the project and the risk aversion among the sponsors and lenders involved in each project. It is also to be hoped that, in the medium term, most African public entities will be able to structure projects without extensive recourse to public support. Guarantees are still needed for risks that cannot be covered by private partners. For example, risks relating to political and contractual stability may represent one of the major obstacles to the development of large-scale infrastructure in Africa.[8] It should be borne in mind that exposure to high risk leads project promoters and private companies to seek higher returns.[9] Balancing the allocation of risk is therefore the key to establishing the optimum overall cost and facilitating the success of the project.

230 Granting guarantees. – The granting of guarantees by public bodies in a systematic or overly broad manner can lead to poorly structured risk transfers in infrastructure projects. Some development banks believe that comprehensive insurance against any potential loss can distort incentives to reduce costs and ensure quality maintenance, especially as guarantees tend to entail much higher costs given the number of players involved and the costs they represent,[10] not to mention the difficulty of correctly assessing the financial impact of these guarantees on public finances.

7 *Ibid.*
8 George KARARACH, *op. cit.*, p. 630.
9 *Ibid.*, p. 631.
10 *Ibid.*, p. 630.

Section 2. Financial institutions

231 Financial institutions have a central role to play in this project financing phase, because the SPV will not be able to start and finance the construction of the infrastructure without having mobilised all the resources, and in particular the project debt, unless its shareholders decide to finance from their own funds and then refinance or resort to corporate financing at the level of their shareholders.

There are three main types of financial institution: bilateral or multilateral DFI, which are the first to be involved in infrastructure projects in Africa; credit support or credit guarantee institutions; and private sector commercial banks.

§ 1. Bilateral and multilateral development banks and institutions

232 Support of DFIs. – Bilateral and multilateral development banks and institutions play a key role in the provision of infrastructure finance in Africa. The following section provides an overview of the contributions of the various institutions to infrastructure financing in Africa, as published by the ICA. The ICA is one of the few, if not the only, source of information providing a comprehensive overview of infrastructure financing trends in Africa. Unfortunately, the consortium has not published a new study since 2018. More generally, questions arise as to the need to reform multilateral support to project finance in Africa. Some studies indicate that reforms to the way multilateral financial institutions approach project finance could help overcome some of the most intractable barriers to the electrification of Africa, including fears of default and high project financing costs which drive away many potential investors.[11]

A. Multilateral institutions

233 The World Bank (WB). – The WB committed a total of USD 6.6 billion in 2020 to Africa's infrastructure sector, 18% more than in 2019, but 14% less than in 2018. On average, WB commitments to infrastructure financing remain stable: over the period 2019–2020, WB commitments average USD 6.1 billion compared with USD 6.3 billion between 2016 and 2018. In 2020, WB commitments are concentrated in the energy (34%), water and sanitation (26%), transport (23%) and ICT (15%) sectors. The International Finance Corporation (IFC), the WB's private sector arm, has announced commitments of USD 416 million in 2019 and USD 391 million in 2020. The energy sector accounted for 95% of its commitments in 2019 but only 28% in 2020. In 2020, the IFC's commitments were spread over several sectors, such as transport (33%) and ICT (24%).[12]

11 African Energy, Issue 512, John Hamilton: "Reforms at multilateral development banks could meet Africa's project financing challenges", Reforms at multilateral development banks could meet Africa's project financing challenges | African Energy.

12 IAC, "Trends in infrastructure financing in Africa – 2019–2020", *op. cit.*

An example of mixed public/private financing: the Dakar BRT project[13]

The financing of Dakar's 100% electric BRT (bus rapid transit) network, worth a total of more than 500 million euros, is an example of the use of public-private finance instruments in the field of transport infrastructure.

The project was managed by the State, represented by CETUD, acting as the organising and regulatory authority for urban transport in the city of Dakar. As part of its remit, CETUD was responsible for building the project's infrastructure (i.e. the BRT reserved lane, the 23 stations, the interchanges, etc.).

The project was carried out in the form of works contracts thanks to the mobilisation of a number of public funding sources (the WB to the tune of around 280 million euros, the Green Climate Fund to the tune of around 30 million euros, the EIB to the tune of around 80 million euros and the Senegalese government to the tune of around 4 million euros).

The purchase of rolling stock (i.e. the bus fleet, equipment, battery replacement, etc.) and the operation of the BRT were entrusted to a private company (Dakar Mobilité) by means of a concession contract, following an international call for tenders organised by CETUD.

The concession company has raised around €135 million in private financing, divided between bank financing, subsidies and shareholder contributions (two loans from Proparco and EAAIF, a subsidy from Private Infrastructure Development Group (PIDG) and the EU, with the balance provided by the concession company's shareholders, Meridiam and Fonsis). In addition, the State has undertaken, with the support of a WB grant, to guarantee the concession company's loss of income in the event of traffic falling below a certain threshold. The two banks participating on the private side (Proparco and EAAIF) were thus able to benefit from several public instruments to mitigate the project's risks (subsidies and traffic guarantees).

The BRT project demonstrates that it is possible to carry out projects as complex and risky as urban transport infrastructure in Africa, using "blended" financing from public and private sources (infrastructure financed from public funds under project management and rolling stock financed by the concessionaire from private funds with risk mitigation mechanisms).

13 This development has been prepared with the kind assistance of Olivier Fille-Lambie, a partner at Hogan Lovells who was involved in this case.

234 The African Development Bank (AfDB). – The AfDB's commitments on the African continent increased by 20% between 2018 and 2019 to reach USD 5.4 billion. This sharp increase needs to be qualified, as commitments in 2020 will be relatively low, at USD 1.2 billion.

The AfDB's commitments focused mainly on the energy and transport sectors. The energy sector accounted for 44% (USD 2.4 billion) of AfDB investments in 2019 and 55% (USD 0.6 billion) in 2020. Commitments to the transport sector accounted for 46% (USD 2.5 billion) of investments in 2019 and 25% in 2020 (USD 0.3 billion). Commitments to the water and sanitation and ICT sectors were smaller, accounting for 9% (USD 0.5 billion) and 2% (USD 0.1 billion) of AfDB commitments in 2019 respectively.[14] The AfDB therefore plays a very important role in financing infrastructure in Africa *through* the provision of loans, but also certain guarantees (partial credit guarantee, partial risk guarantee and hedging products).[15] Like other development banks, the AfDB set up the ADF in 1972 with 29 contributing countries. It is very involved in climate finance. It has set up the Africa Green Fund, with which it supports pioneering industrial-scale renewable energy projects and energy efficiency projects.[16] Together with a number of African countries, the AfDB has launched a pan-African investment fund, Africa50, with the aim of accelerating the development of infrastructure projects on the continent. This international organisation, which acts like a fund, mainly finances these projects by taking equity stakes in project companies. Its role is also to release private funds for high-impact projects and accelerate their delivery.[17] Africa50 has completed its first *closing*, with commitments totalling $222.5 million from 16 pan-African institutional investors (sovereign wealth funds, pension funds, banks, IDF, etc.).[18]

The LNG Zone 1 project in Mozambique is an example of one of the most significant project financings to have been completed in Africa

Although the conventional oil and gas sector is not necessarily the most popular sector in times of energy transition, projects in this sector are continuing and, along with mining projects, are still the largest project finance deals of the last decade. The Mozambique Zone 1 project involves the construction of a liquefied natural gas (LNG) plant with a production capacity of 12.88 million tonnes of LNG per annum (mtpa), including offshore extraction, pipeline, gas processing and liquefaction facilities, as well as an

14 IAC, "Trends in infrastructure financing in Africa – 2019–2020", *op. cit.*

15 Mthuli Ncube, *op. cit.*, p. 606.

16 *Ibid.*, p. 606.

17 *Ibid.*, p. 603.

18 Africa50, "An African first: Africa50 infrastructure accelerator fund reaches first closing with USD 222.5 million – backed by strong support from mainly African institutional investors", 9 January 2024.

LNG export terminal, primary domestic gas supply infrastructure and other related facilities. It is the largest foreign direct investment on the African continent to date and the largest project finance deal in Africa (total project cost estimated at USD 24.1 billion). The sheer volume of gas discovered and the expected LNG production will make Mozambique the third largest supplier of LNG in the world. The project is sourcing gas from the Golfinho-Atum field in "Area 1", which is located 40 km off the coast of Mozambique. Zone 1 contains approximately 75 trillion cubic feet of recoverable gas, implying a resource life of approximately 120 years at an initial production rate of 12.88 mtpa. The project will supply gas for export (mainly to Europe and Asia) and domestic consumption of LNG, fuelling the industrial development of the country and the Southern African region.[19]

235 The European Investment Bank (EIB). – The EIB has committed USD 1.6 billion to Africa's infrastructure sector in 2019 and 2020. In 2020, the EIB devoted USD 768 million to the transport sector (47%), USD 519 million to the water and sanitation sector (32%) and USD 269 million to energy (17%).[20]

236 The West African Development Bank (BOAD). – The BOAD, a development finance institution for the member countries of the WAEMU, committed a total of USD 468 million in 2020, an increase of 50% compared with 2018. In 2020, the majority of WADB commitments went to the transport sector (54%), followed by energy (38%).[21]

237 The European Bank for Reconstruction and Development (EBRD). – After concentrating its activities on Europe, this bank has seen its mandate extended over the last ten years to the Mediterranean basin and in particular to North African countries. It has been involved in a large number of infrastructure projects in North Africa. In 2019 and 2020, the EBRD's commitments in North Africa have fallen significantly. They amounted to USD 345 million in 2019 and USD 421 million in 2020, a decrease of 53% and 44% respectively compared with 2018 (USD 744 million).[22]

238 Credit alternatives with multilaterals. – Joint financing arrangements between commercial banks and multilateral institutions have become prevalent in the project finance sector. Often, commercial banks and multilaterals provide loans concurrently. However, some multilaterals have introduced A-loan/B-loan

19 Source: https://projectsportal.afdb.org/dataportal/VProject/show/P-MZ-FD0-003?lang=en
20 IAC, "Trends in infrastructure financing in Africa 2019–2020", *IAC Report*, 2022.
21 *Ibid.*
22 *Ibid.*

frameworks that allow them to utilise the liquidity of commercial banks while maintaining their role as the official lender on the loan.[23]

B. Bilateral institutions

239 The Development Bank of South Africa (DBSA). – The DBSA has committed USD 1.5 billion in 2019 and USD 1.1 billion in 2020 for infrastructure financing. DBSA commitments increased significantly by 36% between 2018 and 2019 but returned to 2018 levels at USD 1.1 billion in 2020.[24]

240 Involvement of bilateral institutions. – The commitments of French institutions[25] amount to USD 1.9 billion in 2019 – the same amount as in 2018 – and USD 1 billion in 2020. The energy sector accounts for a large proportion of these commitments, with 62% of commitments in 2019 and 46% in 2020. The German KfW Group's commitments fell significantly, from USD 1.6 billion in 2018 to USD 739 million in 2019 and USD 588 million in 2020. In 2019, a large proportion of KfW's commitments were dedicated to energy (59%), while the water and sanitation sector accounted for the majority of its commitments in 2020 (54%). The US development agency, USAID, has committed USD 227 million in 2019 and USD 243 million in 2020, most of which will go to the water and sanitation sector.[26] USAID has also launched a programme of aid for electrification in Africa, Power Africa.

The Arab Funds Coordination Group comprises ten financial institutions from Arab countries, of which four are national institutions[27] and six are regional organisations.[28] In total, they have committed USD 0.6 billion in 2020, 4 times less than in 2019.[29]

241 The emergence of Islamic infrastructure financing. – Islamic finance represents a market estimated at USD 3,250 billion in assets under management in 2022, which has grown by a strong 20% since 2020.[30] Its role in the infrastructure financing sector in Africa therefore deserves to be emphasised, as its scale on the continent could increase as a result, for example, of the Islamic Development Bank's growing activity in this market. Islamic finance embraces principles based on the values of social justice and human progress and is therefore particularly suited to the development of public-private partnership (PPP) projects with a high social and environmental impact.[31]

23 John Dewar, *op. cit.*, p. 249.

24 *Ibid.*

25 Agence française de développement and Proparco.

26 IAC, "Trends in infrastructure financing in Africa 2019–2020", *op. cit.*

27 The Kuwait Fund for Arab Economic Development, the Saudi Fund for Development, the Abu Dhabi Development Fund and the Qatar Development Fund.

28 The Arab Fund for Economic and Social Development, the Islamic Development Bank, the OPEC Fund for International Development, the Arab Bank for Economic Development in Africa, the Arab Gulf Programme for Development and the Arab Monetary Fund.

29 IAC, "Trends in infrastructure financing in Africa 2019–2020", *op. cit.*

30 Ezzedine Ghlamallah, "Croissance et perspectives globales de la finance islamique", *La Tribune*, 9 February 2024.

31 Ashraf Bouajina and Sara Ahmed, "A new tool to harness the growth of Islamic finance for infrastructure development", *World Bank*, 19 February 2020.

In its report *Islamic Finance – Africa: Robust performance and strong sukuk issuance support Islamic banking in Africa*, Moody's notes that Islamic banks are highly resilient, even in the face of difficult operating environments in many African countries. The report suggests that Islamic banks will be able to increase their footprint if African countries reform their financial systems and legal frameworks to allow this form of finance to flourish.[32] The WB has also published a guide in collaboration with the Islamic Development Bank[33] which sets out the procedures for structuring projects using Islamic financing and explains the legal tools involved.

242 Other bilateral development banks. – It is difficult to list all the bilateral organisations, but they include FMO, DEG, Swedfund, Norfund and LuxDev.

243 The example of China. – From 2000 to 2021, Chinese creditors, particularly State-owned commercial banks (SOCBs) and State-owned enterprises (SOEs), lent more than $75 billion in infrastructure loans across Africa.[34] However, as mentioned in the first part of the book, Chinese loans and investment are experiencing a historic decline, with USD 0.9 billion in loans in 2022, compared with USD 28.5 billion in 2016.[35]

244 Volume of IFI operations in Africa. – In 2019, other players played a role in financing infrastructure on the continent, the EU-Africa Trust Fund (USD 83 million), the Dutch (USD 194 million), Danish (USD 175 million), Swedish (USD 93 million), Norwegian (USD 60 million), Finnish (USD 16 million), Belgian (USD 8 million) and Austrian (USD 7 million) bilateral agencies. Nevertheless, the commitments of these seven European bilateral agencies fell by 37% between 2019 and 2020, from $553 million in 2019 to $347 million in 2020. They were mainly involved in the energy sector, accounting for 78% of total commitments in 2019 and 68% in 2020. The EU-Africa Trust Fund quadrupled its commitments between 2018 and 2019, but this increase needs to be qualified as it did not carry out any new operations in 2020. A "New Development Bank" (NDB), a multilateral development bank, was established in 2015 by Brazil, Russia, India, China and South Africa (BRICS) with the purpose of mobilising resources for infrastructure and sustainable development projects in emerging markets and developing countries (EMDCs). This emphasises the new South-South collaboration/investment trend.[36] Specialised funds and other funds-of-funds, often created and/or administered by development institutions, have proliferated in recent years. These include the Green Climate Fund, the *AREI*, the *GEEREF*, the African Water Facility, the Sustainable Energy Fund for Africa and the Global Environment Facility.

32 Moody's report, "Islamic Finance – Africa: Robust Performance and Strong Sukuk Issuance Support Islamic Banking in Africa".

33 Islamic Finance for Infrastructure PPP Projects.

34 Boston University Working Paper, Tianyi Wu and Yunnan Chen: "China's Creditor Diversification in Africa: Impacts and Challenges of Infrastructure Debt–Financing by Chinese Commercial Creditors", China's creditor diversification in Africa: impacts and challenges of infrastructure debt-financing by Chinese commercial creditors | ODI: Think change

35 Boston University Global Development Policy Center, Chinese Loans to Africa Database.

36 Jana Honke, Eric Cezne and Yifan Yang (eds.), *Africa's Global Infrastructures: South-South Transformations in Practice*, Oxford University Press, 2024.

To remember

It is important to remember that these multilateral or bilateral banks can intervene both to finance programmes or funds dedicated to infrastructure in Africa, but also as lenders for infrastructure projects directly and as equity providers. These same banks have also created guarantee and credit enhancement products.

§ 2. Export credit agencies and credit guarantee institutions

245 Export credit agencies (ECAs). – These are State entities, or private entities acting on behalf of a State, whose aim is to help companies finance export operations. Credit guarantee institutions, on the other hand, provide a guarantee to an organisation (private or public) that issues loans on the financial markets. This guarantee reduces the credit risk and the interest rate charged. Credit enhancement is likely to attract new private financing from institutional investors or improve access to bank financing.

Foreign ECAs often play an important role when one of their national companies is involved in the project.

The principles formulated under the auspices of the International Union of Credit and Investment Insurers, also known as the Berne Union, are not of direct and visible relevance to the funding and sourcing of finance from ECAs. The Berne Union is composed of members from both the public and private sectors of export credit and investment insurance providers (including members from the African continent such as the African Trade & Investment Development Insurance in Kenya and the Société Nationale d'Assurances du Crédit et du Cautionnement in Senegal). The Berne Union collaborates with the OECD and the World Bank to facilitate global trade and investment. It promotes the international acceptance of sound principles in export credit and investment insurance and provides a forum for professional exchanges among its members. The Union encourages uniform principles through organised meetings, ad hoc seminars, workshops and the exchange of information and experiences among insurers.[37]

Many export credit agencies (ECAs) have established internal processes to assess the environmental impacts of the goods and services they support. In some cases, they have also developed their own environmental guidelines. The approval of a proposed financing by an ECA's board typically depends on the successful completion of all required environmental assessments.[38]

246 Multilateral and bilateral financial institutions. – Virtually all multilateral or bilateral financial institutions have developed guarantee or credit enhancement products. These products can sometime overlap, creating competition between them

37 John Dewar, *op. cit.*, p. 232.
38 John Dewar, *op. cit.*, p. 236.

to a certain extent. In some cases, it might be more appropriate to consider whether project financing in Africa could be accelerated by a continental guarantee fund that brings together all these products to give them greater weight and traction and to limit the time it takes to mobilise and the cost of implementing these solutions.

247 AfreximBank. – AfreximBank (the African Export-Import Bank) has a supplier and buyer credit programme. This programme supports African manufacturers and importers of engineering equipment and capital goods, as well as promoters of turnkey projects. It aims to encourage African users of heavy equipment manufactured competitively in Africa to purchase this equipment in Africa and to help African importers of equipment for export, by promoting infrastructure projects to obtain this equipment abroad at reduced costs. The bank's guarantee reduces the cost of export credit cover required by foreign shippers. Among other things, the programme seeks to encourage intra-African trade in machinery, engineering equipment and infrastructure services.[39]

248 Export-Import Bank of China. – For example, the Export-Import Bank of China appears to be one of the main channels used by the Chinese State to finance infrastructure in Africa.[40] As part of a strategy to promote the internationalisation of Chinese companies, the Chinese government provides *soft loans* to African countries on condition that the projects are carried out by Chinese companies. These concessional loans are often distributed by the Export-Import Bank of China, with Chinese commercial banks becoming increasingly active in recent years to supplement the efforts of the Export-Import Bank of China. Unlike traditional contributors, China is perceived as being less involved in the internal affairs of the host country.[41] Nevertheless, the technical solutions proposed and implemented regularly fail to meet the needs of the countries concerned, with the risk of poorly dimensioned infrastructures or technological solutions and standards of uneven quality.

Focus: China's key role in financing African infrastructure

After some 20 years of expansion that enabled China to achieve a leading role, Chinese investments and loans on the continent have slowed sharply since the Covid-19 crisis, raising questions about China's future role in financing infrastructure in Africa.

39 George Kararach, *op. cit.*, p. 626.

40 Vivien Foster, "The changing landscape of infrastructure in Africa, Nontraditional sources take on a growing role", *Grid Lines, PPIAF*, October 2008; Economist Corporate Network, Herman Warren, "Spanning Africa's infrastructure gap: How development capital is transforming Africa's project build-out", November 2015, p. 16.

41 George Kararach, *op. cit.*, p. 627.

Strong growth in Chinese investment in Africa since the early 2000s

The first two decades of the 20TH century were marked by a very proactive policy on the part of China in Africa. From the early 2000s onwards, China became a major source of funding for African countries as part of its new official Going Global policy. This policy has encouraged Chinese companies to invest abroad and engage in development projects in order to secure access to natural resources and foreign markets, as well as to increase its global influence. Chinese capital provided African countries with a welcome new source of finance for their infrastructure following the IMF's structural adjustment policies of the late 1990s.

Annual Chinese investment in Africa in billions of dollars[42]

On the African continent, Chinese loans have mainly been directed towards public infrastructure projects, led by energy and transport. These two sectors account for 64% of the amounts lent. For example, 50% of Ethiopia's new energy capacity was financed by China, which invested more than $4 billion in the country's energy sector between 2011 and 2018.[43] China has played a key role in the financing and construction of hydropower plants, wind farms and biomass plants in Ethiopia.[44] Reflecting this dynamic, the share of sub-Saharan Africa's total external public debt held by Chinese players has risen from less than 2% before 2005 to around 17% in 2021,[45] making China the leading bilateral lender to countries in the region.

Main sectors targeted by Chinese loans in Africa between 2000 and 2022[46]

While China's ambitions extend to the entire continent, the majority of its investments are directed towards certain key countries: five African countries (Angola, Ethiopia, Kenya, Zambia and Egypt) accounted for more than half of Chinese loans over the period 2000–2022.

42 Boston University Global Development Policy Center, Chinese Loans to Africa Database, 2023.
43 World Bank Group, "Independent power projects in Sub-Saharan Africa", 2016.
44 According to data from the International Energy Agency.
45 International Monetary Fund, "At a crossroads: Sub-Saharan Africa's economic relations with China", October 2023.
46 Boston University Global Development Policy Center, Chinese Loans to Africa Database, 2023.

Top 10 countries to receive the most loans from China between 2000 and 2022[47]

Types of Chinese loans in Africa

China's loans to Africa take different forms. Firstly, there are bilateral loans, where China lends directly to African States. China also makes commercial loans through its two main financial arms, the Export-Import Bank of China and the China Development Bank (CDB). Beijing also lends to Africa via specific multilateral funds such as the Asian Infrastructure Investment Bank (AIIB) and the China-Africa Development Fund (CAD Fund). Finally, China grants loans to Africa via PPPs in which Chinese companies are involved, sometimes represented by the Chinese Enterprise Group (CEG). Loans are generally made in Chinese yuan (CNY) and, in some cases, in US dollars (USD).

China sometimes uses the natural resources of African countries as quid pro quo for these loans and as collateral for repayment. One contract in particular illustrates this phenomenon particularly well. It is the contract between the DRC and China, often referred to as the "contract of the century". Signed in 2008, it provided for a $6 billion loan for the construction of infrastructure in the DRC. In exchange, China gained access to the DRC's copper and cobalt resources, with Chinese State-owned enterprises investing 68% of the mining company Socomine. With this type of contract, China is counting on future profits from the mining joint venture to repay its loan for infrastructure work.

A sharp slowdown in China's post-Covid-19 expansion, due to both structural and cyclical factors

In 2023, the International Monetary Fund (IMF) noted that the China-Africa relationship was "at a crossroads", and according to Boston University's China Global Initiative, Chinese loans did not even reach $1 billion in 2022, the lowest figure for 18 years. What's more, in June 2023, at the China-Africa Economic and Trade Expo held in Hunan province, only $10 billion in project investment pledges were signed, half the amount recorded at the previous event in 2019. The downturn is also noticeable in the construction sector, illustrated by a 30% drop in gross revenues from Chinese engineering and construction companies in Africa in 2021 compared to 2015. This figure has fallen from a record peak of $55 billion in 2015 to $37 billion in 2021.[48]

This fall in disbursements of official Chinese loans to sub-Saharan Africa can be explained both by a refocusing of China's political priorities, which has had to

47 *Ibid.*
48 According to data from the China-Africa Research Initiative.

divert capital to support its ailing economy (property crisis, youth unemployment, slowdown in exports), and by a change in China's stance, which is concerned about the increased vulnerability of the debt owed by many African countries.

Despite this economic slowdown, it is likely that China will continue to be a major player in the financing of infrastructure projects in Africa, given the scale of its resource requirements and ambitions.

§ 3. Private sector commercial banks

249 The role of private sector commercial banks. – Private sector commercial banks may be called upon to provide part of the debt raised by the project company. However, in the infrastructure sector, they play a limited role in Africa, with the possible exception of Chinese banks. The latter have actively lent to infrastructure projects in 19 African countries over the past four years. Since 2014, loans from Chinese lenders have totalled USD 1.8 billion in Ethiopia, USD 4.8 billion in Kenya and USD 5 billion in Nigeria.[49]

250 Local and international commercial banks. – Local or international commercial banks are generally reticent about the level of risk involved in financing projects in Africa. In most cases, they will only intervene if multilateral or bilateral financial players are involved alongside them.

Another factor to be taken into consideration is the fact that local commercial banks are often limited from a regulatory point of view when it comes to providing financing for projects in Africa, as they cannot exceed certain maturities provided for by local arrangements or harmonised regional rules. The interest rates offered by commercial banks are less attractive than what bilateral or multilateral development banks and institutions can offer on infrastructure projects.

Furthermore, African commercial banks are still too often focused on retail banking, particularly in sub-Saharan Africa, and are not actively involved in infrastructure financing, particularly as these banks cannot offer financing with a sufficiently long maturity. The conversion of deposits into loans is low, and deposits are generally held in foreign banks rather than being deployed in local investments. According to the Bank for International Settlements and the Banque de France, in 2014 residents of the free trade zones (CEMAC and WAEMU) held a total of $14 billion in cash in offshore bank accounts. The level of banking penetration in Africa is also low by global standards. As a result, credit distribution is also very low by global standards[50] even though the AfDB and NEPAD are calling for the structuring of an African bond market to finance infrastructure.[51]

49 ICA c/o ADB, *op. cit.*, p. 54.

50 Paule Biensan, "Project bonds in the OHADA region, an option for funding infrastructure development in the OHADA region?", *White&Case Publication*, 11 September 2017.

51 Cédric Achille Mbeng Mezui and Bill Hundal, *Conditions for Infrastructure Project Bonds in African Markets*, NEPAD, AfDB, 2013.

Section 3. The project company

§ 1. Role of the project company at the financing stage

251 Borrowing company. – The project company acts as a borrower in order to obtain financing, with an equity and debt structure tailored to the cash flows of the infrastructure project.

252 Chain of contracts. – The project company is at the centre of all the contractual and financial relationships of the project finance. In this respect, the project company may not engage in activities that are outside the scope of the project, as the project financing depends on the lenders' ability to value the project on a stand-alone basis. In practice, the project company is responsible for the construction and operation of the project and must obtain the financing required to complete these two phases.[52] There are several types of shareholders in project companies. Some are at the origin of the development and studies, while others are more like financial investors supporting the initial developers and strengthening the equity capital. Finally, some are industrial players with the technology or know-how to carry out the project. These may be manufacturers or maintainers. They may be involved all together or individually, depending on the project. Their priorities in terms of return on investment and the length of time they will remain shareholders are generally different (Figure 6.1).

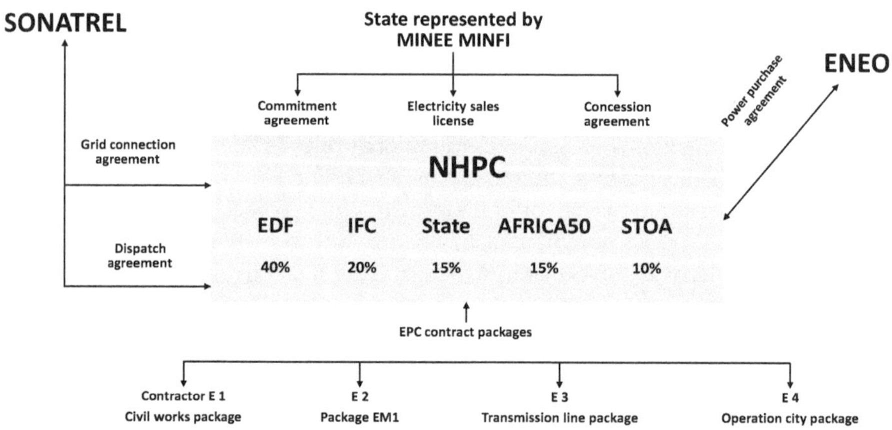

Figure 6.1 Example of contractual structuring: Nachtigal hydroelectric power station project in Cameroon 420 MW

253 Adjustment of project contracts. – The project company will often have to amend the project contracts to satisfy the lenders. In all cases, when public bodies and private sponsors structure projects, it can be useful to involve the lenders very early on in the process so that they can review the project documentation as soon

52 Zine Sekfali, *op. cit.*

as possible, to ensure that it is not subject to too many amendments *after the fact,* at the time of financing.

§ 2. Equity financing provided by the project company

254 Leverage ratio. – The project company's shareholders generally do not finance all the project's requirements themselves. They finance part of it in the form of equity and borrow the remainder from financial institutions. It should be emphasised that the project company must secure the long-term debt maturities with the project's cash flows. In other words, the project company must demonstrate to the lenders how its estimated revenues over the term of the operating contract will cover the project's operating and maintenance costs, taxes and debt repayments, with a sufficient margin to cope with any downturns (the margin required by the lenders depends on all the security and guarantee mechanisms offered by the public partner).[53]

255 Income allocated to repayment. – In terms of cash flow, the project company requires an amount of capital that takes into account the progressive repayment of loan instalments over the life of the project. Revenues normally consist of a unit payment made annually, half-yearly, quarterly or at another frequency agreed by the public sector customer in the case of PPPs with payment by a public counterparty, with, for some of these projects, ancillary revenues generated by rights of use paid directly to the operator.[54] For projects where the users or customers pay the SPV directly, these are the fees, taxes, charges or usage prices paid by these customers to the company. This is regularly the case, for example, in the financing of road projects involving tolls.

§ 3. Setting up the project company

256 Corporate form. – The company will most often be a corporation with shareholders' liability limited to the amount of equity they have contributed, in order to remain consistent with the philosophy of project financing, which is said to be without recourse to shareholders. In the French-speaking countries of North Africa and sub-Saharan Africa, shareholders will most often choose corporate forms such as SA or SAS, and more rarely SARLs, which may prove less practical for structuring relations between shareholders. In English-speaking countries, the company will be a *limited liability company.*

257 Tax structuring. – Sometimes the project company is not directly owned by the sponsors for tax reasons. In some cases, the sponsors use an intermediate holding company in a favourable tax jurisdiction in a third country in order to optimise

53 Laura Turley and Abby Semple, *Financing Sustainable Public Private Partnerships*, International Institute for Sustainable Development, February 2013.

54 *Ibid.*

the payment of financial flows by the SPV.[55] It is true that in all cases, the project company's advisers wish to check the tax structuring, such as the absence of unfavourable tax friction in the holding chain in relation to future flows. This tax structuring is also carried out with due consideration for other local or regional factors, such as exchange regulations, customs unions or specific local tax advantages.

258 Case study. – The Lake Turkana wind farm project in Kenya illustrates the financing structure between equity and debt. It gives an idea of the nature and role of the players involved in financing infrastructure projects in Africa in the renewable energy sector. This project was developed by a consortium of private and public companies and institutions over a period of eight years. It is the largest wind farm in Africa and the largest private investment in the country's history.[56] The government was not one of the developers or lenders. However, it was responsible for negotiating the PPA and building a 400 km transmission line.

The project was funded as shown in Table 6.1:[57]

Table 6.1 Lake Turkana wind farm financing structure

TOTAL (equity, debt)	*Type of institution*	*Country*	*623 m€*	*Remarks*
Shareholders' equity			**125 m€**	**20 %**
KP&P Africa B.V.	Developer	Netherlands	31 m€	
Aldwych Turkana Limited	Developer	United Kingdom	38 m€	
Vestas Eastern Africa Ltd.	Turbine developer/ supplier	Denmark	16 m€	
IFU-Danish Development Bank	IFD	Denmark	7.5 m€	
Norfund	IFD	Norway	16 m€	
Finnfund	IFD	Finland	16 m€	
Sandpiper	GIS developer/ company	Kenya	0.5 m€	
Debts			**498 m€**	**80 %**
Grants				
EU-Africa Infrastructure Trust Fund (EUAITF)	IFD	EU	25 m€	

(*Continued*)

55 E. R. Yescombe, *op. cit.*

56 Britta Klagge and Chigozie Nweke-Eze, *op. cit.*, p. 73.

57 *Ibid.*, p. 72.

Table 6.1 (Continued)

TOTAL (equity, debt)	*Type of institution*	*Country*	*623 m€*	*Remarks*
Senior debt				
African Development Bank (AfDB)	IFD	Africa	115 m€	plus €20m for the EKF (see below)
European Investment Bank (EIB)	IFD	EU	100 m€	plus €100m for the EKF (see below)
Danish Export Credit Fund (EKF)	Export credit bank	Denmark	120 m€	100m via EIB and €20m via AfDB
Netherlands Development Finance Company (FMO)	IFD	Netherlands	35 m€	
Proparco	IFD	France	20 m€	The investor website advertises €50m
The Trade and Development Bank (TDB)	IFD	Africa	10 m€	
Interact Climate Change Facility (ICCF)	Green. The end.	EU	30 m€	
Triodos Bank	Private banking	Netherlands	6 m€	
Subordinated debt				
DEG	IFD	Germany	20 m€	
The Trade and Development Bank (TDB)	IFD	Africa	10 m€	
East African Development Bank (EADB)	IFD	Africa	5 m€	
African Development Bank (AfDB)	IFD	Africa	2 m€	

Sources: investor websites, ICA.

Explanations: DFI = development finance institution; EU = European Union; GIS = Geographic Information System.

7 Principles of bankability

259 Principle of non-recourse financing. – Within the framework of the project, the financial players are keen to limit their risk and the risk of default by the SPV in charge of the project. Given the multitude of both endogenous or exogenous risks to the project in Africa, lenders will carry out very detailed analyses to identify these risks and cover them as far as possible. This is made more complex by the fact that the principle of project financing is based on the fact that the lenders' financial recourse for the payment of the debt is limited to the project company's revenues. Lenders are therefore exposed to numerous risks if the project fails or encounters difficulties during construction or operation. Therefore, before committing to the project, they conduct a thorough review and audit of the project's structuring, contracting and viability, as well as the stakeholders involved. Lenders want to ensure that the risks borne by the project company are limited and properly understood. A "bankable" project necessarily implies a solid financial, economic and technical structure, as well as an appropriate allocation of risks according to the nature of the project, the risks involved and the interests of the lenders. A "bankable" project is one that represents an acceptable credit risk for the various lenders.

Section 1. Concept of bankability

260 Definition. – Bankability is a narrow concept that can be easily overused, misunderstood and widely confused with other concepts such as profitability. Some authors even argue that bankability is an art and not a science,[1] thus demonstrating the subtlety of the concept. Strictly speaking, bankability is a "state" in which a project is sufficiently attractive and solid to benefit from debt financing. If potential lenders consider that the project presents an unacceptable level of risk and uncertainty, they will not provide financing and the project will not be considered bankable.

261 The concept of "better bankability". – A project with better bankability provides easier access to higher amounts of financing and/or better terms in terms of the amount of debt (leverage effect), loan duration and interest rates. The amount of

1 G. Vinter, *Project Finance, a Legal Guide*, Sweet & Maxwell, p. 139.

DOI: 10.4324/9781003616894-10

debt and therefore the level of leverage depend on the cash flow expected each year to service the debt (i.e. the amount of revenue expected and examined by the lenders and/or their advisers as part of a due diligence process), and on the recurrence and reliability of this cash flow in relation to various risk factors.

262 Is there a structuring model? – Given the diversity of projects, the many potential sites and the technical and financial issues involved,[2] there is no single structuring model for achieving bankability. And bankability varies according to the lenders involved. They may have different interests and concerns, as well as different approaches to risk. When lenders are public entities dedicated to development, they are often less fearful of political risk than private sector lenders. They may also have greater flexibility in negotiating with the project company because of the benefits of public sector involvement, particularly in terms of risk management in Africa.

Section 2. Bankability analysis

263 The parameters of the project feasibility study. – To make a project "bankable", the project promoters must carry out a rigorous feasibility study. They clearly understand the demand the facility will attract and the optimal scope and technical specifications, the project's revenue streams, its commercial attractiveness to bidders, stakeholder buy-in and legal requirements such as valid permits and regular land acquisition.[3]

The lenders' analysis concerns the financial, economic and technical viability of the project, the allocation of risks relative to the site and the country, the issues linked to the financial structuring of the project and the contractual structuring of its implementation. The project's viability is therefore assessed from financial, legal, economic, technical, environmental and social perspectives. The banks involved in financing the project will need to have a clear understanding of the sponsors' objectives and their ability and interest in monitoring the project throughout its life.

264 Technical, environmental and social analyses. – The technical analysis will focus, for example, on verifying the design chosen and the equipment planned for the project and ensuring that the project does not present any technical risks. Lenders will check whether the technologies used have a track record, to ensure their reliability and performance in meeting the needs of the project, taking into account the size of the project, its nature or type, the cost of the technologies and their lifespan. Analyses will also be carried out for the lenders by insurance experts to guarantee the capacity to insure existing risks and to properly assess their possible occurrence and magnitude. Similarly, environmental and social management (ESM) experts will be appointed by the lenders to carry out an audit of compliance

2 Michel Lyonnet du Moutier, *Financement de projet et partenariat public-privé*, ed. EMS, 2006, p. 15.

3 Christoph Rothballer and Philipp Gerbert, *Preparing and Structuring Bankable PPP Projects*, p. 66, January 2015.

with environmental and social standards and to check that no risk or element creates a problem in relation to the applicable standards.[4]

265 Economic analysis. – The economic analysis will be sector-specific and country-specific. It will focus on the environmental risk specific to the country of investment, the capacity of the economy to support and absorb the project and, more generally, on the general influence of the project on the local economy to ensure that it meets a need, that the demand is real and that the socio-economic or environmental impact is positive.

266 Legal analysis. – The legal analysis will examine the country's legal and tax system, as well as the project's contracts to ensure there are no clauses that could jeopardise the project company's ability to continue operating and service its debt. It will identify the risks to the project and ensure that a resolution is possible or that a solution for managing these risks can be put in place. Lenders will be assisted by advisors to carry out an audit and to draft financing documents, or even to request amendments to project documents and contracts to make them "bankable".

267 Financial analysis. – The financial analysis will assess the project's financial health and soundness and that of its various stakeholders to ensure that the expected revenues will be sufficient to cover the project's needs. It will enable lenders to check that all the costs associated with the project have been considered during development and structuring. Financial experts will be involved in this analysis to develop a financial model showing all the project's financial flows. This financial model will enable all stakeholders (first and foremost the project promoters and their lenders) to ensure that the estimated revenues over the life of the PPP contract will cover the project's operating and maintenance costs, taxes and duties, payment of debt instalments with a sufficient margin to cope with deteriorating situations (the level of margin required by the lenders depends on all the security and guarantee mechanisms offered by the public partner), while ensuring a satisfactory level of return on equity for the project promoters.

268 Lenders' concerns. – In general, the main concerns of lenders relate to the following elements:

- the robustness of the project's technical design and technological choices;
- certainty about the project cash flows needed to meet debt servicing requirements;
- the sufficiency of the project's cash flow to achieve the expected profit (or a reasonable profit) for the sponsors;
- compliance with the rules governing invitations to tender or the award of the project;
- the solvency of the public sector concerned or of the counterparty paying for the services of the SPV;
- the solidity and stability of the legal framework;

4 See below, technical viability analysis and CSR analysis *infra* n° 229 et seq.

- the effectiveness and enforceability of project contracts;
- confidence in the regulatory regime;
- the robustness of the SPV's financial model;
- the right to intervene if a project fails and availability of other entrepreneurs;
- the ability of contractors to meet their obligations and the quality of their management;
- the solvency of the contractors contracting with the SPV and the quality of their guarantees;
- the existence of understandable, controllable, limited and correctly distributed risks;
- the acceptability of the termination regime and the methods of calculating compensation (offering full protection of the debt);
- the environmental and social impact of the project and the management of these ESG aspects; and
- the availability and effectiveness of insurance cover.

§ 1. Technical viability and CSR analysis

269 Technical analysis. – Lenders will review the infrastructure design and the technologies used. They will be reluctant to finance unproven or experimental technologies. They will want to be able to rely on reliable performance data. They will therefore prefer tried and tested technologies used in similar projects with a documented performance history.

Lenders will also verify that the technology is appropriate to the host country's market and structural needs. This analysis may be carried out by an independent expert appointed by the lenders, who may also review the technical and CSR analyses carried out by the public party where available.

270 Cost analysis. – Lenders will also carry out an economic analysis of the technology, focusing on investment and operating costs, lifespan, maintenance requirements, training needs, usage and wear and tear of the chosen technology.

271 CSR/ESG analysis. – Lenders will also consider the environmental and social risks associated with the technology and the impact on local communities. To this end, upstream ESG audits will be carried out and plans will be put in place to monitor the ESG criteria defined as the standard to be met. Driven by policies in favour of the environment, resource conservation and social risks, development banks want to establish a clear roadmap for project financing that takes into account all environmental, social and governance issues. For example, the AfDB is committed to complying with international standards on ESG by requiring its borrowing counterparties to comply with certain criteria that promote good corporate governance, integrating environmental sustainability into all their operations to improve social conditions on the continent. The AfDB is not an isolated case, and the majority of lenders require their counterparts to comply with ESG criteria in their projects.

However, the CSR or ESG strategy is not necessarily easy to follow, even if it is a strategic priority based on principles that are often similar from one entity to another. At this stage, financing players have not adopted a charter or harmonised CSR rules. As a result, it is not uncommon for banks and borrowers to have to constantly try to accommodate existing local and national rules with the various CSR policies that exist and are becoming mandatory for borrowers in project financing in Africa. The difficulty is compounded in practice by the fact that the ESG standards proposed for certain projects are not always adapted to the development level of each country on the continent. There is sometimes a gap between the laudable wishes of lenders and the reality on the ground in terms of interpreting the chosen benchmark in the context and implementing it as far as possible without distorting it or preventing a project from going ahead.

Furthermore, as there is no common framework for these benchmarks, the ESG ratings carried out each year on lenders are not uniform either. As a result, each agency has developed its own methodology, even if they often use the same basis of international standards to establish a rating criterion. Progress would be welcome to unify the ESG standards applicable to African projects and to make them more agile.

ESG standards frequently used on the continent include those developed by the IFC[5] and the WB.[6]

§ 2. Economic/political viability

272 Local economy. – Lenders will assess the economic context and its interaction with the project, including the effects of the project on the local economy. This includes an assessment of the project's objectives and their incorporation into the government's infrastructure policy. The benefits of the infrastructure include the infrastructure itself, local industrial development, transfers of technology and know-how, the use of local suppliers and job creation.

273 Country analysis. – Lenders will focus on whether the country's economy is "ready" to host the infrastructure, particularly in terms of economic and market maturity. They will look at the following aspects: identification of the buyer or end consumers/users, identification of suppliers, flexibility and skills of the labour market, history and trends in terms of prices, costs, production, quality, competition and demand. Other important factors will also be scrutinised, such as the history of inflation rates, interest rates, exchange rates, labour costs, the state of local infrastructure, pricing and tax policies, foreign investment, the sophistication and stability of the legal system, the regulatory environment and its prospects for change, technical complexity, development costs and the availability of local suppliers.[7]

5 https://firstforsustainability.org/fr/risk-management/implementing-ifc-environmental-and-social-requirements/establish-and-maintain-an-esms/ifc-environmental-and-social-performance-requirements/ifc-performance-standards/

6 https://www.worldbank.org/en/projects-operations/environmental-and-social-policies#safeguards

7 Jeffrey Delmon, *op. cit.*

§ 3. *Legal viability*

274 Local legal system. – Lenders will approach the local legal system with a view to a long-term commercial arrangement which necessarily involves certain public sector commitments and certain assumptions about property rights, collateralisation, asset management and corporate structures.

In practice, project finance contracts have long durations and inevitably involve a high degree of uncertainty during their implementation. The success of project finance often depends on the quality of risk allocation and the regulation of prices, services and investments. There is a fundamental objective here, involving a balance or compromise that can prove delicate: on the one hand, making the operation attractive to the private sector; on the other, safeguarding public interests and optimising the overall economic return to society. Project promoters strive to strike the right balance. They need to determine the optimal type of contract, design prices that are attractive but ensure sufficient profitability, identify and allocate risks effectively, and carefully consider proposals for public sector involvement.[8]

275 Stability risk. – Legislative and regulatory instability increases lenders' risk and requires more protections to be put in place by the host government and/or shareholders. In this regard, lenders will look in particular to the host government's track record in treating foreign investors and protecting their interests.[9]

276 Legal certainty. – Lenders also attach great importance to access to justice in the country where the project is located, both for themselves and for the project company. In this respect, they consider timeframes, costs, the independence of judges and the risks of bias that judges may have towards foreign companies in the event of disputes with the State, national companies and local communities.[10] In any event, in most cases they will opt for international arbitration, taking into account the way the award will be handled by local courts and the ability to enforce the award in the host country. Enforcing foreign judgments or arbitral awards always presents practical difficulties for foreign parties, although certain international conventions provide fluidity and stability, such as the 1968 Washington Convention and the 1958 New York Convention.[11]

Since lenders have limited recourse to the project and SPV assets in the event of project failure, one of their priorities is also to ensure that the guarantees and other security they intend to put in place over the project assets are fully effective. In some jurisdictions, it is impossible to establish security over future assets. This often results in very complex legal mechanisms being put in place to satisfy the lenders. In all cases, various guarantees are examined and

8 Christoph ROTHBALLER and Philipp GERBERT, *Preparing and Structuring Bankable PPP Projects*, p. 68, January 2015.

9 Jeffrey DELMON, *op. cit.*, p. 127.

10 See Part 3, Chapter 4, Dispute management.

11 For further details, please refer to part 3, chapter 4 of the book, *infra* nº 509 et seq.

implemented to create what is commonly known as the security package. These will be examined in Part 2 Chapter 10 Section 2.[12]

It is essential for lenders to ensure that the quality of the collateral held over the project assets is satisfactory, in particular that it is possible to take security over the contracts, or at the very least, over the cash flows generated by the contracts, and that the main contracts do not lapse if the lenders wish to exercise their rights over the project components.[13]

§ 4. Financial viability

277 To convince lenders to contribute to the financing of a project, the financial aspects that matter most are those relating to the structuring of the project, the business plan and the expected revenue stream. This is because the assets of the project company, once completed, may not be worth enough to cover the debt.

278 Financial modelling. – During their audit, the lenders will develop a financial model (or use the financial model prepared by the project developers after the audit) based on available information, including financial inputs and outputs, in order to calculate the project's cash flows. This model will then be tested with the introduction of downgraded cases. This enables lenders to calculate the project's capacity to absorb the impact of a given risk.

Project costs estimated by developers are also scrutinised by lenders, particularly when these are paid to affiliated entities. Lenders may even request that certain payments be made only after the debt has been repaid, treating them as dividends rather than operating costs.

279 Viability with regard to the DSCR. – The project is considered to be financially viable when the project's revenues less costs, expenses and other charges are sufficient to cover the debt service for the lenders by a sufficient margin (assessed in particular by calculating the DSCR[14]) and leave an appropriate rate of return on investment for the shareholders. In addition to ensuring a sufficient DSCR, lenders will carefully assess the financial viability of the project company. The existence and operational capacity of the project company are an essential condition for generating revenue. If the project company's financial room for manoeuvre is too limited and its very existence is threatened, lenders will not be able to lend. In this respect, the robustness of a project's financial model is enhanced when it involves a long-term purchase contract guaranteeing stable revenues over a long period (where the traffic or infrastructure use risk is borne by a third party, compared with models where the project company bears this traffic risk, introducing greater uncertainty into the determination of future revenues).

12 Cf. *infra* n° 302 et seq.

13 Michel Lyonnet du Moutier, *op. cit.*, p. 88.

14 See the discussion of ratios in chapter 5, section 1 of the Credit Agreement.

§ 5. *Study of site and country risks*

280 Site survey. – A site survey carried out at the request of the lenders will look at a number of aspects including the nature of the site (including access rights, ground conditions and works), licences and permissions, local climatic conditions, associated local infrastructure, locally applicable and enforced environmental standards, costs and timescales associated with importing equipment and materials. They will also look at the availability of local staff (including their training and skills) and the costs and local availability of equipment and materials.[15]

281 Local integration. – Lenders will also conduct a more general study of the project's place in the local political context. The government of an African country, while keen to see the new infrastructure built, will often wish to distance itself from the financial burden and risk associated with the project. The State will generally grant the private sector a concession or contract to operate the project, in order to pass on to it the cost and burden of developing such a project, as well as the burden of raising the finance.

Lenders will therefore be keen to verify that the government is a supporter of the project and will examine its policy in this area for questions of clarity and the long-term viability of the project. The government's policy must be in line with the interests of the project. Finally, a stable political system and a solid legal system that is not subject to government discretion also will be fundamental aspects for lenders.

Lenders will also be looking at issues relating to changes in the legal framework, the risk of nationalisation or expropriation, as well as issues relating to administrative procedures, permits and licences to be obtained. All of these issues will be closely examined, as they may generate additional costs that would impact the debt servicing linked to the financing of the project.

282 Risks to financial flows. – In this context, lenders also wish to avoid risks of a financial nature, in particular the inconvertibility of the country's currency, the non-transferability of the project's financial flows, and the adoption of price or trade control restrictions. For example, in the case of a project, the risk of non-transferability of revenues may result from an obligation on the parties to reinvest all or part of the revenues in local projects, a cap on dividends that may be paid by the project company to its foreign shareholders, or an increase in rents, royalties or local taxes for the operation of assets or the resale of products.[16]

Figure 7.1 summarises the main risks a PPP project can face.

15 Jeffrey DELMON, *op. cit.*

16 Zine SEKFALI, *op. cit.*

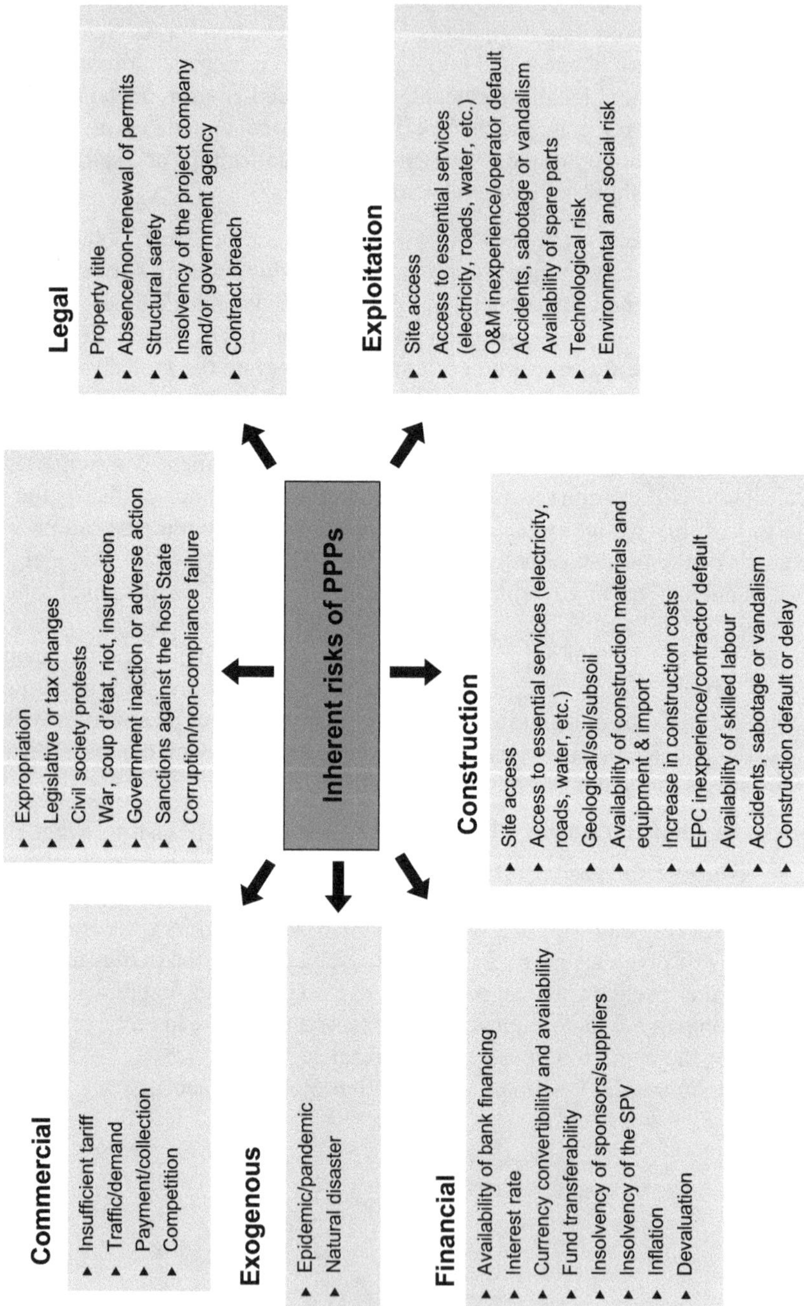

Figure 7.1 Risks inherent in PPP project financing

8 Sources of financing

Section 1. Private funding sources

§ 1. Equity and quasi-equity

283 A Shareholder contribution. – As we saw in Part 1 Chapter 5 Section 2, the project company benefits from equity capital contributed by its shareholders. This is a necessary condition for the banks to commit to financing the project. This contribution reduces the amount of the loan, but it also secures the commitment of the different types of shareholders (developers, financiers, industrialists, constructors or maintainers) in the project company with regard to its public or client counterparties. The level of equity is generally between 10% and 50% of the total financing requirement. This level varies greatly depending on the sector, the maturity of the technology used, the country, the predictability of future cash flows, the sponsor's risk profile and the project risks.

Equity is the capital contributed by shareholders, who receive shares in the company in return. In some projects, there may be different classes of shares with different rights and obligations for each category of shareholder.

In principle, this equity will be disbursed at the financial *closing* or at the first drawdown at the latest. In some cases, however, it may be disbursed over a period of time based on the SPV's needs and, above all, the lenders' requirements. The lenders may allow adjustments to authorise deferred equity contributions to the SPV: payment pro rata to debt drawdowns or, for example, setting up an equity bridging loan. Of course, lenders will seek to penalise any failure to pay in equity through various mechanisms, such as first-demand guarantees from the SPV's shareholders or penalty clauses (Figure 8.1).

284 Subordinated debt. – Shareholders may make shareholder loans available to the company, which are considered to be quasi-equity. These loans usually bear interest and enable the company to strengthen its financial position and meet its cash flow requirements. Repayment of the loans granted by the shareholders will be subordinated to prior repayment of the senior loans disbursed by the banks. This type of financing is known as subordinated debt. In practical terms, subordinated debt

DOI: 10.4324/9781003616894-11

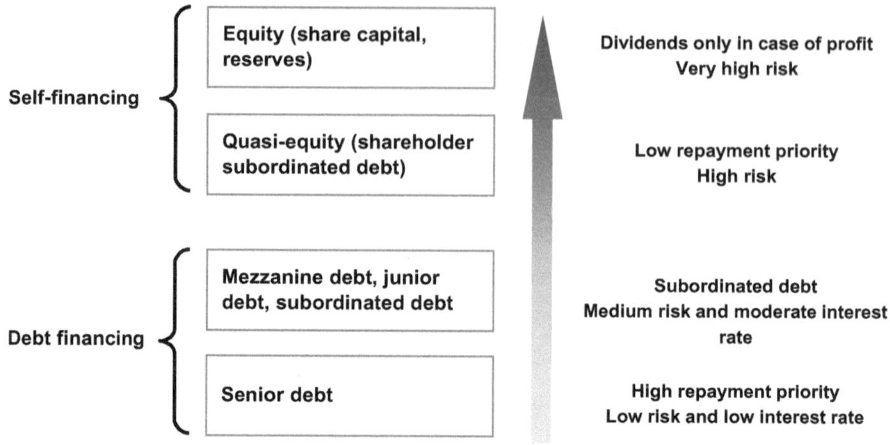

Figure 8.1 The hierarchy of financing in a PPP project

consists of prioritising the repayment of one debt over one or more others. The principle is that when the SPV does not have sufficient funds available to repay all the debts, the subordinated debt will be paid after the other debts. This is also known as junior debt. In particular, the introduction of subordinated debt by the shareholders can prevent cash from being blocked at the level of the SPV, without the possibility of returning it to the shareholders if only share capital had been made available to the SPV. The share capital is remunerated through the payment of dividends, but the constraints on distribution (obligation to have positive retained earnings, to fund regulated reserves, etc.) may mean that the SPV is unable to pay dividends to its shareholders during the first few years of operation, even though it may have a cash surplus. This improves the profitability of the project for the shareholders, as they are paid more quickly, enabling them to offer a more competitive price.

Focus on shareholder loans

The more equity the SPV's shareholders contribute to the company's capital, the greater their powers over the company as partners. They may, however, choose to lend to the company or to combine a capital contribution with a shareholder loan.

Current account advances will not confer shareholder rights in proportion to the sums lent, like a capital subscription, but they will have the advantage of allowing a degree of flexibility in terms of payment and repayment. Similarly, these advances can bear interest and be repaid more easily, which will improve the return on capital invested for shareholder sponsors, especially as the latter are often obliged by lenders to wait several financial years before distributing dividends. The structure of equity and quasi-equity capital will also depend on the obligation to maintain equity capital in excess of half the share capital. Indeed, most of the laws applicable to companies located in French-speaking areas of Africa require joint stock companies to maintain shareholders' equity above half of the share capital. Under these conditions, shareholders will often make a commitment to lenders to capitalise their current account advances. These shareholder loan agreements will therefore need to be formalised to set out their terms and conditions, and will generally be for a fixed term, often extending beyond the term of the loan agreements signed with the lenders. Early repayment may be authorised by the lenders if the SPV has sufficient cash and if the order of payments is respected, since in all cases the SPV shareholders' current account advance agreement remains subject to compliance with the intercreditor agreement and the credit agreement.

285 Pari passu. – However, it should be emphasised that shareholders are not the only ones to set up subordinated financing. In some project financings, subordinated debt may be linked to financing offered by financial institutions or investment funds. In this case, the question will be to determine whether these lenders will be treated on a pari passu basis with the shareholders, or if their financing will be guaranteed by additional elements relative to the shareholders and repayable on a priority basis in relation to the shareholders, so that in this case the shareholders would be subordinate to the junior lenders.

Example of blended financing – the Kigali bulk water supply project

The Kigali Bulk Water Supply Project is part of Rwanda's Vision 2020[1] and its broader development strategy to provide essential public services.

The total estimated cost of the project is USD 126 million, and it is set to provide 40,000 m3 of potable water, contributing to improving water access for approximately 500,000 people in the city. It includes the construction of a new water treatment plant at a site on the Nyabarongo River, along with a 10 km pipeline to transport the treated water to Kigali, along with several associated reservoirs and distribution systems.[2]

Financing for the Kigali Bulk Water Supply Project has been structured through a combination of equity and debt. The financing model involves a PPP between the Rwanda government and the private sector. The equity share in the project is primarily held by the government of Rwanda, while the private sector partner, Metito, a global leader in water management and infrastructure, plays a key role in the development.

1 https://www.minecofin.gov.rw/fileadmin/user_upload/Minecofin/Publications/STRATEGIES/Vision_2020/Vision_2020_.pdf

2 https://www.afdb.org/fr/documents/document/project-brief-rwanda-kigali-bulk-water-supply-project-86770

The financing breakdown is as follows: approximately 40% of the total project cost is financed through equity, while the remaining 60% is covered by senior debt. The project is structured as a Design Build Finance Operate (DBFO) concession, with Metito responsible for the full lifecycle of the project, from design through to the operation and maintenance phase for 25 years. A WPA, lasting for 25 years, has been signed between the Rwanda government, represented by the Rwanda Utilities Regulatory Authority, and the private sector partner. This agreement outlines the terms under which the government will purchase water from Metito, including the tariffs to ensure the financial sustainability of the project.

The Kigali Bulk Water Supply Project benefited from a well-coordinated package of blended finance.[3] EAAIF arranged the financing for USD 61 million, providing a long-term loan of USD 40 million for 18 years, alongside support from the AfDB. Additionally, other PIDG companies helped to galvanise the development. The DevCo (specialist PPP advisory facility under PIDG, implemented by the IFC) provided critical funding to help structure the transaction and manage the competitive tender process. Furthermore, the Technical Assistance Facility (TAF) provided USD 6.5 million in viability gap funding, reducing the up-front costs and allowing the government to expand access to reliable water supply without raising tariffs.

This coordinated financing package is an excellent example of how blended finance can successfully de-risk infrastructure projects in developing countries by combining public funding with private sector involvement.

§ 2. Bank financing

286 Senior loans. – Senior loans are provided by banks and are generally guaranteed by the assets of the project as well as other securities and indemnity mechanisms, as we shall see in Chapter 5. They represent the bulk of the financing for the total amount invested. Senior debt is, in a way, the king of debts, and senior banks will look specifically at the cash flow or income generated by the project and used to service the debt. They will also look at the amounts released by shareholders as equity or quasi-equity.

287 Club deal and syndication. – Given the size of the projects financed, several banks are usually involved in raising the finance for the project company's needs. In some cases, there may be more than 30 banks lending to the largest African projects. These are referred to as syndicated loans for very large financings and club deals for financings with a few banks. Among these banks, one or more arrangers are appointed. They mobilise the other banks on the market on a large scale to finance very large projects. The banks acting as arrangers negotiate the financing directly with the project company and coordinate its implementation through to financial closing. These arrangers are paid an arrangement fee.

3 https://blogs.worldbank.org/en/ppps/kigali-water-lessons-one-sub-saharan-africa-s-first-water-ppps

288 Remuneration. – Project finance syndication involves underwriters who underwrite the debt and are remunerated as such but take less risk than the other participants, in particular the arrangers, even though all parties are remunerated through the interest paid based on the rate granted and the margins or spreads which remunerate the banks. Underwriters will often underwrite the loan before general syndication.

289 Intercreditor agreement. – Given the size of the financing and the different parties involved, it is also common for the financing to include several types of lenders, whether multilateral, bilateral or other, with different credit lines, repayment profiles or maturities. Intercreditor agreements are then put in place to organise the relationships between these lenders and their rights and obligations throughout the financing.

290 Bridge loan. – In some cases, the project company is unable to complete its senior financing within the time required to start building the infrastructure. In these cases, it approaches lenders to obtain a bridge loan to finance construction while it waits for a long-term senior loan to be arranged.[4]

Example of a bridging loan

The pan-African banking group Oragroup SA has raised a bridging loan of CFA 50 billion to finance the completion of the construction of the Malicounda combined-cycle power plant in Senegal. This combined-cycle power plant, located in Malicounda, 85 kilometres from Dakar, will increase Senegal's electricity production capacity by 17%. Oragroup SA, acting as arranger, and the other participating banks (Orabank Togo, Bank of Africa Sénégal, Bank of Africa Burkina Faso, Bank of Africa Togo, La Banque Outarde and La Financière de l'Afrique de l'Ouest) have provided financing of FCFA 22.4 billion. This new financing comes on top of an initial tranche of FCFA 27.6 billion granted by Orabank Senegal, Orabank Benin and Orabank Burkina in December 2020 on a bridging loan totalling FCFA 50 billion.

291 Standby credit. – In senior project finance structures, standby letters of credit are frequently set up to cover unforeseen costs that may arise as a result of changes to the infrastructure financed. In principle, this credit can be drawn down during construction and at the start of operation. Its amount is added to the total senior debt raised by the project company. This standby financing line, set up by the shareholders or by one or more banks, will be very useful in enabling the SPV to deal with the ups and downs of construction activities or any difficulties that may arise when the infrastructure starts operating.

4 In early 2021, for example, Eiffel Investment Group raised $200 million in bridging loans to support developers of infrastructure projects in Africa.

292 PIM and term sheet. – The shareholders of the SPV will often prepare an information document to solicit offers from banks. This is often called a Project Information Memorandum or PIM, or an offering memorandum. Based on this, the banks will be able to prepare their financing offers and will examine the information provided by the project company in this document: description of the project and its development, proposed financing structure, project participants as identified at that date, contractual organisation and description of project contracts, characteristics of the equity and bank financing requested. To respond to this MIP and structure their intervention, the banks first propose a letter of intent or expression of interest to the project company and the sponsors, and then carry out their review of the project, audit, etc. They then develop the financing package and prepare their mandate and a credit term sheet setting out the various financing conditions in greater detail. Among other things, this document will describe the project, the parties who are shareholders in the SPV and in the loan granted, the contractual framework envisaged, the amount of the financing, the proposed rate, the purpose or uses of the financing, the conditions precedent to disbursement, the provisional timetable, declarations and guarantees, the applicable law and jurisdiction and so-called covenants, which require the borrower to enter into negative pledges and positive commitments such as information or reporting obligations or access to infrastructure for the bank or its advisers, for example. Some institutions, such as the Loan Market Association (LMA, see no. 281), have published guides for drafting term sheets, which should be consulted.[5]

§ 3. Bond financing

293 A bond issue for project financing is not common in all African countries, whereas this form of financing has been developed in the infrastructure sector in other regions of the world. However, it is likely that this form of financing will develop more widely in the future on the African continent.

When a bond issue is launched, it may take the form of a private placement if the number and quality of entities invited to participate is limited, or it may be a public issue in certain African regions where market rules are regulated, such as the WAEMU zone.

With the structuring and development of African financial markets and financing players, it is likely that certain project financing operations will increasingly be financed through bond issues by project companies. At present, bond financing remains weak in this sector due to a financial market that is still too fragile or fragmented at the regional level in the OHADA area, for example.[6]

5 *Best Practice Guide for Term Sheet Completeness*, Loan Market Association, December 2021.

6 See for example Paule Biensan, *op. cit.*

Section 2. Public funding sources

§ 1. Public grants and subsidies

294 Subsidies and grants. – Due to the financial constraints of most African States, public aid and subsidies are relatively rare in practice. However, developers and SPVs may receive grants, subsidised loans or subsidies for their projects from multilateral development banks, which are channelled through the State or State-affiliated bodies and *ultimately* used to finance infrastructure projects. It is also common for development banks to provide financing on condition that they obtain a government guarantee for the repayment of loans.

Focus: Financing the Noor solar project in Ouarzazate

The Noor Ouarzazate project is being developed as part of the first phase of Morocco's Noor solar plan, launched in 2009. The aim of the project is to develop, finance, build, operate and maintain a 500 MW *Concentrated* Solar Power (CSP) plant connected to the national grid.

To finance the first phase of the Noor Ouarzazate solar power plant project, several financial instruments have been put in place, in the form of loans guaranteed by the State and subsidies granted by MASEN (Moroccan Agency for Sustainable Energy), which buys the electricity from the IPP and sells it to the national utility ONEE.

AFD has granted MASEN a €100 million concessional loan for the project and a €300,000 grant to finance the development (studies and technical expertise).

The EIB has provided co-financing of €100 million for the project. The KfW Bankengruppe provided €115 million for the project, including a €15 million grant from the German government.

The European Commission has awarded a grant of €30 million under the Neighbourhood Investment Facility (NIF).

The CTF contributed 197 million euros.

The AfDB has granted a loan of €168 million.

Concessional loans granted to MASEN on preferential financing terms, due to the State's involvement in the solar plan and the public guarantees granted associated with these projects, have significantly reduced the overall cost of the project. The financing and exchange rate risk is borne entirely by MASEN. Mitigating these risks has enabled the kingdom to optimise solar energy production costs, increase its attractiveness and attract private partners.

MASEN's equity stake in the SPV and the company dedicated to the management and operation of the Noor solar power plant serves as a risk mitigation factor in the project's financing. This model grants the public authority significant decision-making power in the project company and the authority responsible for protecting the rights of the Moroccan State with, for example, certain specific shareholder rights such as a right for MASEN to buy out other investors wishing to sell their shares, thereby protecting its position in the project and maintaining control over the State's interest in the underlying asset, a right of joint exit as well as a right of veto in strategic decisions on the project.

§ 2. *Public shareholdings in the SPV*

295 Public shareholding in SPV. – Direct public participation in the capital of the project company may be considered. This is still rare in Africa, but capital contributions, subordinated loans or equity loans may be tools to consider when they are possible under the local legislative framework. If a public entity becomes a shareholder in the SPV, the terms of its commitment should be checked against the public accounting rules of the country concerned, and the type of authorisation required to commit the public entity to subscribing to the capital of the project company should be determined. In some African countries, there are very specific restrictions on private sector commitments, and the players involved should have checked the prerequisites and consequences of such guidelines beforehand.

Example of a project company with a public shareholder: the Nachtigal project

Nachtigal is a greenfield project for the construction, financing and operation of a 420 MW dam on the Sanaga River at Nachtigal Falls, 65 km north-east of Yaoundé. It is being developed by SPV Nachtingal Hydropower Corporation SA ("NHPC") under a 35-year concession granted by the State of Cameroon in 2017.

The SPV is owned 15% by the Cameroon government, 40% by EDF International SAS (EDFI), 20% by the IFC, 15% by Africa50 and 10% by STOA Infra & Energy. Initially, the Cameroonian government held 30% of NHPC but informed all stakeholders of the sale of half of its stake at the time of financial closing to Africa50 Project Finance, the investment platform owned by 25 African governments, two central banks and the AfDB. The sale of half its stake enabled the government to free up public funds for other development needs in Cameroon. In addition, the mobilisation of private sector financing is helping to lighten the burden of public investment in this sector, thereby reducing the country's public debt ratio. The State's participation in the capital has significantly contributed to the bankability of the project, as demonstrated by the implementation of significant sectoral reforms by the State of Cameroon, which has facilitated the financial closing of the project.

The Nachtigal project will be connected to the country's Southern Interconnected System (RIS), which transmits around 94% of the national electricity consumed and includes major cities such as Yaoundé and Douala. The project is expected to generate an average of 2,900 GWh per year, meeting

Cameroon's growing electricity needs and contributing to the country's energy transition. The project will increase the share of renewable energies in the country's energy mix from 51% to 75%.[7]

Nachtigal is one of the lowest-cost energy production projects in sub-Saharan Africa (per unit of production)

The total project cost is €1.18 billion, including €114 million in contingency funds, which are created to deal with unforeseen or emergency scenarios that the NHPC may encounter. These contingency funds enhance the monetary stability of projects by providing a safety net. Unused contingency funds will be shared equally between the promoter and the State and will result in savings on customs duties.

Cameroonian electricity operators ENEO and NHPC have signed a PPA for a period of 35 years, at an estimated price of 6.1 EURct/kWh. This is a very competitive price compared with most power generation projects in sub-Saharan Africa.

The project is the first PPP in the hydroelectric sector in Cameroon

The project is financed with a gearing ratio of 76:24 with limited recourse to shareholders, giving creditors a limited claim on the borrower's assets in the event of default.

Table 8.1 shows the indicative project costs and financing structure of Nachtigal hydropower project.

Table 8.1 Indicative project costs, financing structures and IBRD guarantees ($M)

Generating capacity of the power station	420 MW
Estimated project cost	1,383
– including contingency funds	133
Estimated equity @24	319
Estimated VAT receipts	54
Estimated debt	1,010
– of which long-term debt denominated in euros	810
– of which long-term debt in local currency	200
Estimated payment guarantee	100
Estimated local loan guarantee	200
Estimated total warranty	300

Source: World Bank, "Cameroon: Nachtigal Hydropower Project", 22 June 2018.

7 World Bank, "Cameroon: Nachtigal Hydropower Project", 22 June 2018.

The project is supported by a number of WB Group financial instruments to mitigate risk and ensure its bankability

The project is supported by several financial instruments from the WB Group: two IBRD guarantees, debt and equity investments from the IFC, one or more euro interest rate swaps from the IFC and guarantees from the Multilateral Investment Guarantee Agency (MIGA).

The presence of the IFC as co-developer of the project was crucial in (a) reassuring the other developers, (b) ensuring the bankability of the project thanks to its structuring capabilities in the development and financing of IPPs in sub-Saharan Africa, (c) mitigating political and regulatory risks by ensuring a solid and sustainable contractual framework and (d) guaranteeing that the project is developed in accordance with international environmental and social standards.[8]

In addition, the IBRD is providing two guarantees – a payment guarantee and a loan guarantee – to secure the government's payment obligations under the project agreements and to reassure the commercial banks involved. The local banks will provide a 21-year local currency debt tranche with a put option at the 7ᵉ and 14ᵉ year life of the loan. If the local banks activate the put option and cannot be replaced by a suitable lender, then the GoC will have to buy back their loan. The IBRD will guarantee (a) the government's obligation to repurchase the loans at 7ᵉ and 14ᵉ years if the put option is exercised by the lenders and (b) take over the government's payment obligations if the government is unable to pay termination compensation.[9] For its part, MIGA provides guarantees to EDFI and the investors.

This guarantee structure, backed by WB Group institutions, reassures commercial banks, investors and the developer (EDFI) and mitigates the risks inherent in the project.

Figure 8.2 shows the structure of IBRD and MIGA guarantees for the Nachtigal hydroelectric project.

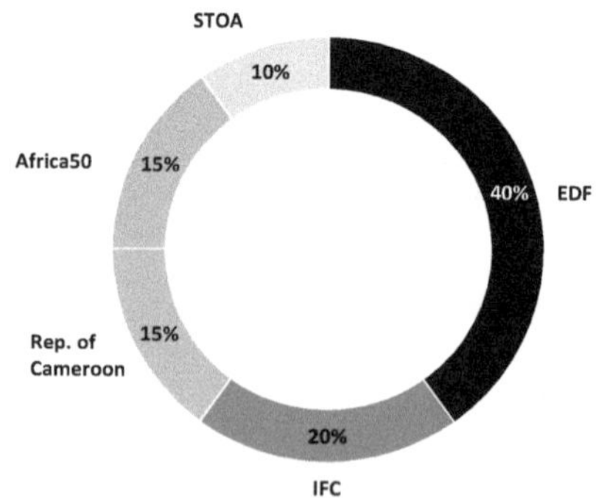

Figure 8.2 Structure of IBRD and MIGA guarantees for the Nachtigal hydroelectric project[10]

8 *Ibid.*
9 *Ibid.*
10 *Ibid.*

296 Interest in public participation. – The contracting authority (or any public authority) may consider taking a stake in the project company to optimise the overall financing of the project. Taking a public shareholding reduces the overall net cost of the project (by participating as an equity partner on favourable terms, in terms of return or rights) and thus reduces the tariff borne by the user. In addition, public participation offers public authorities improved access to information about the project, enhances their involvement in the decision-making process and increases VfM by sharing the benefits.

297 Risks of conflicts of interest. – However, this can also lead to conflicts of interest on the public side and increase the perceived risk to private investors and lenders. Public authorities may be tempted to take decisions that are in the best interests of the public sector, but not necessarily adequate to maximise shareholder value, which can be mitigated by separating the ownership function (as shareholder) from the contract management function (as contracting authority).

Public participation also means that the public party takes on additional risks (construction and operating risks, for example). Therefore, public sector involvement in the SPV needs to be carefully assessed as it has important implications in terms of the financial structure of the project and its attractiveness to bidders and lenders.

Feedback: managing the risk of potential conflicts of interest – example of MASEN in Morocco

As part of its role, MASEN has taken various precautions to manage potential conflicts of interest.

Combination of shareholder and offtaker

- use of separate legal entities as investor in each SPV (Masen Capital) and as lender and offtaker (MASEN);
- Masen Capital does not control the management of the SPVs;
- Masen Capital has a right of veto over decisions that could have an impact on its interests as a shareholder but can only use its right of veto over key decisions taken by the SPV to protect its interests as a shareholder and not as a principal;
- Masen's rights under the PPA are in line with IPP precedents where the purchaser is also a shareholder and principal (limit in the change of ownership of the operating shareholder in the SPV and the possibility to terminate the PPA in case of default of the SPV and to own the power plant).

Combined shareholder/lender

- use of separate legal entities as investor in the SPV (Masen Capital) and as lender/policyholder (MASEN);
- separation of the roles of lender and shareholder;
- segregation of funds used to finance the project;
- Masen Capital has no management control over the SPV;
- Masen Capital has a right of veto over decisions that could have an impact on its interests as a shareholder but can only use its right of veto over key decisions taken by the SPV to protect its interests as a shareholder and not as a lender or originator;
- the loan agreement only deals with cases that would have an impact on Masen's interests as a lender and not as a shareholder.

298 Tax incentives. – Tax breaks are a form of subsidy granted by governments as an incentive for the development of certain sectors. Tax breaks can take many different forms. Tax exemptions are defined according to (i) the tax concerned (VAT on certain equipment, corporation tax, withholding tax, property tax, customs duties), (ii) the duration of the exemption (limited in time or not) and (iii) the level of exemption (total or partial).

To implement such measures, it is often necessary to adopt amendments to the Finance Act initiated by the Ministry of Finance. As with other sources of public funding, their necessity (given the attractiveness of the market) and cost must be accurately assessed against the expected benefits before they are implemented.

299 Guarantees and credit enhancement mechanisms. – Guarantees and credit enhancement mechanisms can be put in place against short-term risks (buyer liquidity risks in the case of a public payment PPP) and long-term risks (force majeure, political risks, early termination).

These guarantees may take the form of a sovereign guarantee, a letter of support/assurance, letters of credit, an escrow account, a put/call option, PRGs (and partial credit guarantees) and political risk insurance. The impact of this public support will vary depending on the stakeholders involved:

- For lenders, the State's contractual support will reduce credit risk, interest rates, the minimum DSCR and therefore the possibility of a higher debt ratio.
- For the sponsors, the contractual support from the State will increase their interest, reduce the risk of the project and therefore result in a lower target IRR.
- For the State, depending on local legislation, public contractual support may be considered as a contingent liability and sometimes included in the amount of public debt.

Example of project financing in the form of a public-pay PPP in Lesotho

This example illustrates the existence of PPPs with public support on the financing side. There is a project finance market for projects of a social nature, such as in the health sector. Lesotho signed a DBFO PPP contract to create a new hospital. This is one of the first private sector breakthroughs in Lesotho's health sector, and undoubtedly in sub-Saharan Africa.

The 18-year PPP contract involves the design, construction, partial financing and operation of a 390-bed hospital unit on a greenfield site as well as the rehabilitation and upgrading of three clinics. The financial advisor was IFC, and financing was provided by the Development Bank of South Africa.

The State of Lesotho obtained support from the WB, the IFC and other development banks to reform its health sector, which required major investment.

The hospital serves a catchment area of around 500,000 people in the Maseru region. The SPV is remunerated by income paid by the State for services rendered, with performance criteria contractually agreed over the 18-year contract period. It benefits from the past experience of its shareholders on similar PPPs developed in South Africa and is creating a pilot project for other comparable projects in Africa.

The strength of the project lies in several factors:

- strong support from the highest levels of government, the community and the medical profession;
- the ability to attract private sector healthcare professionals with international experience;
- the involvement of international, regional and local sponsors and investors.

The 18-year PPP contract to develop, design, build, partially finance and operate the hospital was awarded to the Netcare consortium, comprising Netcare (40%), Exxcel Health (20%), a local investment company, Afri'nnai (20%), Mohloli (10%) and Basotho's Women Investment Company (10%). The financial closing took place in December 2007. It enabled the creation of 390 hospital beds in the State for an investment of USD 107 million.

§ 3. Systematic public participation

300 Public shareholdings in mining projects are becoming increasingly common. – This situation is as much the result of the fact that the subsoil and natural resources are the property of the host country, as it is the host country's desire to benefit from the exploitation of the resources. This has an impact on project financing arrangements.

For the State, the acquisition of a stake has several benefits. It generates additional revenue, either immediately in the case of a non-contributory stake, or after reimbursement of production costs in the case of a contributory stake. What's more, public participation guarantees the State greater involvement in and control over mining projects.

This shareholding may be free or contributory, depending on the natural resource in question, whether the reserves are proven or not, and whether the State is itself a producer.

301 Free non-contributory participation by the host State. – The host State's participation in the capital of a project's operating company is also becoming more common in other sectors. It generally involves the allocation of shares in the project company. No financial contribution is generally required from the host country.

The level of this non-contributory free shareholding is often governed by legislative provisions, but only in the mining sector. The 10% threshold is regularly set, for example, by the Mining Code in Côte d'Ivoire, Benin, Mali and Mauritania. Article 78 of Law No. 2023-040 of 29 August 2023 on the Mining Code in the Republic of Mali provides that "the granting by the State of an operating licence entitles it to a free holding set at a minimum of ten per cent (10%) of the capital of the operating company". However, in Guinea, the maximum limit of 15% has been retained, whereas Ethiopian legislation provides for a non-contributory free shareholding by the State of no more than 5%.

Even if the State benefits from a free, non-contributory stake, it can still request an additional stake, this time a contributory one. In this context, the State will be subject to the same obligations as a traditional shareholder. Its contribution may be in cash or in kind and will be the result of an agreement between the parties. Despite this agreement, the level of additional shareholding may be limited by legislation.

302 Contributory participation by the host State. – In contrast to free non-contributory participation, contributory participation by the host State requires the State to assume the rights and obligations arising from its participation. Generally, the terms of this participation are determined by the terms of the operating contract. An association agreement is sometimes required in addition to the contract.

The texts can provide a firm framework for the State's contributory participation. They may stipulate which entity is competent to decide whether to exercise the option granted to the State, and the deadlines for doing so. Similarly, they may provide for the option to be exercised once resources have been discovered in commercial quantities, or once an exploitation title has been obtained, or when the project company starts production.

9 Financial models

303 Bankability factors. – The implementation of an infrastructure project is subject to a range of factors which help to ensure its bankability, as presented in the previous chapter. The construction of one or more financial models for the project plays a key role in this process. It is the main tool for analysing all the economic and financial criteria, enabling each of the stakeholders to assess the project's sustainability and profitability.

This chapter begins by outlining the architecture and construction of a typical financial model, as found at an advanced stage of the project cycle (raising finance/closing). We will then look at the different types of models used at earlier or later stages of the project cycle, showing that there is not one, but many models for the same project, each with its own specific features and objectives.

Section 1. Architecture and construction of a financial model

304 Hypotheses. – Whatever its level of complexity, the purpose of a financial model is always to produce forecasts over a given time horizon based on assumptions made at the time the model was created. Three "modules" can therefore be distinguished: (i) the assumptions or *inputs*, (ii) the calculations of the various forecasts and (iii) the results or *outputs*. In terms of user-friendliness, the model is built in such a way that it is easy to simulate changes in assumptions, perform sensitivities and present several scenarios. The diagram in Figure 9.1 shows a typical logical architecture for building a financial model.

305 Phases. – As in the case of a project, different phases can be distinguished in the construction of the model: a design or planning phase, a construction phase and a use phase.

In the planning phase, the person responsible for producing the model focuses first on the objectives to be achieved by the model. These objectives will lead to the definition of the desired level of complexity and flexibility, as well as the time horizon and periodicity to be used for the model (ranging from monthly to annual). The

DOI: 10.4324/9781003616894-12

model architecture can then be drawn up. Secondly, the person responsible for producing the model looks at the availability and collection of input data. They define the set of assumptions that will then be used in the calculations, and in particular:

- investment cost estimates (based on the technical studies that will have been carried out), in particular the costs associated with design/development work, construction and financial costs;
- estimates of operating costs;
- revenue estimates;
- the tax and accounting assumptions applicable to the project;
- financing structure and assumptions;
- macroeconomic and market assumptions.

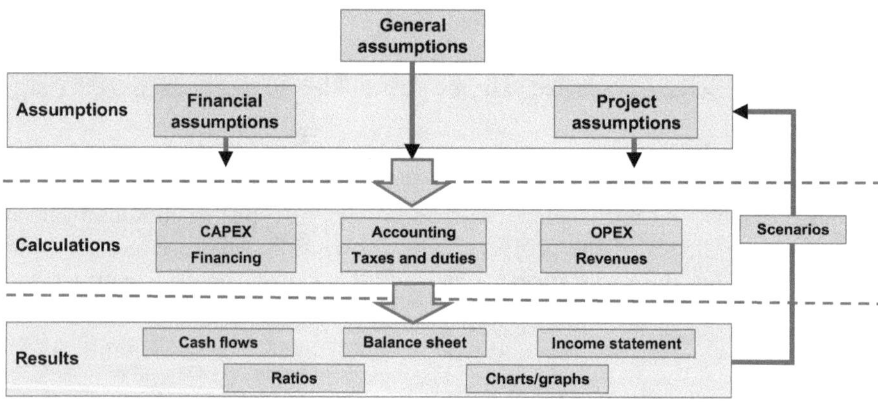

Figure 9.1 Logical architecture of a financial model

306 Model assumptions. – During the model construction phase, the assumptions are fed into a series of calculations whose level of complexity may vary according to the characteristics of the project and the level of detail required. It is relatively common to find a calculation tab for each component of the body of assumptions: investment (CAPEX), financing, revenues, operating costs (OPEX), repayment of financing, depreciation, determination of taxable income and applicable tax, and *ultimately* shareholder cash flows. The logical architecture used by the model is therefore based on the cascade of project cash flows according to the level of priority of the various flows: operating flows making up EBITDA, tax, loan repayments and shareholders.

Finally, the person responsible for creating the model concentrates on the results tabs, which are typically made up of:

- the project's financial statements: cash flow statement, income statement and balance sheet;
- the main indicators for analysing the project: investor IRR and project IRR, debt coverage ratios, WACC, EBITDA margin, etc.;

- a financing plan with a use-resources analysis;
- a "Dashboard" tab presenting these results, certain structuring hypotheses and representative graphs to facilitate analysis.

The finalisation of the model is an opportunity to create a specific tab to facilitate the creation of scenarios. This involves linking certain structuring hypotheses of the project to a matrix defining several scenarios with a "switch" (list of choices) to select the applicable scenario.

The model is then fully operational, providing each stakeholder with a fair assessment of its expected costs and benefits, its financial commitments and the associated risks.

Section 2. The diversity of economic and financial models depending on the stage of the project

307 In practice, however, the nature and objectives of a financial model can vary significantly depending on the project's stage and the stakeholders' objectives. The following stages can be distinguished:

- **The design phase:** this is used to define the overall structure of the project, in particular to understand the economics of the project, its economic sustainability and the major balances between the various stakeholders. This stage provides a preliminary understanding of the project's costs, potential revenue and the level of government involvement (in all its forms) that will be required.
- **The feasibility phase:** this is used to ensure the economic viability of the project and to study the interest aroused by the project in order to facilitate the tendering process. Compared with the design phase, the feasibility phase incorporates additional studies (technical studies, market research, environmental and social impact studies, etc.) to refine the assumptions. It is also at this stage that the various contractual arrangements are evaluated (VfM analysis, as described later) and the structure chosen is defined.
- **The tendering phase** (preparation for consultation and selection of private partners): during the tendering phase, the private partners develop their own financial model on the basis of the project documentation submitted to the call for tenders, the technical specifications, the tariff structure chosen by the public authority, the tax arrangements applicable to the project, the indicative financing terms that the lenders are able to offer them and their own profitability requirements. If all these factors are taken into account, the bidders will be able to formulate their financial offer.
- **The contractual and financial closing phase:** this leads to the finalisation of the financial models, incorporating the lenders' requirements (definitive financing conditions). Depending on the negotiation process and the financial due diligence carried out, the public authority or the lenders may also have to produce their own models at this stage and/or request an audit of the selected bidder's model.

- **The monitoring phase:** this consists of recording actual (completed) cash flows and updating forecast cash flows in line with the project's progress. By updating the financial model, this monitoring can ensure that the private investor's profitability aligns with the initial objectives, with possible adjustment and compensation mechanisms depending on the terms of the agreement.

In the following sections, we will detail the main characteristics and objectives of financial models in relation to each of these stages. The distinctions made between the types of models and the different phases are intended to be schematic and simplistic. In reality, each project responds to its unique market context and project cycle, often making the stages involved in producing a financial model less distinct than they appear here.

§ 1. The business model

308 Overall project economics. – At an early stage in a project, it is common to refer to an "economic" rather than a "financial" model. The economic analysis enables the overall economics of the project to be understood and its feasibility to be studied. The economic feasibility of the project is studied from a public and societal perspective, whoever the promoter may be. More specifically, it is defined in terms of the benefits of the project (whoever the beneficiaries are) relative to the costs (whoever the payers are). To determine the project's costs and benefits, two scenarios are typically established, a situation with a project and a situation without a project, which are then compared.

From the public authority's point of view, the economic analysis must primarily address the following aspects:

- an estimate of the project's economic costs in terms of both initial investment (CAPEX) and operating costs (OPEX). Unlike the models used in the tendering or closing phases, the financing costs are considered here in a simplified manner, while the tax costs/revenues are not included, as they are ultimately neutral from the point of view of the project's economic equilibrium (what is a cost for the private partner will be passed on in its bid);
- the willingness of consumers to pay for the service ("*willingness to pay*") and therefore the revenue that can be generated;
- the added value generated by the project, particularly in terms of economic impact (jobs, growth, etc.) and improved service delivery;
- the costs of an alternative supply providing the same service.

309 Economic model. – The economic model enables the project to be evaluated economically by comparing the cash flows associated with the investment (the costs and benefits) discounted to each period. The net present value (NPV) of the project is calculated by discounting the cash flows at the rate of return required by the market, taking into account the risk of the investment. Initially, this rate of return is calculated by estimating the weighted average cost of capital (or WACC), which is the weighted average of the financing costs of debt and equity.

310 Internal rate of return. – The main indicator used to estimate the economic viability of the project is the "project internal rate of return (IRR)". The IRR indicates the discount rate for which the NPV of the investment is zero. The project IRR helps evaluate the internal rate of return of a project without considering the sources of financing, thus reflecting the intrinsic economic profitability of a project. It takes into account the overall cost of the investment at the outset of the project and the sum of operating cash flows. The project IRR increases when the sum of the project's cumulative cash flows increases over a given period. The project IRR therefore gives an indication of the financial interest in carrying out the project: all that needs to be done is to compare it with the rate of return required for the project, given its risk. The required rate of return can initially be equated with the weighted average cost of capital (WACC).

§ 2. VfM (Value for Money) model: feasibility phase

This model is used in the feasibility phase as a decision-making tool to define the best contractual framework for the project.

311 Project definition. – During the project definition phase, the government's strategic objective is to achieve an optimal allocation of resources in order to minimise the overall costs of the project for society and maximise the benefits. The aim of the VfM analysis is to assess whether a given project structure is likely to offer better value for the public authority than its alternatives.

312 Comparison of management methods. – Once the stage of economic justification for carrying out the project has been passed (§ 1. Economic model), the analysis generally focuses on the contractual and financial scheme to be put in place. This involves evaluating different PPP schemes and estimating the advantages of using a PPP, thus mobilising private investors and/or operators, rather than a public contract in which the execution of the project would be carried out directly by the State (partly internalised and partly via a multitude of purchase contracts with private companies).

313 Qualitative assessment. – This analysis of value for money through the contractual scheme involves a combination of two approaches. Firstly, a qualitative assessment is carried out, verifying the basis for using the PPP for the project according to its characteristics. For example, a preliminary PPP analysis may involve checking certain criteria in three categories: the suitability of the PPP (for example, the suitability of an integrated management approach over the project's life), commercial attractiveness (revenue generation potential) and the potential for optimal risk allocation. This analysis can be initiated at a relatively early stage in the development of the project.

314 Quantitative evaluation. – Secondly, a quantitative evaluation plays a decisive role in the construction of the economic and financial model. In this case, the PPP option(s) are compared with a situation where the project is carried out using conventional public contracts, using a "public sector comparator" (PSC).

The model calculates the discounted State costs associated with each contractual model. It compares the NPV of the public entity's budget costs for each contractual model and establishes the difference compared with a traditional public contractual model. Generally, a "switch" (a list of choices with different scenarios) in the model is used to compare the "base" contractual scheme with the other options.

315 Impact on investment and operating costs. – In addition, the model can include a cost optimisation factor. This optimisation factor will make it possible to quantify the impact of a PPP on investment and operating costs, and to estimate the efficiency gains resulting from a better allocation of risks. Finally, the model can incorporate a risk matrix to identify and quantify:

- risks to be assessed;
- a certain severity threshold for each risk, expressed in terms of cost and time overruns, this severity threshold being associated with scenarios (for example: scenario 1 – No overruns; scenario 2 – Moderate overruns; etc.);
- a probability that the risk will occur;
- the criticality of each risk is then determined by the product of its severity and its probability of occurrence;
- a total of the criticalities of each risk is calculated (total in months, and total as a percentage) and applied in the financial model to the project costs and revenues.

§ 3. Public authority model: feasibility phase

316 Technical studies. – This model is generally refined based on the preferred contractual scheme and the feasibility studies that will have been conducted. The first step is to have the technical studies needed to refine the project's investment and operating cost assumptions. Depending on the type of project, market studies must have been carried out to estimate the project's revenue, based on user demand and ability to pay. In the case of a transport infrastructure project, a detailed traffic study is often a key stage. In the case of a grid-connected power plant project, on the other hand, this assessment of demand is more generally carried out at the level of the regulatory authorities through planning documents (but a market study would be necessary, for example, if an electricity generation project were to be carried out to meet the demand of a specific industrial player or an independent *mini-grid*).

The main objective of the model is to design a pricing structure that minimises costs for the public entity while remaining sufficiently attractive to the private bidder(s).

The results of the model can be divided into two parts: one evaluating the project from the point of view of the public authority and the other from the future private investors' perspective. In this way, the model can be used to predefine the terms of the transaction, which will facilitate the design of the call for tenders and the discussions or negotiations with the partners.

Depending on the case, the tariff structure envisaged for the project is more or less precisely defined in the terms of the call for tenders. For example, in a power plant project, the electricity purchase tariff is proposed by the bidder and will generally be the determining economic factor of its bid. In a transmission project, on the other hand, indications may be given of a tariff that is intended to be socially acceptable. In this case, the goal is to minimise the investment cost of the installations and/or the subsidy level required from the State during the operating phase.

§ 4. Sponsor financial model: tender phase

317 Sponsors' model. – The sponsor's financial model comes into play at the invitation to tender stage (after the feasibility phase) and is a decisive element in the bid submitted by the bidder(s). This model incorporates the cost, production/revenue estimates and, above all, the profitability targets defined by the sponsor when drawing up its bid. While a multitude of indicators and factors can be derived from this model, the key indicator is often the shareholder IRR.

318 IRR. – This IRR is calculated based on the cash flows contributed and received by the investor. It should be distinguished from the project IRR. The shareholder IRR (or equity IRR) is used to assess the internal rate of return on equity invested by shareholders in a project. It is calculated by considering all the equity capital injected by shareholders (share capital, shareholder current account, subordinated loan, equity bridging loan or any other advance of funds made by shareholders) and all the repayment and remuneration flows of this equity capital (interest on subordinated loan or shareholder current account, repayment of subordinated loan or current account, dividends, reduction in share capital, sale price of shares if the shareholder sells the project before completion, etc.). It is used to assess a project's attractiveness to equity providers. Depending on various factors (risk-free rate of return, country risk, counterparty risk, investment strategy, etc.), a shareholder will determine its target profitability and structure the project (in particular the expected revenues) and its financing in order to achieve this target shareholder IRR. A shareholder will only agree to invest in a project if its business model and the financial structuring solutions put in place enable it to achieve its target shareholder IRR.

This IRR is therefore different from the project IRR, as described in the design phase, which is based on the economic costs of the project.

In Africa, depending on the country, the sector and the guarantee scheme in place, shareholder profitability requirements can vary widely. They range from 6% to 12% for projects with no demand risk, such as solar photovoltaic projects. This profitability requirement can rise to 15% or even 20% and more for more innovative projects based on unproven technologies, where the investor bears the demand risk.

At this stage, the financial model incorporates all the components of the final project model, closely aligning with the architecture of a typical model described in section 1.

§ 5. Lender financial model and model audit

319 Once the bidder has been selected, there is usually a due diligence and negotiation phase with the lenders and the government. During this phase the "sponsor" model becomes the reference model for the project, although lenders and governments may have or develop their own models.

During this final phase, discussions with the lenders enable the financing assumptions to be fine-tuned: financing plan for the project (gearing/debt-to-equity ratio), loan maturity, interest rates and fees, and bank covenants. In terms of covenants, lenders pay particular attention to the DSCR, which is the ratio of cash flow available for debt service (CFADS) to annual debt service. Unlike a principal or constant annuity repayment schedule, the debt repayment schedule in project financing is often sculpted to maintain a target DSCR (which will vary according to the predictability of the project's cash flows and the level of risk borne by the project company in particular).

The point of view adopted by lenders is therefore different from that of the State and the investor. Rather than the expected profitability or economic benefit, the primary concern is to guarantee repayment of the debts and associated interest. To this end, lenders require a number of sensitivity analyses to be carried out to ensure that the project is capable of repaying the loans, and may ask for additional guarantees if certain risks are considered too high. For example, in the renewable energy sector, lenders will often consider a production scenario known as "P-90", where the actual annual production level has a 90% probability of being greater than or equal to the forecast level. In contrast, investors will tend to favour a "P-50" scenario, where the production risk is therefore higher.

Finally, lenders will often request an independent audit of the model by an expert. The aim of this stage is to provide stakeholders with a guarantee that the project's financial model accurately reflects its future financial flows, taking into account the assumptions considered. To achieve this, the model audit generally includes:

- a review of the logical and arithmetic integrity of the model;
- an accounting review;
- a tax review;
- checking that all the assumptions are consistent with the project documentation.

The model review results in the issue of an audit report or certificate setting out the work carried out by the auditor and his conclusions. This document is signed by the audit firm, which assumes responsibility for the conclusions reached at the end of the assignment.

§ 6. Implementation monitoring model (operational): monitoring phase

320 Reference model. – The performance monitoring model serves as the "reference model" for the project. On one hand, it provides a reminder of what has actually been achieved (actual cash flows), while on the other hand, it provides information on the updated forecast cash flows. It is submitted to the project's shareholders and lenders for approval. It must be easy to update at each period and facilitate monitoring of the project's overall performance by the various stakeholders. The model can be used to calculate a discounted IRR based on actual and forecast discounted cash flows.

In addition, this model is often referred to in the contractual documentation (financing agreements, concession agreements, etc.) and a monitoring procedure may be defined therein. Updating the financial model ensures that the private investor's profitability aligns with the initial objectives. At the same time, depending on the terms of the agreement, adjustment and compensation mechanisms may be implemented. This may be the case if the investor's profitability deteriorates due to political or macroeconomic risk that he was not initially supposed to bear (the risk of currency exchange or inflation, for example), or on the contrary if it increases due to a surplus of revenue collected from users or reduced taxation.

These issues are therefore closely linked to the contractual arrangements for the project, which are the subject of the next chapter.

10 The main financing contracts

321 Set of contracts. – A project finance transaction involves a series of contracts executed successively or simultaneously in order to guarantee the completion of the project and the rapid materialisation of the cash flows needed to repay the debt and ensure a return on investment for the investors involved in the project.[1]

Financing contracts are drawn up either at the same time as the lenders finalise their audit of the various aspects enabling them to assess the project's risks, or immediately after validation of the results of the audits carried out or confirmation by the parties: the project company and its shareholders and the lenders who have subscribed to the term sheets. Typically, financing contracts include credit documents, sureties and direct agreements. However, there are other ancillary contractual documents which we will attempt to list next but which will not necessarily be among the documents used for all projects.

Section 1. Credit documents

§ 1. Common Terms Agreement

322 Common Terms Agreement. – Credit documents relating to project finance most often include a Common Terms Agreement. This agreement is useful because the transaction involves multiple parties and various categories of lender, as we have seen: commercial banks, multilateral development banks and lenders offering an equity bridge loan.[2]

323 Content. – This is an agreement between the lenders financing the project and the company in charge of the project, drawn up by their advisers. Its purpose is to define and agree on the terms common to all the project's financial documentation and the relationship between the financing parties. Indeed, since each category of lender may have its own model loan agreement, the parties will have an interest in concluding such an agreement on common terms, as long as it can establish the common terminology and conditions applicable to all the lenders as well as to the

1 ALSF, *Public-Private Partnership (PPP) Projects in the Infrastructure Sector*.
2 *Ibid.*

DOI: 10.4324/9781003616894-13

project company. It includes definitions, conditions, drawdown orders, powers of each and the modalities for waiving the exercise of their rights and the modification of the financing contract, as well as financing conditions, financial undertakings, events of default, declarations and other undertakings. The Common Terms Agreement clarifies and simplifies the financing of the project when the loans are from different sources and ensures that the parties have a common understanding of the key definitions and events critical to the management of the financing. It is often a long and detailed document with several annexes and sometimes tables.

§ 2. The loan contract(s)

324 Definition. – The loan contract is the set of financing documents that establish the terms of the loan and govern the relationship between the lenders and the company in charge of the project.

325 Content. – Insofar as project finance transactions always include a portion relating to the construction of the project, the loan agreements provide for the financing of this construction, setting out the manner in which the loan may be drawn down as construction progresses, including the conditions for the advancement of funds by the lenders to the project company. It also includes the term, the repayment profile that will take place once the construction phase is completed, the methods for calculating and deducting interest and charges from the loan amounts, the events of default and the consequences attached to such events of default and the stipulations usually provided for in business loan contracts or loan contracts linked to real estate projects.

326 LMA. – Over the decades, loan contracts have become more standardised, with relatively stable precedents resulting from practice and the efforts of various organisations. One of these organisations, the Loan Market Association (LMA), has been working for nearly 25 years to improve the financing markets in Europe, Africa and the Middle East. This organisation aims to promote and establish market documentation standards that can be used in a harmonised way by lenders and borrowers in all regions. The LMA works with banks, law firms, institutional investors, rating agencies, financial advisors and borrowers to develop precedents for financing documentation applicable to all types of transactions. It comprises some 779 organisations in more than 65 countries.[3] Its objective is to act not only on documentation but also on market practices, the formulation of recommendations, training and interaction with legislators and regulators in each country, including in emerging areas.[4]

The document bases resulting from the LMA's activities have nevertheless largely influenced the financing documents also used on the African continent in project financing. However, as IFIs are often heavily involved in project finance in Africa, they will most often use their own templates.

3 https://www.lma.eu.com/about-us

4 *Developing Loan Markets*, LMA Publication Book, 2013.

327 Special clauses. – Project finance loan agreements contain special clauses that reflect the specific requirements of the project and its financial documentation. As project finance is non-recourse or limited recourse (to equity investors) and relies solely on the project as a source of repayment, the loan agreement sets out restrictions on the distribution of dividends, measures required for the project, ratios and covenants relating to the project. It also outlines the general conditions precedent and the standard loan stipulations concerning the project's progress. It also lists the various securities or guarantees taken out on the assets of the project or the company carrying it. Other clauses are detailed in the credit agreement, which we describe later.

328 Declarations and guarantees. – The agreement typically provides for representations and warranties given by the project company to the lenders. These representations and warranties will generally relate to the status of the SPV, the good governance of the company by its directors, the capacity and powers to bind the company, the absence of any breach of laws or contracts, the validity of the company's commitments, the fairness of the company's financial statements, the absence of default events or adverse changes, the absence of indebtedness, the existence of project contracts in a valid form, the absence of undeclared ancillary activities by the company, compliance with the ESG rules defined by the lenders, etc.

329 Maturity. – Maturity refers to the duration of the loan or the period between the first drawdown and the last repayment of the loan made available to the project company. In Africa, the maturities of project financing vary widely depending on the nature of the project, the identity of the lenders and the currency in which the financing is provided. For example, in the CFA Franc zone, the maturities offered by local banks can range from five to eight years, with very rare cases extending up to ten years (including the construction period). Moroccan banks, on the other hand, can offer euro-denominated loans with maturities of up to around 15 years. IFIs can offer maturities of up to 18 or 20 years (sometimes longer in rare projects) in euros or US dollars.

330 Drawdowns. – These refer to calls made by the SPV on the funds made available to it under the credit agreement. The drawdown period will begin once the credit agreement has been signed and all the conditions precedent have been met. It will generally end when the project company takes delivery of the infrastructure. At this stage, in most projects, the repayment period begins, as operations generate revenues that will service the debt. Credit agreements usually include a model drawdown notice sent by the project company to the lenders, in accordance with the terms and conditions set out in the agreement.

331 Repayment terms. – The SPV sets repayment terms and dates with the lenders in line with the project's cash flows, so that the chosen profile is appropriate. The loan agreement sets out the repayment profile and specifies the repayments based on the final interest rate calculated on the day of the financial closing. The repayment schedule for project finance debt is often tailored to the achievement of a target DSCR (which will vary depending on the predictability of the project's cash flows and the level of risk borne by the project company). More rarely, debt may be amortised on a constant principal basis.

332 Conditions precedent. – The conditions precedent in the credit agreement are conditions precedent to drawings on the financing provided by the lenders. Agreements often contain conditions precedent to the first drawdown, which are the most detailed and strict, and conditions precedent to subsequent drawdowns.

The banks will try to list all the actions or conditions that they would like to see carried out or met before the drawdown. These items usually concern:

- the SPV has taken out the required insurance policies;
- the signing of all direct agreements;
- the subscription and payment by the shareholders of the SPV of the required equity capital;
- the SPV obtains all administrative, regulatory and other authorisations;
- opening and operating the company's *onshore* and *offshore* accounts;
- the implementation of all the securities included in the *security package*;
- the receipt of legal opinions from law firms on the validity and capacity;
- receipt of a satisfactory report from the technical and environmental experts selected by the lenders.

When financing African projects, banks often add to this list:

- approval of the PPP agreement or project by the national authorities, executive and/or parliamentary;
- the submission of an opinion by a State judicial authority on the validity of the contract and the award of the project to the SPV;
- authorisation for currency conversion and entry/exit;
- authorisation for the outflow of financial flows from the SPV to its offshore accounts.

The preceding lists are not exhaustive, of course, and vary from country to country and project to project.

For subsequent drawdowns, lenders often require confirmation that the items requested in the first drawdown have been maintained and confirmation that the project company is not affected by any event of default. They also check compliance with the covenants and ratios set out in the credit agreement.

333 Clauses most frequently negotiated. – There are many clauses that are often the subject of discussion, but we find, for example, the cases of eligibility/cases of default, the purpose of which is to define the situations that allow the lender to demand early repayment of the loan, and the reconsideration of the financing for the amount of the outstanding amounts that have not been drawn down. There are also clauses relating to the very notion or qualification of default, enabling lenders to anticipate changes in the SPV's risk profile. It may be useful to distinguish between cases of default and cases of potential default by proposing a distinction with legal effects specific to each case. From the point of view of the SPV's perspective, it may be appropriate to reiterate that the specific effect attached to events of default should not be automatic but should remain an option for lenders. The

SPV and its advisors will therefore seek to propose wording to mitigate the immediate effect of an event of default, for example by requesting that the credit agreement include a grace period to regularise the default situation, or by requesting that the event giving rise to the event of default be considered as having a significant impact on the SPV's ability to repay its debts or that the event itself be so serious that the SPV will no longer be able to meet its obligations. Other clauses will be discussed frequently, such as the refinancing clause, indemnities in the event of early repayment, fees and commissions relating to unused financing, conditions precedent to drawdown, negative pledges, and sale and change of control clauses.

334 Interest rate. – The credit agreement distinguishes between the base rate (EURIBOR for financing in euros, LIBOR for financing in USD, BCEAO key rate for financing in XOF, etc.) and the bank margin, which is added to the base rate. Banks are generally able to offer either a variable rate (base rate + margin) or the equivalent fixed rate.

335 Effective Global Rate (EGR). – In many countries or regions of Africa, there are rules requiring lenders to disclose the total effective interest rate to the borrower. The acronym of TEG for Taux Effectif Global is often used in French speaking countries. This includes, in addition to the interest rate, any costs, commissions or remuneration of any kind, whether direct or indirect, including those paid or due to intermediaries involved in any way in the granting of the loan. However, it is advisable to check the precise calculation rules in each country.

For example, in the CEMAC zone, Regulation 04/19/CEMAC/UMAC/CM of 10 August 2020 on various provisions relating to the overall effective rate and the publication of bank terms and conditions, governs the obligations of the borrower, who must expressly acknowledge having received a written indication from the lender of the overall effective rate applicable to the loan and confirm that this indication forms an integral part of the loan taken out. In Senegal, for example, this provision is set out in Decree 95-1004 of 7 November 1995 on the overall effective rate for interest-bearing loans.

Various African countries or regional organisations may also regulate the usury rate, which must be carefully monitored by the parties. This is the case, for example, of the WAEMU, which in Article 33 of BCEAO Decision 397/12/2010 recalled the obligation for credit institutions to provide information to borrowers[5] arising from the framework law on banking regulations of 3 December 2010, which has been transposed in the Member States.

336 Default events. – Lenders will endeavour to list the so-called events of default of the SPV, which allow them to suspend their obligations under the financing. Credit agreements often contain the same events of default, such as:

- failure to comply with financial ratios;
- cross default, i.e. a default under a contract other than the credit agreement will give rise to an event of default;
- failure of shareholders to subscribe to the capital or to pay the required funds;

5 Decision BCEAO 397/12/2010 on the Rules, Instruments and Procedures for implementing the monetary and credit policy of the Central Bank of West African States.

- failure to carry out the work planned under the project within the agreed timetable;
- unauthorised changes to the SPV's shareholder structure;
- insolvency, cessation of payments.

In the event of a proven default, lenders will take measures to safeguard their rights, and these will generally be clearly outlined in the credit agreement:

- enforcement of security interests;
- allocation of all SPV income to debt servicing as a priority;
- early repayment, often referred to as accelerated payments, repayments due by the SPV;
- the suspension of all printing.

337 Reserve account. – A reserve account is known as a debt service reserve account (DSRA). The lending institutions oblige the project company, as soon as it is able, to reserve sums acquired more than those allocated in the order defined by the credit agreement for the cascade of payments in the context of the use of income. This is a "thirst quencher", as some authors have called it,[6] which will be useful for dealing with more difficult situations should they arise. The agreement sets out the rules for allocating and calculating the amount to be set aside. Reserve accounts may include amounts drawn down by the project company but not allocated to payments because of certain changes, and they are a kind of complement to the security package by making it possible to locate undisbursed sums in a clearly identifiable way.

An example of payment cascade is provided in Figure 10.1.

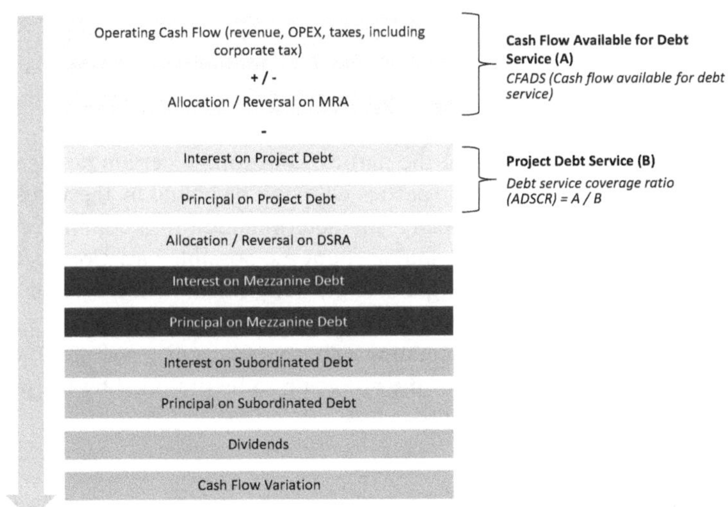

Figure 10.1 Example of a payment cascade

6 D. CORCHIA and I. BÉNICHOU, *op. cit.*

338 Ratios. – Lenders define various ratios that the project company must meet, and failure to do so may trigger post-default measures, such as accelerated debt repayment or the use of security. Typical ratios are often found, such as the equity/balance sheet total ratio, the Debt Service Cover Ratio (DSCR), the Loan Life Cover Ratio (LLCR) or the Annual Debt Service Cover Ratio (ADSR). The Credit Agreement also refers to the *debt/equity* or *gearing* ratio agreed upstream of the project. In the event of cost overruns or a rise in interest rates, for example, the SPV's shareholders may have to increase their equity contributions. Indeed, such assumptions will create an obligation to re-establish the ratio levels defined in terms of gearing in the base case and included in the covenants of the loan agreement.[7]

339 Covenants. – Covenants are commitments made by the project company during the term sheet stage. In most cases, these covenants include an obligation on the part of the company not to sign any new contracts or make any new commitments, not to exit the project, not to grant any new security interests or not to take out any new loans and, in general, an obligation to comply with applicable laws and defined ESG principles and to use the financing for the defined purpose. These obligations will be refined for each project and exceptions may be negotiated and included from time to time.

Focus on compliance with ESG principles and negotiation of related elements[8]

In financing, it is now common for borrowers and guarantors to comply with ESG rules defined as including, in most cases, the laws and regulations of the country hosting the project financing. These same entities also undertake to comply with the ESG policies imposed by the lending banks, to maintain any related authorisations or licences, and to bring their commitments into line with any changes or updates to the standards.

It will therefore be usual for the parties to negotiate certain points under these commitments, such as: the parties who will be bound by these commitments beyond the project company; the determination of a common definition of ESG obligations, taking into account the possible variations between existing standards and local obligations; the determination of the scope of the ESG commitments made (commitment to do, obligation of means or result); and the timetable for implementation. The parties will also often negotiate the content and frequency of the reporting to be provided by the project company.

7 V. Haubert-McGetrick and G. Ansaloni, *Financement de Projet, Enjeux juridiques et bancabilité d'une opération*, *op. cit.*, p. 107.

8 Cf. supra nº 231.

340 Use of funds. – Lenders will attach importance to ensuring that the funds they provide are used for the design and construction activities planned by the SPV. They will also seek to qualify in the credit agreement the structure that the project company must follow in order to use the funds made available, indicating precisely the path that the funds must follow, starting with the financing disbursement account, then the payments of the various investment and operating commitments, the commissions (referred to later in this chapter), the reserve accounts and the repayments to the shareholders of their subordinated debt. The balance of the funds lent and paid may then remain to the credit of the SPV's account. For each project, the banks build their own payment cascade structure, but there are common features in the various clauses governing the use of the funds. It is important to ensure that the payment dates for the various debts coincide as closely as possible so that, in the event of an exceptional payment taking priority over the others, this payment does not subsequently prevent the other debts from being paid in the normal order provided for by the cascade.

Focus: negative pledges

In this case, the lenders shall ensure that the borrowing project company undertakes not to carry out certain actions that could devalue or affect the value of the assets, or not to participate in certain activities. This also very often concerns the undertaking not to encumber the assets of the project company with securities other than those granted to the lenders as part of the project financing. In addition, lenders often require an additional undertaking in the form of a *pari passu* clause whereby the project company undertakes that if third-party creditors were to request a preference in relation to security interests or otherwise, such third parties will not benefit from rights different from those conferred on existing creditors.[9]

341 Involvement of local lenders. – In some cases, local lenders may be involved in African projects to stimulate the local or regional financial system of the country in which the project is being developed. A specific local loan contract may be adopted to involve local banks. This contract includes specific conditions linked to the fact that the maturity of the local loans and the financing terms may be different and require certain adjustments, as indicated earlier.

There are other ways of involving State-owned local banks and financial institutions. These play a key role in some countries, where they have built up a large financial base and a broad reach in the national economy. One example is the Caisse de dépôt et gestion (CDG) group in Morocco, which is involved in the capital of

9 *Also refer to developments herein on Quasi Security n°337-2 hereinafter.*

SPVs but also provides them with financing in the form of bank loans. In the coming years, many banks and State-owned financial institutions in sub-Saharan Africa are likely to play an increasingly important role in the financing of infrastructure projects.

342 Commissions. – There are different types of commission paid to financial institutions involved in project financing:

- the agent's commission, which remunerates the administrative activities involved in managing the loan and financial flows, mainly drawdowns and repayments of the SPV;
- the arranger's fee, which remunerates the arranging bank for the time spent structuring the loan and arranging the syndication for the project financing;
- the participation fee, which compensates the lenders for all their efforts in studying the project financing, as well as the provision of the financing, which commits the lenders' own funds;
- the commitment fee for funds made available for drawings but not yet used by the SPV;
- the cancellation fee for funds made available for drawdowns but not ultimately used by the SPV.

343 Applicable law. – Regarding the law applicable to credit agreements, there is considerable competition on the African continent.[10] It is very rare for credit agreements to be governed by the local law of an African country, except in cases where the financing is provided by African financial institutions and/or the host country of the project is considered by the lenders to be a country with sufficient maturity and legal certainty. More and more development banks are asking for agreements to be governed by English or New York law, although many bilateral development institutions lending in Africa choose to govern the agreement by the law of their own home country.

§ 3. Intercreditor agreement

344 Scope of the intercreditor agreement. – Project finance documentation often includes an intercreditor agreement where several lenders will be involved. In all cases where the project financing involves a consortium or syndicate of lenders, specific terms governing their relationship must be determined. An intercreditor agreement is concluded between the lenders financing the project to organise their respective roles. It governs the common conditions and the relationship between the lenders with regard to the borrower's obligations. If the financing includes mezzanine financing, the intercreditor agreement sets out the conditions of subordination and all the principles that may

10 Cf. *infra* n° 487 et seq.

apply between the senior lenders and the subordinated lenders. The intercreditor agreement classifies the rights of each party in respect of security interests and deals with any specific security interest such as a security interest granted to a creditor or group of creditors. It may include provisions relating to the appointment of a trustee or security agent if such provisions are not governed by a separate security trust deed and it regulates the coordinated decision making of the lenders.[11]

> **To remember**
>
> Subordination means that one of the creditors undertakes not to request repayment of its claim in favour of another creditor until the latter has been paid in priority. This form of stipulation in favour of third parties should be relatively easy to recognise in most African countries. However, if a subordination mechanism is set up, it may be useful to include a clause stating that if the stipulating creditor is reimbursed by a third party by preference, it must pay the sums received to the creditor who has priority under the subordination.
>
> A distinction is often made between general subordination agreements, under which the subordinated creditor is paid only after the other creditors, and specific subordination agreements, under which the subordinated creditor is entitled to recover the debt in the event of the debtor's default and is responsible for paying the sums recovered to the priority creditor. In most cases, subordination agreements are incorporated into the intercreditor agreement.[12]

345 Differing objectives by type of lender. – Different types of financial institution will have different ambitions. IFIs will often be concerned with the environmental, social and impact orientations of project finance, even if they wish to earn a return on the finance. More traditional commercial lenders will tend to favour a stricter approach. Mezzanine or subordinated lenders, on the other hand, will have more limited ambitions due to their decision-making rights and the limits of the guarantees they benefit from.

346 Governance of relations between lenders. – The intercreditor agreement governs the relationship between the lenders and regulates the lenders' voting and decision-making rights. It provides for the distribution of the proceeds from the enforcement of security interests and guarantees between the various

11 ALSF, *Public-Private Partnership (PPP) Projects in the Infrastructure Sector.*

12 For more details on subordination in project finance, see in particular V. Haubert-McGetrick and G. Ansaloni, *Financement de projet, enjeux juridiques et bancabilité d'une opération, op. cit.*, p. 133 et seq.

parties to the financing. In practice, to avoid a negative impact on the day-to-day management of the project, the project company must ensure that the lenders' decision-making process does not lead to unnecessary delays in its ability to make amendments to the concession contract and all documents relating to the project.[13]

Section 2. Security documents

347 Security package. – The lenders require a number of security interests to be granted over the project company and most of its assets as a condition of the loan. They want the right to receive repayment before reimbursement of any shareholder debt. The lenders require a set of securities known as a "security package". The type of security varies based on the applicable law, but in most project financings, security will be taken over the company's shares, movable and immovable property, and all contracts and rights relating to the project. The most common types of security are pledges, assignments or delegations of receivables. Depending on the applicable law in the African country concerned, it may be necessary to register the securities, inform third parties (such as government entities and contractors) of the creation of security interests by the project company and, in some cases, it will be appropriate to ensure that such third parties take note of, or consent to, such security interests.

Sous-section 1. The strategy to adopt when choosing securities

348 Bankability and structuring of financing. – Lenders wish to analyse the identity and nature of the shareholders and the chain of ownership of the legal entities, their financing plan and the contractual structure, including the allocation of risks and limitations of liability, in order to better study which securities are relevant to protect them.

Taking security to protect themselves is not the only objective of lenders. As we have seen, they ensure that the sponsors have the appropriate experience, sufficient financial solidity and the technical expertise needed to carry out the project, so that the SPV can manage the project profitably and protect the interests of the lenders. The involvement of the sponsors in the project is scrutinised, regarding the capital invested and the lock-up period, i.e. the period during which the sponsors retain a stake in the SPV. Above all, the solvency of the shareholders and the potential conflicts of interest they may face as shareholders and co-contractors of the project company are checked.

In terms of financial structuring, they focus on ensuring the adequacy of capital contributions, the reliability and stability of the project company's income, the creation of adequate reserves at the start of the project, and the prioritisation of debt repayment.

13 ALSF, *Public-Private Partnership (PPP) Projects in the Infrastructure Sector.*

With regard to the contractual structure, the lenders will review the project contracts, insurance and other contractual arrangements in detail with a view to verifying that the planned risk allocation is appropriate and seeking the relevant security from the project company and its shareholders.

349 Lenders due diligence. – To achieve this, they require audits conducted by experts across various disciplines. These are often referred to as "lender" audits. In practice, in Africa like anywhere else, most of these audits are carried out by international and local teams with expertise on the continent. There are still many African markets where local expertise is not sufficient, even if it can be considered that it is increasing with each passing year and project, and that certain African markets, by virtue of their size, the number of operations and the quality of the local teams, have recently acquired significant maturity.

The legal due diligence carried out on the project will cover the following elements in particular:

- identification of project risks;
- analysis of project contracts entered into or to be entered into by the SPV to ensure that risks are properly allocated and mitigated by the various parties involved;
- indication of contractual items to be reviewed or unallocated risks to be mitigated;
- analysis of the project's contractual structure in relation to the proposed financing.

The lenders will summarise the legal, financial and technical due diligence reports received and will check the reliability of the financial flows organised by the various contracts concluded or to be concluded, ensure that sufficient budgets are available to meet the SPV's commitments, and commission additional studies to confirm the assumptions relating to the SPV's income. On this basis, they may ask the SPV to make contractual adjustments to the documentation and changes to the structure if necessary to ensure that the project is bankable, with risk-taking controlled by each party and in line with standards. The lenders will then be able to propose progress on the financing contracts and reflect any specific features of the project by requesting appropriate security.

350 Security arrangements. – Various solutions are available to guarantee the lenders repayment of the loans granted to the project company to finance the infrastructure.

However, in the context of project financing, where the financing is non-recourse to the project company's shareholders, lenders cannot, as a matter of principle, request personal guarantees or sureties from the project company's shareholder sponsors.

The idea is to consider that the infrastructure built and the income it is expected to generate are the sole collateral of the creditors. In practice, exceptions are sometimes made to this principle and shareholders often give limited undertakings to lenders in the form of comfort letters or undertakings to do or not to do something. The absolute principle must therefore be qualified, as exceptions are sometimes made depending on the project and the associated risks, and particularly in Africa, where country risks are generally higher.

Security interests and debtors' ability to use them reassure creditors, who prefer liquid security interests, which are automatic and easy to use, as in the case of stand-alone guarantees[14] which we will examine later.

351 The different types of security available in project financing. – In view of the principle of financing without recourse to shareholders, lenders need to be satisfied with more targeted securities and to study precisely which securities are most appropriate, depending on the project and the sector in which it operates. Different types of security exist in different African countries, whether in the form of movable, immovable or personal property. Guarantees facilitate access to credit by reducing the potential losses associated with the risk of non-payment by the lender. In this sense, collateral law promotes lender confidence, which is the cornerstone of credit activities, and access to financing and the development of credit, which are largely determined by a debtor's ability to freely offer reliable collateral to lenders.[15]

352 OHADA securities law. – In this respect, there is a unified legal area in Africa within OHADA, which comprises 17 African countries applying the same rules in business law and in particular in the law on securities.[16] The OHADA securities system, established in 1997, was reformed by the OHADA Uniform Act on the Organisation of Securities of 15 December 2010 ("Uniform Act on Securities"), which introduced new definitions and concepts to modernise the legal framework governing securities. There is no other example of unified security law on the continent, covering 17 countries. This is also a unique example on a global scale.

353 Variety of securities depending on the country. – In the other countries of the African continent with a civil law tradition, the securities taken are generally very similar to the rules applicable in France or in the OHADA countries, often with slightly less modern mechanisms. These include countries such as Morocco, Algeria, Tunisia and Madagascar. In English-speaking African countries, the securities used by lenders are largely inspired by English law and common law. Reference is often made to the concept of "Universal Security Interests", which refers to the possibility of including all the assets of the SPV and the project within the scope of the guarantees taken by the lenders. This is often the

14 Guillaume Feld, *op. cit.*

15 Lionel Yondo Black, "L'enjeu économique de la réforme de l'Acte Uniforme OHADA portant organisation des sûretés: un atout pour faciliter l'accès au crédit", *Droit & Patrimoine*, no. 197, p. 46. *Revue du Barreau du Mali*, no. 1, January–April 2011, p. 13.

16 OHADA Member States: Benin, Burkina-Faso, Cameroon, Central African Republic, Chad, Comoros, Congo, Congo D.R., Côte d'Ivoire, Equatorial Guinea, Gabon, Guinea, Guinea Bissau, Mali, Niger, Senegal and Togo.

implementation of the concept better known as the *floating charge* or any similar legal instrument.[17]

354 OHADA security agent. – The new Uniform Act has introduced a new method of managing security interests through the possibility of appointing a security agent, a role attributed solely to national or foreign financial institutions or credit institutions that manage security interests or other guarantees for the performance of an obligation. Thus, the security agent will be involved in syndicated loans, structured finance and international project finance.[18]

355 Security management. – The security agent may be set up in many other countries outside OHADA. However, in the OHADA zone, a uniform legal regime exists on this subject. More generally, given the size and complexity of project financing in Africa, the management role of the security agent is key, as in practice there are very often many lenders with different rights and many securities to manage. The creation of the security agent facilitates the syndicated credit activities used in infrastructure, commodities or other structured finance. The security agent facilitates the management of security interests where the secured claim is held by several creditors, and creditors remain protected in the event of the debtor, or the security agent being placed in insolvency proceedings through the introduction and recognition of the concept of special purpose assets.[19] Where the assigned debtor is subject to collective proceedings, the assignee, as a creditor in the estate, will be obliged to comply with the requirements relating to the suspension of individual proceedings, the prohibition of payments and the production of claims applicable to the said proceedings. In the event of collective proceedings against the assigned debtor, the realisation of the claim will be based on its ranking in accordance with the provisions of Article 167 of the Uniform Act Organising Collective Proceedings for the Settlement of Debts.[20]

17 For more details on the typical security package in English law: https://www.lexisnexis.com/uk/lexispsl/bankingandfinance/document/391289/55KB-65S1-F185-X04X-00000-00/Security_in_project_finance_transactions_overview

18 Mactar Sakho, "Le nouvel Acte Uniforme OHADA portant organisation des sûretés: Propos introductifs autour d'une refonte d'envergure du droit des sûretés", *Revue de l'ERSUMA: Droit des affaires – Pratique Professionnelle*, n° Spécial – November–Décember 2011, Législation.

19 Lionel Yondo Black, *op. cit.*, p. 13.

20 Article 167 of the UAOC: Without prejudice to the exercise of any right of retention or exclusive right to payment, the proceeds from the realisation of movables are distributed in the following order:

1° creditors benefiting from the preferential right provided for in articles 5-11, 11-1 and 33-1 above (conciliation agreement approved or executed by the court or competent authority, approval of a composition agreement, new cash injection, etc.);

2° to creditors for the legal costs incurred in realising the property sold and distributing the proceeds;

3° to creditors for costs incurred for the preservation of the debtor's property in the interest of the creditor whose titles predate the date;

4° to creditors of super-privileged wages in proportion to the value of the furniture in relation to the total assets;

This mechanism is particularly useful in the context of project financing, where many creditors will be involved in the financing and where numerous arrangements shall be put in place to promote the proper application of the agreements reached between these creditors. In practice, however, it should be noted that there are not many financial institutions that accept this role in Africa at present, which can sometimes cause difficulties in finding reliable agents available for project financing. Conversely, in the event of the assignor's insolvency proceedings, the effectiveness of the assignment of a claim by way of security is certain vis-à-vis the assignor placed in insolvency proceedings, as the claim is deemed to have already left the assignor's assets and entered those of the assignee on the date of the deed. The assignee of a claim assigned by way of security is therefore *a priori* a creditor protected from the ban on payments and the suspension of individual proceedings.[21]

Sous-section 2. Types of security

Having studied the strategy for taking security and considered certain points in the structure of the security package, we need to look at the types of security that will be taken in project financing in Africa. Classically, a distinction is made between personal sureties and sureties on project assets.

§ 1. Personal sureties

356-1 Definition. – Personal sureties are commitments by natural or legal persons to guarantee obligations contracted by another natural or legal person.[22]

357 Cases of use. – In general, these securities are not used to guarantee the SPV's bank financing, as the shareholders refuse to support the project company in the context of project financing by granting sureties, independent guarantees or other direct commitments. However, they may be more likely to be used in the relationship between the project company as project owner and the builder with regard to the guarantees that the builder must provide for the performance of its obligations. Similarly, this bond is more frequently requested by public parties during the call for tenders to obtain a bid bond from the project company, for example.

It is advisable to check in each country concerning each party to the project what personal guarantees are included in the arrangements applicable to these parties. In

5° creditors guaranteed by a general lien subject to publication, a pledge or a charge, each on the date on which it becomes effective against third parties; 6°creditors with a special movable lien, each on the item of movable property to which the lien relates;

7° creditors of the estate as defined in article 117 above;

8° creditors with a general lien in the order established by the Uniform Act on the organisation of securities;

9° unsecured creditors with a writ of execution;

10° to unsecured creditors without a writ of execution.

21 "Les sûretés à l'épreuve de la réforme OHADA des procédures collectives du 10 septembre 2015", *Revue Le Penant*, 1er October 2018.

22 Boris Martor, Nanette Pilkington, David Sellers and Sébastien Thouvenot, *Le droit uniforme africain des affaires issu de l'OHADA*, 2e ed, Litec, p. 234.

civil law countries, it is common to find surety bonds and first demand guarantees. In common law countries, surety bonds are referred to as "guarantees" and *contracts of indemnity* are also used.

358 OHADA. – In OHADA countries, the Uniform Act on Securities recognises surety bonds, autonomous guarantees and autonomous counter-guarantees as personal securities, which are understood to be an undertaking by a person to meet the obligation of the principal debtor in the event of the latter's default or at the first request of the beneficiary of the guarantee.

359 Distinction between suretyship and guarantee. – The Uniform Act provides a clear distinction between suretyship, which is ancillary, and guarantees or counter-guarantees, which are independent of the main contract. However, this autonomy is not absolute, since the writing recording the guarantee or counter-guarantee must mention, on pain of nullity, "the basic agreement, act or fact in consideration of which the autonomous guarantee or counter-guarantee is issued".[23]

360 *Cautionnement.* – It defines suretyship as a contract where the guarantor undertakes to the creditor, who accepts the performance of a present or future obligation contracted by the debtor, if the debtor does not himself fulfil it (art. 13 of the Uniform Act on Guarantees) and retains the principle of the accessory nature of the guarantee, which means that the guarantor may not enter into a contract under conditions that are more onerous than the principal obligation, failing which the guarantee will be reduced and may not exceed what is owed by the principal debtor (art. 17 of the Uniform Act on Guarantees).

361 Future obligations. – In addition to the admission of surety bonds for future obligations, a novelty enshrined in the latest Uniform Act, the OHADA legislator has also relaxed the conditions for the validity of surety bonds, removing the requirement for a written document, the signature of the parties and the handwritten signature of the guarantor in words and figures. These are now conditions of proof, since Article 14 provides that

> a guarantee shall not be presumed. . . . It shall be proved by a deed bearing the signatures of the guarantor and the creditor and a handwritten statement by the guarantor, in words and figures, of the maximum sum guaranteed covering the principal, interest and other ancillary sums.

362 First demand guarantee. – The framework of the autonomous guarantee and counter-guarantee in OHADA law reveals an undertaking and not a mere agreement, since these are undertakings incumbent on the guarantor and counter-guarantor by which they undertake "in consideration of an obligation entered into by the principal and on the instructions of the principal to pay a specified sum either on first demand or in accordance with the agreed terms".[24]

23 Art. 41 of the Uniform Act on Security Interests.

24 Art. 39 of the Uniform Act on Security Interests.

This is an effective instrument for mobilising the funds allocated as collateral to cover the debtor's obligations to the creditor. It can be issued by a credit institution or by any type of legal entity.

It is most often used for the repayment of deposits, performance bonds or completion bonds, or for the restoration of assets covered by project financing. This tool was essentially developed by practice over years last century.

Focus: the autonomous guarantee, an instrument codified by practice[25]

The system of back-to-back guarantees and counter-guarantees has been developed and used in international contracts for decades when a performance bond is required from a foreign co-contractor. In such cases, the client generally requires the company carrying out the work to provide a performance bond issued by a local bank. This bank in turn requires a counter-guarantee to be given by a bank in the construction company's home country, so that it is itself guaranteed if the main guarantee is called. In practice, the foreign co-contractor asks its own bank to act as counter-guarantor, which then arranges for the main guarantee to be obtained from a local bank. Letters of guarantee can also be used as overdraft guarantees, customs duty payment guarantees or bid guarantees for tenders, where bidders are sometimes required to provide such a guarantee in order to demonstrate the seriousness of their bid.

The OHADA Uniform Act on securities was highly innovative when it first came into force in 1998, as it was one of the first laws to codify, with a specific legal framework, the law applicable to letters of guarantee and counter-guarantees, which are very useful instruments in international trade. Indeed, the creation of harmonised rules can be of invaluable assistance to practitioners in their efforts to draw up effective guarantees, even if the existence of a legal framework does not always resolve all the legal problems arising in practice. The provisions of the Uniform Act governing the letter of guarantee were ahead of many legislations and are largely inspired by the definition of the first demand guarantee in the related Uniform Rules drawn up by the International Chamber of Commerce (ICC).[26]

It was not until 2006, for example, that the French legislature codified the principles governing autonomous guarantees, as derived from practice and case law, in Article 2321 of the Civil Code.

25 On autonomous guarantees, see also M. Audit, S. Bollée and P. Callé, *Droit du commerce international et des investissements étrangers*, *op. cit.*, n° 640 et seq.

26 Uniform Rules for Demand Guarantees (UDRG) drawn up by the International Chamber of Commerce (ICC) and Model Forms, 2010 edition, Revision no. E758EF.

363 Autonomous undertakings. – Understood as "autonomous undertakings, distinct from the agreements, acts and facts likely to form their basis",[27] OHADA legislation has enshrined the independence of the obligations of the guarantor and counter-guarantor from those of the principal debtor. Recently, it has become possible to issue guarantees of this type for both fixed and indefinite periods. However, these guarantees can be very costly in practice if they are issued by a bank, which will charge fees for the entire term of the guarantee. It is therefore more common to apply for stand-alone guarantees of limited duration or to provide for renewals. In projects, these guarantees are often used for the period during which the assets are made available or for the period during which the project assets are taken over by the public entity, in order to ensure that the assets are compliant and operational.

364 Performance guarantee. – In practice, in the context of project financing, the performance guarantee may take the form of a bond, often in the form of an indemnity guarantee in favour of a customer, the amount of which corresponds to a percentage of the price of the contract concerned, issued by a bank at the request of the economic operator. In the event of the economic operator's default, the bank undertakes to pay the beneficiary all or part of the amount under the contract concluded between the contracting authority and the economic operator.[28] This may sometimes take the form of a bond or guarantee for the return of the deposit paid by the public-sector client to the project company holding the contract.

To remember

In all cases, the autonomous nature of the first demand guarantee and its less restrictive formalities make it a preferred tool compared to surety bonds for the commitments of the SPV or its subcontractors.

365 Letters of intent or comfort. – Banks may request a written personal undertaking from the shareholders of a project company, without asking for a personal guarantee from them. This commitment is generally referred to as a letter of credit or letter of comfort. This type of letter provides the shareholder's subsidiary project company with reassurance that the group financially supports it and will provide it with the necessary funds. This type of commitment has little legal effect, depending on the wording chosen by the issuer. A distinction is made between letters that are similar to an obligation to act (e.g. to provide current account capital if necessary), to a moral commitment (e.g. to monitor the subsidiary's financial situation to ensure that it is in good health) or to a surety or guarantee (e.g. to undertake to

27 Art. 40 of the Uniform Act on Security Interests.
28 Guillaume Feld, *op. cit.*, p. 160.

pay in place of the project company, in which case it must include all the obligatory information specific to this type of surety).[29]

This type of commitment is found in project finance mainly where the lenders ask the shareholders of the project company to reassure them of their group's support for delivery and operation. Because of the non-recourse nature of project finance, shareholders are very reluctant to give more than a fairly general commitment of support.

On the other hand, the letter may be slightly more binding when the project company requests it from the EPC contractor in order to obtain guarantees from the latter's shareholder to ensure performance of the obligations under the construction contract.

Depending on the company law applicable to the issuing company, this commitment may require approval from its governance bodies, such as the Board of Directors.

Additionally, for some riskier projects, although project finance is normally structured without direct recourse or guarantees from the sponsor, lenders may consider the project risk cannot be mitigated or it may be considered beyond the creditors' ability to absorb. In such cases, sponsor guarantees may be extended to creditors before the physical or financial completion of the project, usually after COD. Guarantees will take the form of a partial loan guarantee, which guarantees only a portion of the loan principal and interest payment. This reduces the lenders' exposure somewhat and adds a portion of risks sharing to give lenders an additional inducement to finance a project.[30]

§ 2. Security interests in project assets

366 Types of securities. – Different forms of security are available for project assets, depending on whether the security is in the form of movable or immovable property. The value of a mortgage depends, however, on the nature of the project and the project's financing structure. If the project involves a production facility, the value of the mortgaged land, plant and equipment might secure a large portion of the project's debts. However, in some other situations, it may be less useful and practical for the creditors to realise a mortgage. As a consequence, step-in rights and assignment of concession or similar agreements will be more appropriate.

A. Property security

367 Mortgages. – It is often impractical for lenders to take mortgages or security interests over the project company's real estate assets. This is particularly true in Africa. On the one hand, since these assets are used for public service purposes, it may be impossible or difficult to take out such security over them. If the project is part of a concession with delegated management of a public service, the principle

29 On the classification of letters of intent, see M. Audit, S. Bollée and P. Callé, *Droit du commerce international et des investissements étrangers*, *op. cit.*, no. 651.

30 IFC, Lessons of Experience, Project Finance in Developing countries.

of the inalienability of the public domain, which exists in many civil law countries, entails a risk which crystallises in the fact that if the assets essential to the operation of the project are encumbered by security, the realisation of the security will lead to the assets being diverted from their proper purpose.[31]

368 Fees. – On the other hand, it appears that in most African countries the costs of registering mortgages and related property security can be very high. As a result, the cost/benefit ratio of such security interests in Africa often leads to their exclusion from the guarantees chosen to provide security to lenders. Lastly, the specific situation of certain land rights in Africa, which may be governed by customary law in some cases, can also complicate the enforcement of property security.

369 OHADA mortgage. – It should be noted, however, that the OHADA Uniform Act on Securities provides a framework for mortgages, which may be legal, contractual or judicial and may be constituted on future assets.[32] It covers all types of immovable property rights and envisages the possibility of constituting a mortgage on a share of an undivided immovable property, thereby providing additional protection for mortgage creditors such as banks. In this respect, in most OHADA Member States, real estate assets are an essential criterion for a bank's assessment of the solidity of the guarantees to be offered to a customer wishing to obtain a bank loan.[33] In the context of project financing in Africa, these assets are often estimated by taking as a reference the property rights conferred by the concession or operating contract or by a long-term title relating to the site on which the project is being operated (communications networks, relay antenna sites, land on which a solar power plant sits,[34] etc.).

The OHADA Uniform Act on Securities allows "the possibility of creating mortgages on buildings and structures erected on the public domain or the national domain", which makes it easier to create mortgages on assets built by the project company, even if they are on the public domain, whereas in many other French-speaking countries, this option is not allowed by virtue of the principle of inalienability of assets allocated to the public service.[35]

370 Common law mortgages. – In the common law system as applicable in many English–speaking countries of the continent, a mortgage involves transferring the title of an asset as security for specific obligations. There are often two main types of mortgages: legal and equitable. A legal mortgage transfers the legal title to the lender (mortgagee) and restricts the mortgagor from dealing with the asset while it is under the mortgage. Notably, a legal mortgage cannot be taken

31 Zine Sekfali, *op. cit.*, p. 573.

32 Articles 190 and 203 of the OHADA Uniform Act on Securities.

33 Pierre Crocq, *Le nouvel acte uniforme portant organisation des sûretés*, Lamy, coll. Lamy axe droit, 2012, p. 280.

34 See Guide for project developers on solar project development and financing: IFC, *Commercial solar photovoltaic power plants*, available at ifc.org, July 2015.

35 Tony Giustini, "La réforme des sûretés en droit OHADA – Considérations pratiques", *Droit et Patrimoine*, no. 213, 2012.

over a future property, but an equitable mortgage can. An equitable mortgage arises when the formalities for a legal mortgage are not fully met or when the asset is an equitable interest. It transfers only the beneficial interest to the mortgagee, while the legal title remains with the mortgagor. For an equitable mortgage, the assets must be clearly identified.[36] In Table 10.1 are detailed a few examples of legal mortgage options in several African countries.

Table 10.1 Legal regime of mortgages in a couple of African countries

	Scope of concerned assets	*Registration*
Mauritus	• Immovable property (and their accessories considered as immovable property); • The usufruct of the same accessories for the duration of its term.[37] **Note**: *Future assets cannot be mortgaged. However, if current assets are insufficient, the debtor can agree to allocate future acquisitions as security.*	1. A deed/judgment giving rise to the mortgage with a memorandum annexed setting out details of the mortgage must be prepared and presented to the Conservator of Mortgages. 2. These documents must be registered in the Registration of Deeds and Documents System (RDDS).[38]
Ethiopia	Immovable property.[39]	Entered in the Immovable Property Registry at the place where the immovable mortgaged is situated.[40]
	Certain kinds of movables (for example: business or business flows).[41]	Two major conditions:[42] • The grantor must have rights in the asset to be encumbered or the power to encumber it. • The security agreement is evidenced by a written agreement that is signed by the grantor and: • identifies the secured creditor and the grantor; • describes the secured obligation; and • describes the collateral.

(*Continued*)

36 Thomson Reuters, *Practical Law*, Taking Security, 2024.
37 Mauritius Civil Code, chapter 3, Mortgages.
38 Inscription of Privileges and Mortgages Act, Act 73 of 1946.
39 Civil Code of Ethiopia, art.3047.
40 Civil Code of Ethiopia, art.3052–3053.
41 Commercial Code of the Federal Democratic Republic of Ethiopia, art.143.
42 Article 4 of the Movable Property Security Right Proclamation no. 1147/2019.

Table 10.1 (Continued)

	Scope of concerned assets	*Registration*
		The obligations of the secured creditor are as follows:[43] • to register, amend and cancel the notice with the Collateral Registry; • upon termination of the security right, to return the asset to the grantor or release its control over the security; • to provide adequate proof to the debtor regarding the securitisation of receivables that a security right has been created over the receivables. **Note**: *The notice with respect to the security right over corporeal assets (including cash) registered in the Collateral Registry by the secured creditor is necessary to be effective against third parties.*
Ghana	Immovable property.[44]	1. Registered in the Collateral Registry[45] and the Registrar of Companies for companies' properties.[46] 2. The mortgage shall be in writing and signed by the mortgagor or the authorised agent.[47] 3. Every writing evidencing a mortgage may be registered in accordance with the Land Registry Act, 1962 (Act 122).[48] 4. The security interest shall be registered with the Land Registration Division of the Lands Commission.[49] 5. The lender shall affix a stamp to the credit agreement before or after registering the security interest.[50]
	Mortgages on shares do not seem to be prohibited.[51]	Those are then registered in the Collateral Registry[52] and the Registrar of Companies.[53]

(*Continued*)

43 Article 13 of the Movable Property Security Right Proclamation no. 1147/2019.
44 Section 1 of the Mortgages Act – 1972 (NRCD 96).
45 Borrowers and Lenders Act 2020 (Act 1052).
46 The Companies Act, 2019 (Act 992).
47 Section 3 of Mortgages Act – 1972 (NRCD 96), Section 82 of The Land Act, 2020.
48 *Ibid.*
49 The Land Act, 2020.
50 Section 22 of the Borrowers and Lenders Act 2020 (Act 1052).
51 The Companies Act, 2019 (Act 992).
52 Borrowers and Lenders Act 2020 (Act 1052).
53 The Companies Act, 2019 (Act 992).

Table 10.1 (Continued)

	Scope of concerned assets	*Registration*
Kenya	Immovable property;[54] Uncalled share capital, company's book debts + ship or aircraft + company's goodwill or intellectual property.[55]	Its filing may be completed in physical or electronic form, different possibilities:[56] • Documents related to immovable property outside the Coast Province must be registered in the Principal Registry at Nairobi. • Documents related to immovable property within the Coast Province must be registered in the Coast Registry at Mombasa. • If a document pertains to properties in both areas, it can be registered in either or both registries. • Original documents shall be presented for registration. **Note**: *Company charges shall be registered at Register of Companies (the Companies Act lists the types of charges and mortgages that are registrable).*[57]
	Movable property.[58]	Registration of an initial notice or an amendment notice at the Office of the Registar that should contain in particular: the identifier and address of the grantor, the identifier and notice of secured creditor, a description of the collateral and the period of effectiveness of the registration.[59]
Nigeria[60]	Immovable property;[61] Movable property;[62] Lagos State: Immovable and movable property.[63]	1. Registered at the Land Registry office of the State in which the property is situated. Where a company is involved, registration is also required to be done at the Corporate Affairs Commission (CAC).[64]

(*Continued*)

54 Chapter 85 of the Registration of Documents Act, Revised Edition 2020 (Cap.285), Article 78 of The Land Act n°6 of 2012, Chapter IV of The Transfer of Property Act, 1882.

55 Article 878 et seq. of The Companies Act, n°17 OF 2015.

56 Registration of Documents Act, Chapter 85, Revised Edition 2020.

57 Article 878 et seq. of The Companies Act, n°17 OF 2015.

58 Article 4 of The Movable Property Security Rights Act n°. 13 OF 2017.

59 Article 20 et seq. of The Movable Property Security Rights Act n°. 13 OF 2017.

60 Note: In Nigeria, the Secured Transactions in Movable Assets Act "regulates the creation and perfection of movable assets' security assets such as equipment, raw material, account receivables etc. and where a charge document is in respect of a movable asset and required to be perfected in accordance with the SETIMA, then documents should not be stamped".

61 Property and Conveyancing Act of 1959.

62 Secured Transactions in Movable Assets Act, 2017 and Property and Conveyancing Act of 1959.

63 Article 1.2 of the Mortgage and Property Law of Lagos, 2010.

64 Section 191 of the Companies and Allied Matters Act, 2020.

Table 10.1 (Continued)

	Scope of concerned assets	*Registration*
		2. The deed of legal mortgage shall also be registered at the Lagos State Mortgage Board.[65] 3. A legal mortgage requires the governor's consent and registration at the land's registry.[66] 4. A charge document is required to be stamped within 30 days of execution if it has been executed in Nigeria. Where the charge document is executed outside Nigeria, it is required to be stamped before the expiration of 30 days, "after it has been first received in Nigeria" after the applicable stamp duty has been paid.[67]
South Africa	Immovable property.[68]	Registered in at deeds registry, received by a Deeds Office.[69]
	"Notarial Bonds" are used to hypothecate corporeal movable property.[70]	The notarial bond sufficiently recognisable is registered in accordance with the Deeds Registries Act, 1937.[71]
Uganda	Land, any estate or interest in land.[72]	Registered at the Registrar of Titles under the Registration of Titles Act and received by the Office of Titles. The date of registration determines the priority between the charges. Some documents are required for registration to be done such as for example two original copies of the charging instrument or mortgage deed or a copy of the certificate of title.[73]
	Movable property.[74]	1. The Registrar General appointed under the Uganda Registration Services Bureau Act, Cap. 210, shall be the registrar of security interests in movable property under this Act.[75] 2. A security interest in movable property shall be registered electronically using an initial notice or amendment notice, in the order submitted.[76]

65 Section 53 of the Mortgage and Property Law of Lagos State, 2010.
66 Section 22 and 26 of the Land Use Act of 1978.
67 Section 22 and 23 of the Stamp Duties Act, 1939.
68 Deeds Registries Act 1937.
69 Deeds Registries Act, 1937 and Deeds Registration Systems Act, 2019.
70 Security by Means of Movable Property Act, 1993 and Deeds Registries Act, 1937.
71 Article 1 of the Security by Means of Movable Property Act, 1993 and Deeds Registries Act, 1937.
72 Mortgage Act, 2009.
73 Mortgage Act, 2009 and Registration of Titles Act, 1924 revised in 2023.
74 Security Interest in Movable Property Act, 2019.
75 Security Interest in Movable Property Act, 2019.
76 *Ibid.*

To remember

The process of registering a mortgage is relatively complex and costly in Africa, since it very often requires a notarial deed, which in turn requires the payment of taxes and registration fees, which are often high. In addition, enforcing a mortgage can sometimes be lengthy and difficult, particularly because of the means of protecting the debtor's rights and the possibility of appeal. For all these reasons, creditors generally prefer to use other, more flexible types of security.

B. Movable collateral

371 Securities strategy. – There are various types of personal property security that lenders can take out. The choice generally depends on the type of project, its location and the value of the assets, although there are some types of security that are systematically selected by lenders. These include pledges of the project company's shares or pledges of the bank accounts through which the project company's income will flow. In practice, the creditors ask the sponsors for a general security over all the assets of the project company, such as the main contracts entered into, which will enable the lenders to exercise the rights and obligations of the project company if it defaults.[77] There is therefore a real strategy to choose the guarantees granted and required by the parties depending on the country's legal framework, the costs of implementation and the effectiveness offered in practice.

372 Ohada securities. – Regarding countries, in 2010, the OHADA Uniform Act on Securities reformed the concepts of pledge and collateral security, since they are no longer distinguished by the requirement or absence of dispossession of the grantor[78] but now relate to the assets to which they relate: pledge relates to tangible movable assets and collateral security to intangible movable assets. On pain of nullity, the Uniform Act requires these two types of security to be evidenced in writing.[79] The non-possessory pledge has several advantages, such as allowing the debtor to retain the use of the asset that he is pledging. It also encourages the creation of successive pledges on the same asset, which necessarily means strengthening the creditworthiness of the pledgor. Another new feature is that the pledge may relate to future assets, so that the classification of the pledge as a real contract, implying that the pledge could only be validly constituted at the time of delivery of the asset – the subject of the pledge – has been abandoned.[80] This shift in the nature of the pledge contract allows the pledgor to

77 Zine SEKFALI, *op. cit.*, p. 181.

78 Pierre CROCQ, *op. cit.*, p. 46.

79 Articles 96 and 127 of the Uniform Act on Securities.

80 Mactar SAKHO, "Le nouvel Acte Uniforme OHADA portant organisation des sûretés: Propos introductifs autour d'une refonte d'envergure du droit des sûretés", *Revue de l'ERSUMA: Droit des affaires – Pratique Professionnelle*, n° Spécial, November–Décember 2011, Législation.

continue to use the asset offered as collateral while benefiting from liquidity and thus does not require him to divest himself of it.[81] The Uniform Act broadly recognises the scope of pledges, which may cover receivables, bank accounts, shareholders' rights, transferable securities, securities accounts, goodwill and intellectual property rights.[82]

It must be noted that, for some countries that apply the common law system, only assets that can be transferred through delivery of possession may be pledged (including for example tangible moveable property such as goods, furniture, aircraft and ships but excluding future assets and intangible assets such as registered securities in contrast to bearer securities).[83]

C. *Pledge of company rights and pledge of financial securities account*

373 Possible options. – Even if the shareholders of the project company do not give guarantees on their own assets, they are most often mobilised to grant securities on their shares held in the project company. These shares are therefore pledged as security, with two options available if we refer to most French-language or civil law instruments such as the OHADA Uniform Act on security interests: pledging of company rights or pledging of financial securities accounts. The share pledge is particularly useful if lenders feel that the value of the mortgaged assets is not providing enough security or when it could be uncertain to enforce such a mortgage.

374 Pledge of company rights. – This is governed by Articles 140 to 145 of OHADA law, which regulate pledges of non-dematerialised, non-account-entry securities, which are governed by the pledge of financial securities accounts described later in this chapter. It can be set up for any type of shareholder rights, company shares or securities. Even though registration with the RCCM is no longer a condition of validity, in practice it is registered with the RCCM because this guarantees its enforceability against third parties and with the tax authorities. Some African countries maintain prohibitively high registration fees in proportion to the secured debt, making it more difficult for lenders to obtain security and borrowers to obtain credit. This pledge is valid for a maximum of ten years and then renewed, and its registration is notified to the project company.

In Morocco, Articles 537 et seq. govern the pledging of securities. The same principles and distinctions between pledges of securities accounts and pledges of corporate rights can be found in most French-speaking African countries.

375 Pledge of financial instruments accounts. – In general, where local security law is applicable to the project company's securities, lenders require the pledge of financial instrument accounts which attracts all rights and sums derived from the shares within its scope. This is also more flexible than the pledge of company rights and is governed by Articles 146 to 155 of the Uniform Act on Securities in the OHADA zone. This security may be combined with an intercreditor agreement to govern the

81 Pierre Crocq, *op. cit.*, p. 203.

82 Art. 126 of the Uniform Act on Securities.

83 Thomson Reuters, *Practical Law*, Pledges: A quick guide, 2024.

ranking of repayments and the privileges of each lender or creditor in the event of seizure of the account(s) where several lenders are involved in financing the project.

376 Pledge base. – The advantage of this type of pledge is that the basis on which it can be seized by lenders does not consist solely of the securities, as in the case of a pledge of company rights, but of all the sums received on the securities account, i.e. all the debt securities attached to the ownership of the share held and all the sums received by the shareholder, such as the fruits or income received, such as dividends, for example.[84]

377 Enforceability. – For a pledge governed by OHADA as well as in most French speaking African countries to be valid and enforceable, it must be the subject of a pledge declaration signed and dated by the holder of the securities account and by the owner of that account. It is common practice to attach this declaration to the pledge agreement signed between the parties so that it is the accessory implemented as soon as the agreement is reached to create this security. Under penalty of nullity, the declaration includes the names of the parties, the amount of the secured debt, the securities identified as initially forming part of the pledge and details of the special pledged account enabling it to be identified. The agreement signed by the parties sets out how the account is to operate during the pledge period, and in particular any freedoms that the pledgor may have during the pledge period, generally until the debt has been repaid by the project company.

D. Pledging of equipment or stocks

378 Securities over project's assets. – In some cases, if certain assets of the company are clearly identified or need to be secured, pledges of equipment[85] or inventories may be preferred. For example, as part of project financing for a railway line, lenders may ask for security to be taken over equipment such as locomotives or carriages used to operate the line, or over stocks of spare parts.

The pledging of material or equipment can have certain limitations for lenders, even if the goods are identified in the absence of dispossession. While wagons and locomotives are difficult to disappear, other assets such as vehicles and machinery can be more easily removed from lenders' seizures.

379 Ohada securities over stock or equipment. – The Uniform Act on Secured Transactions provides that stocks of raw materials, agricultural or industrial products and stocks of goods in the possession of the debtor[86] may be pledged. The non-possessory pledge of stocks is constituted by the stock pledge slip issued by the registrar or the head of the competent body in the Contracting State. Finally, the inventory pledge must be registered in the RCCM and it is after this registration that the slip will be given to the debtor.[87] In practice, it may be useful to combine the inventory pledge with a third-party holding mechanism, which is very common in Africa, to

84 Art. 148 of the Uniform Act on Security Interests.

85 OHADA law organises the pledge of business equipment in Article 118 of the Uniform Act on Security Interests.

86 Art. 120 of the Uniform Act on Securities.

87 Art. 122 of the Uniform Act on Securities.

allow a third party to control the entry and exit of inventory. This can be useful, for example, for high-value goods such as ores, petroleum products or other products intended for export such as coffee or cocoa.

Pledging professional equipment or stock has a number of advantages for the project company, where it makes sense in the context of the project: firstly, by providing a guarantee on its stock to a lending institution, the latter enables the company to finance its cash flow and optimise its lending capacity while retaining the right to dispose of its stock; secondly, by having the borrower take out a guarantee on its stock, the lending institution will be able to call on the guarantee if necessary.[88]

380 Moroccan securities over assets or equiment. – In Morocco, Article 355 of Moroccan law governs the pledging of materials and equipment, and most laws in African countries include similar provisions for pledging materials and stocks.

Focus: lien of equipment or stock

The OHADA legislator has established the lien as a security by clearly and definitively specifying its legal nature, which has been the subject of a long doctrinal debate. Article 50 of the OHADA Uniform Act on the Organization of Security Interests (AUS) provides that movable securities include the right of retention.

In English speaking countries of Africa applying a common law system, a lien is the legal right to retain possession of property until a debt is repaid, arising by operation of law. Liens are generally less significant in financial transactions because they typically occur automatically by law, rather than being granted by a security provider. However, lenders must be mindful of any liens affecting the assets they secure, as in some cases, liens may take priority over the security granted to the lender. The main types of liens that may arise include:[89]

- **legal or common law lien**: the creditor's right to retain possession of the debtor's property until the debt is paid;
- **equitable lien:** a right based on principles of equity, rather than strict legal rules;
- **statutory lien:** a right established by specific legislation;
- **contractual lien:** extends a legal lien by providing enforcement rights (such as the ability to sell the goods) in case of default or is used to create a lien when a lien under general law cannot be established.

In South Africa, there are no specific perfection requirements for a lien. A lien is established by the existence of an obligation owing to the lien holder and the lien holder's possession of the asset over which the lien is held.[90]

88 Sylvie Bissaloué, "Le gage de stocks, un instrument juridique innovant pour les entreprises relevant du droit OHADA", *Wolters Kluwer*, 18 April 2019, legal news, Africa, national law.

89 Thomson Reuters, *Practical Law*, Pledges: A quick guide, 2024.

90 Latham & Watkins, *Taking Security in Africa*, 2024.

E. Pledging of receivables or bank accounts

381 Pledge of receivables. – This is particularly useful for pledging any type of receivable, whether existing or future, held by the project company.[91] Under OHADA law, it is governed by Articles 127 to 135 of the Uniform Act on Security Interests. To be enforceable, the debtor of the claim must be notified of the pledge, who may also intervene in the pledge deed. While this formality is not an obligation, it provides greater security by preventing the debtor from paying another creditor after being notified or intervening in the deed. To be enforceable against third parties, it must be registered with the RCCM in the OHADA zone. This formality may raise questions because it is not certain that all creditors can easily be aware of the existence of this security, but also because very often the costs of registering these securities on receivables are high in Africa and in some OHADA member countries.

The pledge of a claim gives the pledgee a priority right to payment of the claim. However, the claim remains in the pledgor's assets until the pledge is realised. As a result, in the event of insolvency proceedings, all of the pledgor's previous creditors may not take individual legal action, claim payment of their debts or levy seizures. In addition, the prohibition on individual lawsuits applies to all unsecured claims and to claims secured by a general lien, a special movable lien, a pledge, a charge or a mortgage.[92] The realisation of a claim secured by a pledge will be organised according to the creditor's rank on the date the proceedings are opened, in accordance with Article 167 of the UAOC referred to earlier. In short, the assignment of a claim as security may offer better protection to the lenders of the project company of their security interests in the event of insolvency proceedings.

382 Pledge of the SPV's bank accounts. – Insofar as the creditors' main pledge is linked to the project company's income, taking security over the flows paid into the company's bank accounts is crucial. The remuneration received by the project company is in fact its main asset, provided that it is certain and can be seized, and lenders seek to take every precaution to seize all possible income from all the company's bank accounts in the event of default.

383 Ohada securities over accounts. – The pledge of a bank account is widely used in international project financing, as it offers a degree of control over the financial flows of the borrower/project company while allowing it to use them.[93] Under OHADA law, this pledge of a bank account is assimilated to a pledge of a claim by the very wording of Article 136 of the Uniform Act on Security Interests. Its regime is therefore similar to that of a pledge of a claim. All countries in Africa enable this pledge to be structured.

91 See Marine Zammith, "L'intérêt des sûretés sur créances du nouvel acte uniforme portant organisation des sûretés de l'OHADA pour les financements de projet", *Revue trimestrielle de droit africain* (Penant) ex. n° 902, pp. 34–54.

92 "Les sûretés à l'épreuve de la réforme OHADA des procédures collectives du 10 septembre 2015", *Revue Le Penant*, supra; Acte Uniforme portant organisation des procédures collectives d'apurement du passif, art. 9.

93 Olivier Fille-Lambie and Ariane Marceau-Cotte, "Les sûretés sur les meubles incorporels: le nouveau nantissement de l'Acte Uniforme sur les Sûretés", *Droit et Patrimoine*, no. 197, 1er November 2010.

384 Scope of pledge. – The basis of the pledged claim arising from the pledged account for this security is understood to be "the credit balance, whether provisional or definitive, on the day of realisation of the security, subject to the regularisation of current transactions", and the same rule is applied in the event of the opening of collective proceedings against the debtor of the pledged claim since "the rights of the pledged creditor relate to the credit balance of the account on the day of such opening".[94]

385 Use of pledged sums. – Another special feature of bank account pledges is that the parties can agree that the pledgor will continue to have access to the sums available in the pledged account. However, such a practice can be risky: on the day of realisation, the credit balance on the account may not be sufficient to fully pay off the pledged creditor.[95] In any event, it should be emphasised that this is simply an option left to the parties and that they may also opt to freeze the bank account, so that financial inflows will be possible and will increase the pledge base.[96]

386 Realisation. – This pledge is usually set up in accordance with the same formalities as those for the pledge of receivables, and the pledged receivable is equal to the amount shown on the account on the day of realisation.

F. Security interests in foreign or offshore accounts

387 Opening foreign accounts. – In some projects, the project host State may allow the project company to open bank accounts outside the country in which it operates. This facility is often eagerly awaited by lenders and shareholders in cases where the country represents a high level of risk in terms of conflict or compliance.

388 Application of the rules of the place where the account is located. – In this case, the pledging of these accounts should be organised in accordance with the rules applicable in the "offshore" State, often France, the United Kingdom or Mauritius, for example.

389 Prior authorisations for opening offshore accounts. – Depending on the rules of the country in which the project is located, it should also be checked whether there are any restrictions on the company opening offshore accounts and whether any authorisations are required. Foreign exchange rules are quite extensive in some jurisdictions. For example, this may be necessary in the case of projects located in one of the countries in the CEMAC zone. In the WAEMU zone, certain authorisations may be required from the BCEAO in order to validate the principle of the use of an offshore account by a project company established in the zone. In Morocco, the *Office des Changes* also enjoys a wide spectrum of action.

94 Art. 137 of the Uniform Act on Securities.

95 Art. 138 of the revised Uniform Act on the organisation of securities; J.-E. Bakatuinamina, "Les apports de l'OHADA dans l'évolution du droit congolais: le nantissement de compte bancaire", Kinshasa, 2015, Ohadata D-15-04.

96 O. Fille Lambie, "Les nantissements de meubles incorporels", *Le nouvel acte uniforme portant organisation des sûretés*, Lamy, 2012, p. 239.

G. Assignment and delegation of receivables

390 Assignment of SPV income. – In project financing, the assignment of receivables mechanism is frequently used, since it enables lending institutions to benefit from the assignment, by way of security, of all or part of the receivables arising from the project company's income under contracts entered for the delivery of its goods or services to its customers during the project's operating phase.[97] Under OHADA law, the Uniform Act on Security has introduced the assignment of receivables by way of guarantee, which is defined as

> a receivable held against a third party that may be assigned by way of guarantee for any credit granted by a national or foreign legal person that carries out banking and credit transactions on its behalf and in the course of its usual professional activities.[98]

391 Assignment of receivables. – According to Article 80 of the Uniform Act on Securities, the assignment of a claim by way of security makes it possible to assign ownership of a claim by way of security for any credit granted by a legal person carrying on banking or credit transactions for its own account and as part of its usual business. The assignment assigns ownership of the receivable to the assignee until the security is released. Under Moroccan law, Article 529 of the Code du Commerce authorises the assignment of business receivables as security and is frequently used for project financing.

392 Scope of application. – Insofar as Article 80 of the Uniform Act on Security Interests envisions it solely for securing loans, this security interest cannot be used to cover creditors of the SPV who are not its lenders.

393 OHADA assignment regime. – The OHADA legislator has provided in the legal regime for this security for rules of protection in favour of the non-professional assigned debtor (which will sometimes be difficult to grasp) in the event of his acceptance of the assignment, the consequence of which is that he waives the possibility of asserting against the assignee defences based on his relationship with the assignor. In this respect, the Uniform Act provides an exception to unenforceability if the assignee has "knowingly acted to the detriment of the debtor" when acquiring or receiving the claim and, secondly, adds to the sanction of nullity the requirement that the assignment must be evidenced in writing (the deed of acceptance of an assignment of a claim by way of security) and "reproducing in sufficiently clear characters the provisions of this article".[99]

394 Enforceability. – The rules governing the effectiveness of the claim against third parties differ from the French rules governing Dailly assignments in that the latter are not subject to any formalities.[100] Under Article 82 of the Uniform Act, the assignment can be

97 Zine Sekfali, *op. cit.*, p. 571.

98 Art. 80 of the Uniform Act on Security Interests.

99 Art. 85 of the Uniform Act on Security Interests.

100 Art. L. 313-27 of the French Monetary and Financial Code.

relied on from the time it is entered in the trade and real estate credit register, and the law applicable to the claim and the law of the debtor's country of residence are irrelevant.

395 Distinction from delegation of claims. – A distinction must be made between assignment and delegation of receivables. In most projects, lenders request for certain types of financial flows to be delegated by the project company. These may include insurance indemnities arising from insurance policies taken out by the project company, even if in some cases the insurance policies do not allow the delegation technique prohibiting the payment of indemnities to third parties to the SPV. In such cases, the lenders fall back on the obligation for the SPV to receive the insurance indemnities in a bank account pledged to them by the project company. Article 48 of the Moroccan Insurance Code authorises this.

This type of mechanism can be considered highly flexible, since in most countries it will be subject to very little regulation. This is one of the advantages of setting it up. However, for receivables where the lenders may be in competition with other creditors, the assignment of receivables will be preferred because it will provide the creditors with greater legal certainty.

H. Pledging of business assets

396 Goodwill. – Lenders rarely require the project company's goodwill to be pledged as collateral. This pledge, which is fairly broad in scope since it covers all the assets of the SPV, is often considered cumbersome to organise, often costly in practice in many African countries and not very effective in the event of default. One of the major advantages of this pledge is that it covers the assets attached to the business, such as intellectual and industrial property, which for some SPVs can be of significant value, particularly in the context of project financing for telecommunications or technological assets.

397 Floating charge. – The pledge of goodwill is commonly compared to the floating charge known in English-speaking countries. However, it is important to distinguish between them on one fundamental point, which is that the floating charge pledges a set of receivables belonging to the debtor and really encompasses all the assets and financial flows. The pledge of a business does not provide the same advantage in terms of scope.[101]

398 Fixed charge. – In common law countries, there is also the more secure mechanism of the fixed charge. In contrast to the floating charge, the fixed charge gives the lender control over the charged asset. A deed which establishes a fixed charge grants the lender the right to prevent the chargor from disposing of the asset without the lender's consent, sell the asset if the chargor defaults on repaying the secured liabilities, require the chargor to maintain the asset while it remains in his possession, claim the proceeds from the sale of the charged asset in priority over other creditors, and thus fulfil the purpose of taking security.[102]

101 Paul Lignières and Anne-Marie Toledo, *Le financement de projet*, ed. Joly, 2002, no. 247, p. 145.
102 Thomson Reuters, *Practical Law*, Pledges: A quick guide, 2024.

Focus on fixed charges in Nigeria

In Nigeria, a fixed charge generally has priority over a floating charge, unless the floating charge restricts later charges and the fixed chargee is aware of this. Floating charges shall be registered under section 222 of CAMA, while fixed charges only need registration if they cover specific asset classes.[103]

I. "Quasi-security"

399 The quasi-security refers to various methods a creditor might use to improve its position in the event of a debtor's insolvency without taking a formal security interest. Quasi-security can influence the security provided by the debtor and their access to the affected assets. The rights it creates are rights usually against a person and not against assets. There are lots of types of quasi-security, including but not limited to:[104]

- **finance lease**: that transfers substantially all of the risk of ownership of a fixed asset to the lessee because generally the lender buys the asset to the borrower, and then leases it to him;
- **negative pledges**: commitments not to do certain things for the borrower;[105]
- **the sale and leaseback method**: that is a form of finance leasing where one party sells property to a buyer and the buyer immediately leases it back to the seller.

J. Sub-security

400 Cases where sub-security intervene. – Sub-security may arise when a person (the sub-security holder) benefits from another person's (the original security holder's) a security, as allowed by the terms of the original security. This can happen: (i) by taking security over the original security or (ii) by having the original security transferred to them. In both cases, the resulting interest in the original security is known as sub-security.[106]

Section 3. Direct agreements

401 Tripartite agreements. – Tripartite agreements are part of project finance documentation. They are usually required by lenders to create a direct relationship between themselves and the counterparties (usually between the lenders and the project company and third-party public authorities or counterparties of the project company). Tripartite agreements are sometimes referred to as consent deeds, direct

103 *The Gravitas Review of Business & Property Law, a Review of the Nigerian Law and Practice on Perfection of Charges, September 2021.*

104 Thomson Reuters, *Practical Law*, Pledges: A quick guide, 2024.

105 *See further developments herein on Negative pledges n°XXX.*

106 Thomson Reuters, *Practical Law*, Pledges: A quick guide, 2024.

agreements or side agreements. Since lenders are not parties to the project contracts entered into by the project company, they have no relationship with the parties to these contracts, which are key to the continued operation of the project. For their rights in relation to the project to be recognised, the lenders require the signing of direct contracts with the parties to certain project contracts such as the EPC or O&M contracts and, above all, the public parties.

402 Purpose. – The tripartite agreement sets out the circumstances in which the lenders financing the project can intervene in these contracts signed by the project company to remedy a breach or difficulty and avoid problematic impacts on the conduct of the project and the project finance documents. Although direct agreements often give rise to difficult negotiations, they are essential documents for the proper constitution of the project's financial documentation, ensuring its bankability.

403 Content. – Direct contracts generally contain one or more of the following stipulations:

- acknowledgement by the counterparty (e.g. buyer, host State, builder, O&M contractor) of the lenders' guarantee of the project company's rights under each relevant contract;
- an agreement by the counterparty not to terminate or suspend the contract concerned without first informing the lenders or obtaining their agreement;
- an acceptance that the lenders may substitute themselves for the project company or substitute a third party to perform or continue to perform the project company's obligations under the relevant contract, in the event of default or any other scenario unfavourable to continuity of service or concerning the execution[107] of the project.

404 Parties to direct agreements. – All the major parties to the project (whether builder, operator, purchaser, supplier, concessioning authority or host State) generally enter into direct agreements with the lenders (to which the project company may also be a party). The purpose of these agreements is to secure recognition of the lenders' position, and to agree to the assignment of the contracts as security for the benefit of the lenders. These contracts are usually negotiated at the same time as the other project contracts, and the form of the direct agreement is often appended to the underlying contract in question.

Under these agreements, the lenders' counterparty acknowledges that the underlying contract with the project company is secured for the benefit of the lenders. It also undertakes that any payments will be made to specific bank accounts (pledged for the benefit of the lenders) and that no changes will be made to the underlying contract without the consent of the lenders.[108]

107 ALSF, Energy Level 2.

108 E. R. Yescombe, *op. cit.*, pp. 133–135.

405 *Cure periods.* – It is often the case that lenders are notified if the project company is in default under the underlying contract and have the right to join discussions with the counterparty where appropriate. As such, lenders are granted "cure periods". These periods are relatively limited in the case of default by the project company on a payment obligation and longer for other types of obligation.

406 Step-in right. – Lenders often ask to be granted a "step-in" right, to intervene in the project contract to take control of the project or to appoint a third party to do so, in the event of default by the project company. The length of the step-in period is at the discretion of the lenders, and they can often exit at their convenience. The financial and technical capabilities of the new co-contractor must be acceptable to the other counterparties to the project in particular.

It is more of a guarantee or an assignment of contractual rights than a security, and this means of substitution by the lenders or their nominees will often be more of a deterrent than an effective measure, as the lenders will often want to avoid directly taking over the risks inherited from an ongoing operation. A step-in clause may be limited by the effect of insolvency law or the public procurement law of the country in which the project is being developed. Insolvency law often protects the project company from its creditors by mandating the continuation of contracts with the debtor, potentially preventing lenders from appointing a third party to take over control of the project. Similarly, national public procurement law may prevent the lenders from appointing a third party without first authorising a competitive tendering procedure for the operating contract.

Section 4. Instruments for securing SPV remuneration flows

407 Securing financial flows. – Securing the SPV's remuneration streams is crucial to the success of a project finance transaction. Investors and lenders alike are keen to ensure that these flows are as predictable and certain as possible. These flows must remain unaffected by exogenous factors beyond the control of investors. Several hedging instruments can therefore be put in place to cover these risks. As part of their due diligence, lenders identify the hedging instruments they wish to see put in place to enable them to participate in the financing of the project.

§ 1. Currency hedging

408 Fluctuations. – Lenders require the project company to hedge the risks associated with fluctuations in exchange rates, interest rates and/or commodity prices.

409 Hedging instruments. – Hedging can be achieved in various ways, through *swaps* or other types of hedging instruments. The financial institutions providing these instruments for financing a project are very often the same ones supplying the senior debt.[109] Hedging banks are generally part of the banking *pool* and, in return for a fee, will provide hedging instruments to protect the project company against all of these fluctuation risks.

109 ALSF, Energy Level 2.

410 Hedging foreign exchange risk. – For example, if the SPV's income is in local currency but the financing is in another currency, it will be crucial to be able to find instruments to hedge this exchange rate risk. In project financing, the aim will always be to obtain income in a currency identical to the repayments due to the lenders. However, there are cases where the SPV's income will be in local currency. In such cases, exchange rate *swaps* may be considered. This would involve a forward contract with a swap exercise period. It should be noted, however, that there are many different types of swaps, including open forwards, currency swaps and non-deliverable forwards. It is also possible to take out options to hedge this risk, giving you the freedom to buy or sell currencies at a set price with a defined exchange rate. This option, as its name suggests, is not a firm commitment, unlike a *swap*. The instruments available and chosen by the parties will depend on the situation in the country, the local currency and the project risks.

However, these swap instruments are not always available or may not be offered for long enough periods in Africa. An alternative often used is for public authorities or users to bear the exchange rate risk by incorporating ad hoc indexation arrangements into the infrastructure pricing mechanism.

§ 2. Hedging of interest rate risk

411 Interest rate hedging. – Similarly, in practice, the project company may be required to pay a variable interest rate to the lenders under the loan agreement and will therefore have an interest in fixing the interest rate under hedging arrangements in order to guarantee the certainty of future payment flows.[110] If rates rise without hedging, the SPV could face significant risks, particularly during the construction period, leading to an increase in interim financing costs. It is therefore very common for interest rate risks to be fully hedged during the construction period.

Key points to remember about hedging instruments

There are two main ways of hedging interest rate risk: *swaps* and *caps*. The swap is used to hedge by exchanging a variable interest rate on the market for a fixed rate at a certain price. This is often used for large-scale project financing. The cap will be used to hedge by capping the interest rate to limit its potential rise.

Where the dates of use of the financing are uncertain, certain option mechanisms may also be considered.

In practice, when formalising hedging tools, it will be common to refer to framework contracts and models drawn up by professional associations such as ISDA111 (International Swaps and Derivatives Association), which was set up in 1985, is based in New York and has 900 members covering around 70 countries. ISDA and its models can be used for all types of hedging (interest rates, exchange rates, commodity prices, etc.).

110 ALSF, *Public-Private Partnership (PPP) Projects in the Infrastructure Sector*.
111 https://www.isda.org/

§ 3. Hedging of counterparty risk (debt hedging)

412 Partial risk guarantee (PRG) and partial credit guarantee (PCG). – There are a series of guarantees that can be deployed by DFIs to reduce the counterparty risks encountered by the project company. These guarantees can enhance credit by mitigating risk and are known as partial credit guarantees (PCGs), partial payment guarantees or PRGs.[112] These guarantees involve organising the relationships between the host State of the investment, the offtaker, the lenders, the project company and the development finance institution providing the guarantee.

These tools are only available in limited quantities, as they are often the result of a multilateral agreement between a State and the multilateral banks concerned covering a capped envelope. Moreover, due to their cost and the procedure required to set them up, these tools are only available to very large projects capable of absorbing the associated transaction costs, leading to a form of race to the top.[113]

PRGs cover lenders and bondholders against the risk of non-payment of part of the debt service obligations for private loans or bonds over a period specified in the financing terms. These guarantees can take different forms, such as *bullet* payments of loan principal, subsequent maturities, rolling guarantees and non-repayable rolling guarantees.

PRGs are mainly used to cover debt default resulting from a risk of a State – or one of its agencies or entities – failing to meet its obligations.[114]

This makes it possible to extend the duration of private debt financing. Their longer maturity and lower borrowing costs can significantly improve the terms of commercial debt, resulting in lower rates for consumers and purchasers of the product.[115]

These instruments are used to hedge the government's contractual obligations towards the project, such as losses resulting from the government's failure to pay its obligations under a contractual commitment.

In addition to traditional political risks, these instruments can also cover:

- government decisions or failure to act that could adversely affect the project: changes to the law or regulations, taxes or incentives, etc;
- performance in relation to public counterparty contracts; or
- the impossibility of recourse to arbitration.[116]

413 Example of the ADF. – By way of illustration, the ADF, administered by the AfDB, has set up its own partial risk and credit guarantees.

112 ALSF, *Understanding Power Project Financing* – Version 1.1.

113 Antoine Huard and Benjamin Fremaux, *Solar energy in Africa: A Bright Future*, Institut Montaigne, 2019, p. 56.

114 PPIAF, *Public-Private Partnership Programmes: Creating a Framework for Private Sector Investment in Infrastructure*.

115 *Ibid.*

116 Tomoko Matsukawa and Odo Habeck, "Instruments de réduction des risques liés au financement des infrastructures: tendances récentes – Les innovations des prestataires ouvrent de nouvelles possibilités", *Gridlines*, note no. 20, May 2007.

In this respect, the partial risk guarantee was put in place to encourage private investment in low-income countries, with two objectives: to mobilise resources from the private sector and other co-financing institutions for ADF member countries, and to encourage governments to undertake strategic and budgetary reforms to mitigate the risks of not meeting their commitments.

The partial risk guarantee covers private creditors against certain political risks linked to the failure of a government or one of its agencies to honour its contractual commitments. These risks include: force majeure, currency inconvertibility, regulatory risks (changes to the legal framework) and various forms of breach of contract. This guarantee is therefore a leveraged instrument that only consumes a portion of the resources of the ADF of the beneficiary member country. However, it requires the latter to reimburse to the Fund any amount paid under the guarantee.

The Partial Credit Guarantee (PCG) was introduced by the ADF as an instrument designed to enable high-performing ADF countries and State-owned enterprises to overcome the obstacles they face in mobilising domestic and international commercial finance for their development needs.

In practice, this instrument partially guarantees the debt service obligations of low-income countries and efficient State-owned enterprises in these countries. The PCG thus enables low-income performing countries and SOEs to mobilise more financing on more attractive terms to meet their development needs. In practice, ADF countries are considered eligible for CCMs only if they are categorised as countries at low risk of debt distress (green light countries, according to the International Monetary Fund/WB debt sustainability framework) and recognised as having adequate debt management capacity.[117]

414 Indemnity agreement. – In addition to the PRG, which is signed between the development finance institution and the beneficiary, an indemnity agreement is signed between the host State of the project and the development finance institution and provides that the State agrees to indemnify the development finance institution if the latter intervenes to pay in respect of a payment claim made under the guarantee.

Some institutions may offer guarantees without an indemnity agreement at a cost that is nevertheless usually higher for the project, due to the absence of an indemnity granted by the government to cover the obligation.

As an alternative to an indemnity agreement, some DFIs may enter into a bilateral or treaty agreement with the government, which may also have an impact on the cost of cover.[118]

§ 4. Hedging of counterparty risk (hedging of payment obligations)

In addition to covering debt servicing, solutions are implemented to ensure that the obligation to pay invoices issued by the private partner is met. These liquidity

117 https://www.afdb.org/fr/projects-and-operations/financial-products/african-development-fund/guarantees

118 *Understanding Power Project Financing* – Version 1.1.

instruments make it possible to avoid triggering mechanisms for implementing guarantees under the PRG, which are lengthy and provide flexibility before the project defaults.

415 Letter of credit (LC). – In most cases, a letter of credit issued by a local bank will be put in place. It can be used by a project company if the public purchaser counterparty to the concession contract, for example, fails to honour a payment due on a regular basis. In the case of an IPP project, the amount covered by the letter of credit is generally equal to a few months' payments under the PPA.

If the purchaser fails to make payment within the contractual timeframe, the project company can directly demand for payment under this letter of credit. The project company can continue to be solvent and carry on business while being able to meet its overheads and service its debt, even if the buyer fails to pay. The buyer is usually required to replenish such a letter of credit fairly quickly after a drawdown, by paying the issuing bank under the credit and repayment agreement.

416 Reimbursement and Credit Agreement. – The Reimbursement and Credit Agreement refers to a specific loan agreement that can be put in place between the buyer and the bank issuing the letter of credit, providing that any drawdown made under the letter of credit is converted into a loan owed by the buyer to the issuing bank.

This loan is generally required to be repaid within six to 12 months from the date of the drawdown under the letter of credit. The agreement includes at least the standard restrictive clauses, events of default and conditions precedent as in any loan agreement.

This agreement will detail the cases giving rise to the bank's right of substitution. Termination or cancellation of the guarantee constitutes an event of default under the terms of the credit and repayment agreement, giving the bank the right to accelerate repayment and to mobilise any guarantees it may have taken out to secure itself: pledging of accounts, cash collateral or guarantee deposits, for example.

417 Guarantee for the benefit of the bank issuing the letter of credit (LC). – In addition, if the bank has concerns about the buyer's creditworthiness, the letter of credit can be guaranteed by another entity, such as the project host government or a development finance institution. In this way, if the buyer fails to repay the issuing bank, this entity will step in and reimburse the bank.[119]

Thus, if the buyer fails to repay the bank by the due date under the credit and repayment agreement, the bank may request payment from the development finance institution under a guarantee issued by the latter. Where appropriate, the development finance institution will then make payment to the issuing bank to settle the amount owed by the buyer.[120]

418 Indemnity agreement. – As in the case of RPMs, the development finance institution that has provided the counter-guarantee for the benefit of the bank issuing

119 ALSF, Energy Level 2.

120 *Understanding Power Project Financing* – Version 1.1.

the LOC may request in return (but not necessarily) that an indemnity agreement be put in place with the State, under which the latter agrees to indemnify the development finance institution if the latter intervenes to pay in respect of a demand for payment made pursuant to the guarantee for the benefit of the bank issuing the LOC.

419 Direct agreement. – Finally, to ensure the buyer's/client's commitment to the project and impose specific obligations in the project's interests, the development finance institution may request direct agreement to be drawn up.[121]

420 Illustration of payment risk hedging arrangements. – The diagram in Figure 10.2 illustrates the contractual structuring of the guarantee instruments between the parties involved in the case of a project finance PPI.

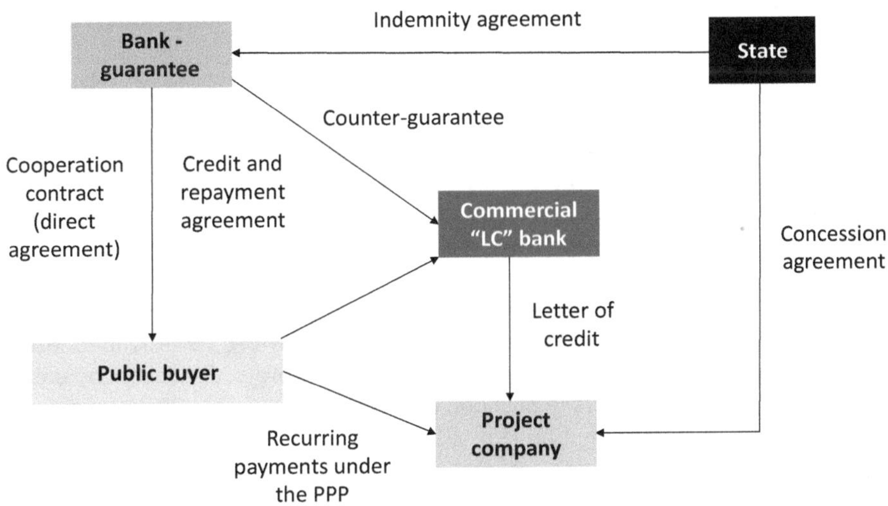

Figure 10.2 Illustration of payment risk hedging arrangements

Section 5. Other financing documents

§ 1. Account agreement

421 Order of payment. – Lenders seek to control the cash flow of the project company by stipulating the order in which payments of project revenues may be made and may therefore impose restrictions on the project company, particularly on the management of incoming and outgoing financial flows.

422 Cash waterfall. – Lenders require certain bank accounts to be opened and funds to be moved between the accounts in accordance with this payment cascade.

121 See details of direct agreements *above*, no. 344 et seq.

This movement of funds is regulated in the account agreement. The account agreement sets out the terms and conditions relating to the project's accounts, and the bank managing the account is responsible for maintaining the project's accounts, as a party to the account agreement.

When international lenders are involved in a financing, especially in situations where there are concerns about political stability or the enforceability of local security in the host country, the lenders often require that most of the project's financial accounts be held offshore. Debt and equity proceeds, along with project revenues, are generally deposited and held in the offshore accounts. Periodic transfers are then made to the onshore accounts to ensure that they contain sufficient funds to cover budgeted onshore expenses. Local sales are usually paid into the onshore accounts first, with any excess amount transferred to the offshore accounts once local expenses are covered.[122]

§ 2. Equity contribution agreement

423 Cash contribution. – This is the contract often signed by the project company's shareholders, in which they commit to subscribe equity. This document is key because it determines whether the project's structure and financing comply with the gearing debt/capital ratio. This contract involves several parties: the project company, the initial shareholders, the lenders' agent (also sometimes referred to as the *Global Facility Agent*), the *Offshore Security Trustee* and the *Onshore Security Agent*. In this way, the SPV's capital movements and the rights of each party subscribing to the capital or lending to the company can be structured. Such equity contribution agreement is also key to ensure the project's success by creating obstacles for the sponsors to abandon the project, encouraging them to remain involved on the long term and remedy difficulties if they arise and increasing the confidence of other parties in the project. Generally, banks will oblige sponsors to maintain a certain level of project ownership and cash contribution. This requirement typically lasts for the entire period of the loan agreement.[123]

424 Contributions in kind. – In some cases, shareholders may wish certain "in-kind contributions", such as land provided by a local partner, to be recognised as equity. In such cases, shareholders and lenders must agree on the valuation of the in-kind contributions, and lenders may require an audit of any valuation carried out.[124]

§ 3. Shareholders agreement

425 Although this document will often have been negotiated and put in place during the development of the project, it will be reviewed by the lenders to ensure the

122 John Dewar, *op. cit.*, p. 194.
123 IFC, Lessons of Experience, Project Finance in Developing Countries.
124 ALSF, Energy Level 2.

availability of equity or quasi-equity shareholder financing in the SPV and to verify the terms of its organisation and governance.

The shareholders' agreement can therefore reiterate the obligations regarding the provision of equity capital to the project company. However, as we saw earlier, a separate financial document such as the capital subscription agreement will often specify the equity contributions required, making it possible to establish a direct contractual relationship with the shareholders and make the equity contributions binding.

Shareholders' agreements take the form of a contract between the shareholders who are going to contribute capital to finance the project in order to form the SPV for the development, financing and operation of the project.

426 Contents. – The shareholders' agreement shall include *at least*:

- contributions of share capital;
- voting requirements;
- dividend distribution policy;
- management of the SPV;
- the terms of sale of the shares.

Shareholders' agreements regulate the relationships among shareholders and stipulate their rights and obligations; capital subscription agreements govern the movement of shares and the rights of each provider of capital. OHADA company law recognises their existence.

427 Conflict of interest. – It should be noted that conflicts of interest may arise if one of the shareholders is also a contractor or the host State. In such cases, the shareholders' agreement may exclude this party from taking certain decisions. The shareholders' agreement can also protect a minority shareholder, such as a local partner.

As part of the project, if lenders are concerned about cost overruns or the risk of a financing default, shareholders may be forced to commit contingent or reserve equity, which will probably have to be secured by a letter of credit or a guarantee.

Part 3

Project implementation

42-8 Managing the contractual life of the project. – Once the project financing is in place, the banks will disburse funds as the project progresses and as the project company's needs change. The infrastructure or project can then be developed, built and, in principle, carried out and delivered until it is completed and put into operation. However, the contractual life of this project financing continues and many events may occur.

429 Content. – In this Part 3 we deal with five main topics relating to the execution and management of project financing after financial close: Monitoring project implementation (Chapter 11), Managing changes and project completion (Chapter 12), Refinancing of the project (Chapter 13), Managing disputes arising from project financing (Chapter 14) and Insolvency of the project company (Chapter 15).

DOI: 10.4324/9781003616894-14

11 Monitoring project implementation

430 Importance of project's monitoring. – Project financing involves a very broad chain of contracts that can be divided into two categories, as described earlier: project contracts and financing contracts. It requires a large number of authorisations, as projects are often carried out on public land or in regulated sectors. The challenges of monitoring are just as critical as those of development or financing, because they involve a large number of parties over a long period and determine the success of the projects. To meet these challenges, it is important to refer to the backbone of the project, the main contract for managing the infrastructure: the PPP or concession contract. Issues of coordination and interfaces between the parties during operation must also be addressed.

431 Content. – In this chapter, we will examine the issues involved in this monitoring (section 1), the procedures for setting up an efficient monitoring interface (section 2), the principles of contractual management (section 3) and the specific monitoring of lenders (section 4).

Section 1. Monitoring issues

432 Chain of contracts. – The interlocking nature of the various contracts and authorisations makes project monitoring particularly delicate, as many of the players already identified will remain involved in overseeing progress. The more recent nature of project financing techniques on the African continent can make monitoring more difficult and implementation sometimes delayed, prevented or constrained. Local players in Africa do not always have full control over these global contracts and the human and operational structures that ideally need to be put in place to take advantage of them.

Monitoring during both construction and operation is one of the crucial issues for those involved in the project.

433 Construction phase. – At the construction stage, time is, more than ever, money, because delays in construction mean delayed operation, and every day without operation will represent an additional cost without revenue for the project company that has taken out financing, not to mention the increase in interim financial costs and the start of debt repayment where applicable. The risk during this phase is particularly sensitive for the project company, its shareholders and its

DOI: 10.4324/9781003616894-15

lenders. Similarly, in the event of delay or non-performance, the public party and users are unable to benefit from the project and the possible payment of royalties. The key to covering this risk is to ensure the quality and references of the builders, to transfer the risks to them[1] to cover them at the level of the project company and to follow the defined timetable closely to avoid any drift. In the first instance, it is the chosen construction companies that will be best placed to manage this risk and be accountable to the SPV and, in turn, to the public party during this phase.

The FIDIC Yellow Book model contract can be used as a basis by SPVs entrusting a third-party company with a construction project. The third party is obliged to produce reports containing precise information on the progress of the work, the state of human and operational resources, the controls carried out and to issue assessments in terms of quality, health and safety on the site or to indicate whether changes to the work have been proposed and whether there are any complaints, for example from subcontractors. When a project is financed by a PPP, the project owner is the SPV, and it is important to check how this information is to be transferred to the PPP contract and how it is to be implemented so that the parties are easily informed.

434 Operation phase. – During the project operation phase, it is essential that the project operates satisfactorily, so that there is sufficient revenue for debt service, and the project company is not in default or liable to be penalised or terminated. Similarly, as users and the public sector have delegated an activity that can often be described as a public service, proper performance is crucial to improving the economic and social environment. Commentators often note issues in terms of performance monitoring on Africa mega projects.[2]

435 Monitoring over time. – In this respect, it should be remembered that project financing can be considered a success not at the stage of financial closure but only when the construction phase is completed and a satisfactory level of service quality is ensured on a regular basis with satisfactory operation.[3] Indeed, to achieve VfM throughout the project's lifecycle, the public party must ensure that the planned allocation of responsibilities and risks is instituted, controlled, recorded and continually analysed and verified.[4]

1 As we saw in Part 1 Chapter 5 Section 1, it is therefore common practice to provide for lump sum turnkey construction contracts, with performance indicators and precise timetables, sanctioned by lump sum penalties which are often called *liquidated* damages in English-speaking jurisdictions and which can be likened to penalty clauses.

2 *Project Leadership and Society, 2024-12*, Vol. 5, p. 100123, Article 100123; Jackson Sekasi, Steven Harrod, Victor Andrade and Jacob H. Madsen, "Performance controls and accountability in African transport infrastructure megaprojects: A systematic literature review", *Performance Controls and Accountability in African Transport Infrastructure Megaprojects: A Systematic Literature Review – ScienceDirect.*

3 World Bank Group, *Promoting African Public-Private Partnerships to Investors*, 2009.

4 World Bank 2017, *Public-Private Partnerships: Reference Guide Version 3*, World Bank, Washington, DC, © World Bank [online]. https://openknowledge.worldbank.org/handle/10986/29052. License: CC BY 3.0 IGO.

436 Continuity of monitoring. – More generally, project financing is backed by very long-term contracts, often for more than 20 years. In these circumstances, it is important to bear in mind that project contracts will rarely anticipate all circumstances or events likely to occur during implementation, and those who initiated the project may no longer be working after the project began. The memory of the project then remains the contractual memory, without it often being possible to call upon the memories of the people who were initially at the table at the start of the negotiations and who have since left.

437 Performance monitoring. – Documented contract management and performance monitoring are essential for all parties committed to the project's success. This need seems even more obvious insofar as the infrastructure, once built and operated for a certain period, very often reverts to the assets of the public entity, which is most often responsible for operating it directly. To establish their rights and ensure that they meet their obligations, it is in the interests of all parties to ensure that they collect data relating to the monitoring of operations in a secure and permanent manner. They can use collaborative platforms and take advantage of modern digital tools.

Section 2. Establishing an efficient interface

§ 1. Organisation of a precise interface

438 References in the contract. – When assessing the stipulations included in the main contract (concession or PPP), it is essential to define the means that will enable the public entity and the SPV to establish a monitoring system throughout the project cycle, with tools that must be deployed during operation to manage effectively the partnership with the project company and ensure an efficient operational interface. This is even more critical given the scattering of responsibilities that is a constant in most African countries or projects, with numerous ministries responsible for different aspects, regulatory authorities and other public players potentially involved. It is imperative that the project company knows who to contact and who to answer to, and that it is sanctioned, if necessary, in the event of failure to comply, within the framework of a clear, transparent process that the contract identifies perfectly. Conversely, the project company and the lenders must be able to activate the defined communication channels in the event of default by the public entity or its representatives.

To remember

When drafting the clauses of the contract, an attempt should be made to concentrate the responsibility for monitoring for each party around a specific circle of restricted players coupled with a centralised storage tool containing all the data, correspondence, contracts and amendments relating to the project. For example, in the case of a public transport project in the form of a concession or PPP, it is advisable to clearly identify the responsibilities of the project company with regard to each public player, while indicating that the main counterparty of this company remains the ministry in charge of transport (or a transport organising authority) to facilitate the monitoring of the contract.

439 Managing crises that could affect the continuity of the project. – Unanticipated transient or permanent events can negatively impact the economic equilibrium of the contract and weaken the financing of the project. Examples include repeated acts of vandalism by users or acts of line piracy or sabotage, which are not uncommon in some African countries. The public sector/SPV interface makes it possible to create a rapid and effective link between the parties in order to jointly find solutions. It can be a more or less structured interface, as detailed later.

440 Risk management plan. – Very often, a risk management plan is drawn up by the SPV before the start of the project to then serve as a resource and guide throughout its execution. As part of this process, the public contract manager can gather relevant risk monitoring information from the private party, as well as relevant external information (such as economic trends in visitor numbers, for example), in order to regularly update the plan.[5] Among the major risks to consider, the prevalence of terrorist acts across Africa is a significant factor to take into account.

As part of a broader risk management plan, the contract manager must:

- monitor indicators against expected levels to identify emerging risks. For example, the fact that traffic levels are not increasing as expected may signal a potential risk of a public payment guarantee being triggered;
- take planned mitigating action where there are risks that the executing agency can control (or ensure that the private sector does). For example, if the host State is responsible for the associated infrastructure that is falling behind schedule, the plan may be to transfer responsibility for that infrastructure to a senior team within government, or to the private party;
- even when risks cannot be controlled, possible actions and responses should still be considered. For example, if flooding threatens essential water service facilities, the public party can begin to work with the private sector on an emergency response, including replacement supplies, rationing and a plan to restore services. The usefulness of the interface can be particularly marked when temporary or permanent actions have not been anticipated and may call into question the economic equilibrium of the contract.[6]

5 World Bank Group, "Implementing PPP projects", *in Guide de référence des partenariats public-privé*, version 3, PPP Knowledgelab, 2017, pp. 178–186. https://pppknowledgelab.org/fr/guide-kl/sections/75-monitoring-and-managing-ppp-delivery-and-risk
6 *Ibid.*

§ 2. Structuring the interface

441 Project appraisal. – In PPP projects for project financing in Africa, the evaluation carried out during the project feasibility stage is essential. On the one hand, it can be a means of ensuring that the objectives set by public policy are achieved and, on the other, a means of realising the benefits sought. In addition, such evaluations can be an essential source of data providing lessons that can be used at a later stage to develop the partnership process and improve the approach to the market, as well as increasing feedback on project financing so as to increase its volume on the continent.[7] As early as the appraisal stage, it is therefore possible to outline the contractual monitoring required during construction and then during operation of the infrastructure.

442 Classification of interfaces. – The activities involved and the skills required to ensure the viability of project financing vary depending on the stage of contract execution. The stages of project execution can be listed as follows: design, construction, operation, preparation of financial closing and execution of project construction.

443 Monitoring committee. – To ensure that service performance and compliance with the contract are monitored, it may be useful to designate a person or form a team, such as a monitoring committee, comprising a representative from the public entity, the private entity and the users or customers.[8] The size and importance of this interface is determined by the scale of the investment involved, the duration of the contract and the technical nature of the services provided.

It is important to provide for a relay from the original project team to the project team dedicated to contract monitoring. Unfortunately, however, this is rarely done in practice. This original team is often called upon if requests are made during implementation. You must always ensure that you can mobilise the people from the initial project team who were involved in the feasibility and structuring of the project.

444 Committees. – The interface can thus be ensured, either through an informal monitoring committee or by the creation of a joint monitoring committee as stipulated in the contract. A real entity with its own budget, possibly financed under the public-private partnership contract, may be envisaged for the largest projects. In any event, the role, resources and composition of the interface must be detailed in the contract.

For example, at the commissioning stage, in order to monitor the project's performance, it is appropriate to carry out regular monitoring operations, which make it possible to report to the public authority on issues relating to the project's progress, safety and environment. Both the public authority and the lenders are directly involved in ensuring that the construction phase is properly managed, so that it can be brought to an efficient operating phase as quickly as possible and under the best possible conditions.[9]

7 World Bank Group, *op. cit.*
8 *Ibid.*
9 *Ibid.*

Practical tip

The role of the interface or committee may be more or less important, depending on the direction taken by the public authority, the scope of the outsourced services and the duration of the project funding. In particular, the interface is responsible for the following tasks:

- receive documents for examination;
- commission contradictory expert reports;
- check compliance with the obligations of the public authority and the private partner;
- make comments to the SPV and request additional information or explanations;
- give formal notice to the SPV or receive formal notices and complaints from the SPV;
- confirm the application of penalties affecting the remuneration of services;
- negotiate or compromise;
- terminate the contract if necessary and handle litigation.[10]

445 Role of expert bodies. – Most African countries that are developing or promoting PPPs using the project finance model have set up or are still developing public bodies to support the development of privately financed infrastructure.[11] These bodies are often experts in the legal and financial structuring of general interest infrastructure investment projects, particularly those requiring private finance. Its tasks are usually as follows:

- promote the development of investment projects desired by public authorities and provide specific expertise in financing techniques, engineering, financial modelling of projects and knowledge of the infrastructure market;
- help to optimise the value and overall cost of investment projects for public bodies, drawing on external expertise;
- help to identify and manage the legal, financial and budgetary risks for public bodies in relation to various public contracts (concession contracts, PPPs, global public contracts), financing law and public business law.

446 Attachment. – These bodies support the international economic development and cooperation activities of government departments in their areas of competence and carry out activities in conjunction with the relevant departments of the economic and financial ministries and other ministerial departments. In some countries, these bodies may be attached to the Presidency of the Republic, the Prime Minister's Office or the Ministry of Finance.

10 François Lichère, Boris Martor, Sébastien Thouvenot and Gilles Pédini, *Pratique des partenariats public-privé – Choisir, évaluer, monter et suivre son PPP*, LexisNexis/Litec, 2009.

11 See Annex 4 on the various African PPP laws.

447 Purpose. – They can help public bodies to optimise the legal and financial structuring of their investments, particularly when they use a global contract – design, construction, maintenance, operation – and/or when they call on external financing (bank debt, equity).

448 Advisory services. – In practice, these bodies offer their services to public bodies such as ministries of state, local authorities and public establishments. They also act as a point of contact for all public and private players in the field of public infrastructure and financing.

449 African expert bodies. – In Africa, PPP units often play an essential expert role in their institutional framework by providing support and expertise to public ministries or entities carrying out PPP projects with public or concessionary payment.[12] In practice in Africa, these bodies are unfortunately often more involved in the project procurement phase than in the implementation phase.

450 Centre of resources and expertise. – The PPP unit is setting up a resource and expertise centre to assist with the legal and financial aspects of setting up PPPs. Its area of activity can be divided as follows:[13]

- by providing support and assistance to the authorities responsible for the projects, in particular by advising the authorities directly or by developing methodological models and guides, or by developing training courses;
- in a role of validating the implementation options proposed by the project leader.

451 Role. – In this context, it should be noted that the PPP unit may become involved at various points in the life cycle of project financing in the form of a PPP:[14]

- for the validation of studies prior to the launch of a PPP award procedure;
- during the key stages of the award procedure;
- to issue an opinion on the PPP contract before it is signed; and
- during performance monitoring.

452 Capacity building. – The PPP unit can take on tasks relating to capacity building for institutional players, the provision of decision-making support tools and the standardisation of practices to enable the implementation and monitoring of balanced contracts that best protect the interests of the contracting public entity.[15]

453 African PPP units. – Many African countries have a PPP unit: Benin, Burkina Faso, Cameroon, Côte d'Ivoire, Gabon, Mali, Niger, Senegal, Kenya, Ghana, Mozambique, Uganda, Egypt and Zambia.

12 Africa PPP Initiative, *Public-Private Partnership, Definitions and tools: PPP Unit.* http://www.initiative-ppp-afrique.com/Partenariat-public-prive/Definitions-et-outils/Unite-PPP

13 *Ibid.*

14 *Ibid.*

15 *Ibid.*

454 Guinea. – In Guinea, the PPP Unit is responsible for monitoring projects at each stage of their life cycle introduced by Law No. 2017-32 of 4 July 2017 (0032/PRG/SGG/2017/AN). The Unit works alongside the PPP Committee, which oversees PPP policy in the Republic of Guinea, and the Public Procurement Regulatory Authority (ARMP), which ensures and guarantees independent regulation of PPP award procedures in line with Decree D/2014/167/PRG/SGG on the organisation and operation of the ARMP and the Public Procurement Code.

455 Côte d'Ivoire. – In Côte d'Ivoire, the National Steering Committee for Public-Private Partnerships, abbreviated to CNP-PPP, is the decision-making, validation and guidance body of the institutional steering framework, responsible for assisting the government in implementing strategies and actions aimed at developing public-private partnership projects.

456 Senegal. – In Senegal, a PPP unit equipped with legal and financial expertise assists public authorities with PPP projects. Its remit is based on the latest PPP law standardising the PPP system, No. 2021-23, adopted on 21 February 2021, and the implementing decree of 27 October A 2021.

Although most African countries have established such units, in practice the question arises as to the actual resources and skills available to these units to effectively help monitor the contracts signed for project funding, given their complexity.

Focus on OFPPP and UNAPP in Senegal

Taking Senegal as an example, the country has developed a toolbox containing the essential documents for preparing public-private partnership projects, as well as information on the procedures and legislation applicable to them.

Against this backdrop, Senegal's Ministry of Investment Promotion, Partnerships and Teleservices Development has created the Department of Financing and Public-Private Partnerships (DFPPP). The DFPPP acts as the PPP Unit, helping to define and implement the State's PPP policy. It provides technical and legal support to the contracting authorities during the preparation, negotiation, management and monitoring of partnership contracts.

Rationalisation of the bodies involved means that the National Public-Private Partnership Support Unit (UNAPPP) will be responsible for providing advice and technical assistance to the contracting authorities throughout the project cycle. In practice, this Unit will provide support to the contracting authorities in identifying, preparing, negotiating and monitoring projects.

Section 3. Contract management

§ 1. Principles derived from long-term contracts

457 Contractual monitoring. – Project finance management also involves monitoring the stipulations of the main contract governing the delegated service, such as the concession contract or PPP signed between the project company and the public party. This contract necessarily contains elements relating to deadlines, the monitoring of the application of its requirements, and the management of the relationship between the public and private sector partners from the date of effective implementation of the contract until the end of the contract term.

458 Contractual clauses. – The clauses included in the contract concluded between the SPV and the public sector have numerous consequences for its performance over a relatively long contractual period. It is therefore important to ensure that there is close monitoring and control between the partners to ensure that the contract evolves and is implemented on a long-term basis throughout the life cycle of the project.

In practice, throughout the duration of the project, contract management aims to ensure:

- uninterrupted delivery of services to a high standard in accordance with the contract, with payments or penalties calculated accordingly;
- the maintenance in practice of contractual responsibilities and risk allocation, and effective management of the responsibilities and risks assumed by the public sector;
- detection of changes in the external environment, both risks and opportunities, and effective action as a result.[16]

459 Time and cost management. – In particular, the parties must ensure that all phases of the project are completed within the deadlines set out in the PPP contract and within the projected costs. The project company is obliged to deliver quality goods and services and to respect the expected quantity, while making any necessary adaptations made essential by changing needs or events not anticipated when the contract was evaluated and awarded. All these elements are also subject to verification by the lenders.

§ 2. Monitoring the achievement of performance targets

460 The characteristics of performance monitoring. – Performance is essential when the private partner is delivering the service or project to ensure the quality of the goods built or equipment developed, which must last throughout the contractual period. In this context, if the goods built or the equipment developed

16 World Bank 2016, *Public-Private Partnerships: Reference Guide Version 2*, World Bank, Washington, DC, © World Bank [Online]. https://ppiaf.org/documents/2968.

are returned to the public entity, control seems particularly essential. As the PPP contract is performance-based, it is necessary, as part of the monitoring process, to ensure that the contractually defined performance levels are achieved. The performance criteria clearly define what is expected of the private entity, in terms of the quality and quantity of the assets and services to be provided.[17] They are sanctioned by penalties or, in the case of better performance, by bonuses in certain contracts. These may, for example, relate to deadlines, costs, or quality and quantity standards. In practice, this may involve defining standards for road maintenance or the quality required in terms of service, or even targets for extending connections as part of public services provided directly to users.[18] In addition, the relevance and rigour of the contractual clauses must enable the smooth running of the public-private partnership to be monitored, and thus the proper repayment of the funding that enabled it to be set up.

461 Practical difficulties encountered in monitoring performance. – The difficulty in verifying performance can be explained by a lack of technical expertise within the public entity, which is nevertheless essential to fully understand the management of the project. In addition, the public entity may struggle to access the accounting and financial information needed to fully understand the true costs of the SPV, as well as the productivity gains. Among the items that can be identified as the most difficult to assess are structural costs, internal re-invoicing (between the SPV and the parent company), IT costs, provision of services (premises, cars, staff), assistance services (IT maintenance), provisions for major repairs, renewal, obsolescence, etc.[19]

These difficulties necessarily mean that the contract must detail the different degrees and methods of control.

Focus on the MMR account

In infrastructure projects, the concession or PPP contract stipulates that the SPV must maintain and service the project assets on a regular basis and carry out periodic renewal and maintenance operations if necessary. Remuneration for this service is generally clearly identified.[20] An MMR programme is therefore usually appended to the concession contract, which will be periodically updated and monitored by the parties. A specific guarantee may be required from the SPV to ensure that the works are restored to their original condition. In addition, a specific bank account may be required to ensure that the SPV makes the necessary provision for MMR items. At the end of

17 World Bank Group, "Implementing PPP projects", in *Public-Private Partnerships Reference Guide*, version 3, PPP Knowledgelab, 2017, pp. 178–186 [online]. https://pppknowledgelab.org/fr/guide-kl/sections/62-performance-requirements

18 World Bank 2016, *op. cit.*

19 François Lichère, Boris Martor, Sébastien Thouvenot and Gilles Pédini, *op. cit.*

20 V. Haubert-McGetrick and G. Ansaloni, *Financement de Projet, Enjeux juridiques et bancabilité d'une opération*, *op. cit.*, pp. 74–75.

the concession contract, the grantor receives any positive balance in this account. This positive balance can be offset against other amounts that may be paid by the parties at the end of the term.[21]

462 The use of evaluation data. – As we have seen, upstream evaluation of the management method should make it possible to clearly provide the key performance indicators, which should be confirmed when the contract is put out to tender or possibly adapted during the dialogue or negotiation. Thus, the evaluation serves as an investment in the future of the project if it makes it possible to anticipate needs and performance indicators[22] which will be sanctioned by bonuses/maluses.

§ 3. Monitoring and control procedures

463 Controls at the level of the public entity. – The PPP laws in each country may provide, at the level of the public entity, for controls to oversee the procurement and execution of projects. The texts relating to PPPs in Kenya[23] and Egypt[24] provide examples of such controls.

464 Controls at private partner level. – Generally, the SPV is responsible for submitting performance data related to the project to the contracting authority in the form of regular reports. The content, format and frequency of these reports must be specified in the contract[25] but they may also be taken from national texts relating to PPP law. For example, the PPP contract may stipulate that the SPV is responsible for drawing up a site organisation plan before the public facilities are built, or a monthly report on the progress of the works, with site meetings organised. Checks can also be carried out at the time of acceptance of the work by the public authority. During the operating phase, monitoring may take the form of an operating report including, in particular, incidents and equipment faults, the procedures to be implemented and followed by staff in the event of a fault, the actual working hours of the operating and maintenance staff assigned to the service, or an inventory of the equipment replaced, for example.

465 Contractual controls. – Beyond traditional performance monitoring tools of the PPP contract, specific contractual clauses may allow for more detailed monitoring of contract performance. The parties may provide for a *benchmarking* mechanism enabling them both to assess and compare the costs of providing the services

21 See no. 465 *below*.

22 *Ibid.*

23 See in particular the mandate and function of the Kenya PPP Unit at the URL: Mandate & Functions – Public Private Partnership Unit (https://www.pppunit.go.ke/).

24 Ministry of Finance, *Public Private Partnership PPP & The Egyptian Experience*, 2013, [online], accessed 17 Sept. 2021. https://www.mcit.gov.eg/Upcont/Documents/20134151031MoF-%20 11%20Apr%202013.pdf

25 World Bank 2016, *op. cit.*

entrusted by the SPV on the market to different third parties. These costs are likely to change during the performance of the contract, and to modify the contractual stipulations in financial and technical terms if the choice of service providers is modified.

To remember

In practice, the public party may ask the SPV periodically to provide, or on certain specific dates, information on the cost of providing the services in relation to the market prices for the same services, which will enable the private partner to specify the average price for each service. Project contracts can also include "performance clauses" that allow the private partner's remuneration to vary according to the achievement of a certain number of contractually defined objectives (level of patronage, quality of service, etc.). In this respect, the performance criteria for the execution of the PPP project must necessarily be "SMART" (Specific, Measurable, Achievable, Relevant and Time-bound).[26]

466 Control levels. – Control can occur at several levels:

- by providing the contracting authority with performance data relating to the project in the form of an annual report or any other document listed in the contract;
- by carrying out site visits. Independent experts can carry out checks on service standards in the fields of construction and maintenance;
- by organising accounting and financial audits;
- by sending satisfaction questionnaires to users. Service users have important information about the quality of the service and the prevalence of faults.[27]

467 Sanctions. – If the SPV fails to fulfil its obligations, the public authority must necessarily impose penalties. In practice, such sanctions may take the form of specific penalty payments or penalties under the concession contract, particularly in the event of failure to provide documents or access to premises or information. In the case of a PPP with public payments, it would be useful for the contract to provide that the amount of these penalty payments may be set off against the sums due as remuneration to the private partner.[28] These penalties must, however, be calibrated so as not to affect the continuity of the service and to retain an incentive role that does not prevent the project company from having sufficient cash flow to service the project debt taken out with the lenders.

26 World Bank 2016, *op. cit.*

27 *Ibid.*

28 *Ibid.*

468 Meeting clauses. – The parties may include so-called rendezvous or meeting clauses to allow the partners to meet and check that the partnership is progressing in accordance to the performance criteria determined contractually. In the event of difficulties, these same clauses can usefully be combined with clauses for renegotiating contractual amendments and/or mediation and dispute resolution if the difficulties persist.

469 External audits. – Carrying out[29] external audits by independent consultants can give the public authority an overall view of the project finance operation and enable it to check the actual conditions under which it is being carried out.

Section 4. Specific monitoring of lenders

470 Risk monitoring. – After the conclusion of project financing, the risks for lenders remain high, despite having negotiated various protection mechanisms or guarantees in the financing documentation and even directly in the project contracts, which they have reviewed during their audits and sometimes asked to modify.

471 Monitoring the work. – In particular, it remains critical for them to ensure that the infrastructure is properly built and handed over, and that it is operating correctly to generate the revenues required to service the debt. Monitoring both construction and debt servicing is particularly important from the lenders' point of view. They will therefore closely monitor the construction and handover operations, requesting information directly or through their technical advisors.

472 Meeting deadlines. – Lenders want to monitor the progress of the work and ensure the project company is meeting its contractual obligations on time. The importance of meeting deadlines is particularly evident during the construction phase of an infrastructure project. In Africa, given the difficulties involved in managing PPP contracts, the time taken to implement project financing can often be long, requiring particular attention to be paid to the timetable. Similarly, problems with the delivery of goods can generate tensions on the timetable, to which lenders will be very sensitive. For example, lenders will want to monitor the timetable for completion of the work and may order audits to look more closely at the *reporting* that the project company has been able to provide on a regular basis.

473 Provision of documents and alerts. – Lenders require the SPV to provide audited financial statements to assess its operational and financial situation on a regular basis. Under the terms of the financing agreements, the SPV is often responsible for issuing warnings if certain thresholds are exceeded, such as non-compliance with certain ratios. As we shall see later, the lenders will also be called upon in the event of changes to the project.

474 Cost control. – Another critical element particularly closely monitored by lenders is cost control. Even if the project company has included elements in its model that allow room for manoeuvre, the risk of cost overruns can put the SPV

29 See example sequence *below* n° 514.

and the lenders at risk. These can arise from modifications to the project required to correct design problems, changes to the execution of the project or an underestimation of the costs of the goods and services required for the work.

Focus

Cost control means that particular care must be taken when drafting the clauses of the PPP contract used to finance the project, in particular to mitigate the following risks:

- maintenance risk: maintenance clauses must be extremely detailed, particularly with regard to the regularity of interventions;
- asset insurance risk borne by the private partner making the infrastructure it has financed available to the public sector and users;
- service quality risk: in the event of failure to meet its obligations, the SPV will have to pay sufficiently significant compensation so that the risk is always borne by the private partner; a bonus-malus system may also be envisaged;
- risk linked to the operating costs borne by the SPV: the contract must stipulate that the price paid will not fluctuate according to the additional costs incurred by the project company (operating or maintenance cost drift, structure or financing).[30]

475 Verification of quality and quantity standards. – Lenders also want to verify that the borrowing project company meets the quality and performance standards required by its contractual commitments to the project host country, as well as the quality standards of the sponsors and international norms. The quality of the service provided, as well as the quantity, are governed by precise contractual clauses allowing the public entity to carry out regular and unannounced checks, but such possibilities are also often offered to lenders in the financing documentation.

In quantitative terms, they may also require the company to confirm that it has achieved a certain level of technical performance (minimum performance ratio, for example).

476 Compliance with the terms of the credit agreement. – Among the elements provided for in the credit agreement, lenders want to ensure that the representations and warranties granted by the SPV are complied with. In addition to identifying breaches of these representations and warranties, the financial institutions involved aim to prevent any issues that could jeopardise the SPV or the project they are financing. They therefore want to ensure that they can suspend or stop drawdowns, exercise their security or take any other

30 François Lichère, Boris Martor, Sébastien Thouvenot and Gilles Pédini, *op. cit.*

appropriate measure as quickly as possible. The various ratios defined (DSCR, LLCR, leverage, for example) will serve as monitoring tools for the lenders throughout the repayment of the financing. If certain ratios fall below the levels accepted by the lenders, the latter may require the amount of the debt to be reduced, request partial repayment of the loan by exercising a *cash sweep* on available cash or notify an event of default likely to result in the loan becoming due and payable.

477 Operational compliance with ESG criteria. – We saw in section 2 that ESG criteria are decisive for lenders. They require lenders to verify the reality of the project company's and the project's compliance with the Equator Principles[31] and/or environmental and social safeguard policies and relevant international environmental standards that have been accepted by the parties. This check may also encompass the conditions under which the private partner effectively involves local companies, in compliance with national legal requirements and the rules defined contractually with the host State.

478 International sanctions. – It is not uncommon in Africa for certain countries to be subject to international sanctions, such as those imposed by the UN, the European Union, the United States of America or ECOWAS. However, lenders will usually require, as part of the financing documentation, that the borrower does not use the loan proceeds to directly or indirectly finance (or otherwise making available) the activities of any person or entity on the UN sanctions list, nor contribute to or make available the proceeds of the loan to any other party known to use them for such purposes. If the situation of a State and the project company's counterparties changes and such commitments can no longer be met, the lenders must then decide on the fate of the loan granted for project financing.

479 Renegotiation during a health crisis. – In most African project finance cases, the impact of the health crisis from 2020 onwards may require the renegotiation of the SPV's financial commitments, a revision of the ratios accepted by the SPV in the credit agreement, a request for a *waiver*, i.e. for the bank to waive the exercise of certain rights, or even the introduction of refinancing or the granting of additional deadlines for the repayment of certain instalments. It may also be necessary to make broader adjustments to contracts as a whole, for example by extending contractual deadlines, agreeing to waive penalties for late payment, granting advances or sharing additional costs. In many cases, these exceptional measures have to be chosen by the parties to the project so that they apply until the crisis is over, or on a more permanent basis until the end of the contract. A case-by-case approach is usually adopted.

31 *The Equator Principles,* first published in 2003, are a set of provisions for sound risk management in project finance, adopted by financial institutions. They enable the identification, assessment and management of social and environmental risk in project financing. For a French version of their detailed content: https://equator-principles.com/app/uploads/EP4_French.pdf. The measures they propose are graduated according to the type of project implemented.

12 Managing changes and project completion

480 Almost inevitable changes. – Throughout the term of a PPP contract – generally ten to 30 years – and during the period of repayment of the financing, events may occur which could not have been foreseen at the time the contract was signed. These can make it necessary to negotiate changes to the project documentation and sometimes to the financing documentation.

The parties must also manage the end of the project as entrusted to the private partner. In some cases, difficulties or disputes will require changes to be made, and if these cannot be agreed, they may lead to arbitration or even termination of the contract. Nevertheless, even if it is impossible to avoid such risks, it is possible to control them and thus avoid blockages or the failure of the project.[1] Cases where litigation becomes a reality are dealt with below in Chapter 14.

481 Plan. – We will look at the cases of modifications initiated by the parties (section 1), modifications due to the occurrence of external events (section 2), the procedures for introducing riders (section 3), then the cases of assignment of the contract (section 4) and finally the management of the end of contracts (section 5).

Section 1. Modification by the parties

§ 1. Renegotiation opportunities

482 Renegotiation obligation. – Project financing in the infrastructure sector is conducive to recurring renegotiations, given its long duration, in order to allow adjustments to be made in the light of new information or new circumstances relating to the project environment. This is because PPPs involve complex, long-term commercial and financial arrangements in highly regulated sectors and sometimes involve rapidly evolving technological assets. The projects are also influenced by political considerations and are often surrounded by uncertainties about the condition of existing assets or the lack of commercial data and information about the situation on the ground. By way of illustration, on other emerging continents comparable to Africa, around 75% of PPP contracts in the transport sector and 87%

1 World Bank 2016, *op. cit.*

DOI: 10.4324/9781003616894-16

of PPP contracts in the water and sanitation sector are renegotiated at some point during their contractual life.[2]

483 Impacts on the project. – The consequences of poor management or implementation of the renegotiation process can have adverse effects on the project, including reduced revenue streams or service standards, and public or government opposition to private sector participation in other projects, which would reduce the range of tools available to the State to improve and transform infrastructure services.[3]

However, renegotiation has many advantages, such as adjusting the terms and conditions of a project to take account of the requirements of that project or the needs of the public or enabling the parties to adapt the documentation in the face of unexpected events and changes.[4]

484 Influence of lenders. – It should be noted that lenders may wish to prevent changes to the PPP contract that they believe would impact the bankability of the project by altering the creditworthiness of the project company or the risk profile of the project.[5] In practice, lenders may wish to veto any changes that would require the project company to materially alter its risk profile, which may include an amendment to significantly increase the size of the project as an example.[6]

§ 2. Terms of renegotiation

485 Purpose of general interest or related to the public service. – Since PPP contracts are classified as administrative contracts in most French-speaking countries, the contracting authority may legitimately make unilateral changes to the conditions of performance of the contract or terminate it on the grounds of public interest or public service, provided that it financially compensates the loss suffered by the private partner, as we shall see below in section 5 on managing the end of the contract.

486 Other reasons for modification. – Apart from these cases, modifications at the initiative of the public entity may be motivated by changes affecting the performance of services, by the impact of refinancing the project company's debt or linked to the consequences of a change in the legal or regulatory regime applicable to the project.[7]

2 Straub, Laffont and Guasch, *Infrastructure Concessions in Latin America: Government-Led Renegotiations*, World Bank Policy Research Working, 2005.

3 Jeffrey Delmon, *Public-Private Partnerships in Infrastructure, a Practical Guide for Policymakers*, The World Bank, PPIAF, 2010.

4 *Ibid.*

5 *Main PPP Guidelines October 2006: Guidelines for the Provision of Infrastructure and Capital Investments through Public Private Partnerships: Procedures for the Assessment, Approval, Audit and Procurement of Projects Government of Ireland.*

6 See in particular, ALSF, *Public-Private Partnership (PPP) Projects in the Infrastructure Sector*, Norton Rose Fulbright. https://alsf.academy/sites/default/files/2020-06/PPP%20Handbook%20-%20FR_0.pdf

7 See in particular, *Le guide EPEC des PPP: Manuel de bonnes pratiques.*

In any event, the project company must not be forced to make a change that might be impossible to carry out or that would result in a breach of the legislation applicable to it.

487 Limits on the right to amend. – It should be emphasised, however, that the public entity cannot unilaterally amend all the clauses of the PPP contract without upsetting its general structure. Thus, legitimate amendments can only be minor, so that the essential clauses of the contract, such as the purpose clause or the remuneration clause, cannot be fundamentally called into question by the public entity.

488 The consequences of the amendment. – The outcome of the modification procedure by the public entity often leads to the project company being compensated if modifications are made. This compensation may take the form of a direct compensation payment or an adjustment to the revenue-sharing mechanism provided for in the PPP contract.

The project company may have the right to propose changes itself, but the public authority is generally not obliged to consent to them, unless the change is necessary to comply with a change in the law and there is no increase in cost for it and the users. It may also be tempting to consider requiring that a proportion of the savings made be passed on downwards in the tariffs paid by it or by users as a condition of its consent.[8]

Section 2. Modification by external events

489 Types of external impacts. – Certain events beyond the control of the project company may also occur and have a negative impact on the completion of the project.

In contracts relating to large-scale projects, such events can be divided into the following categories: force majeure (§ 1); fait du prince and legislative and fiscal changes (§ 2); disruption of the general scheme of the contract or unforeseeability (§ 3); and unforeseen circumstances (§ 4).

§ 1. Cases of force majeure

490 Distinction. – Beyond the classic definition of force majeure by reference to the civil codes applicable in French-speaking jurisdictions or by reference to stipulations and case law in English-speaking countries, it is common practice in African project documents to circumscribe, on the one hand, traditional cases of force majeure in order to better explain them and organise their consequences and, on the other hand, to develop a separate definition for what is commonly called political force majeure.

In common law countries, the doctrine of frustration may terminate a contract if an unforeseen event occurs after the contract is concluded, through no fault of either party, which makes performance either physically or commercially

8 See in particular, ALSF, *Public-Private Partnership (PPP) Projects in the Infrastructure Sector*, *op. cit.*

impossible, or radically alters the obligation. English courts may find that a contract includes an implied term allowing for discharge if an event significantly changes the nature (in addition to the cost or burden) of the contractual obligations. However, the doctrine's application is often limited by the widespread use of force majeure clauses, which specifically address such unforeseen events.[9]

491 Ordinary or traditional force majeure. – In order to organise the terms and conditions relating to changes in the execution of the project, project contracts usually make a distinction between cases of ordinary force majeure and cases of political force majeure, with each case being dealt with differently.

In most countries, recognition of a case of force majeure will be based on the fulfilment of three cumulative conditions:[10]

- unforeseeability: first of all, the SPV must be faced with an unforeseeable event on the date the contract is concluded;
- externality: the event must be external to the co-contracting parties;
- irresistibility: the consequences of this event, which could not be foreseen at the time the project was concluded, must be irresistible, i.e. the debtor of the contractual obligation was unable to avoid its effects by implementing appropriate measures.

In practice, the parties will therefore refer to these criteria when reviewing the project contracts and checking that they do not include more detailed clauses for interpreting any force majeure situation. It is advisable to ensure that all project and finance contracts include force majeure clauses drafted as closely as possible, if not identically, in order to facilitate their interpretation and enforcement.

Example of a classic definition of force majeure from a concession agreement in a French-speaking sub-Saharan African country

Force majeure refers to an event that meets the conditions listed in the French Civil Code. In addition, the parties have agreed that the following events will be considered as cases of force majeure if the conditions of this code are met:

- lightning, fires, earthquakes, tsunamis, floods, storms, cyclones, typhoons, tornadoes and other natural disasters;
- chemical contamination or explosions unless caused by the fault or negligence of the affected party or its representatives;
- epidemics, quarantines or health scourges in the territory of [X];

9 John Dewar, *op.cit.*, p.96.
10 CE, 29 January 1909, *Cie des messageries maritimes*.

- accidents (such as air or rail disasters and shipwrecks) unless caused by the fault or negligence of the affected party or its representatives;
- strikes taking place outside the territory of [X];
- any act of war (declared or not), invasion, armed conflict, revolution or embargo, occurring in any case outside the territory of [X];
- any act of rebellion, riot, insurrection, act or series of acts of terrorism or sabotage, occurring in any case outside the territory of [X].

492 Case of Covid-19. – In the case of the Covid-19 crisis, the conditions relating to exteriority and unforeseeability often appear to be fulfilled. On the other hand, irresistibility is often more difficult and must be assessed on a case-by-case basis to demonstrate that the SPV is unable to continue performing the public contract.[11] If we refer to laws applicable in France, which is often a benchmark in French-speaking Africa, the administrative judge assesses force majeure very strictly and did not automatically apply force majeure in recent epidemics, hence the importance of drafting and qualifying it in contracts relating to project financing in Africa. Force majeure is used more in the case of natural disasters, again depending on the exceptional nature of the climatic phenomenon: the storm of December 1999 in France[12]; pollution affecting a spring water catchment site, which prohibits its use for a period that could last up to two centuries[13]; a tidal wave in a port causing waves of up to seven metres in amplitude as a result of a drop in sea level of more than two metres.[14] As French-speaking African States often refer to the case law of the French Conseil d'Etat, force majeure is rarely accepted in these States in the absence of a clause expressly providing for its application and authorising it more broadly than the strict criteria of the law or those commonly accepted.

493 Political force majeure. – Given the sometimes unstable nature of certain countries in Africa and the greater local risk factors in certain areas, it is common to anticipate that certain risks caused by the State or which could be avoided, controlled or limited by the State or its subdivisions, such as obtaining certain approvals, authorisations or the occurrence of political unrest or events for which the State or public parties can be held entirely responsible, such as the expropriation of assets or the imposition of capital controls, are subject to compensation as soon as they have an impact on the project company. They are often referred to as political force majeure or sometimes as adverse State events.

11 F. Linditch, "Crise sanitaire et contrats publics: libres propos sur la force majeure", *JCP* A 2020, 2123, Contrats-Marchés publics, 2020, 14.

12 CAA Nantes, 5 November 1998, *Mutuelles du Mans Assurances*, req. no. 94NT00398.

13 CE, 14 June 2000, *Commune de Staffelfelden*, no. 184722.

14 CE, 11 December 1991, *Sonexa*, no. 81588.

Example of a definition of political force majeure

Political force majeure means any act or omission of a public authority occurring in the course of the performance of the agreement and preventing one of the parties from performing all or part of its major obligations in the territory.

This includes, in particular, the following, provided they meet the aforementioned two conditions:

- any international sanction, embargo, act of hostility, act of terrorism or act of sabotage that may occur in the territory;
- industry-wide strikes, national strikes of political origin, riots, demonstrations, popular uprisings, which may occur in the country;
- any failure to issue, renew or reinstate any of the authorisations and permits or the issue of such authorisations and permits;
- a change in the law that would make it impossible to perform the main obligations of this agreement;
- the expropriation, requisition, confiscation, compulsory acquisition or nationalisation of all or part of the concessionaire's shares or all or part of its assets or rights in the project;
- any security or health situation in the country requiring an alert to be issued to foreign nationals by their respective Ministries of Foreign Affairs recommending that they do not travel to the country or region in which the project is built and operated.

494 Management of ordinary or political force majeure. – Most of the time, the parties provide for a mechanism of notification and exchange with specific forms allowing the situation of force majeure to be justified in order to characterise it, even if this means refining the assessment initially made. The parties generally meet to find ways of continuing or reorganising the contractual relationship. If, after a certain period, no solution is found or there is no change in the situation, compensation is determined on terms such as those defined below in section 5 for the termination of contracts. From the lenders' point of view, debt servicing can, to a certain extent, be covered by the amounts available in the DSRA.

495 Extended force majeure. – The parties must manage the changes or sometimes the termination of the contract as a result of a situation of force majeure known as "prolonged force majeure", i.e. including a period beyond the fixed period for meeting, finding solutions and organising changes in performance. In general, if the project is no longer viable and/or if the parties cannot agree to modify their relationship, and depending on the reasons for the force majeure situation, the contract may be terminated by mutual agreement, with different compensation consequences depending on whether the situation is one of ordinary or political force majeure.

496 Insured events. – In principle, insurable events are excluded from the force majeure clause. In the majority of cases of property damage, these events are likely to be insured by the licensee. Consequently, business interruption insurance must be taken out to cover subsequent loss of revenue. Because of the existence of insurance or insurable risks, these events generally do not necessarily give rise to compensation from the State, at least if insurance can cover all or part of the losses, additional costs or damage. It should be emphasised that where insurance is taken out, it is also limited in time. In the absence of insurance – as is the case for events that do not give rise to compensation by the State, such as a strike by the project company's own staff – the State may envisage that the concessionaire bears part of this risk and that the lenders ask the concessionaire to set up a debt service reserve account to control this risk. However, if the case of force majeure persists and the project remains in financial difficulty, the lenders may no longer be able to meet this risk with the SPV and, for this reason, most PPP contracts provide for termination without fault.

§ 2. The fait du prince and compensable legislative and tax changes

497 French origin. – A brief development is devoted to this theory because it can be used in most of the French-speaking countries of the continent even if it is less developed than in France. The theory of fait du prince *stricto sensu* refers to a measure taken by the public authority, the contracting authority, outside the PPP contract binding it to its co-contractor, but which affects the conditions of performance of the contract.[15] It should also be remembered that many judges and arbitrators often refer to French case law as a basis for their interpretations. We therefore set out in the following several French contextual elements and references that have been taken up by many African laws.[16] For example, Article 51 of the Constitution of Cameroon, which appears in Title XII relating to transitional provisions, states that the texts previously in force on the date on which the Constitution took effect (largely French law) continue to apply until they have been replaced by legislative or regulatory texts adopted pursuant to the said Constitution. Insofar as Cameroonian public contract law has been largely inspired by French public law, we believe it is possible to draw on certain case law solutions developed by the French administrative courts to interpret certain provisions of contracts governing the financing of an African project if they are not sufficiently clarified by Cameroonian case law and administrative doctrine in this area.[17] The same approach also applies to many French-speaking African countries.

15 CE, 1er mars 1967, *Société des Ets Petitjean*, *Rec.* 97.

16 Jean-Marie Mboko Dj'Andima and Félix Vunduawe te Pemako, *Traité de droit administratif de la République démocratique du Congo*, Bruylant, no. 1920 et seq.

17 For more perspectives on the influence of French public law in post-independence Francophone Africa, see Lukas Perichon, *Les entreprises françaises et la commande publique en Afrique*, Université Paris Saclay (COmUE), 2019.

498 Distinction. – This theory of fait du prince differs from force majeure, unforeseeability or unforeseen circumstances in that the external nature of the parties is not a criterion for qualification. However, this theory may be useful in interpreting the concept often found in contracts relating to project financing of "compensable legislative or regulatory changes" or unfavourable decisions which sometimes give rise to the right to compensation in certain contracts developed on the continent.

499 Verification of the nature of the administrative intervention. – The application of this theory first requires consideration of the nature of the intervention likely to give rise to the application of the theory of the fait du prince and, more particularly, whether a legislative change taken by the contracting authority is likely to constitute a fait du prince:

> It may happen that a general measure, legislative or regulatory, has the effect of modifying the very provisions of certain administrative contracts, of paralysing some of them or of putting a premature end to their performance. The general nature of such measures does not prevent the doctrine of fait du prince from being applied in such cases, provided however, in the case of formal legislation, that the legislature did not intend to exclude compensation.[18]

500 Right to compensation. – For example, the Conseil d'Etat has recognised a printer's right to compensation following the termination of a contract by the entry into force of a law[19] unless the law itself excludes all compensation.[20] As long as the law does not exclude compensation, it is necessary to check whether the conditions for applying the doctrine of fait du prince have been met:

- the existence of damage caused by the administrative measure taken by the contracting authority[21];
- the unforeseeability of the harmful event[22];
- the harmful event is attributable to the contracting public authority.[23]

Once the conditions are met, the rule is that the loss is compensated in full, which corresponds to the amount of the expenditure actually incurred by the project company and caused by the act of God, as well as the lost profit that it could legitimately expect,[24] unless the loss is only partly due to the co-contracting administration.[25]

18 A. De Laubadère, F. Moderne and P. Delvolvé, *Traité des contrats administratifs*, LGDJ, T. II, 2e ed. 1984, p. 529.
19 CE, 12 févr. 1886, *Société des publications périodiques, Rec.* 137.
20 CE, 7 déc. 1894, *Cie algérienne, S.* 1896, 3, 89; CE, 28 juin 1967, *société des Ets Skalli, Rec.* 284.
21 CE, 8 March 1941, *Amat, Rec.* 99.
22 CE, 14 May 1926, *Rec.* 498.
23 CE, 9 July 1929, *Le Clainche, Rec.* 706; CE, 4 March 1949, *Ville de Toulon, Rec.* 197.
24 CE, 23 avr. 1948, *Ville d'Ajaccio*; CE, 25 janv. 1953, *sté des alcools du Vexin, Rec.* 50.
25 CE, 28 nov. 1928, *Tanti, Vaudron et Brûlebois, Rec.* 940.

501 Contractual protection against legislative changes. – Changes in legislation may lead to an increase in a project company's costs or a reduction in its revenues and, in some cases, reduce the internal rate of return for shareholders. In practice, the change may apply to all project companies operating in the country concerned, or it may be considered discriminatory if it affects only one category of project company. By way of illustration, most electricity purchase contracts concluded in emerging markets include stipulations protecting the project company against the effects of such a change. In practice, they allow an increase in the tariff or, in some cases, a lump-sum payment from the purchaser or the State to the project company. Alternatively, PPAs may provide for an increase in the presumed availability of a project, a decrease in the target availability, particularly when the legislative amendment limits the amount of energy that can actually be produced, and/or an extension of any relevant deadline that the project company is required to meet.[26] Where a legislative change makes it impossible to perform the project contract, the project company will normally have the right to terminate the contract and will obtain a level of compensation assessed in the same way as in the case of termination for force majeure of a political nature.[27]

502 Compensation. – Thus, the project company must not find itself in a better or worse situation than it would have been without the legislative change, so that this event cannot be assimilated to a default by the project company. Similarly, for example, to the extent that the change causes a delay in the COD, the plant will have to be considered as operating on the initial date. Or, again in the case of an IPP project, if the plant is unavailable due to a change in legislation, the project company will be able to rely on deemed availability or payments for deemed energy generated. Finally, the project company will, in the presence of appropriate contractual stipulations, receive either (i) direct compensation to reimburse the cost or shortfall, or (ii) an appropriate tariff increase.

503 Compensable tax changes. – Project contracts often provide for a form of fiscal stability. In this way, a tax change that may have a negative impact on the revenues of a project and make it economically untenable should be compensated. Compensable forms of tax change may arise from a revision of the tax rate, the creation of a new category of tax or the abolition of tax concessions, or the imposition of customs duties that increase the price of goods to be imported by the project company. In general, in order to establish a compensation mechanism for the project company, reference is made to significant changes likely to have a negative impact on the project's return on investment and/or its ability to service its debt beyond a certain threshold to be defined. In practice, the consequences of such a tax change must lead to an increase or reduction in project costs, maintenance and operating costs and/or revenues expected by the project company[28] and must be demonstrated in order for the contractual compensation mechanisms to operate.

26 V., ALSF, *Training materials – Level 2 – Power Course Handbook.*
27 *Ibid.*
28 *Ibid.*

To remember

In the practice of project financing in Africa, the contractual clauses will most often provide for cases of compensation events that can be assimilated to fait du prince or compensable legislative changes, taking care however to define them and to circumscribe their application by means of compensation ceilings and/or thresholds for application.

§ 3. Disruption of the contractual terms

504 Economic disruption. – A disruption to the general scheme of the contract may give rise to compensation if an unforeseeable event beyond the control of the parties at the time the contract was entered into has occurred, causing a temporary disruption to the general scheme of the contract. In this respect, the circumstances in which compensation may be triggered and the methods for determining and paying this type of indemnity may usefully be set out in detail in the concession or PPP contract. For example, this compensation can be used to cover all extra-contractual costs, defined as those that were not foreseen by the parties at the time the contract was entered into.[29]

Even if, in practice, in the event of difficulties encountered during the execution of the project by the SPV arising solely from a disruption to the economic equilibrium of the contract linked to a macroeconomic shock, the two partners must reach a compromise within the framework of the renegotiation of the contractual terms,[30] it is preferable to provide for contractual clauses organising such cases in order to deal with them. This is all the more true given that for instance the scale of the Covid-19 health crisis and its consequences on certain sectors, such as transport, have created significant imbalances.

In lending transactions, a clause, often referred to as a Material Adverse Change (MAC) clause, allows the lender to declare a default if there is a significant negative change in the borrower's financial situation or circumstances (such as a substantial decline in successive financial statements). MAC clauses are commonly included in facility agreements. They are typically subject to extensive negotiation; they are rarely used to trigger a default.[31]

505 Contingency. – In the absence of a contractual mechanism for unforeseeable circumstances and in French-speaking African countries, the SPV may try to refer to the theory of unforeseeability. This theory originated in French administrative law and was developed to allow "the holder of an administrative contract to ask the

29 François Lichère, Boris Martor, Sébastien Thouvenot, Gilles Pédini, *op. cit.*

30 Frédéric Marty, Arnaud Voisin and Sylvie Trosa, *Les partenariats public-privé*, La Découverte, 2006.

31 Thomson Reuters, *Practical Law*, Material adverse change (MAC) clause: share purchase agreement, 2024.

Administration for partial compensation for the loss it suffers, in the event that the occurrence of unforeseeable events outside the control of the parties disrupts the cost price of the services".[32]

Several conditions must be met:

- the unforeseeable nature of the event that makes it difficult to perform the contract;[33]
- the event is external to the parties to the contract;[34]
- continued performance of the contract by the administration's co-contractor despite the difficulties encountered, provided that the administration has not suspended or terminated the contract;[35]
- the economy of the contract must be "absolutely disrupted" regarding the contract in question alone, thus creating an operating deficit.[36]

If these conditions are met, the co-contractor can generally claim compensation before the courts for part of the operating loss strictly linked to the unforeseeable event. Unforeseeable events never allow for full compensation.

This theory, which originated in France, is found in most French-speaking African countries. For example, under the terms of Article 121 of Senegal's Code des obligations de l'administration, unforeseeable circumstances exist

> when circumstances beyond the control of the contracting party and unforeseeable at the time the agreement is concluded upset the economy of the contract, resulting in a shortfall for the contracting party, the latter may obtain that the contracting authority bear part of the loss it has incurred in order to ensure the continuity of the public service.

Initially applied to public service delegation agreements, unforeseeability can also be used in the case of another public contract.[37] The Senegalese code was drawn up after independence but incorporates elements of French administrative law, in particular to facilitate the management of public contracts.[38]

This theory of unforeseeability has been adopted and used in public law in other African countries. For example, the Egyptian Council of State was the first of the

32 CE, 30 March 1916, *Compagnie générale d'éclairage de Bordeaux*, no. 59928.

33 CE, 22 févr. 1963, *Ville d'Avignon*, *Rec.* 115.

34 CE, 8 nov. 1935, *Ville de Lagny*, *Rec.* 1026.

35 CE, 9 déc. 1932, *Compagnie de tramways de Cherbourg*, n° 89655.

36 CE, judgment, 30 March 1916, *Cie générale d'éclairage de Bordeaux*, aforementioned; CE, 21 Oct. 2019, *Société Alliance*, no. 419155.

37 Binty Diop and Seynabou Samb Tosco, "Regards croisés sur le contrat administratif et le contrat de droit privé éprouvés par la crise", 12 April 2020.

38 Alioune Badara Fall, "Le Code des obligations de l'administration au Sénégal", *in Mélanges en l'honneur de Jean du Bois de Gaudusson*, Presses universitaires de Bordeaux, 2014, p. 225.

African Arab Councils of State to adopt the theory of unforeseeability in administrative law.[39] It is also found in Moroccan law.[40]

506 Case-by-case analysis. – Unlike force majeure, we have not to date identified any case law in Africa based on unforeseeability to compensate co-contractors in connection with the financing of projects that suffered operating deficits during the Covid-19 pandemic. While in the case of Covid-19, the conditions relating to unforeseeability and external factors are often met, those relating to the disruption of the contractual economy and the suspension or termination of the contract require a case-by-case assessment, often involving detailed financial expertise, in order to separate the causes and attribute the additional costs or loss of revenue associated with these different causes.

§ 4. Unforeseen circumstances

507 Distinction. – This theory is similar to the theory of unforeseeability but differs in that it is applied mainly in works contracts and always concerns difficulties of a material nature, whereas the events giving rise to the theory of unforeseeability are circumstances of an economic nature or sometimes of a natural nature.[41] Once again, this theory, which originated in France, can be used in most French-speaking African countries. It is even codified in Senegal[42] as for unforeseeability.

508 Conditions. – The conditions for applying the theory of unforeseen circumstances are as follows:

- an unforeseen difficulty is a material difficulty resulting essentially from a natural phenomenon (unforeseen terrain problems, unexpectedly large quantities of excavated earth, bodies of water to be drained, etc.);[43]
- the unforeseen hardship results from a circumstance external to the parties;[44]
- the unforeseen hardship is a difficulty that could not have been initially envisaged by the parties;[45]
- the unforeseen hardship is a difficulty of an absolutely abnormal nature.[46]

509 Compensation. – Under the theory of unforeseen circumstances, the compensation that may be claimed by the co-contractor from the government must

39 Salma Seifelnasr, *Regards croisés sur la théorie de l'imprévision en droit des pays arabes et en droit français*, Université Montpellier, 2020.
40 Mohamed Amine Benabdallah, "Contribution à la doctrine du droit administratif marocain", *Revue marocaine d'administration locale et de développement*, coll. Manuels et Travaux Universitaires, vol. 3, 2020.
41 A. De Laubadère, F. Moderne and P. Delvolvé, *op. cit.*
42 Code des obligations de l'administration du Sénégal, art. 118 et seq.
43 CE 29 avr. 1953, *Commune de Moissac*, *Rec.* 724.
44 CE, 22 June 1945, *Belvisi, Rec.* 133.
45 CE, 22 déc. 1976, *Depussé, Rec.* 575.
46 CE, 30 July 1948, *Rol Lister*, *Rec.* 359.

cover the resulting expenses that exceed those that should normally have resulted from the contract[47] but in fixed-price contracts, there must be a disruption of the economy of the contract as in the case of unforeseen circumstances.[48] The application of this theory to PPP contracts in French-speaking African countries is the subject of debate, and some authors limit its application to public works contracts, thus excluding global contracts.

To remember

In order to apply all these theories and elements of compensation, it is useful to check in the risk matrices established during the development of the project how the treatment and allocation of these risks have been determined from a contractual point of view before proceeding with any request for compensation or contract amendment.

Section 3. Setting up endorsements

510 Impact of amendments on legal documentation. – In addition to the cases of external events discussed later, or of indemnification by the public entity, cases of revision of signed contracts may arise. Renegotiation to change the structure of the project and the contracts requires the drafting and signing of amendments to the project contracts. These changes may also require amendments to the financing contracts or the obtaining of waivers, if certain impacts in terms of investments and financial capacities of the project company are envisaged as a result of the changes or if these changes have an impact on the coverage ratios, in particular, the financing documents through the covenants clauses.

511 Competitive tendering for amendments. – If the amendment has an impact on the balance and scope of the project, another question that may arise is whether the amendment and the rider should be subject to an advertising and competitive tendering procedure under the national system for PPPs or public contracts. In general, it is considered that the amendment does not substantially change the purpose of the initial contract or alter its structure, unless it constitutes a new contract that is subject to a new and independent competitive tendering procedure. It is advisable to check the rules applicable to public procurement and PPPs at the local level to see whether any elements need to be considered in order to comply with a specific competitive tendering procedure in the event of an amendment. This is often tricky, as most countries in Africa do not always have specific rules or case law in this area.

It should also be noted that the issue of riders, their quantification and the organisation of the correlative consultation procedures can usefully be resolved

47 CE, 2 déc. 1964, *Port autonome de Bordeaux*, *Rec.* 936.
48 CE, 6 May 1936, *Régnier*, *Rec.* 508.

by inserting contractual clauses in the project documentation, in particular in the concession contract.

> **Focus**
>
> If we refer to the principles generally applied in France, it is often considered that an amendment made by means of a rider for an increase of more than 15% in the amount of the initial investment represents an upheaval in the economy of the contract which is likely to require a competitive tender.

Section 4. Assignment of contract

512 Change in the public entity. – Given the often delicate financial situations of public companies and governments in Africa, one of the risks for the SPV is insolvency on the part of these entities or dealing with a reorganisation of the public sector. Such reorganisation may result from financial challenges that lead to reforms and modifications of existing contracts. The contracting public entity may also disappear for other non-financial reasons, given the number of events likely to occur during the term of the contracts.

> **Example**
>
> This may be the case of a national public electricity company which purchases the electricity produced by the project company which holds a concession contract with the State in the same country. In the event of the restructuring of the national company, the State may be asked to continue to guarantee the obligations of the restructured entity, even if the concessionaire cannot oppose such restructuring, if the restructured entity has sufficient financial capacity and technical skills and makes a commitment to the concessionaire to fulfil the obligations of the substituted entity under the PPA. It may be stipulated that if the public party fails to comply with such stipulations, the concession contract may be terminated to the detriment of the State.

In such cases, the lenders necessarily require to be consulted at the same time and before any changes are made to the contractual documents linking the project company with the public parties.

513 Assignment of contracts by the SPV. – It is rare that the parties intend to assign the contracts that are the subject of the project, given that the structure of the project is set up in a specific manner and is dependent on existing entities. There are cases linked to step-in situations, as we have seen, or to the implementation of direct agreements at the initiative of the lenders. If a contract transfer occurs in other circumstances not envisaged in the initial documentation, the public authority must ensure that the new project operator has adequate technical and financial capacity and that the lenders have accepted the change. It is therefore always subject to prior authorisation. In some countries, such a transfer may also involve a competitive tendering process.

> **To remember**
>
> The transfer of a contract should not be confused with the transfer of shares in the project company, which is often subject to authorisation but may be more easily granted depending on the criteria set out in the concession contract, which may set authorisation thresholds based on the percentage of shares transferred or on an actual change in control of the SPV.

Section 5. Managing the end of the project

514 Stakes for the parties. – The project may come to an end naturally, or the parties may wish to terminate it at the initiative of one of them, by mutual agreement or due to the occurrence of a triggering event. In general, the public authority wishes to anticipate taking over the project, either on a public-private basis or by adding teams of its own to take over the management of the assets covered by the project financing, or to put the project out to tender and choose a new concession operator to take over the management on an outsourced basis.

The public authority wants to be sure that, when it leaves, the project company in place will leave it with assets in a condition that complies with the contractual requirements, while guaranteeing the takeover of staff, potential customers and equipment.

A distinction must be made between early termination and termination at the end of the contract.

§ 1. Early termination of the project

515 Unilateral right of termination. – In principle, in most French-speaking countries, the public party has the right to terminate the main contract unilaterally, due to the administrative nature of the contract. Sponsors, the SPV and lenders are often concerned by this concept and, as a result, they seek to contractualise a whole series of undertakings enabling them to organise precisely the pecuniary consequences of a termination decided by the public party unilaterally. While the value of such arrangements has been discussed in French administrative law, French case law does not always have an equivalent in Africa, even though many countries can refer to it.

516 Cases of termination. – The PPP or concession contract most often distinguishes several cases of termination: termination for reasons of general interest or public service, termination for fault on the part of the project company and termination for fault on the part of the public entity, as well as cases of force majeure. As we have seen, termination indemnities may vary in each case, and we set out in the following some guidelines for calculating them.

517 Compensation. – In the event of a reason relating to the general interest or a fault on the part of the public entity, the project company is generally compensated for all costs incurred as a result of the termination, the investments made, including all amounts of debt and financial costs, as well as all or part of the loss of revenue over the remaining term of the contract. In the event of fault on the part of the project company, only the elements relating to the value of the unamortised investments or the repayment of the debt and the payment of the financial costs are due to it.

518 Example of an indemnity clause. – The following example shows one possible method of calculating the compensation due to the SPV in the event of early termination of the contract.

> In the event of early termination of the Concession Agreement, the State pays the Concessionaire a termination indemnity calculated in accordance with the terms and conditions of this article.
>
> For the purposes of this article, the following words and expressions shall have the meanings set out below:

"A"	All outstanding amounts of credit granted by the Lenders to the Licensee under the terms of the financing agreements, as well as all amounts (other than the outstanding amounts of credit mentioned above) not yet paid and due by the Licensee to the Lenders under the terms of the financing agreements, including the following amounts: The entire outstanding principal under the financing agreements, plus accrued and capitalised interest under the same financing agreements as at the Termination Date; – Interest, late interest, credit breakage costs, additional costs, fees, taxes and incidentals owed by the Licensee to the Lenders under the financing agreements and due as at the Termination Date; and – Expenses, costs, penalties and indemnities incurred by the Lenders for the termination of *swaps* securing the Financing Agreements or other hedging instruments and payable by the Licensee as a result of the termination of this Agreement.
"B"	The amount of equity, consisting of the sum of the amounts invested in the Project by the Shareholders on the Termination Date, whether in the form of capital contributions or loans granted by the Shareholders in favour of the Concessionaire, less the sums reimbursed or paid to the Shareholders.
"C"	An amount corresponding to compensation for loss of earnings is calculated [method of calculating compensation for loss of earnings].

"D"	The amounts necessary to fully compensate the Licensee and the Lenders for all taxes of any kind (income tax, withholding tax, etc.) due in the Host State, as well as all other costs, deductions or compulsory levies in connection with the payment, conversion or transfer abroad of elements "A", "B" and "F" of the Termination Fee.
"E"	Costs associated with the early termination of contracts signed by the Concessionaire to carry out the construction and operation of the licensed assets, but only to the extent that: 1) these costs are the direct consequence of the termination and fall into one of the following categories (a), (b), (c) and (d): a: costs resulting from the cancellation of orders for any materials, equipment or goods, or any sub-contracts entered into, where the cancellation of such orders or the termination of such sub-contracts cannot be effected without incurring such costs; b: any expenditure incurred in anticipation of the future provision of services or the future performance of work, where such expenditure is not reimbursable; c: demobilisation costs, including the cost of moving equipment used in connection with the Project; and d: redundancy payments. 2) these costs result from the application of agreements entered into in the normal course of the Concessionaire's business and on the basis of reasonable commercial terms, and excluding any loss of profits calculated over a period exceeding one (1) year from the Termination Date; and 3) the Concessionaire and its sub-contractors have made their best efforts to mitigate these costs where possible.
"F"	On the Termination Date, the value of the Power Plant shall be assessed by an independent expert (appointed by agreement of the Parties or, failing that, by the International Centre for Expertise of the International Chamber of Commerce). If this amount is greater than the sum of the items (A + B + C) defined above, the positive difference between these two amounts is added to the Termination Indemnity. On the other hand, if the value of the concession assets (as determined by the Independent Expert) is less than the sum of the elements (A + B + C) defined above, the negative difference is deducted from elements B, C, D and E as long as their payment to the Concessionaire by the State is stipulated in the following table.

The amount of the Termination Fee is determined according to the cause of the early termination. The Termination Indemnity is then calculated on the Termination Date as follows:

Circumstances of termination	*Amount of termination indemnity*
a. Termination of this Agreement by the Concessionaire for an Event of Default by the State or for prolonged Political Force Majeure or for reasons of public interest	If F is positive: = A + (B + C + D + E +F) If F is negative: = A + (B + C + D + E – F), with the proviso that (B + C + D + E – F) cannot be less than zero to ensure that the project is bankable.
b. Termination for prolonged Ordinary Force Majeure	If F is positive: = A + ([. . .] % B + D + E + F) If F is negative: = A + ([. . .] % B + D + E – F), with the proviso that ([. . .] % B + D – F) may not be less than zero to ensure that the project is bankable.
c. Termination by the State for default by the Concessionaire	If F is positive: = A + (D + F) If F is negative: = A + (D – F), with the proviso that (D – F) must not be less than zero to ensure that the Project is bankable.

It is specified that the amount of the Termination Indemnity will be reduced by the sum of the following elements assessed on the date of its payment, and unless the corresponding amounts have already been charged to the debt relating to the Financing of the Project:

(i) all sums received by the Concessionaire or the Lenders under insurance policies or indemnities for any reason whatsoever in connection with the Project and which have not been allocated to the repair or replacement of the Power Plant or to the reimbursement of the Lenders;
(ii) on the date of payment, any sum standing to the credit of the Concessionaire's accounts and available for repayment of the debt relating to the Project Financing (including any sum standing to the credit of the debt service reserve account relating to the Project Financing);
(iii) where applicable (and without double counting), any amounts received from hedging banks for the unwinding of hedging instruments (including SWAPs);
(iv) the amount of equity called and not injected by the Concessionaire's Shareholders;
(v) any amount received by the Concessionaire or the Concessionaire's Shareholders as compensation for expropriation in accordance with Guinean law;
(vi) the Restoration Costs as defined in the Concession Agreement.

The Concessionaire will calculate elements "A", "B", "C", "D", "E" and "F" with reference to the date of the Termination Notice. The Parties have agreed that in all circumstances, the Termination indemnity will be at least equal to the amount of element A referred to above.

The State is deemed to have accepted the calculation if it does not notify the Concessionaire of its disagreement within thirty (30) days of the sending of the Notification of Termination, accompanied by all the documentation on which the Concessionaire based its calculation.

If the State questions the Concessionaire's calculation within this thirty (30) day period, the calculation of elements "A", "B", "C", "D", "E" and "F" will then be carried out by an Independent Expert of international renown in accordance with the Article providing for his intervention. In any event, the French State must pay the Termination Indemnity as specified in the Concession Agreement.

It should be noted that these terms and conditions, as given in the preceding by way of example, must be defined taking into account the specific nature of each project, the relevant precedents in each country and the contracts already signed or accepted by the sponsors and lenders in the country for comparable projects.

519 Payment arrangements. – Given the sometimes very rapid implementation of this termination and the continuity of the SPV's financial commitments to the lenders, it is important to provide for a mechanism for the rapid payment of indemnities and associated guarantees. The direct agreement between the State or the public entity and the lenders can deal in particular with this case.

The amount of the termination indemnity may, for example, be paid within a short period of time from the notification of termination as follows: for the amount of the indemnity whose calculation is not called into question, the State must transfer this amount to the concessionaire's bank account, and for the amount of the indemnity that is called into question, the State may transfer the disputed amount to an escrow account designated by the lenders, specially opened for this purpose, and which may in some cases be located abroad. The sums placed in escrow may then be paid to the project company or to the State depending on the findings of the independent expert, if this is provided for in the PPP contract and appointed, and if the parties agree. In the event of a manifest error on the part of the independent expert, invoked by one of the parties, they may have recourse to the dispute resolution procedure. This is only one of several possibilities that can be established contractually and must be adapted on a case-by-case basis.

520 Disputes. – In the event of a dispute over the amounts of compensation, the parties may, depending on the case, use the means of mediation, expert appraisal or dispute resolution described later, as chosen by the parties in the legal documentation.

In addition to the aforementioned elements specific to the early termination of the project, the elements described as follows for the termination of the project at the end of its term may also apply in the event of an early termination.

§ 2. The consequences of ending the project early or at the end of its term

When the project comes to an end, and even in the case of early termination, other areas of focus are staff, assets and the business including customers.

521 Inventory of assets. – In order to transfer operation, the public party may ask the concessionaire to transmit all data such as the list of current contracts, operating files, work and maintenance reports and supply contracts.

522 Fate of assets. – The PPP or concession contract also governs the fate of the assets according to a distinction inherited from the practice of concessions in France: the return assets, which automatically revert to the public party, the trade-in assets, for which a balancing payment may be made, and the own assets, which in principle remain the property of the project company.

This distinction is not found in all countries or in all contracts in Africa, but in practice it has the merit, upstream and at the time of the transfer, of raising questions about the materiality of the assets, their future usefulness and their decisive nature for the takeover and transfer of the project.

The parties may have organised in advance a site audit, joint on-site visits to review ongoing maintenance work and exchange related documents.

It may be agreed between the parties in the concession contract, or during this takeover period, that any work that has not been completed will remain the responsibility of and be financially borne by the project company in place if it is the latter that has undertaken the work, in order to retain responsibility for its completion.

523 Responsibility during the contractual period. – Regarding the activities of the project company, the contract may usefully have provided for the handover of all types of internal operational documents such as files of customers or subscribers using the infrastructure. The concessionaire is responsible for the service provided and for collecting the invoices relating to all the obligations it has entered into during the contractual period. It is also responsible for all disputes arising or to arise during this same period.

524 Accounts. – The concession agreement may provide that, at the end of the concession, the parties will settle their reciprocal claims, thereby offsetting existing claims and debts between the SPV and the host State. The claims that may be asserted by the SPV include, for example, termination indemnities if applicable, any balances relating to provisions for the renewal of works recorded in the MMR account, and amounts relating to the purchase of trade-in assets or assets that have not been depreciated. The State may claim the amount of scheduled work that has not been carried out before the end of the concession contract, outstanding penalties, costs charged to the SPV for restoration if these costs are deemed relevant following the inventory carried out at the end of the concession, or claims relating to concession assets that may be missing as a result of the same inventory.

To remember

To avoid difficulties relating to settlement operations, it may be appropriate to provide for a contractual settlement mechanism whereby the parties notify their claims, can then carry out their reconciliations or disputes within a certain period, and then agree on the accounting reconciliations. It will be useful to have a deadline beyond which no dispute can be made and to organise a mechanism such as expert appraisal or mediation/conciliation to settle disputes, as we shall see later in the context of dispute management procedures. In the absence of a contractual mechanism, the parties can easily find themselves in delicate situations. In practice, however, few project contracts in Africa specifically organise end-of-contract settlement operations.

525 Transfer of personnel. – The legal systems of many African countries often provide for the automatic transfer of personnel related to the activities being taken over. However, it may be contractually arranged for the outgoing concessionaire to hand over a detailed list of staff employment contracts and the benefits granted to them, to the public party or to the new concessionaire if a competitive bidding process is organised. Ideally, this information should have been anticipated when the concession contract was drawn up.

13 Refinancing

526 Refinancing strategies. – Project debt represented by bank financing is the largest in terms of volume and maturity. It represents a very significant cost item. It is therefore in the interest of the SPV and its shareholders to reduce this cost if possible. In some cases, refinancing may therefore be in the interest of reducing costs in order to improve the SPV's financial situation, but also, depending on the commitments made to the public party, to reduce the costs of building the infrastructure or providing the services. The purpose of this chapter is to examine the circumstances in which opportunities to refinance project debt raised as part of a project finance package can be considered and then implemented. Although refinancing strategies are sometimes very much in the minds of investors, the way in which they are carried out and how the gains are allocated between the public authority and the private partner are often uncertain, limiting the incentives to carry out such a transaction. In some cases, however, refinancing operations can significantly improve the economics of the project and generate gains for all parties.

527 Plan. – This chapter is structured around the following sections: (1) the reasons for refinancing, (2) characterising the (re)financing offer, (3) calculating the refinancing gain, (4) sharing the gains and finally (5) the associated contractual provisions.

Section 1. Reasons for refinancing

528 Components of initial financing. – As discussed in part 2, a typical project financing scheme generally consists of:

- equity financing provided by the investor(s);
- senior debt financing, generally long-term, provided by one or more banks.

529 Comparison with the situation at financial *closing*. – The refinancing opportunities discussed in this section relate to the renegotiation of bank debt, the terms of which were defined by reference to a market and transaction context at a given point in time at the time of financial *closing*.

DOI: 10.4324/9781003616894-17

530 Changes in financing conditions and risks. – In particular, two major factors must be distinguished and may vary over time after the financial closing:

- changes in the financing terms available on the markets at the time of the transaction: interbank rate, terms of hedging instruments (swap rates).
- the level of risk in the transaction, particularly in typical project financing cases, includes the evolution of:
  - country risk: during the life of the project, the risk linked to the host country may vary upwards or downwards, in the latter case presenting a refinancing opportunity;
  - construction risk: as the financing is mainly raised before the completion of the project and the installations, this risk has been incorporated into the pricing of the banking offer, generally in the form of an additional premium. The post-construction project is therefore intrinsically less risky, since the facilities will generally already be in operation and generating income. The project company can therefore legitimately consider raising finance at a lower cost;
  - operating risk: depending on the type of project, this risk may be linked to the availability of the facilities and the level of production (power plant project) or to demand in cases where the partner bears the traffic risk (motorway transport project, for example). Once the project enters the operating phase, it can be reassessed on the basis of the operating results actually achieved.

It is often the favourable evolution of these factors in relation to their reference level at the time the loan was set up at the financial closing that will determine the interest of a refinancing.

531 External factors. – Other external factors may also come into play. This includes the competitive environment, the project company's market positioning and the strategy of lenders, which may have changed over the years. A simple re-evaluation of these commitments and the search for a more aggressive or specialised loan offer may therefore prove to be a virtuous circle.

532 Optimising the financing structure. – Finally, refinancing offers an opportunity to review certain financing conditions to optimise the financial structure of the project. Typically, this may involve extending maturity or increasing gearing (the ratio of equity to debt). Increasing gearing is a classic case of optimisation, making it possible to increase financial leverage by reducing the amount of equity required from the investor, thereby increasing profitability.

To speed up the implementation of the project (to meet the requirements of the host State benefiting from the infrastructure), the SPV's shareholders can provide full equity financing to start construction as quickly as possible, while at the same time raising senior bank financing. The project is then refinanced using senior debt as soon as the financial closing is reached, and the investors take advantage of this to reduce their financial exposure and free up capital that they can then deploy on other projects.

Example of the refinancing of a project initially financed entirely from equity: the Essakane solar power plant

Background: the mine has been managed since 2009 by IAMGOLD Essakane SA, a Canadian company. It is 90% owned by IAMGOLD and 10% by the government of Burkina Faso. Essakane began commercial production in July 2010. The Essakane gold mine in Burkina Faso had a thermal power plant running on heavy fuel oil to meet its energy needs. Given the good exploration results obtained, IAMGOLD is continuing to explore the Essakane area (1,300 km²) with a view to extending the life of the mine. In view of growing energy needs, a project to increase energy production capacity has been studied and has taken the form of a 15 MW solar power plant to combine with the existing thermal power plant.

An IPP developer, TOTAL EREN, was selected to sign a 15-year PPA following a restricted tender process. The IPP undertook to (i) develop, finance, build and operate the solar power plant and (ii) manage the SCADA system between the solar power plant and the oil-fired power plant. The PPA will be paid in CFA francs, partly indexed to changes in the USD/euro exchange rate. This is a "Take or Pay" type PPA between IPP and IAMGOLD.

Solar production is favoured over the use of the HFO plant in order to minimise the use of fuel oil and reduce production costs. IAMGOLD sends a daily forecast of its electricity requirements to the IPP, which is then able to better manage production from the PV plant and the HFO plant.

The mining group had a time constraint that did not allow IPP to finance the project partly with bank debt before construction. IPP therefore financed the construction of the project with its own funds and then refinanced the project after construction. IPP signed a credit agreement for 9.2 billion CFA francs (around USD 16.5 million) with the Banque Internationale pour le Commerce, l'Industrie et l'Artisanat du Burkina (BICIAB), the Burkina Faso subsidiary of the BNP Paribas group.

Section 2. Characterisation of the (re)financing offer

533 Analysis of existing financing. – In order to study refinancing opportunities, it is first necessary to have detailed understanding of the pricing conditions of existing financing.

Analysis of these conditions allows for the assessment of an *all-in* debt financing rate, which can be broken down into several components:

- **the base rate** (or swap rate), generally set at the end of the loan disbursement period, corresponding to the financing conditions applicable on the interbank market (generally EURIBOR and LIBOR);
- **the bank margin**, which remunerates the bank for the transaction based on its assessment of the risk and its management costs;

- **the swap margin**, which is the cost of the hedging instruments, in particular the conversion of the transaction into a fixed rate (*compared with* initial financing at a variable rate for the bank);
- **applicable bank charges**: application fee, commitment fee, non-utilisation fee, etc.

534 Calculation of penalties and breakage costs. – In order to define the cost of breaking off existing financing, the following elements must be considered and analysed:

- **Any penalties** that may be applied by the banks that granted the loans, in particular for early repayment and replacement penalties. These indemnities are intended to offset the opportunity cost to the bank of terminating the loan. The level of these indemnities depends on the terms and conditions of the banking partner and may be subject to negotiation.
- **The cost of unwinding interest rate hedging instruments (SWAPs)**: the unwinding of interest rate hedging instruments results in the payment of a penalty (either positive or negative) calculated based on the market value of the interest rate hedging instruments. Estimates of the associated amounts are provided by the banks but can be estimated in advance. The accounting impact of breaking the swap, and in particular whether or not the swap balance can be amortised, may also vary.

In order to assess the benefits of refinancing, these break-up costs must be compared with the profits from the operation.

Section 3. Refinancing gain

535 Estimating the gain. – The decision to refinance primarily hinges on estimating the refinancing gain by comparing the net value of shareholders' cash flows in scenarios with and without refinancing.

In particular, elements (A), (B) and (C) can be defined as follows:

- (A) is equal to the **net present value (NPV)** of the projected **shareholder cash flows** from the refinancing date until the expiry of the contract, as derived from the base case of the financial model updated to **take account of the refinancing conditions**.
- (B) is equal to the **NPV** of the projected **shareholder cash flows** from the refinancing date until the expiry of the contract, as derived from the base case of the financial model updated **without considering the refinancing conditions**.

536 Discount rate. – In both cases, the discount rate used for the calculation is the shareholders' IRR as set in the base case of the model, excluding refinancing. Furthermore, the only difference between the financial model used to determine (A) and that used to determine (B) lies in the financing conditions adopted. The fees to be paid by the private partner to the public entity or, conversely, the payment granted by the public entity, therefore remains unchanged in both cases.

- (C) is equal to the **direct or indirect fees, commissions and disbursements incurred by the project company in connection with the refinancing** (both for the termination of the previous contracts and for the implementation of the new ones), including the costs associated with the termination of the debt instruments, the termination or readjustment of the hedging instruments, bank commissions, as well as the tax costs generated, research costs, amendment procedure costs and consultancy costs. As item C is not capped and the method of calculation is not contractually agreed, it is an estimate which generally involves a degree of uncertainty and risk.

537 Calculation of the refinancing gain. – The refinancing gain will then be equal to the positive difference between (A) and the sum of (B) and (C). The refinancing option will be chosen if it provides sufficiently significant gains in relation to the risk of the transaction.

Section 4. Sharing refinancing gains

538 Payment sharing arrangements. – The terms for sharing refinancing gains between the private partner and the public entity must be defined in the concession or PPP contract. These sharing arrangements must be defined in such a way as to provide the private partner with sufficient incentive to optimise the structuring of the project while ensuring that part of the gains obtained can benefit the State.

Profit sharing may be negotiated on a case-by-case basis for certain projects, particularly if the refinancing is carried out directly at the initiative of the private partner. However, it is also common to introduce a sharing clause (50/50 for example) between the two parties to the initial contract, to avoid further negotiation at the time of refinancing.

539 Methods for allocating gains. – In addition to allocating the refinancing gains between the parties, the terms and conditions for realising these gains, particularly to redistribute them to the public entity, must be defined. Depending on the characteristics of the project, this may involve a change in the tariff, an increase in the charge levied or a reduction in the payment/rate granted to the project.

540 Difference between NPV and public authority cash flows. – To determine the realisation of these gains, the level of the fee or payment is adjusted to balance the difference between the NPV of the shareholder cash flows and the public entity's cash flows (with a discount rate corresponding to the IRR of the base case of the model without refinancing).

Section 5. Impact of contractual stipulations

541 Participation in documentation. – Refinancing can serve as an optimisation tool and may occur at various stages of the project, either at the initiative or request of the parties. It is advisable to foresee refinancing possibilities in the contractual documentation, and in particular to define:

- the possibility of refinancing at the request/initiative of either party;
- the conditions, if any, under which a decision may be made to use it; and
- the terms and conditions for sharing gains in the event of refinancing.

542 Incitations to refinance. – *A fortiori*, it is also desirable to include provisions requiring the partner to study refinancing opportunities. This obligation may be provided for at regular intervals (every five years, for example) or at different phases of the project (post-construction, after the first years of operation, etc.). In such cases, the partner must report on the actions taken to assess refinancing opportunities.

14 Managing disputes arising from project financing

543 Dispute avoidance strategy. – All the documents relating to the project finance structure are designed to ensure that the parties work together over a long period. Over a long period, the possibility of the parties disagreeing profoundly on the content of the contracts or their performance cannot be ruled out.

544 Preventive priority. – Disputes can be disastrous for infrastructure projects, as they can threaten project completion and operation, destroy dialogue between the public and private parties and jeopardise the fate of the debt incurred to finance the works. Priority is therefore given to preventing any difficulties that may arise, using a wide range of tools that have been detailed in the previous sections on monitoring and drafting project documents.

Sometimes, however, disputes cannot be avoided. In such cases, other tools must be used and appropriate dispute resolution mechanisms implemented.

545 Content. – It will be necessary to check which law applies to the management of disputes and then to determine how to prevent them before studying the preferred mechanisms for resolving them in the context of project financing.

Section 1. The law applicable to contractual documents

546 Variety of legal influences in Africa. – The applicable law poses numerous questions of choice given the variety of African countries, actors and contracts. Before outlining guidelines on the law applicable to project finance, it is necessary to give some perspective on the continent's legal situation. Africa is all too often referred to as if it were just a country. Yet Africa is a vast continent made up of 54 States. It incorporates a multitude of languages, cultures and legal traditions, inherited from the history and culture of each nation. In some cases, different historical influences are superimposed on one another, influencing the laws and regulations that apply. Apart from customary influences, which

DOI: 10.4324/9781003616894-18

generally have little impact on business law, most African States have developed their law on the basis of their colonial origins. They have subsequently undergone various modernisations while, more often than not, retaining their linguistic and legal roots in the country to which they were attached. There are four main legal areas on the African continent:[1]

- The civil law zone of influence, with a legal system similar to that in force in France, which applies in over 30 countries, mainly in North, West and Central Africa, around half of which have adopted French as their official language (either alone or co-existing with other official languages). Portuguese-speaking countries such as Angola and Mozambique are also part of this zone. The civil law system is based on a division between private law (commercial law, contract law, company law, banking and financial law, etc.) and public law (constitutional law, administrative law, etc.). The law in these civil law countries is written and generally codified, with the rules applicable in a given area grouped together in a "code", such as the Civil Code or the Commercial Code.
- The area of influence of common law, which operates on the basis of a legal system similar to that in force in the United Kingdom, and which includes around 20 countries, mainly in East and Southern Africa (although some countries in West Africa, such as Ghana and Nigeria, are also affected). The official or business language of these countries is generally English. This common law system is, in principle, based more on case law, although many "Acts" are adopted as specific laws, particularly in business law.
- The Romano-Dutch zone, which stems from the Romano-civil law tradition, is based on the "jus commune" as it was applied in the United Provinces of the Netherlands in the 17th and 18th centuries (before the Napoleonic Code of 1804) and applies to an area comprising South Africa and neighbouring countries such as Namibia, Zimbabwe, Lesotho and Swaziland. The Romano-Dutch system can be described as a hybrid between a civil law system and a common law system.
- Finally, some African countries, such as Cameroon, Mauritius and Rwanda, have adopted a legal and linguistic system of mixed influence (Figures 14.1 and 14.2).

1 Cf. *Guide du Développement sur le continent africain*, Publication France Invest, 2020. https://www.franceinvest.eu/wp-content/uploads/2021/03/Guide-Developpement-sur-le-continent-africain–2020.pdf

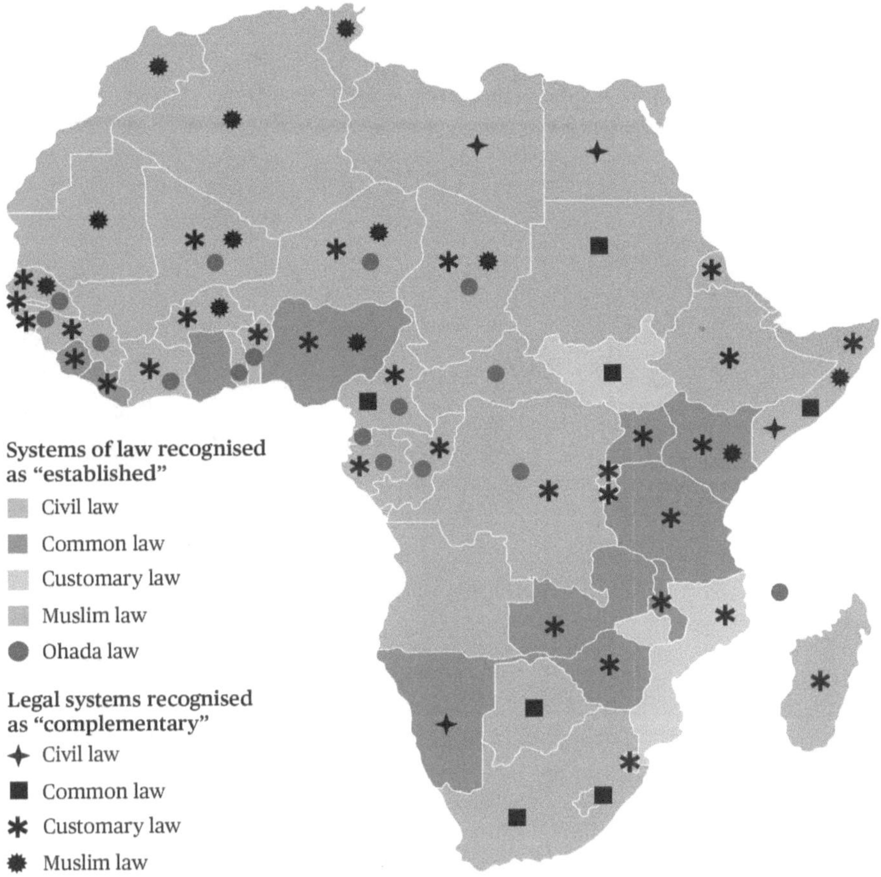

Figure 14.1 Legal systems in Africa

547 Variety of disputes. – Disputes may arise, for example, when a State takes an unfavourable decision affecting the operation of the infrastructure or when there is a disagreement between the shareholders of the project company or a difficulty relating to construction under the EPC contract. The typology of disputes is almost infinite, given that project financing involves a multitude of players and contracts, and therefore of situations likely to generate disputes.

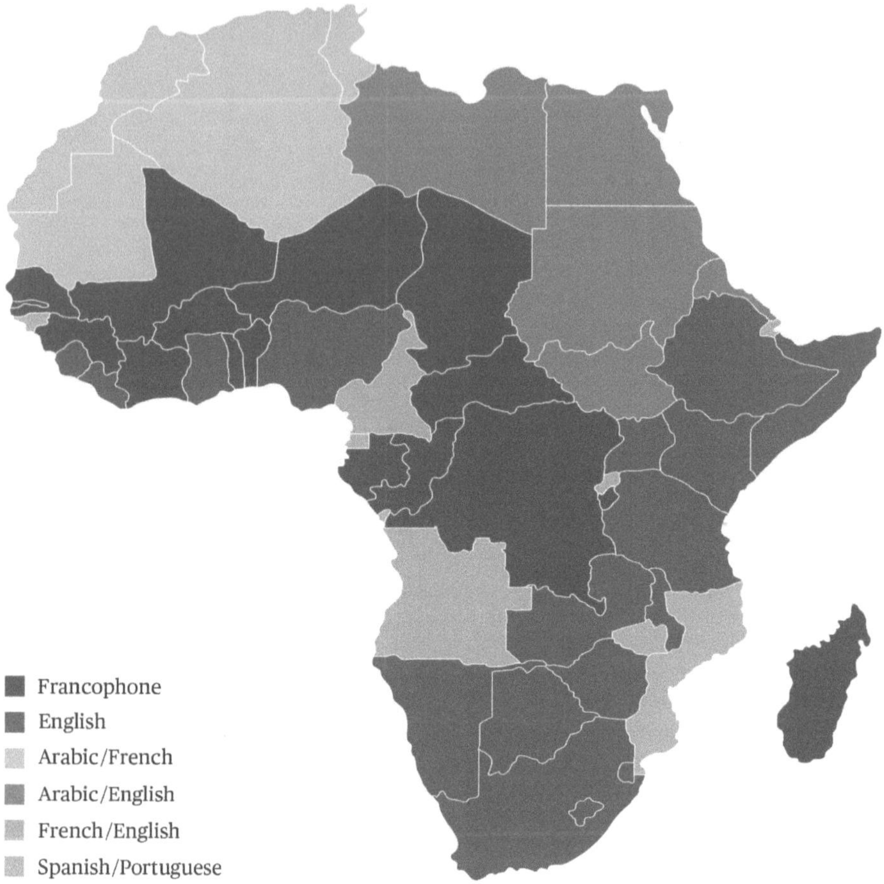

Figure 14.2 Languages spoken on the continent

548 Variety of nationalities involved. – This phenomenon is exacerbated by the fact that many different nationalities are involved. It is therefore advisable and prudent to include in each contract a clause defining, on the one hand, the law to which it is subject and specifying, on the other hand, the court that must be seized in the event of a dispute or litigation. The question of the choice of applicable law is all the more sensitive as the parties involved in the project are often of different origins and nationalities. We will look at these issues of foreignness, what documents are generally governed by non-African law and what documents will most often be governed by local law.

§ 1. Foreign issues

549 Multitude of parties. – In most African projects, there is a variety of nationalities: the first parties are the sponsors, who are often foreign; the nationality of the country or countries where the project is being developed is often different; the other shareholders, often minority shareholders, are not necessarily of the nationality of the country where the infrastructure is being built; and finally the lender or lenders, who are often numerous, are of different nationalities and, for many of those involved in project financing, located outside the African continent.

550 International and cross-border nature of projects. – Project finance is often international in nature and has links with several countries because of the nationality of the various parties involved and the cross-border nature of many infrastructure projects financed by project finance. Given the international nature of project and financing contracts, where the elements to which they relate can be connected to more than one State, it is important to consider the approach to be adopted when choosing the applicable legal clauses.

551 Autonomy of the will of the parties. – African legal systems do not always provide rules (statutes and case law) relating to party autonomy for the choice of the law applicable to such international contracts. However, in African countries where civil law is influential, reference to Article 1103 of the Civil Code (used in many countries) and to the principle of correlative party autonomy will lead to the conclusion that it is easy to choose freely the law applicable to such contracts.

552 Impact of choices made. – The choice of applicable law is not always neutral, as it may have an impact on the validity of the contract, on a clause or on the way it is implemented. The law chosen can also have an impact if the court designated as having jurisdiction to deal with disputes relating to the contract is not in the same country as the law chosen in the contract and does not necessarily have jurisdiction. These few points illustrate the importance of the choices made in terms of applicable law for the various contracts linked to project financing.

In view of the criticism regularly levelled at national legal frameworks in Africa, which are often considered old, outdated and unstable, project finance players are often opportunistic in choosing the law applicable to legal documentation on a case-by-case basis. Let's see which documents are generally subject to non-African law and which remain traditionally subject to local law.

§ 2. Documents governed by non-African law

553 Choice of developer's right of origin. – Among the project documents, it is common, prior to the creation of the company, to find consortium agreements or development agreements between the development players. They often use the reference law that they consider to be the most reliable and choose their own law to govern their relations during this study, structuring and organisation phase. This is often a law of European or American origin, or that of the main player behind the development.

554 Financing contracts. – As we saw in Part 2, financing contracts are most often subject to competition between the laws preferred by lenders depending on their origin and national preference. However, it is very common for finance contracts to be governed by English, French or New York law. It should be noted that in this case, it is correlatively common to choose the same law for certain derivative agreements linked to the financing, such as the intercreditor agreement.

§ 3. Documents governed by local law

555 Precedence of local law for the main contract. – The PPP contract and the entire procedure for awarding the project, even if they are mainly financed by multilateral or bilateral funds, cannot escape the application of local law. States or public bodies are always determined to ensure that their rules prevail; their local public procurement law, the rules applicable to the launch of a PPP procedure or a concession inherent in the financing of an infrastructure project will be of national origin.

556 Construction contracts and O&M contracts. – Construction contracts and O&M contracts may be the subject of debates on the choice of applicable law.[2] If the project company's co-contractors to these contracts are established or set up local bases to perform their obligations with a project company that is essentially locally established, then consideration may be given to choosing a local applicable law. This really depends on the free choice of the parties, the influence of each party and, above all, their willingness to rely on the local legal framework. The parties will then determine in practice whether the local law is reliable, recognised and stable in order to make their choice. However, in Africa, most suppliers of goods and services and construction companies, as well as their counterparties within the SPV, are of international origin and often want to use their law, but also to apply models that they are familiar with and for which the applicable law has been adapted according to standard clauses that they know well from having negotiated them for other project financing. In this contract, a link will have to be found between contract law and the mandatory provisions of local law.

557 Documents relating to the SPV. – On the other hand, the parties often choose local law for certain documents that can be directly linked to local company law obligations. This is the case for the articles of association of the project company. As the project company is registered locally, it is difficult not to govern relations between shareholders by reference to foreign law. This could be envisaged for countries where the law would be totally inadequate, but it could give rise to difficulties in the event of local court cases. Furthermore, the choice of applicable law for the project company's articles of association should be considered in relation to the choice made for the company's shareholders' agreement.

558 Security interests. – Similarly, it is difficult for security interests in the project company's assets located in the host country to avoid being governed by local law, as security interests must still be governed by national law in order to be effective.

2 On the law applicable to construction contracts, see M. AUDIT, S. BOLLÉE and P. CALLÉ, *Droit du commerce international et des investissements étrangers*, *op. cit.*, n° 519 et seq.

It should be emphasised that over the last 20 years, the law in the majority of African countries has been strengthened and modernised, and its reliability is less in doubt with the advent of regional organisations such as OHADA, but also thanks to legal and institutional reforms often financed by international organisations or development banks. This is creating a positive dynamic in securities law, for example in certain countries that are undertaking reforms.

Section 2. Dispute prevention: planning and information

559 Continuing the dialogue. – As we saw in Chapter 11, in order to prevent disputes, it is advisable to put in place precise monitoring tools for each of the parties involved and to carry out effective and regular checks. Dialogue and the use of formalised and digital tools in project and finance contracts are assets in preventing disputes and enshrine the principles of good practice in contract management.

560 Contractual inaccuracies. – Disputes often arise due to documentary inaccuracies, such as errors in technical specifications or insufficient initial data on which projects are based.[3] This can be the case, for example, of a faulty design due to inadequacies in the basic data supplied to the SPV. The most frequent causes of disputes are errors or inadequacies in the contractual documentation or the failure of the parties to manage the contracts,[4] such as (i) errors or omissions in the contractual documentation, (ii) incomplete information on the design and/or the client's requirements, (iii) the failure of the parties to understand and comply with the contractual obligations or (iv) performance conditions different from those anticipated.

561 Contract management. – The first step in preventing disputes is to ensure that the data provided by the host State during the tender phase are accurate, complete and reliable, particularly data that are crucial to the design of the works (e.g. data relating to soil conditions). In particular, the submission of tenders, design, construction, price and construction schedule depend on these data. These initial data are also important because they determine the technical, financial and operational feasibility of the project, particularly the timescales for completion and the budget envisaged. Properly defining all the contractual aspects of the project at an early stage helps to avoid numerous disputes, as does rigorous and regular contract management by all parties, also commonly known as contract management.[5]

§ 1. Recourse to regulatory or PPP authorities

562 Roles of authorities. – Sectoral regulatory authorities have developed rapidly and significantly on the African continent over the last 20 years. As the infrastructure financed on the continent most often belongs to regulated sectors, the

3 Guillaume Feld, *Droit et pratique des grands projets à l'international, Une perspective civiliste*, Legitech, 2020, p. 795.

4 *Ibid.*, p. 801; Arcadis Global construction Disputes Report 2016, 2017 and 2018.

5 For more information on the importance of *contract management*, see Guillaume Feld, "Le *contract management*, levier de réduction des délais et coûts de l'arbitrage commercial international", *RDAI*, 2021, p. 299.

specialised authorities in charge of it (for example in the energy sector,[6] transport, telecommunications[7]) intend to play a role in preventing disputes or settling them. They also have the power to impose sanctions or to monitor.

We should also mention the authorities specifically dedicated to PPP or public contracts[8] whose role, as we have already seen, is to monitor projects and act as an upstream control authority, and as a sanctioning or dispute settlement authority, prior to the implementation of contractual mechanisms.

It is useful to check whether their involvement is compulsory in certain disputes or whether their intervention may be necessary or desirable in certain cases, depending on the type of dispute.

§ 2. Amicable negotiations

563 Authorised exchanges. – As mentioned previously, in project finance contracts, as in many other sectors, communication is the key to preventing disputes. The parties involved are therefore strongly encouraged, at any stage in the life of the project, to resolve difficulties as quickly as possible in order to avoid escalation of the dispute. Given this evidence, we may well wonder whether it is appropriate to make amicable discussions compulsory.

564 Clauses for resolution by management. – The advantage of such arrangements is that they allow the directors to be included in the discussions at an early stage and prevent one party from being put in a weak position by requesting an amicable discussion. However, there are significant limits to these provisions, which relate to their mandatory nature: how can the other party be forced to come to the negotiations and negotiate in good faith? This is why discussions are generally limited in time, so as not to block the resolution of the dispute.[9]

§ 3. Expertise

565 Recourse to an expert. – Halfway between preventing disputes and settling them, the parties may sometimes provide in their contracts for disputes to be referred to an expert, who may propose a contractual, technical and financial assessment of the claims submitted to him.[10] Although these assessments are generally contractually binding, they have no jurisdictional authority, unlike an arbitration award.

6 See for example, at regional level, the ECOWAS Regional Electricity Authority (ARREC).

7 See, for example, the *Independent Communications Authority of South Africa* in South Africa.

8 See, for example, the Autorité nationale de régulation des marchés publics in Côte d'Ivoire, the equivalent of which exists in most countries.

9 On the question of amicable negotiations, see J. Jenkins, *International Construction Arbitration Law*, Kluwer Law International, 2021, pp. 66–68.

10 C. Freedman, "Expert Determination", *in* F. e Ly and P.-A. Gélinas, *Dispute Prevention and Settlement through Expert Determination and Dispute Boards, Dossiers of the ICC Institute of World Business Law*, Vol. 15, 2017, pp. 27–38; D. Jone, "Expert Determination and Arbitration", *Arbitration: The International Journal of Arbitration, Mediation and Dispute Management*, 2001, vol. 67, no. 1, pp. 17–29.

As with negotiations, mediation and other methods of dispute resolution, this process can be used for dilatory purposes. The expert can enlighten the courts on the technical aspects of the dispute and/or provide proof of factual elements that could not be established without his report. The expert's report can thus become a key piece of evidence in the resolution of the dispute.[11] An expert may also give advice to a party to enable it to prepare its case. In the event of difficulties, it will often be useful to prepare for the expert's involvement beforehand, especially if a settlement is envisaged.

566 Scope of the expert appraisal clause. – The difficulty in contracts is knowing what scope to give to these clauses, what powers to confer on an expert, what support body can appoint him and within what timeframe, and on what subjects he can intervene. One of these issues is often more delicate than the others: whether or not expert reports are binding. If the expert's report or opinion is not binding, it may be overridden, and the parties may feel that they have wasted time in resolving their difficulties. However, even in the latter case, if a party does not submit to a non-binding expert's decision and decides to take the case to the arbitral tribunal or court at a later date, the expert's conclusions may still be taken into consideration by the court.

567 FIDIC and CCI expertise. – Among the centres of expertise that can be consulted are FIDIC[12] and the CCI.[13]

Examples of expert appraisal clauses

- Simple clause:

In the event of a dispute arising out of or relating to [clause X of the present contract], the parties agree to submit the dispute to *ad hoc* expert determination. The expert shall be appointed by the ICC International ADR Centre in accordance with the ICC Rules for the Appointment of Experts and Third Parties.

- More detailed clause:

The Parties undertake in good faith to seek an amicable settlement of any dispute (hereinafter the **"Dispute"**) that may arise between them in connection with this Concession Agreement.

Failing an amicable settlement within thirty (30) days of notification by one Party to the other of the existence of a Dispute, such Dispute shall be submitted, as the case may be, to an Independent Expert in accordance with

11 For more information on the procedures for selecting experts, their role and the means of involving them, see P. Rosher and V. Thieffry, "Arbitrage: les questions à se poser pour faire intervenir un expert dans un litige", 4 April 2019. www.lemoniteur.fr/article/arbitrage-les-questions-a-se-poser-pour-faire-intervenir-un-expert-dans-un-litige.2033290

12 https://fidic.org/node/814

13 https://iccwbo.org/dispute-resolution-services/experts/

the procedure described in Article X below or to Arbitration in accordance with the procedure described in Article Y below.

Disputes for which referral to an Independent Expert is expressly provided for in this Concession Agreement or which the Parties decide by mutual agreement to submit to an Independent Expert (including those concerning the calculation of the Termination Indemnity) will be submitted to an Independent Expert for decision in accordance with the expertise procedure provided for below. To this end, the following is specified.

The Independent Expert must be chosen from the list of experts registered with the International Chamber of Commerce (ICC) and appointed in accordance with the provisions of the ICC Rules for the Administration of Expertise Procedures.

The procedure to be followed by the Independent Expert is that set out in the ICC Rules for the Administration of Expertise Proceedings. The procedural timetable will be established by the Independent Expert in accordance with these Rules.

It is specified that the findings of the Independent Expert will be binding on them and the Parties undertake to comply with them without possibility of appeal, unless there is a manifest error, in which case the Dispute between the Parties (including the calculation of the Termination Indemnity) may be submitted by either of the Parties to arbitration, solely on the basis of manifest error, in accordance with Article Y of the concession contract. In the latter case, in the context of the submission of the Dispute (including the calculation of the Termination Payment) to the arbitration procedure stipulated in Article Z hereof, the findings of the Independent Expert shall be admissible and may be submitted to the arbitral tribunal for consideration.

The fees and costs of the expertise proceedings will be determined in accordance with the provisions of the ICC Rules for the Administration of Expertise Proceedings.

Section 3. Dispute resolution: arbitration the preferred route

568 Arbitration domination. – International contracts concluded as part of major infrastructure projects in Africa generally contain detailed and precise stipulations on dispute resolution.[14] Eighty-eight percent of projects in Africa[15] include a method of resolving disputes through arbitration.[16] Care must be taken to ensure that these mechanisms do not compete with the powers of regulatory authorities

14 See for practical development of African arbitration the comments in Inter-African dispute settlement mechanisms Sebastien Manciaux I.B.L.J. 2022, 3/4, 399–410.

15 Georgios Martsekis, "Arbitration in International Project Finance Transactions: The Path to Financial Arbitration", *in* Stavros Brekoulakis (ed), *Arbitration: The International Journal of Arbitration, Mediation and Dispute Management*, (© Chartered Institute of Arbitrators (CIArb); Sweet & Maxwell, 2018, Volume 84, Issue 2), pp. 142–158.

16 Partenariats Public Privé, Cadres juridiques et institutionnels en Afrique, comparative study, ALSF, p. 36.

that may be competent to resolve disputes. In some cases, referral to these authorities may be a necessary prerequisite. The use of arbitration in loan agreements that was initially uncommon as the banking community preferred to resort to court litigation instead became more and more frequent.[17]

569 Multiple stages of dispute resolution. – These stipulations often set up a mechanism with several gradual stages, in order to give the parties the opportunity to resolve their dispute as early as possible and use procedures that are more or less contentious. Indeed, these contracts often contain clauses at several levels, combining negotiation, expert appraisal, mediation and, *ultimately,* arbitration.[18]

§ 1. The need for graduated dispute resolution with recourse to arbitration

570 Preferred recourse to arbitration. – In contracts relating to project financing, financial institutions often require disputes to be resolved by arbitration. Given the lack of confidence in local courts, the need for confidentiality and the high financial stakes involved, promoters, investors, lenders and the State generally agree on the need to resort to arbitration to ensure that the project is bankable.

Arbitration remains the preferred method of dispute resolution, although dispute resolution commissions and mediation are increasingly popular.[19] In the infrastructure sector, for example, participants in the SOAS Arbitration in Africa Survey Report ranked arbitration as the preferred dispute resolution method in 36% of cases, ahead of mediation (19.4%) and dispute resolution committees (15.5%).

571 Institutional support for arbitration. – The increased use of arbitration has led to the updating of arbitration legislation in several countries. These include the Tanzanian Arbitration Act 2020[20] and the Nigerian Arbitration and Mediation Act 2023.[21]

These recent laws are part of a modernisation of the arbitration framework, based on international standards and the UNCITRAL Model Law.

Without necessarily enacting legislation specific to arbitration, other States continue to sign the New York Convention. This is the case for Ethiopia and the Seychelles in 2020 and Malawi in 2021.

17 Court litigation was supposed to provide more favourable outcomes to lenders who, being the party with the stronger bargaining power, would be able to impose their choice of law and forum. Lenders tend to select the law governing the loan agreement rather than the law of the borrower's State to avoid any "home court" advantage. Most often they opt for the laws of New York or England and Wales, two of the leading banking centres worldwide, due to their advanced and developed legal systems based on common law. This, in turn, increases the predictability of the outcome of proceedings as a result of their long histories of case law precedent, established procedural laws and unbiased judicial oversight. See Maria Davies, "The Use of Arbitration in Loan Agreements in International Project Finance: Opening Pandora's Box or an Unexpected Panacea?", *Journal of International Arbitration*, (© Kluwer Law International; Kluwer Law International 2015, Volume 32, Issue 2), pp. 143–172.

18 Bernd Ehle, Benjamin Ng'eno, Baptiste Rigaudeau, "Projets d'infrastructure en Afrique de l'Est et règlement des litiges", *Revue de droit des affaires internationales*, no. 4, 2021, pp. 482–483.

19 E. Oneyma, "SOAS Arbitration in Africa Survey Report – Africa-connected Arbitration Perspectives on Major Global Issues", SOAS University of London, 2022.

20 "The Arbitration Act, no. 2, 2020.

21 "Arbitration and Mediation Act, 2023.

572 Conduct of arbitration hearings. – The Covid-19 pandemic has allowed virtual hearings to flourish in arbitration proceedings. The "Virtual Hearing Protocol" developed by the Africa Arbitration Academy was known to 46% of respondents to the 2022 SOAS Arbitration in Africa Survey Report, 37.5% of whom had already used it. As this protocol was set up specifically for African parties, the proportion of respondents aware of it remains relatively low.[22] Other protocols are nevertheless used for virtual hearings in arbitration in Africa, including the *ICC Checklist for a Protocol on Virtual Hearings and Suggested Clauses for Cyber-Protocols and Procedural Orders Dealing with the Organisation of Virtual Hearings*, the *Seoul Protocol on Video Conferencing in International Arbitration* and the *CIArb Guidance Notes on Remote Dispute Resolution Proceedings*.

573 The need for a single procedure. – Project financing involves contracts with several parties: the State, operators, suppliers and builders. They also involve numerous agreements and contracts with financial institutions, which are linked to the basic contracts through direct agreements. All these contracts form part of the same operation and are interdependent. As far as possible, it is important to choose a single, uniform method of dispute resolution. In the event of a dispute, unified procedures will enable the parties, and the project, to limit the impact in terms of timetable and costs, and above all to ensure consistent treatment of the various disputes that may arise. The parties must therefore try to converge on a single, coherent method of settlement, and recourse to arbitration is often the preferred option. To a certain extent, it is even a key condition for setting up infrastructure project financing.

574 Resolution steps. – Lenders and IFIs require two types of clauses in structured project finance contracts: (i) a multi-stage dispute resolution clause, including recourse to arbitration as a last resort; and (ii) a waiver by the State, its public entities and, more generally, entities in which the State holds an equity interest, of all immunities from jurisdiction and enforcement.

Generally, the parties describe in their contract an entire dispute resolution process prior to arbitration. If, despite all their efforts, the parties are unable to put an end to their dispute, they plan to use a dispute resolution clause containing several stages: (i) an amicable settlement phase within 30 or 60 days, often with recourse to the ultimate managers or decision-makers; (ii) recourse to an independent expert under certain conditions; and (iii) as a last resort, submission of the dispute to an arbitration tribunal, often favoured for its efficiency.[23]

575 An example of a dispute resolution mechanism that can be put in place. – This mechanism is only one possible sequence that can be adapted on a case-by-case basis. It provides for the possibility of recourse to expertise, mediation/conciliation and/or dispute boards before moving on to arbitration.

22 The 194 respondents have been involved in arbitrations in Africa during the period 2019–2021 as arbitrators, lawyers, tribunal secretaries, expert witnesses, parties to the dispute or as administrators. Some respondents have been involved in arbitrations in more than one capacity in different Africa-related cases.

23 V. J. El Ahdab, "L'efficacité des sentences arbitrales", in *Vingt ans d'arbitrage OHADA: bilan et perspectives* – Actes du colloque des 17 et 18 octobre 2019 de la Conférence des Barreaux de l'Espace OHADA et JUS AFRICA, LexisNexis, 2019.

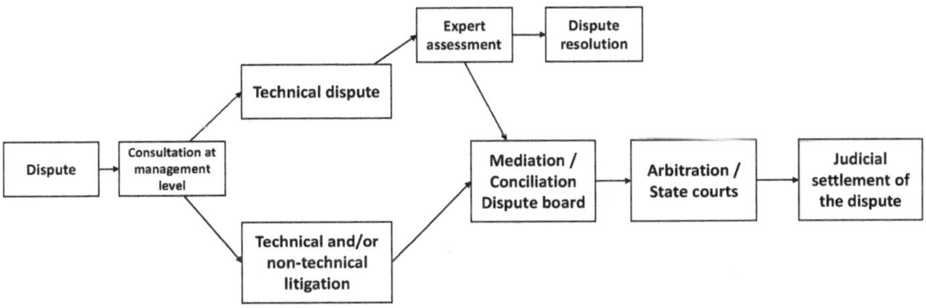

Figure 14.3 Dispute resolution scheme

576 Impact on financing. – In practice, the multi-stage dispute settlement clauses are the result of a common desire on the part of the State and the various parties involved in the project, given the high financial stakes borne by each of them. The financial penalties and the "acceleration" of senior and subordinated loans are likely to dissuade the project's investors and promoters from immediately initiating litigation with the State.

577 Risk for governments. – Amicable negotiations, or even non-judicial dispute resolution methods, resulting in the establishment of agreements with the State and the lenders are generally preferred. For its part, the State is rather inclined to enter into such dispute resolution arrangements given the potentially substantial amount of termination compensation and other penalties that it would have to pay if the project were terminated as a result of contractual breaches, whether attributable to it or not.

578 Wary of arbitration. – In addition, African governments are increasingly concerned about the legal and financial effects of a possible arbitration ruling, in a context where commitments made at the request of lenders to ensure the bankability of projects are becoming more and more important. The effect of these arbitration rulings is to weaken the economic capacity of African countries and to make them more wary of recourse to arbitration.[24]

579 Immunities. – It is frequently requested by sponsors and lenders that the project host State irrevocably and unconditionally waive any claim of immunity from jurisdiction and immunity from execution so that, in the event of any proceedings, legal action or arbitration claim being brought against that State in respect of contracts to which it is a party, no claim of sovereign immunity or other proceedings (including suits, attachments before judgment, judgments of any court or arbitral awards, whether on the merits, provisional or conservatory) may be asserted by or on behalf of the State in respect of itself or any of its property. Contracts sometimes authorise the State to list a series of so-called protected assets that may not be seized or assigned.

580 Waiver of immunity. – In most cases, the State irrevocably and unconditionally waives, to the fullest extent permitted by the laws applicable to it, any immunity which it could normally claim in respect of any of its property other than the

24 Sylvie Bebohi Ebongo, "L'appréciation des condamnations contre les Etats africains dans l'arbitrage", *Revue trimestrielle de droit africain*, January–March 2017.

protected property listed. Thus, the State generally consents to the enforcement of any award rendered against it in accordance with the arbitration procedure chosen, as we shall see later, and to the measures taken in the context of such procedure, including in particular the compulsory enforcement of any award concerning any of its property other than its protected property, regardless of its actual or potential use.

581 Development of litigation. – As African public parties have undergone numerous proceedings over the last few decades, the issue of this waiver of immunity is creating more and more difficulties and negotiations in practice when finalising certain project contracts to which they are party. Governments and their agencies or institutions, as well as publicly owned companies, are increasingly reluctant to accept this waiver. Numerous disputes are therefore developing around these issues.

For example, the CCJA recently ruled[25] that a company constituted in one of the forms governed by the OHADA Uniform Act on commercial companies and EIGs, classified as a State company by a national law, and whose capital is wholly owned by an OHADA Member State, is neither a public law entity nor a public enterprise. It thus confirmed its case law to the effect that, although the company has a public service mission, it does not enjoy immunity from execution. The CCJA appears to adopt a restrictive interpretation of immunity.[26]

§ 2. Arbitration systems

A. The existence of local systems

582 African arbitration centres. – Recourse to arbitration is often motivated by a concern for neutrality. However, this does not mean that the solutions proposed are completely delocalised. Many jurisdictions are trying to develop arbitration centres in order to promote this method of dispute resolution and offer a solution to contractors.[27] In Africa, for example,[28] the Arbitration Foundation of South Africa in South Africa,[29] the Cairo Regional Centre for International Commercial Arbitration in Egypt,[30] the Mediation and Arbitration Center of the Mauritius Chamber of Commerce and Industry in Mauritius,[31] the Casablanca International Mediation and Arbitration Centre in Morocco[32] or the African Court of Mediation and Arbitration (CAMAR) created in April 2019, or even more specialised alternatives such as

25 CCJA, 2e ch., 29 April 2021, no. 076/2021.

26 See Ramss Akono Adam, *L'Esssentiel Droits Africains des Affaires*, no. 11, December 2021, p. 4.

27 On the development of arbitration in Africa, see J. Miles, N. Muriuki and L. Lusiji, "The Development of International Arbitration in Africa", *in* Menaker (ed.), *International Arbitration and the Rule of Law: Contribution and Conformity*, Kluwer Law International, 2017.

28 For an overview of arbitration in Africa, see M.-A. Ngwe, "État des lieux de l'arbitrage en Afrique", AFA conference, 19 September 2018; Gregory Travaini, "Arbitration centres in Africa: too many cooks?", *Kluwer Arbitration Blog*, 1 October 2019.

29 https://arbitration.co.za/

30 https://crcica.org/

31 https://marc.mu/

32 http://cimac.ma/

the China-Africa Joint Arbitration Centre in Johannesburg and Shanghai, focusing on disputes relating to the New Silk Road initiative.[33] This highlights the desire to deal with disputes locally, but also a concern for cost management, as international institutions are often more expensive and less close to the disputes and the players involved. New legislation and the development of African arbitration centres also support this desire for local management of arbitrations relating to Africa.[34]

As a result, while international systems are still predominant (see the next section), African arbitration practice is accelerating. This is due as much to the enactment of more favourable legislation as to the increase in the number of local practitioners, as well as to a desire to develop an arbitration practice "centred on Africa".[35] When it comes to infrastructure projects, arbitration is no exception to the trend towards the Africanisation of disputes.[36]

583 OHADA institutional arbitration. – More than 20 years ago, the OHADA system also acquired a modern arbitration law and a centre administered by the CCJA. OHADA arbitration covers arbitration law that is directly applicable in OHADA member countries and is embodied in the Uniform Act on Arbitration of 23 November 2017 and the Arbitration Rules of the Common Court of Justice and Arbitration ("CCJA Rules"), under which the CCJA acts as an arbitration centre. It must be said that this institutional arbitration by the CCJA has not managed to establish itself in infrastructure project financing contracts, with the parties involved (including governments) often preferring to use a more international centre such as the ICC, even though such arbitration is expressly provided for in certain legislation (for example, certain public procurement codes). For example, in November 2020, an ICC arbitration tribunal heard the dispute between Douala International Terminal (DIT) and the Douala port authority, following DIT's exclusion from the call for tenders for the renewal of the concession.[37]

584 The dual role of the CCJA. – There appear to be several reasons for the reluctance to use CCJA arbitration. Firstly, the dual role of the CCJA, which acts both as an arbitration institution – and as such will review the arbitration award – and as the "Supreme Court" of the OHADA zone – and *ultimately* the judge reviewing the award – is not likely to reassure lenders, promoters and investors. What was supposed to be an advantage of the OHADA institutional system seems in reality to be misinterpreted, no doubt wrongly, by the business community.

585 Organisational changes at the CCJA. – The CCJA has recently undergone an internal reorganisation in order to revitalise its arbitration practice. The

33 http://www.shiac.org/CAJAC/index_E.aspx

34 Bernd EHLE, Benjamin NG'ENO and Baptiste RIGAUDEAU, "Projets d'infrastructures en Afrique de l'Est et règlement des litiges", *Revue de droit des affaires internationales*, 2021.

35 Amne SUEDI, "The need for 'Africa-focused' arbitration and reform of Tanzania's Arbitration Act", *Investment Treaty News*, 5 October 2020.

36 Bernd EHLE, Benjamin NG'ENO and Baptiste RIGAUDEAU, "Projets d'infrastructure en Afrique de l'Est et règlement des litiges", *op. cit.*, n. 4, pp. 482–483.

37 Bernd EHLE, Baptiste RIGAUDEAU and Maël DESCHAMPS, "Projets d'infrastructure en Afrique de l'Ouest et centrale et règlement des litiges", *Revue de droit des affaires internationales*, 2023.

CCJA's arbitration centre now reports to the Secretary General of the CCJA, who is responsible for its day-to-day management. In addition to this internal reorganisation, more human resources have been made available, and a monitoring committee has been set up to oversee the implementation and completion of arbitration proceedings and the review of draft awards.[38]

586 Competence of the arbitral tribunal. – Secondly, it seems that the quality of arbitration tribunals, and even the impartiality and neutrality of arbitrators, may be a cause for concern for investors, promoters and lenders. The appointment of the chairman by the CCJA can leave parties sceptical, not to mention the low fees involved, which keep out the best candidates.[39] The CCJA also seems to suffer from a panel of experts that is not sufficiently varied to interest professionals in the sector.

587 Immunities of enforcement. – Thirdly, the position of OHADA law regarding immunities from execution is a real subject. It is true that the CCJA has taken steps to reassure investors and economic operators in the area.[40] The case law of the CCJA tends to reduce the scope of the immunity from execution provided for in Article 30 of the Uniform Act on the organisation of simplified recovery procedures and enforcement,[41] but it is not certain that this is sufficient to reassure investors who expect to be able to seize certain assets of the State acting as a commercial and economic player.

38 Alexis Ndzuenkeu, "Un nouveau règlement intérieur pour redynamiser l'arbitrage CCJA – Règlement intérieur de la CCJA en matière d'arbitrage", *L'Essentiel Droits africains des affaires*, no. 1, 2024, p. 1.

39 Moreover, a famous dispute has arisen between arbitrators and the CCJA concerning the payment of their fees, v. CCJA judgment no. 139/2015 of 19 November 2015, in which the CCJA held that: "When the parties have agreed to have recourse to arbitration by the Court, they thereby submit to the provisions of Title IV of the OHADA Treaty, these Rules, the Rules of Procedure of the Court, their annexes and the schedule of arbitration costs, in their wording in force on the date of the commencement of the arbitration proceedings indicated in Article 5 above. . . . Whereas it is common ground, as appears from the case file, that after the Court had fixed the arbitrators' fees at 40,480,332 FCFA, the Chairman of the Arbitral Tribunal negotiated directly with counsel for the parties in dispute and obtained their agreement to increase the amount of the said fees to 450,000 €, i.e. 295,180,650 FCFA; that, having then applied to the Court for regularisation of this increase, its applications were successively rejected by decisions no. 081/2013/CCJA/ADM/ARB dated 1[er] August 2013 and no. 096/2013/CCJA/ADM/ARB dated 3 October 2013; that notwithstanding these decisions, the President of the Arbitral Tribunal obtained payment from GETMA of its share of the sum claimed, in addition to ordering GETMA to pay the Republic of Guinea's share; That by deliberately disregarding the essential provisions of the Arbitration Rules to which the parties agreed to subject the handling of their dispute by means of the arbitration clause inserted in the concession contract, the Arbitral Tribunal did not comply with its terms of reference; that the Award should be set aside, without there being any need to examine the other pleas in law in the appeal".

40 Mahutodji Jimmy Vital Kodo, "Sur le revirement de la jurisprudence de la Cour commune de justice et d'arbitrage de l'OHADA en matière d'immunité d'exécution", *Revue trimestrielle de droit africain*, Pénant, no. 906, January–March 2019, pp. 102 et seq.

41 Judgment no. 103/2018 of 26 Apr. 2018; CCJA Judgment no. 032/2019 of 31 Jan. 2019; CCJA Judgment no. 039/2019 of 31 Jan. 2019; CCJA Judgment no. 260/2018 of 13 Dec. 2018.

588 Seat of CCJA arbitration. – Fourthly, the current wording of the CCJA Rules indirectly requires that the seat of the arbitration be chosen within the OHADA zone in order to avoid the risk of a possible double action for setting aside, even though practitioners advising lenders or investors often wish to impose a seat outside the OHADA zone in order to reassure their clients in terms of neutrality. Article 29 of the CCJA Rules gives the CCJA jurisdiction to rule on any action to set aside an award made under its auspices. This poses two major problems for investors, promoters and lenders, which flow from one another. Firstly, investors, promoters and lenders do not want a seat in the OHADA zone when their dispute is precisely with a Member State of the OHADA zone. Secondly, they do not want to run the risk of having two possible actions for annulment if they decide to choose a neutral place outside the OHADA zone as the seat of arbitration.

588 Access to judgments. – Fifthly, the difficulty of predicting the legal positions of the CCJA due to the difficulty of accessing its judgments in real time is also one of the problems raised in the negotiations between all the stakeholders.

590 Resources of the CCJA. – Lastly, foreign investors often complain about the lack of resources allocated to the CCJA, which can probably explain the slowness with which arbitration cases are managed, and sometimes even the lack of organisation that is often criticised by clients and players in the African market. Without any real hindsight on the effects of this, the CCJA's rules of procedure on arbitration of 20 September 2023 and the resulting reorganisation of the arbitration centre should nevertheless help to alleviate the CCJA's lack of human resources.[42]

B. The pre-eminence of international systems

591 International arbitration centres. – More often than not, investors and governments prefer to use the services of reputable international centres, which provide a framework for and organise the arbitration process. These institutions play a regulatory role by adopting precise arbitration rules and an administrative role by managing the proceedings. The International Chamber of Commerce, based in Paris but with branches in Hong Kong, New York, Sao Paulo, Singapore and Abu Dhabi, is a resolutely international institution.[43] This institution remains one of the most popular, with 929 cases registered in 2021.[44] It is also versatile, in the sense that it can serve as an institution in commercial as well as investment arbitrations, and is accustomed to hosting arbitrations involving States or State entities.[45]

42 Alexis Ndzuenkeu, "Un nouveau règlement intérieur pour redynamiser l'arbitrage CCJA – Règlement intérieur de la CCJA en matière d'arbitrage", *op. cit.*

43 https://iccwbo.org/dispute-resolution-services/arbitration/

44 *ICC Dispute Resolution 2020 Statistics*, p. 9.

45 V. *Arbitration Involving States and State Entities under the ICC Rules of Arbitration* (2015).

592 LCIA, SIAC, HKIAC, SCC. – Mention should also be made of the London Court of International Arbitration[46] which, although more closely linked to London, is a solution frequently used in international arbitrations relating to project finance. There are also several other fast-growing centres that may be a useful option, such as the Singapore International Arbitration Centre in Singapore,[47] the Hong Kong International Arbitration Centre in Hong Kong,[48] the Stockholm Chamber of Commerce in Stockholm,[49] etc.

593 ICSID. – In addition to these centres, which deal mainly with commercial arbitrations, i.e. based on contractual breaches, PPPs, generally involving foreign investment, frequently give rise to investment arbitration proceedings based on breaches of international investment protection treaties.[50] Such arbitrations may take place on an ad hoc basis, i.e. without being administered by centres, or they may be administered by the International Centre for Settlement of Investment Disputes ("ICSID").[51] In this respect, the decisive contribution of the African States in the establishment of the ICSID[52] should be noted. The African States immediately acceded to the Washington Convention, which established ICSID.[53]

Most of the first cases recorded by ICSID concern investments in African countries. This is not so much the result of a greater number of disputes as of the frequent inclusion of ICSID arbitration clauses in local investment laws and contracts.

Focus on bilateral investment treaties

Bilateral investment promotion and protection treaties are proliferating across Africa.[54] These treaties aim to accelerate and increase the number and flow of cross-border investments in the world.[55] Their scope may vary from one treaty to another, and their rules on protection and dispute settlement may be more or less developed and binding, even though their content is

46 https://www.lcia.org/Dispute_Resolution_Services/LCIA_Arbitration.aspx

47 https://www.siac.org.sg/

48 https://www.hkiac.org/

49 https://sccarbitrationinstitute.se/en/

50 V. Bernd Ehle, Benjamin Ng'eno and Baptiste Rigaudeau, "Projets d'infrastructure en Afrique de l'Est et règlement des litiges", *Revue de droit des affaires internationales*, 2021, no. 4, pp. 475–478.

51 On the different options for investment arbitration, see J. El Ahdab, "Les institutions arbitrales alternatives au CIRDI et les arbitrages d'investissement", *Le CIRDI – 45 ans après*, Pédone, 2011.

52 U. Ewelukwa Ofodile, "African states, investor-state arbitration and the ICSID dispute resolution system: Continuities, changes and challenges", *ICSID Review – Foreign Investment Law Journal*, 2001, vol. 34, no. 2, pp. 296–364.

53 "Introductory Report: ICSID and Africa", *in* W. Ben Hamida, A. Ngwanza and J.-B. Harelimana (eds.), *Un demi-siècle africain d'arbitrage d'investissement CIRDI, regards rétrospectifs et prospectifs*, LGDJ, EJA, 2019.

54 The African State, weak party to the foreign investment contract Eustache Da Allada, International Business Law Journal, IBLJ 2022, 3/4, 295–304.

55 M. Audit, S. Bollée and P. Callé, *Droit du commerce international et des investissements étrangers*, *op. cit.*, n° 287 et seq.

often very similar. In all cases, they will be important elements in the structuring of projects. African countries are signatories to a large number of bilateral treaties for the promotion and protection of investments between the company's country of origin and the country where the project is to be set up.[56] The United Kingdom, for example, has signed around 26 bilateral treaties of this type with African countries.[57]

C. A crisis in the legitimacy of international arbitration in Africa?

594 Investment arbitration. – International arbitration is experiencing a crisis of legitimacy throughout the world, being perceived, wrongly, as an opaque method of settling disputes and a breeding ground for corruption, criticised by civil society and even by certain institutions and States. It is investment arbitration in particular that has to face up to this criticism, as the stakes involved are often higher, due to the amounts involved, the strategic sectors concerned and the presence of a defendant State. However, investment arbitration is often the type of arbitration that will be used in project financing when difficulties arise between the State and the project company or its investors.

595 Increased transparency. – In response to criticism of the opacity of arbitration, a clear trend has emerged in recent years towards greater transparency in arbitration proceedings, particularly investor-State arbitration. The publication of awards and other procedural documents is encouraged,[58] not to mention the possible participation of civil society in certain proceedings.

However, States may suffer from a lack of representation. The management of such proceedings requires a certain degree of responsiveness, a large budget, invitations to tender for representation, and the establishment of a strategy and follow-up. Some governments, particularly in Africa, are not sufficiently equipped and/or accustomed to dealing with this type of litigation, which requires dedicated teams and skills.

596 African States and ICSID. – Without restricting the analysis to the African continent, it can be noted that ICSID arbitrations frequently involve African States,[59] while noting that they are condemned in only 33% of cases.[60] For the calendar year 2023, 12% of ICSID cases registered involved a State or regional economic integration organisation from sub-Saharan Africa.[61]

56 The specificities of investment protection in Africa Michel Trochu I.B.L.J. 2022, 3/4, 305–318.
57 Kluwer Law International – Bits.
58 See in particular the UNCITRAL Rules on Transparency in Investor-State Arbitration of 1er April 2014.
59 In 2023, States in sub-Saharan Africa and the MENA region accounted for 12% and 17%, respectively, of registered proceedings, see "The ICSID Caseload – Statistics Issue 2024-1".
60 ICSID, "The ICSID Caseload – Statistics Special Focus Africa", May 2017.
61 ICSID, "The ICSID Caseload – Statistics Issue 2024-1", February 2024.

This does not mean that African States are over-represented.[62] However, this type of intra-African dispute is tending to develop, thanks in particular to the greater number of investment treaties, regional and continental initiatives and the increase in trade and exchanges between African States.[63]

597 Low number of African referees. – On the other hand, there is a real crisis in the representativeness of African arbitrators. Few African arbitrators are appointed to tribunals and ad hoc committees. The latest ICSID statistics show that specialists from sub-Saharan Africa account for only 3% of appointed arbitrators, conciliators and ad hoc committee members (around 60), and 3% for the MENA region.[64] In the ICSID statistics for 2023, Africa accounted for fewer than 100 appointments made by ICSID.[65] In fact, African arbitrators accounted for only 3.6% of appointments.[66] It should also be noted that African arbitrators are almost exclusively appointed in the case of disputes in Africa, but very few in the case of disputes on other continents, which contrasts with the case of European or American arbitrators who are frequently appointed for arbitrations linked to the financing of African projects. We can only hope that diversity and representativeness will increase in the decades to come.

D. Other dispute resolution methods

1. RECOURSE TO THE COURTS

As judge of the merits of the case

598 Role of the administrative courts. – Local courts may have jurisdiction to settle disputes relating to PPPs. As PPP contracts are often administrative in nature, they are subject to special regimes, or even, in countries with a duality of jurisdictions, disputes may come under the jurisdiction of the administrative courts.[67] This is the case in Benin and Côte d'Ivoire[68] as in most civil law countries on the African continent.

599 Single jurisdiction. – On the other hand, in countries with a single jurisdiction, such as Senegal or Cameroon,[69] disputes, although administrative, may come under the jurisdiction of the ordinary courts. However, the jurisdiction of local courts is

62 For example, Central American and Caribbean States accounted for 23% of cases in 2023, see "The ICSID Caseload – Statistics Issue 2024-1".

63 W. Ben Hamida, A. Ngwanza and J.-B. Harelimana, *op. cit.*

64 ICSID, "The ICSID Caseload – Statistics Issue 2024-1", *op. cit.*

65 *Ibid.*

66 ICC dispute Resolution 2019 statistics.

67 See in French law Ph. Delelis and L.-M. Nicolas, *JCl. adm.* – Fasc. 728: Partenariats public-privé, 2021, no. 161 et seq.

68 Law no. 2016-24 of 28 June 2017 on the legal framework for public-private partnerships in the Republic of Benin; Decree no. 2012-1151 of 19 December 2012 on public-private partnership contracts (Côte d'Ivoire).

69 Art. 37 of Law no. 2014-09 of 20 February 2014 on partnership contracts (Senegal); Decree no. 2008/0115/PM of 24 January 2008 specifying the terms of application of Law no. 2006/012 of 29 December 2006 setting out the general regime for partnership contracts (Cameroon).

not automatic, and legislation relating to partnership contracts often leaves it up to the parties to choose in the contract the desired method of dispute resolution, which is often arbitration. Indeed, as explained earlier, and as in other areas,[70] arbitration is often the chosen method, and recourse to the courts to decide on the merits of the dispute is in the minority, and the parties to the project most often wish to avoid it for reasons of jurisdiction, compliance and neutrality.

A single resolution system should be preferred to cover all or as many of the contracts covered by the project finance, to ensure that a single procedure settles all disputes between the parties.

Prior to or in parallel with arbitration proceedings

600 Provisional and conservatory measures. – In all cases, the State courts remain involved. Prior to the constitution of an arbitral tribunal, the court retains jurisdiction to order provisional and protective measures.[71]

601 Supporting judge. – The State judge with jurisdiction over the seat of the arbitration may also act as a "supporting judge" when the arbitration is ad hoc. In this capacity, he or she is responsible for assisting the parties and, where appropriate, the arbitral tribunal in the event of procedural difficulties (constitution of the arbitral tribunal, challenge of arbitrators, etc.).[72]

As a judge of control and enforcement

602 Supervision of the arbitration award. – Finally, the judge's intervention remains critical as the judge reviewing the arbitration award, in the context of appeals to set aside or appeal against the *exequatur* order.[73] The arbitral award is still subject to review by the court of first instance, on specific and limited grounds. In order to have full effect in a given legal system, the award must be *exequatur*, which also entails a review of the award.

603 Judge of enforcement. – The State court retains jurisdiction as an enforcement judge when it is a matter of resorting to forced execution of the award.

2. OTHER ALTERNATIVE DISPUTE RESOLUTION METHODS

Mediation

604 Distinction from arbitration. – Mediation differs from other methods of dispute resolution in that it aims to resolve disputes amicably (rather than through the courts) through the intervention of a third party. It is a method of dispute resolution

70 On this subject, see J. El Ahdab and D. Mainguy, *Droit de l'arbitrage: Théorie et pratique*, LexisNexis, 2021, n° 77 et seq.

71 Art. 13 of the OHADA Uniform Act on Arbitration Law of 23 November 2017; art. 9 of the UNCITRAL Model Law on International Commercial Arbitration (2006).

72 Ch. Seraglini and J. Ortscheidt, *Droit de l'arbitrage interne et international*, LGDJ, 2019, n° 265 et seq.

73 See generally J. El Ahdab and D. Mainguy, *op. cit.*, nos. 1520 et seq. and 1662 et seq.

that aims to be effective. The aim is not to reach a fair decision, but to resolve the dispute. For this reason, international infrastructure contracts regularly include clauses on negotiation, arbitration and mediation, with mediation being a prerequisite for another method of dispute resolution should the latter prove unsuccessful.

Mediation is booming and is being promoted by legislators, economic players and international organisations. As such, mediation enjoys genuine international recognition, as demonstrated by the adoption of the United Nations Convention on International Mediation Settlement Agreements (known as the Singapore Convention). Mediation has also been recognised and adopted in Africa, where it has traditionally been used to settle disputes.[74]

The OHADA Uniform Act on mediation follows this trend[75] and the introduction of an "*ad hoc* mediation process is clearly an excellent method of resolving a crisis between two contracting parties who wish to continue or terminate their relationship without recourse to judicial or arbitral proceedings".[76]

Dispute boards

605 The Dispute Resolution Board (DRB). – This is a dispute resolution panel most often used originally in construction contracts or projects[77] in English-speaking countries. It is generally made up of three experts (technical or legal), appointed in the same way as arbitrators, at the start of a project or for specific disputes. The role of these adjudicating experts is to monitor the progress of the project at all stages (site visits, meetings with the parties, etc.) and to be able to intervene at any time to prevent and resolve difficulties between the parties, on a temporary basis, with a view to ensuring the continuity of the project.

606 Power of investigation and facilitation. – As such, the dispute board has significant investigative powers and can play a facilitating role in that it generally has useful technical knowledge. Dispute boards also have the power to issue a binding, but not final, decision, which allows the parties to have recourse to other dispute resolution mechanisms if necessary.

74 A. Fénéon, J.-M. Tchakoua and N. Aka, *Le nouveau droit de l'arbitrage et de la médiation en Afrique (Ohada)*, LGDJ, 2018.

75 Cf. A. Fénéon, *op. cit.*

76 Danyele Palazo-Gauthier and Alain Fénéon, "Pourquoi la médiation peut faciliter la reprise des relations d'affaires en Afrique dans le contexte post-Covid", *La Tribune Afrique*, 29 May 2020.

77 For an overview of this alternative dispute resolution method, see J. Jenkins, *International Construction Arbitration Law*, Kluwer Law International, 2021, p. 72 et seq. and 121 et seq.; J. Perry, "Dispute Boards", *in* F. de Lys and P.-A. Gélinas, *Dispute Prevention and Settlement through Expert Determination and Dispute Boards, Dossiers of the ICC Institute of World Business Law*, 2017, vol. 15, pp. 97–105.

15 Insolvency of the project company

607 Insolvency of the SPV. – In project finance, the insolvency of the SPV, established to manage a specific infrastructure, presents significant legal consequences and risks for continuation of the infrastructure service which can be critical. It represents also a major issue for lenders and probably the worst scenario which they have tried to prevent by carefully allocating and mitigating any risks. We provide in the following an overview of its implications, focusing on the unique aspects of insolvency within the realm of project financing.

Section 1. Risks associated with insolvency

§ 1. Operational disruptions

608 Operational disruptions. – Insolvency can cause significant operational disruptions, affecting the project's ability to deliver services or meet performance standards. These disruptions can lead to breaches of contractual obligations and further financial losses. Ensuring continuity of operations during insolvency proceedings is a critical risk management challenge.

609 OHADA AUPC. – To fix these challenges, in the OHADA Member States, the OHADA AUPC provides a framework for restructuring and continuing business operations. Similarly, in African common law countries such as South Africa, the Companies Act of 2008 (Chapter 6) provides for business rescue procedures, allowing for the restructuring of debts and the continuation of business operations during insolvency proceedings. The first objective always must be to ensure continuity despite financial difficulties.

§ 2. Reputational damage

610 Reputational Damage. – The insolvency of a project company can tarnish its reputation and that of its stakeholders, including sponsors, lenders and contractors. Reputational damage can affect future business opportunities, investor confidence and stakeholder relationships. Managing communications and stakeholder expectations, particularly of public and finance parties, is vital to mitigating reputational risks and restoring trust in any restructuring.

DOI: 10.4324/9781003616894-19

§ 3. Financial losses

611 Impact of financial losses. – Financial losses are a significant risk in insolvency scenarios. Stakeholders may face write-offs, reduced recoveries and increased costs associated with legal proceedings and asset management. The financial implications extend beyond the immediate insolvency, potentially affecting the broader financial health of involved parties.

§ 4. Legal and litigation risks

612 Legal and Litigation Risks. – Insolvency often leads to legal disputes and litigation, as stakeholders seek to protect their interests and recover losses. Litigation can be protracted and costly, with uncertain outcomes. Engaging experienced legal counsel and adopting a proactive approach to dispute resolution are essential strategies to manage legal risks.

Section 2. Legal consequences

§ 1. Impact on contracts and agreements

613 Insolvency legal impact. – One of the primary legal consequences of a project company's insolvency is the effect on its contracts and agreements. The insolvency may trigger default clauses in various contracts, including financing agreements, construction contracts, and operation and maintenance agreements. These defaults can lead to the termination of contracts, accelerated repayment obligations and potential legal disputes.

614 Insolvency in OHADA countries. – In many francophone countries, especially OHADA ones, the legislation sets a principle of continuity of contracts. This principle aims not only to maintain the activity of the debtor company but also to sustain its contractual framework. According to Article 107 of the Uniform Act Organizing Collective Proceedings for Wiping off Debts (AUPC), this principle is explicitly applied in the curative phase of collective proceedings (judicial reorganisation and liquidation). The AUPC distinguishes two main types of procedure in case of restructuring:

- Judicial Reorganisation: This curative phase aims to reorganise the company to continue its operations and settle debts while maintaining contractual relationships.
- Liquidation: This involves winding up the company's assets and business to pay off debts. The liquidation process prioritises the payment hierarchy, determining how creditors are compensated.

615 Insolvency in common law countries. – In most of the African countries applying common law, the legal system usually distinguishes between administration aiming at rescuing the company, voluntary arrangements when a company is insolvent and the directors propose to the company's creditors the best way to save the company from liquidation, receivership where the objective is to realise and sell the company's assets and help settle the outstanding debts, and liquidation where the whole assets and business are to be liquidated to settle the debts. Often, the laws in anglophone countries also provide no right of termination in the event of insolvency or financial difficulty. There are, however, some limited exceptions such as if the supplier can show to a court that continuing to supply will cause it hardship (although demonstrating this is likely to be challenging).

§ 2. Rights of creditors

616 Creditors, including lenders, suppliers and contractors, have specific rights in the event of insolvency.

617 Claims. – If a project is not a typical project finance type of project without recourse to the sponsors, then lenders and creditors can claim on shareholders' assets if the SPV defaults, offering high security but posing significant risk to shareholders, especially if they granted some securities on their assets. In contrast, a typical project finance is said to be a non-recourse financing and this limits lenders' claims to project assets, safeguarding shareholders but heightening lenders' risk if the project fails.

618 Creditors in OHADA Countries. – The AUPC applicable in OHADA countries introduces unified important legal elements for creditors in the event of insolvency. Particularly, the insolvency process will prioritise the payment hierarchy, affecting how and when creditors are paid.

Senior lenders may have first claims on the assets of the project company due to their secured positions. Unsecured creditors may face significant recoverability issues, leading to potential losses.

619 Imperative rules. – Each country might have specific imperative rules which may not be avoided through the contractual scheme set up initially. In particular, under the revised AUPC, there exist rules that protect payments to employees (AUPC section 4) and to social security and tax authorities (AUPC art.149) before secured creditors. For common law countries, the administration process will usually freeze the proceedings against the insolvent company.[1]

620 Receiver's role. – Usually an administrator or receiver will be appointed to manage the insolvency proceedings and the interaction to reorganise the SPV and/or restructure debts in order to prevent a liquidation. Its rights and obligations will vary according to the legal framework applicable in the concerned country.

§ 3. Project assets and liens

621 Collateral on assets. – Project assets, which are often the collateral for the financing, may be subject to liens and claims by creditors. The insolvency proceedings will determine the disposition of these assets, which can include the transfer or sale of the infrastructure project. The legal complexities surrounding liens and

1 See for instance in Ghana, Corporate Insolvency and Restructuring Act 1015, 2020, 32.

security interests must be navigated carefully to protect the interests of all stakeholders. On top of this, the banks financing the project will usually have requested a right to step in and take over the project or the SPV. This right is actually rarely implemented by banks which do not wish to be exposed to financial and management risks in case of insolvency of the SPV. However, it can enable banks to organise takeover and restructuring in order to reorganise the SPV's activities or create a new one and benefit from the provisions of all direct agreements negotiated with all stakeholders to facilitate the continuation of the SPV's business.

622 Impact over PPP agreements. – In PPP contracts, payment is usually staggered over the life of the contract, and the unpaid portion can act as a security mechanism. In the event of the project company's insolvency, the public authority may, subject to imperative insolvency rules and rights of creditors, take possession of the infrastructure built on its land without being obliged to pay the remuneration balance. However, the public entity will always need to repay the financing if such financing has not yet been fully repaid.4 Regulatory and Compliance Issues – change of control

623 Regulatory and compliance issues. – Insolvency can lead to regulatory and compliance issues, especially if the SPV operates in a highly regulated sector such as energy, transportation or utilities. Regulatory bodies may impose additional requirements or penalties, and the SPV may need to undergo a regulatory review or approval process for any restructuring or transfer of ownership. This adjustment period can affect the project's timeline and budget, as new shareholders may have different priorities or financial constraints. However, they will need to comply with sectoral regulatory frameworks.

For example, in Togo, the Water Code[2] stipulates that in the event of a change of owner, beneficiary or holder of a concession relating to the operation of public water, the new owner or beneficiary must notify the Minister responsible for water within three months from the date of the transfer.

Effective change management is essential to address these challenges and ensure regulatory compliance.

Section 3. Mitigation strategies

624 Management of SPV insolvency. – The insolvency of a project company managing infrastructure financed through project financing presents complex legal consequences and risks. Proactive risk management, comprehensive due diligence and robust contractual protections are essential to mitigate these challenges. By understanding and preparing for the potential implications of insolvency, stakeholders can navigate the process more effectively and protect their interests.

§ 1. Comprehensive due diligence

625 Comprehensive Due Diligence. – Conducting thorough due diligence before project inception can help identify potential insolvency risks and assess the project's

2 Article 22 of the Water Code, Togo.

financial viability. Understanding the legal and regulatory environment, as well as the project's contractual framework, provides a foundation for risk management.

§ 2. Robust contractual protections

626 Contractual protections. – Incorporating strong contractual protections, such as default and termination clauses, step-in rights and financial covenants, can safeguard stakeholders' interests in the event of insolvency. Clear contractual terms help manage expectations and provide mechanisms for addressing insolvency-related issues.

627 Purpose clause. – Including a "purpose clause" in a credit agreement may more clearly protect lenders to avoid the project company to become insolvent using improperly any loan proceeds outside the specified purpose.[3]

628 Conditions precedent. – Moreover, in cases where there has been a significant deterioration in the project company's risk profile, conditions precedent to subsequent drawdown can give the lender the option to continue, change the terms or terminate with the project. The risk of insolvency can be mitigated by having conditions that require evidence or suitable confirmations showing that applicable financial and other forecasts continue to ensure that the project will meet the agreed financial ratio requirements. Other protective conditions include ensuring that the representations set out in the financing agreements remain accurate and that no event of default is ongoing.

629 If an event occurs that prevents any of the condition's precedent, the project company will need to request the lenders to waive that condition before it can borrow additional funds for the project. Usually, lenders will grant the requested waiver. However, before doing so, they will seek additional information or assurances from the project company. By including conditions precedent to subsequent drawdowns, lenders are entitled to request additional information or assurances, even if they do not have a specific right to do so. This allows them to withhold funds without breaching their obligations under the credit agreement.

630 Credit agreement specifications. – Typically, the credit agreement requires that the initial conditions precedent documentation be "in form and substance satisfactory" to the lender.[4] Moreover, the contracting authority can seek assurance that the project company's articles of association properly reflect the obligations assumed under the contract. For this reason, some contracts specify that any modification to the company's articles of association will only take effect once approved by the contracting authority. Also, the lender often wants the shareholders to remain tied to the fate of the project company for as long as possible so that their interests align as closely as possible with his own (for example, ensuring the project's long-term financial viability).

3 John DEWAR, *op. cit.*, p. 162.
4 John DEWAR, *op. cit.*, pp. 163–164.

631 Laws. – Also, usually, the law outlines steps that the borrower and/or secured lender(s) must take to "perfect" the security. "Failure to 'perfect' these security interests may have severe repercussions for the lender, especially in the event of the borrower's insolvency. Such 'unperfected' security for corporate entities will generally be void against the liquidator and other creditors".[5]

§ 3. Contingency planning

632 Contingency strategy. – Developing contingency plans for potential insolvency scenarios ensures readiness to respond effectively. These plans should outline steps for maintaining operations, managing communications and navigating legal processes which might be particularly challenging in some African countries. Regularly reviewing and updating contingency plans is crucial to adapt to changing circumstances and is key to gain trust from partnering financial institutions.

5 The Gravitas Review of Business & Property Law, *A Review of the Nigerian Law and Practice on Perfection of Charges*, September 2021.

Bibliography

1. Reports

Attracting Investors to African Public-Private Partnerships, "A Project Preparation Guide", The World Bank, ICA, PPIAF, 2009.

BCG and AFC, "Infrastructure Financing in Sub-Saharan Africa, Best Practices from Ten Years in the Field", BCG and AFC, 2017.

Luis GRAVITO, Jared HADDON, Andrew ALLI and Alice USANASE, "Infrastructure Financing in Sub-Saharan Africa – Best EST Practices from Ten Years in the Field", BCG and AFC, May 2017.

Antoine HUARD and Benjamin FREMAUX, "Solar Energy in Africa: A Bright Future", Institut Montaigne, 2019.

ICA c/o AfDB, "Infrastructure Financing Trends in Africa – 2018", ICA Report, 2018.

ICA c/o AfDB, "Trends in Infrastructure Financing in Africa – 2019–2020", ICA Report, 2022.

Caitlin MACLEAN and Katie OLDERMAN, "Innovative Financing Models for Energy Infrastructure in Africa", Milken Institute, May 2015.

Tomoko MATSUKAWA, Robert SHEPPARD and Joseph WRIGHT, "Foreign Exchange Risk Mitigation for Power and Water Projects in Developing Countries", The World Bank Group and The Energy and Mining Sector Board, December 2003.

Paris Europlace, "Marché mondial des infrastructures, Les enjeux de la Place de Paris", Report of the Paris EUROPLACE Working Group on Infrastructure Financing, 9 January 2020.

Partenariats Public Privé, "Cadres juridiques et institutionnels en Afrique", Comparative Study, ALSF.

"Renewable Energy Finance Sovereign Guarantees - renewable energy finance brief 01, IRENA 01", January 2020.

The Economist Corporate Network and Herman WARREN, "Spanning Africa's Infrastructure Gap: How Development Capital Is Transforming Africa's Project Build-Out", PPIAF, World Bank, November 2015.

"16 Infrastructure Projects for African Integration", United Nations Economic Commission for Africa and NEPAD, 2016.

2. Works

Nick MERRITT and Simon Currie Mark MOSELEY, *Allocating Risks in PPP Contracts*, Global Infrastructure Hub, Global Infrastructure Hub 2016.

Lise Bosman, *Arbitration in Africa: A Perspective Guide*, Wolters Kluwer, 2013.

Mathias AUDIT, Sylvain BOLLÉE and Pierre CALLÉ, *Droit du commerce international et des investissements étrangers*, 2nd edition, LGDJ, 2016.

David Corchia and Ivan Bénichou, *Le financement de projets – Project Finance*, Eska, 2000.

Developing Loan Markets, LMA Publication Book, 2013.

Défis du droit des affaires en Afrique, Mélanges I, Collective Work, L'Harmattan, 2020.

Jeffrey Delmon, *Private Sector Investment in Infrastructure, Project Finance, PPP Projects and Risk*, Wolters Kluwer, 2nd edition, 2009.

Jalal El Ahdab and Daniel Mainguy, *Droit de l'arbitrage, Théorie et pratique*, LexisNexis, 2021.

Guillaume Feld, *Droit et pratique des grands projets à l'international, Une perspective civiliste*, Legitech, 2020.

Pierre-Henri Ganem, *Sécurisation contractuelle des investissements internationaux, Grands Projets*, Bruylant, 1998.

PPP Reference Guide Version 2.0, World Bank Group – PPIAF, 2016.

Virginie Haubert-McGetrick and Guillaume Ansaloni, *Financement de Projet, Enjeux juridiques et bancabilité d'une opération*, Revue Banque, 2011.

Paul Lignières and Anne-Marie Toledo, *Le Financement de projet*, Ed. Joly, 2002.

Michel Lyonnet du Moutier, Clement Fourchy and Charlotte Mauviot, *Financement de projet et partenariats public-privé*, 3rd edition, EMS Management & Société, 2023.

Charlotte Mauviot, *Infrastructures: stratégies d'investisseurs*, EMS Management & Société, 2022.

Cedric Achille Mbeng Mezui and Bim Hundal, *Structured Finance: Conditions for Infrastructure Project Bonds in African Capital Markets*, NEPAD, 2013.

Mthuli Ncube and Charles Leyeka Lufumpa, *Infrastructures in Africa, Lessons for Future Development*, Bristol University Press, 2017.

Nicholas AVERY, *Public Private Partnerships, A Practical Analysis*, Globe Law and Business, 2006.

Ronald F. Sullivan, *International Project Financing*, 3rd edition, Juris Publishing, 2009.

Vingt ans d'arbitrage OHADA: bilans et perspectives, Proceedings of the Symposium Organised by the Conférence des barreaux de l'Espace OHADA and Jus Africa, 17–18 October 2019.

Graham Vinter, *Project Finance, a Legal Guide*, Sweet & Maxwell, 2005.

E. R. Yescombe, *Principles of Project Finance*, Academic Press, 2013.

E. R. Yescombe and Edward Farquharson, *Public-Private Partnerships for Infrastructure: Principles of Policy and Finance*, Butterworth-Heinemann, 2018.

Paul D. Clifford, *Project Finance: Applications and Insights to Emerging Markets Infrastructure*, Wiley, 2020.

John M. Niehuss, *International Project Finance in a Nutshell*, West Academic, 3rd edition, 2020.

Stefano Gatti, *Project Finance in Theory and Practice: Designing, Structuring, and Financing Private and Public Projects*, Academic Press, 4th edition, 2023.

Edward Bodmer, *Corporate and Project Finance Modeling: Theory and Practice*, Wiley, 2014.

Scott L. Hoffman, *The Law and Business of International Project Finance*, Cambridge University Press, 3rd edition, 2007.

Neil S. Grigg, *Infrastructure Finance: The Business of Infrastructure for a Sustainable Future*, Wiley Finance, 2010.

3. Articles

Rabah Arezki and Amadou Sy, "Financing Africa's Infrastructure Deficit: From Development Banking to Long-Term Investing", *Journal of African Economies*, 2016, vol. 25, AERC, Supplement 2.

Laure Bergala, "Infrastructures en Afrique, combler le gap de financement", *Revue Banque*, October 2020.

Vivien FOSTER, "The Changing Landscape of Infrastructure in Africa, Nontraditional Sources Take on a Growing Role", *Grid Lines, PPIAF*, October 2008.
Julian GREGORY and Benjamin K. SOVACOOL, "The Financial Risks and Barriers to Electricity Infrastructure in Kenya, Tanzania and Mozambique: A Critical and Systematic Review of the Academic Literature", *Energy Policy, Elsevier*, 2019, vol. 125, 145–153.
Britta KLAGGE and Chigozie NWEKE-EZE, "Financing Large-Scale Renewable-Energy Projects in Kenya: Investor Types, International Connections, and Financialization", *Geografiska Annaler: Series B, Human Geography*, 2020, vol. 102, no. 1, 61–83.
Kannan LAKMEEHARAN, Qaizer MANJI, Ronald NYAIRO and Harald POELTNER, "Solving Africa's Infrastructure Paradox", *McKinsey & Company*, 6 March 2020.
Johann Lübbe PR ENG, "Project Finance as Driver of Economic Growth in Africa", *Civil Engineering*, October 2016.
Abebe Aemro SELASSIE, Luc EYRAUD and Catherine PATTILLO, "How to Attract Private Funds to Finance Africa's Development", *International Monetary Fund Blog*, 14 June 2021.

Appendices

Appendix 1

Financing an infrastructure project: the project life cycle

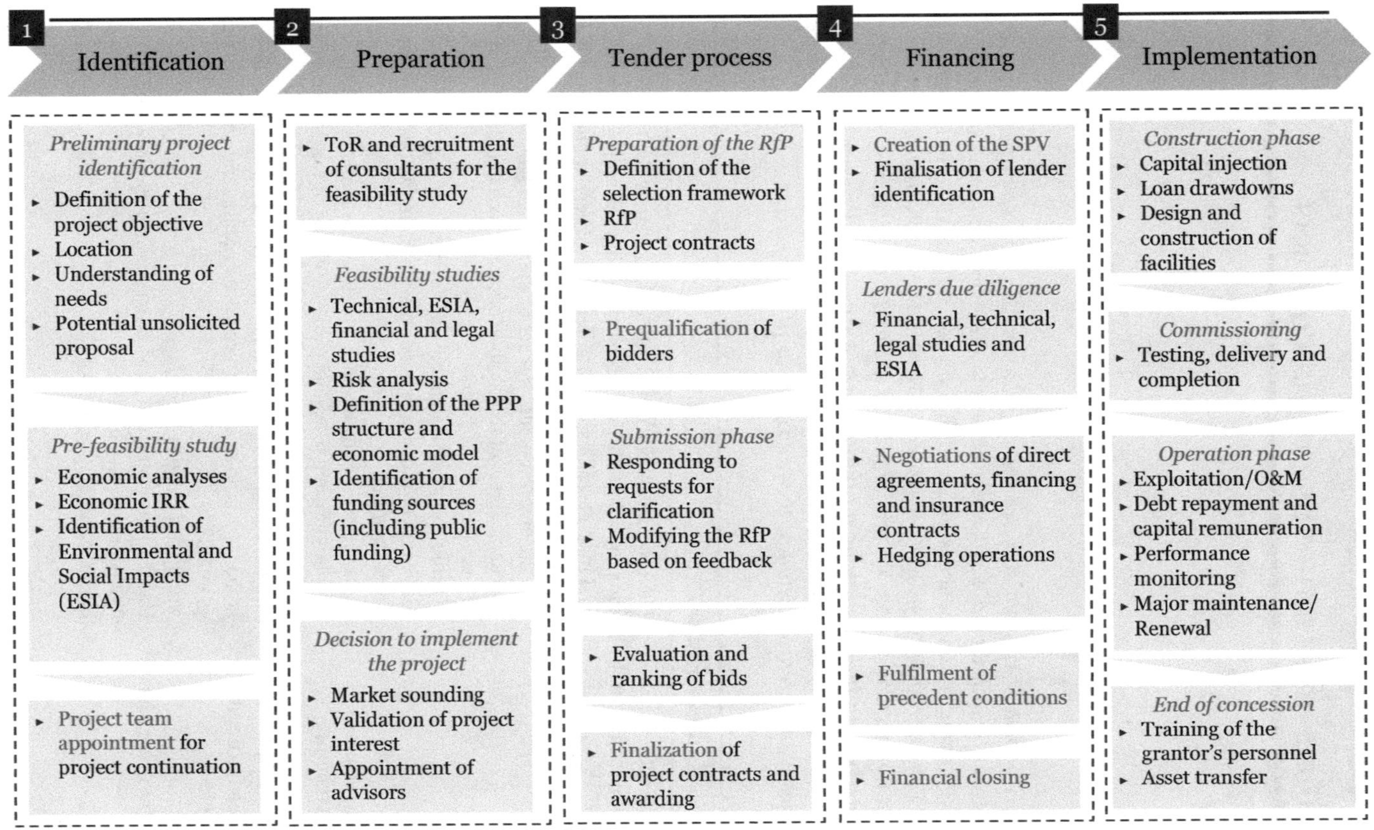

Figure A.1 Financing an infrastructure project: the project life cycle

Appendix 2

Points of attention on project contracts

This appendix sets out some of the main questions that the parties may ask themselves about three main project contracts in order to ensure that the project is running smoothly: the concession or PPP contract, the construction contract and the O&M contract. It does not necessarily cover all the points that need to be checked (and in particular does not go into detail about the allocation of risks between the parties), but it does provide an initial overview of the main checks that need to be made to ensure that the project can be implemented under good governance conditions with a clear division of the prerogatives of each party.

Concession contract or PPP	
Project environment	– Have studies been carried out to demonstrate the feasibility of the project? Have they been carried out (technical, economic and market studies, demand forecasts where applicable, financial analyses)? Have site visits been organised? – Has the environmental impact of the project been assessed? – Has an analysis of the socio-economic costs and benefits of the project been carried out? – Is senior political leadership and interest in the project assured? Have one or more members of government who support the project been identified?
Governance structure	– Does the proposed structure comply with applicable laws? – Are the different roles and responsibilities of the parties clearly defined and appropriate?
Planned construction phase	– Are the construction milestones and deadlines clearly defined? – Is the transition phase between construction and commissioning well planned? – Are there penalties for delays?
Operating phase	– Has a comprehensive O&M programme been drawn up? – Are penalties provided for? – Is subcontracting authorised?

Concession contract or PPP	
Involvement of the public sector	– Has the host country defined a coherent political strategy? Does it plan to launch several infrastructure projects? Does it draw on the experience of other countries? Can it be stable over the long term? – Is there a centralised unit responsible for infrastructure development in the country? – Can subsidies be provided for projects requiring public support? – How is the public sector involved (appointment of a project director, identification of the main representatives of the public parties)? – Is the involvement of users or beneficiaries planned (dissemination of a clear message about the objective and public interest of the project)?
Applicable laws and regulations	– What are the existing regulations? How are they interpreted by the host country? – Are the key concessions, permits and authorisations validly issued? – How are the assets covered by the contract managed? – Does the legislation allow private financing of infrastructure? Does it encourage it? Does it clearly define the roles, responsibilities and rights of the various parties? Are its terms open to unambiguous interpretation by the regulatory authorities? – Are advertising and competitive tendering procedures provided for? Have they been observed? – Are there independent regulatory authorities? – Is international arbitration possible?
Contracts	– What are the contracts to be concluded (for supply, sale of services, etc.)? – Are the co-contractors technically and financially reliable? – Do the co-contractors understand all their contractual obligations? Are they able to meet them? – Are there any restrictions in the event of a change of control?

Construction contract (EPC type)[1]	
Sponsors and investors	– Are the project team and sponsors reliable? – Are the investors and the various advisors chosen a competent and diverse group of professionals? Is the expertise mobilised by the external and internal sponsors sufficient to accurately assess the project's opportunities and risks? – Is the relationship between the various players appropriate (coverage of all the project's subjects, including niche subjects, clear distribution of roles and responsibilities)? – Is the project fully funded? – Has a clear, structured funding strategy been defined (identification of the target sector, definition of the expected IRR, etc.)? – Has the financial modelling been completed?

1 For more details on the practice of EPC contracts, see *Engineer, Procure and Construct (EPC) Contracts: Key Issues*, Practical Law Construction, Thomson Reuters.

Construction contract (EPC type)

General	– Does the builder have the necessary experience and resources to carry out the contract? – Is the contract comprehensive and turnkey? – What are the obligations of each party under the EPC contract? – Does the EPC co-contractor assume the risks of the SPV within the scope of the contract?
Subcontracting	– Can the contractor subcontract certain contracts? – If so, will the SPV/public party need to approve the main subcontractors? – Do subcontracts have to reflect the terms of the main EPC contract? – What happens to subcontracts if the main contract is terminated?
Duration	– What is the duration of the contract? – Can it be extended? – When does the contract come into force? – Are there any conditions precedent linked to other contracts?
Applicable law	– Which law governs the contract? – What does the contract say about the risk of a change of law?
Prices	– Does the contract include a fixed price? – What, if anything, is excluded from the fixed price? – Can the parties adjust the price, and if so, when?
Contractual payments	– What currency is used for payments? Is there currency hedging if necessary? – Does the contract include a payment schedule? – Does the contract provide for an invoicing and advance payment mechanism? – Does the SPV owe the contractor interest for late payment? – How is late payment interest calculated?
Changes of control	– Does the contract include a change of control clause? – Is the change of control subject to notification or authorisation by the SPV? – Can the contract be assigned to the lenders by direct agreement? What rights do the lenders have?
Guarantees and insurance	– What guarantees are provided under the EPC contract? – What legal guarantees must the contractor comply with? – Does the contractor have to provide a performance bond? – Is the contractor obliged to provide a completion guarantee? – Is the contractor obliged to provide a ten-year guarantee for all defects affecting the work? – What type of financial guarantee must the contractor provide (independent guarantee, bond, other) under the contract? – Is there a ceiling on the contractor's liability for defects? – Are insurance policies required? – Does the contract provide a means of checking the insurance policies taken out by the contractor? – Do the insurance policies taken out comply with lenders' requirements?

Construction contract (EPC type)

Defects	– What are the construction deadlines? – How are they governed by the contract? – Can construction deadlines be extended? – In the event of serious or repeated default by the contractor, can the SPV continue to perform the contract by appointing a substitute third-party contractor to carry out all or part of the work at the EPC's expense? – When can the contract be terminated? – How can the project owner terminate the contract? – How can the contractor terminate the contract?
Penalties	– What does the contract stipulate in terms of penalties for non-performance of contractual obligations? Do they at least reflect the amounts set out in the concession contract for the SPV vis-à-vis the public party?
Force majeure	– How is force majeure defined? – How is the risk of force majeure shared between the parties? – Does the contract provide for other grounds for contractual exemption?

Operation & maintenance contract (O&M)

Settlement of disputes	– Does the contract clearly provide for recourse to arbitration to settle disputes between the parties? – What are the terms and conditions of arbitration?
General	– Does the O&M company have the necessary experience and resources to carry out the contract? – What is the nature of the O&M contract (lump sum, other, etc.)? – What are the operator's obligations under any public service obligations? – Does the O&M co-contractor assume the risks of the SPV within its scope of operation?
Duration	– What is the effective date of the O&M contract? – Can it be extended? – Are there any conditions precedent to entry into force?
Applicable law	– Which law governs the contract? – Are disputes submitted to arbitration or to an independent court? – What does the contract say about the risk of a change of law?
Change of control	– Does the contract include a change of control clause? – What rights do the lenders have? Can the contract be assigned to them?
Subcontracting	– Can the operator subcontract certain contracts? – If so, will the SPV (and host State) need to approve the main subcontractors? – Do subcontracts have to reflect the terms of the O&M contract? – What happens to subcontracts if the O&M contract is terminated?
Payments	– What currency is the contract denominated in? – Can pricing be adjusted during the term of the O&M contract?

Cancellation	– When can the O&M contract be terminated? – How can the contract be terminated? – How is force majeure defined? – How is the risk of force majeure shared between the parties?
Penalties and transfer of risk	– What does the contract stipulate in terms of penalties for non-performance of contractual preventive/curative maintenance obligations? – Are the penalties in line with those usually proposed on the market? – The SPV could suffer for lack of maintenance under the concession contract? – Are all maintenance risks transferred to the operator by the SPV?
Guarantees	– What guarantees does the operator provide under the O&M contract? – What legal guarantees must the operator comply with? – Does the operator have to provide an independent warranty under the contract? – Is there a cap on the operator's liability to repair defects?
Insurance	– Are insurance policies compulsory under the contract? – Does the operator comply with all the terms and conditions of the insurance policies required by the government and lenders?
Intellectual property	– What intellectual property licences, if any, must the operator provide to the SPV? Does the operator guarantee the SPV against any lack of licence or ownership of the intellectual property relating to it?

Appendix 3

Financing term sheet

This is an example of a term sheet, but lenders may each have more or less developed models depending on their practice and the nature and scale of the project.

Important note

This indicative term sheet contains the principal terms and conditions of the financing offered by the "**Lender**" or "**THE BANK**" to SPV [X] ("**the Borrower**"). It is not a contract or an offer to contract and does not purport to summarise all of the terms, conditions, undertakings, warranties, representations, promises and other provisions which will be contained in the definitive agreements executed in respect of the proposed loan or financing transaction contemplated hereby. It is specifically understood and agreed that the proposed financing or financing contained herein requires the prior written approval of the management and board of directors of the BANK (or any personnel of the BANK empowered to make such commitments) and is, therefore, subject to modification, adaptation or variation by the BANK and to such other terms and conditions as may be included or excluded by the BANK in its sole discretion in the executed definitive agreements relating to the facility or financing. The information contained in this term sheet is highly confidential and proprietary to the BANK and shall not be disclosed to anyone other than [**insert**] and its employees, agents and advisors without the prior written consent of the BANK. Upon execution of this term sheet by the Borrower, the fee and confidentiality clauses shall apply.

The loan

1	**Project**	Project description
2	**Shareholders of the SPV**	[. . .] [. . .] hereinafter referred to as the "**Shareholders**".
3	**Loan amount**	Minimum: [. . .] EUR Maximum: [. . .] EUR
4	**Currency**	EUR (euros)
5	**Maturity**	[. . .] years old

The loan

6 Availability period	[. . .] months from the date of the first disbursement
7 Capital grace period	[. . .] months from the date of the first disbursement
8 Disbursements	Disbursements will be made in accordance with the payment schedule or as otherwise agreed with the Borrower and subject to the terms and conditions of the loan.
9 Loan offer expiry date	Unless otherwise agreed between the Lender and the Borrower, the loan offer will lapse in its entirety: – if the financing documents are not signed by: [XX/XX/XXXX], the deadline set for the signature of the financing documents; – if the Borrower does not satisfy the requirements set out under the conditions precedent within 180 (one hundred and eighty) days from the Signature of the Financing Documents; – if any of the conditions precedent are not satisfied as provided herein, unless waived by the Lender. However, the Borrower shall remain liable to pay the Lender the Cancellation Costs, as well as any costs and expenses contemplated by the Lender.
10 Base interest rate	EURIBOR – three or six months (depending on how often the loan is repaid. Furthermore, in the case of financing in another currency, the interbank rate used as a reference will itself be different, for example LIBOR for loans in USD).
11 Margin	[. . .] basis points
12 Interests	Interest is payable on the Loan at [6 (six)] monthly intervals (on dates determined by the Lender) starting from the month immediately following the month in which the first disbursement was made. Interest accrues progressively and is calculated on the basis of a 360-day year and the actual number of days elapsed.
13 Interest Payment Date	Each date, as determined by the Lenders, on which interest is due and payable, with intervals of [6 (six)] months between such dates (except in respect of the period between the penultimate Interest Payment Date and the Maturity Date). The Maturity Date is also an Interest Payment Date.
14 Interest period	Refers to: Firstly, the period between the date of the first disbursement and the first interest payment date. Thereafter, each period between 2 (two) consecutive interest payment dates. Finally, the period between the penultimate interest payment date and the maturity date.
15 Loan repayment	The Loan is repaid on each Interest Payment Date following the expiry of the capital grace period. The repayment profile may be in fixed semi-annual instalments or a fixed principal amount, or it may be sculpted. In the latter case, the repayment profile of the principal and interest of the Loan will be determined by the Lenders in accordance with the Financial Base Case for the project without the weighted average life of the debt exceeding that of a loan of the same amount repayable in fixed semi-annual instalments.

The loan

16	**Expiry date**	[. . . years/. . . months] from [. . .] All amounts outstanding under the Loan must be repaid in full no later than thc Maturity Date.
17	**Voluntary advance payments**	The Borrower may prepay all or part of the Loan for a total amount of at least [. . .] million euros and multiples of [. . .] million euros, subject to payment of the Break Costs and the Standard Settlement Costs, plus a prepayment fee of [. . .] % of the amount prepaid, upon [90 days' written notice] to the Lender.
	Early repayment charges	Amounts paid in advance will be applied to the remaining repayment tranches in reverse order of maturity. Amounts paid in advance cannot be re-borrowed.
18	**Mandatory Early Repayment**	In the event of mandatory early redemption, in particular as a result of early redemption due to an Event of Default, Break Costs and Settlement Costs will apply.
19	**Voluntary cancellation**	The Borrower has the right, at any time, to terminate in full or reduce the unused portion of the Loan by giving at least [30] days prior written notice to the Lender. In the event of partial termination, the Borrower must certify to the Lender that it has sufficient funds to complete the Project and that no Event of Default has occurred or is continuing.
	Cancellation fees	Such a reduction is subject to the payment of a cancellation fee of [. . .] % of the capital amount cancelled.
20	**Commitment fee**	[. . .] % per annum, calculated on the undrawn balance of the Loan, from the date of signature and payable [quarterly], on the applicable interest payment date, in arrears, until the Loan is fully drawn down, cancelled or lapses (including completion of the Availability Period).
21	**File commission**	A fee of [. . .] % of the amount of the Loan due and payable to the Lender on the earlier of (i) financial close or (ii) the date falling [30] days after the date of signature. If accepted by the Lender, this fee may be deducted from the first disbursement.
22	**Financial base case**	Means the financial model agreed between the Lender and the Borrower which, based on certain technical, economic and other assumptions, establishes a financial forecast for the Project.

General terms and conditions

23	**Capital contribution**	The shareholder(s) of the SPV shall provide a minimum of EUR [. . .] million of equity or fully subordinated debt on terms acceptable to the Lender. Interest on any subordinated debt must be cumulative. Failure to pay any amount due under any subordinated loan agreement shall not, under the terms of such agreement, trigger an event of default under this document, so long as the Loan remains outstanding. The Shareholders may transfer the subordinated debt to any person acceptable to the Lender. The consent of the Lender to any transfer of subordinated debt shall not be unreasonably withheld or delayed. The consent of the Lender will not be required for any transfer of subordinated debt to any reputable bank which meets objective rating criteria to be agreed.

24	**Financing of cost overruns/ contingency**	A commitment to provide funding for cost overruns up to [. . .] will be required until the Project Completion Date. This commitment will cover any capital cost overruns or delay costs incurred during the construction of the Project. The cost overrun may be funded by equity or debt (or a combination of both), provided by the Borrower's Shareholders on the same basis as their shareholding or on a basis agreed by the Borrower's Shareholders.
25	**Increased costs**	The Lender will be indemnified for any increase in costs or reduction in income resulting from changes in laws or regulations (other than increases in tax on taxable income) and any changes in reserve requirements or capital adequacy regulations, if any.
26	**Default interest**	Base interest rate plus Margin plus [. . .] basis points.
27	**Fees and transaction costs**	The Borrower shall, within [30] days of the Lender's demand, pay to the Lender the amount of all costs and expenses (including attorneys' fees) reasonably incurred in connection with the negotiation, preparation, printing, execution and syndication of the Financing Documents, whether or not the Financing Documents are executed, and after financial close, the costs of any modification or enforcement of the Lenders' rights.
28	**Gross taxes**	All payments of principal, interest, fees and any other amounts shall be made in full, without set-off, counterclaim or other restriction and free from any applicable tax, charge, deduction, withholding or other levy, subject to customary exclusions. If any withholding tax is required by law (including withholding tax on interest), the applicable payments will be grossed up to ensure that the Lender receives the amount it would have received if there had been no such deduction or withholding.
29	**Financial commitments/ Ratios**	Customary for this type of transaction, including, but not limited to (a) Debt Service Coverage Ratio (**"DSCR"**) of not less than [. . .]. (b) Leverage Ratio of not more than [. . .]. (c) Interest coverage ratio not less than [. . .], which will apply after the capital grace period. Any breach by the Borrower of the covenants relating to the financial ratios shall constitute an event of default and shall entitle the Lender to charge default interest for as long as the breach continues.
30	**Debt Service Reserve Account (DSRA)**	The Borrower shall open an account with the Bank [. . .], and shall deposit and maintain in this account, at all times, a total amount equal to [. . .] months' debt servicing.
31	**Transaction Documents**	Refers to the Project Documents, the Financing Documents and the Security Documents.

32	**Project documents**	Means each of the following documents: (a) [to be inserted]; (b) [to be inserted]; (c) the shareholders' agreement of the Borrower; and (d) any other document designated as such by the Borrower and the Lender.
33	**Financing documents**	Refers to the legal agreements which document the conditions under which the Loan is to be provided: [to be inserted].
34	**Security interests** **Security documents**	The first-ranking security package will include, but is not limited to, the following: (a) the assets of the Borrower; (b) a pledge of the shares of the SPV in favour of the Lender; (c) a pledge of the shareholders' receivables; (d) an assignment or delegation of the receivables under the Project Documents; (e) an assignment or delegation of insurance indemnities; (f) a delegation of payment on [X]; (g) the DSRA; (h) a guarantee of the Shareholders' obligations to contribute to the costs of the Project; (i) etc. The structure of the securities and guarantees will be customary for transactions of this type and will be finalised upon approval of the project by the lender's credit authorities.
35	**Declarations and guarantees**	Representations and warranties customary for a transaction of this nature, including but not limited to the following (subject, where applicable, to such qualifications as to materiality and reasonableness as the parties may agree), or as disclosed to the Lender prior to the first disbursement: (a) The Borrower is a limited liability company, duly incorporated and validly existing under the laws of [name of country]. (b) The Borrower has the power to own its assets and to carry out the Project. (c) The Borrower has the power and authority to enter into and perform its obligations under the Transaction Documents to which it is or will be a party. (d) The Borrower has all necessary consents, authorisations, licences, registrations, filings, registrations, permissions and approvals. (e) The obligations expressed to be assumed by the Borrower in each financing Document are legal, valid, binding and enforceable obligations. (f) The entering into and the performance by the Borrower of the transactions contemplated by the Transaction Documents do not and will not conflict with any law or regulation applicable to it, its constating documents or any agreement binding on its assets.

35 more

(g) All consents required or desirable to enable the Borrower to enter into, exercise its rights and comply with its obligations under the Finance Documents to which it is a party and to make the Finance Documents to which it is a party admissible in evidence in the relevant jurisdiction(s) have been obtained and are of full force and effect.
(h) It is not necessary under the laws of the relevant jurisdiction(s) for the Finance Documents to be filed, registered or recorded with any court or other authority in that jurisdiction or for any stamp, registration or similar fee to be paid on or in connection with the Finance Documents or the transactions contemplated by the Finance Documents.
(i) There is no security interest in the Borrower or any of its assets.
(j) The Borrower has no business activities, debts or other financial liabilities other than those contemplated by the Project Documents.
(k) No litigation, arbitration or administrative proceeding by or before any court, arbitral tribunal or agency which, in the event of an adverse decision, could reasonably be expected to have a Material Adverse Effect has not (to its knowledge) been commenced or threatened against the Borrower.
(l) No Insolvency, Insolvency Proceedings and Creditor Arrangement Proceedings.
(m) The Borrower is in compliance with all applicable laws, including the Indigenisation and Economic Empowerment Act, tax laws and regulations and environmental laws.
(n) No Default is outstanding or will result from the completion or execution of any transaction contemplated by any Transaction Document.
(o) There are no events or circumstances outstanding which constitute a Default under any other agreement or instrument binding on the Borrower or to which any of its assets is subject and which could have a Material Adverse Effect.
(p) The Borrower is not in default or breach of any Transaction Document and no person has disputed, repudiated or disclaimed liability under any Transaction Document to which it is a party or has indicated an intention to do so.
(q) There has been no material adverse change in the financial condition of the Borrower since the date on which the last financial statements of the Borrower were prepared.
(r) The legality, validity and enforceability of the Transaction Documents.
(s) Completeness and accuracy of information.
(t) Accuracy of the most recent audited financial statements of the Borrower.
(u) All insurance required for the transaction is in place.

35 more

(v) The Borrower has good and undisputed title to or freedom to use under the laws of [name of country] or other appropriate jurisdiction such property and assets as are necessary, customary or desirable to implement the Project in accordance with the Transaction Documents and that such assets are free from encumbrances, restrictions and onerous covenants.

(w) The payment obligations of the Borrower under the Finance Documents rank at least pari passu with the claims of all of its other unsecured and unsubordinated creditors, except for obligations mandatorily preferred by law applicable to corporations generally.

(x) The Borrower shall not be entitled to claim immunity from suit, execution, attachment or other legal process in any proceedings brought in [name of country] in connection with any Transaction Document.

(y) It is not necessary under the laws of the relevant jurisdiction(s) for any financial party to be authorised, qualified or otherwise entitled to carry on business in such jurisdiction(s) in order to enforce its rights under any Finance Document or by reason of the entering into of any Finance Document or the performance by it of its obligations under any Finance Document.

36 Information commitments

Customary for a transaction of this nature, including, but not limited to

(a) Provision of monthly management accounts within [15] working days of the end of each month prior to completion of the project and quarterly management accounts within [15] working days of the end of each quarter thereafter, for the duration of the project.

(b) The Borrower's audited annual financial statements as soon as they are available.

(c) Provision of such other financial and other information as the Lender may require including site visits on reasonable notice.

(d) Notification of any event or circumstance, which could be expected to have a Material Effect on the performance by the Borrower of its obligations under the Finance Documents and of any event or circumstance which has or could reasonably be expected to have a Material Adverse Effect.

(e) Provision of details of any pending, threatened litigation, arbitration or administrative proceeding which has or could, in the event of an adverse decision, have a Material Adverse Effect.

(f) Provision of information, promptly upon request by a Financial Party, to enable the Financial Party to perform and be satisfied with the results of all applicable Know Your Customer and credit information requirements.

The time periods required for the delivery of the information required under the Information Commitments will be agreed between the parties taking into account the nature of the information required.

37	**Additional commitments**	Customary for this type of transaction (subject, where applicable, to such qualifications as to materiality and reasonableness as the parties may agree), including but not limited to: (a) Implementation of the Project in accordance with the agreed Project Development Plan. (b) Obtaining and maintaining all necessary authorisations, approvals, licences and consents. (c) Compliance with all applicable laws and regulations. (d) Immediate notification to the Lender of any issues relating to material approvals and consents, and the obtaining of required approvals. (e) Undertaking to ensure that the payment obligations of the Borrower under the Financing Documents shall at all times rank at least pari passu with all other present and future unsecured payment obligations of the Borrower, other than obligations mandatorily preferred by law applicable to general partnerships. (f) Compliance with all environmental laws and obtaining and maintaining all environmental authorisations. (g) Compliance with the Equator Principles, the environmental and social safeguard policies of the [African Development Bank/International Finance Corporation/Other] and relevant international environmental standards. (h) Indemnification of the Lender against any material loss or liability incurred by the Lender as a result of any actual or alleged violation of any Environmental Law by the Borrower or any officer of the Borrower which would not have occurred had a Financing Document not been entered into. (i) Implementation and maintenance of appropriate insurance for the Project. (j) Access to inspection of the Project by the Lender or its agents, attendance at progress meetings, completion tests and other meetings. (k) Tax compliance of the Project and the SPV. (l) Compliance with all obligations under the Project Documents.
38	**Negative commitments**	Typical for this type of transaction including but not limited to: (a) Restrictions on: (i) the declaration or payment of any dividends or payments to Shareholders whatsoever prior to the Completion Date, subject to a specific exemption agreed with the lender in respect of bridging loans granted by certain Shareholders; (ii) the repayment of inter-group loans other than the operating costs incurred by Shareholders in the ordinary course of the Borrower's business and the fee for arrangement on the Loan; (iii) the payment of interest on inter-group loans.

38 more

(b) Restriction on changes in the ownership and/or control of the Borrower or the Shareholders/Promoters (other than Permitted Transfers and the creation of an employee share option scheme approved by the Board of Directors), without the prior written consent of the Lender, which shall not be unreasonably withheld.
(c) No amendment to the shareholders' agreement without the prior approval of the Lender, which shall not be unreasonably withheld.
(d) No change in the shareholder's agreement without the prior written consent of the Lender, which shall not be unreasonably withheld.
(e) No change in the financial year of the Borrower.
(f) No change in the governing documents.
(g) Restriction on borrowings by the Borrower other than borrowings under the Finance Documents, such approval not to be unreasonably withheld by the Lender.
(h) The amount of the Loan must not be used for transactions with prohibited nationals or countries or to finance military zones, prohibited narcotics or terrorist activities.
(i) Restriction on disposal of all or part of its assets. This restriction shall not apply to (i) the disposal of property or assets which are worn out and replaced by equivalent assets the total value of which does not exceed **[to be determined by the Lenders]** million euros in any financial year; or (ii) the disposal of obsolete or redundant assets; or (iii) the disposal by the Borrower in the ordinary course of its business.
(j) Restriction on acquisitions and investments by the SPV subject to allocations agreed with the Lender.
(k) Restriction on entering into any merger, demerger or restructuring.
(l) A restriction on the issue of third party guarantees by the Borrower other than in the ordinary course of business.
(m) Restriction on entering into material contracts (other than the Project Documents) which are outside the ordinary course of business.
(n) Restriction on entering into derivative transactions (this restriction shall not apply to hedging arrangements entered into in connection with the Loan).
(o) Restriction on amendments, waivers, assignment, transfer, termination, suspension or abandonment of the Project Documents.
(p) Restriction on amendments to the statutory or constitutive documents of the Borrower.

39	**UN sanctions**	The Borrower shall not: (a) use the amount of the Loan for the purpose of directly or indirectly financing (or otherwise making available) the activities of any person or entity currently on the UN sanctions list (as hereinafter defined); or (b) contribute or otherwise make available the proceeds of the Loan to any other person or entity if the Borrower has actual knowledge that such party intends to use such proceeds for the purpose of financing the activities of any person or entity currently on the UN Sanctions List. For the purposes of this paragraph, the term: **"UN Sanctions"** means sanctions imposed at any time by the United Nations.
40	**Project completion Completion date**	Project Completion is defined as the successful completion of a Mechanical/Technical Completion Test and an Operational/ Economic Completion Test to be developed jointly by the Borrower, the ITA and the Lender. The purpose of the Completion Test is to demonstrate that the Project has reached a stable state of operation and that it is capable of maintaining that stable state of operation for the duration of the Project. The completion of the Project will include requirements that: (a) financial covenants are met for a period set by the Lenders; (b) all payments to the Lender are up to date; (c) the DSRA is fully funded; (d) there are no defaults or potential defaults. (e) the ITA appointed by the Lenders has certified all operational/technical/mechanical aspects of the test.
41	**Provisions relating to distribution blocking**	Following completion of the project, the Borrower may make distributions/payments to shareholders provided that: (a) no default or potential event of default is outstanding or would result from the distribution/payment; and (b) the Borrower is in compliance with the Distribution Undertakings.
42	**Distribution commitments**	(a) At the time of the proposed distribution/payment: (i) the DSCR is not less than **[insert]**; (ii) the debt to EBITDA ratio is not more than **[insert]**. (b) Immediately following the proposed distribution/payment: (i) the DSCR would not be less than **[insert]**; (ii) the interest cover ratio is not less than **[insert]**.
43	**Fault Events**	Typical for this type of transaction (subject, where applicable, to qualifications as to reasonableness, materiality thresholds and recourse periods), including, but not limited to: (a) non-payment; (b) breach of financial covenants; (c) breach of other obligations under the financing documents; (d) misrepresentation; (e) insolvency, insolvency proceedings or creditors' process affecting the Borrower or any debtor;

43 more

(f) the Borrower or any debtor ceases or threatens to cease trading;
(g) it becomes unlawful for the Borrower to perform any of its obligations under the Financing Documents and such obligations cannot be restructured to the satisfaction of the Lender;
(h) it becomes unlawful for any person (other than a Finance Party) to perform any of its obligations under the Finance Documents and such obligations may not be restructured to the satisfaction of the Lender;
(i) any Transaction Document is not binding and effective in accordance with its terms or is alleged by any party not to be binding and effective in accordance with its terms for any reason;
(j) the Borrower terminates any Finance Document or indicates an intention to terminate any Finance Document;
(k) a change in the ownership or control of the Borrower other than as a result of an Authorised Transfer;
(l) the occurrence of any event or circumstance which may reasonably be expected to have a Material Adverse Effect on the ability of the Borrower or any Group Company to perform its obligations under the Financing Documents;
(m) failure to complete the Project by the deadline of [. . .] months following financial close;
(n) expropriation of the Project or any part thereof or any action by the Borrower;
(o) the occurrence of an event or circumstance which constitutes a default under a Project Document where such default has or would be likely to have a Material Adverse Effect;
(p) suspension of work on the Project for one or more continuous periods of more than 45 days in aggregate;
(q) the occurrence of any event of *Force Majeure* which could reasonably be expected to result in the termination by any person of any Project Document;
(r) abandonment of the Project;
(s) any litigation, arbitration or administrative proceeding is pending or, to the knowledge of the Borrower, threatened against any person which, in the opinion of the Lender, has or, in the event of an adverse decision, is reasonably likely to have a Material Adverse Effect;
(t) the occurrence of any event or series of events which, in the opinion of the Lender, has or is reasonably likely to have a Material Adverse Effect.

44 Conditions precedent

As is customary for this type of transaction, all documents must be in form and substance satisfactory to the lender, including:

(a) the concession agreement;
(b) the government support agreement;
(c) the supply contracts;
(d) and so on. **[to be completed]**

45	**Market conditions**	After the date of this *term sheet* but prior to financial *close*, if the Lender, acting reasonably, determines, having regard to the conditions then prevailing in the national and/or international banking or capital markets, that changes in the pricing and terms of the Loan are necessary to permit its continued participation, then it shall, after consultation with the Borrower, be entitled to make such changes. These changes include any event or circumstance (including any Material Adverse Effect or the continuation of any circumstance) which has had or may have an Adverse Effect (in each case, materially) on: (a) the business, condition (financial or otherwise), operations, performance, assets or prospects of the Borrower since the date on which its last audited financial statements or the Group's last audited consolidated financial statements were prepared; (b) the ability of the Borrower or any other obligor to perform its obligations under this Agreement or any Financing Document; or (c) the relevant international or domestic syndicated loan, debt, banking or capital markets which, in the opinion of the Lender, may adversely affect syndication, during the period from the date of this *Term Sheet* to the Financial Close Date.
46	**Break-up costs**	"Breakage Costs" means the amount (if any) by which: (a) the interest which would have accrued on such part of the Loan from the date on which such part of the Loan became due and payable until the last day of the current interest period for such Loan, at a rate equal to LIBOR for such interest period interest; exceeds (b) the amount of interest that such Lender would be able to earn if it placed an amount equal to such part of the Loan on deposit with a leading bank in the London interbank market for the period commencing on the date on which such part of the Loan became due and payable and ending on the last day of the then current Interest Period for such Loan.
47	**Settlement costs**	Means all actual costs, expenses and disbursements incurred by the Lender in taking a new hedging position, closing, settling or unwinding all hedging transactions, deposits or financing transactions that may have been entered into by the Lender in order to provide part of the Loan or to reacquire all negotiable instruments that were issued in connection with the financing of part of the Loan.

48	**Economic failure**	Means any Material Adverse Effect, determined at the sole discretion of the Lender, on the South African or international capital markets or on South African or international monetary, financial, political or economic conditions, which adversely affects the Lender's access to the relevant local or international capital markets or which makes it unlawful or impracticable for the Lender to advance any part of the Principal Amount on any Disbursement Date.
49	**Significant adverse effect**	Means any event or circumstance, or combination of events or circumstances, which, in the reasonable opinion of the Lender, is likely to have a material adverse effect on: (a) the business, prospects, assets or financial condition of the Borrower; (b) the ability of the Borrower or any debtor to perform its obligations under any Transaction Document; (c) the validity, enforceability, effectiveness or priority of any security granted or purported to be granted under any Financing Document; or (d) any right or remedy of the Lender under any Financing Document.
50	**Independent Technical Consultant ("ITC")**	To be appointed at the expense of the Borrower. The scope of the ITA's work includes: (a) formulation (in consultation and agreement with the Borrower and the Lender) of the Project Completion Tests; (b) signing of the Project Completion; (c) monthly monitoring of the Project prior to Project Completion; and (d) annual review of the Project following Project Completion.
51	**Applicable law Jurisdiction**	Law [X] applies to all agreements and local law applies to the Security Documents. The agreements must be executed in English and in the event of any translation, the English version shall prevail. The Borrower submits to the non-exclusive jurisdiction of the *English* courts in respect of the execution of this *term sheet*. Arbitration provisions are to be negotiated and agreed at a later date in respect of the Transaction Documents.

To confirm your agreement with the terms and conditions, please sign and return a copy of this *term sheet*. If it is not signed and returned to the BANK before [XX/XX/XXXX], it will lapse.

Appendix 4

African tour of PPP texts for structuring project finance with the public sector

Algeria

- Executive Decree No. 18-199 of 20 Dhou El Kaâda 1439, corresponding to 2 August 2018, relating to the delegation of public services.
- Presidential Decree No. 15-247 of 2 Dhou Zl Hidja 1436, corresponding to 16 September 2015, regulating public contracts and public service delegations.
- Preliminary draft law on public-private partnerships (PPP) (postponed by Presidency).

Angola

- Law No. 11/2019, of 14 May, approves the Public-Private Partnerships ("PPP Law").
- Presidential Decree 316/19 of 28 October, which approves the Regulation of PPP Law No. 11/2019, of 14 May ("PPP Regulation").
- Executive Decree No. 229/20 of 2 September approving the bylaws and regulations of the Office for Public-Private Partnerships ("PPP Unit Decree").
- Law No. 41/20, of 23 December 2020, which approves the Law of Public Contracts ("PC Law").

Benin

- Law No. 2024-30 of 23 July 2024 on the legal framework for public-private partnership in the Republic of Benin.
- Law No. 2009-02 of 7 August 2009 on the Public Contracts and Public Service Delegations Code.

Botswana

- Public-Private Partnership Policy and Implementation Framework, 2009 (PPPPIF, 2009).
- Public Procurement and Asset Disposal Act, 2001 (PPADB Act).
- Public Procurement and Asset Disposal Regulations, 2006 (PPADB Regulations).

Burkina Faso

- Decree No.° 2024-0980/PRES promulgating Law No. 020-2024/ALT of 2 August 2024 amending the Law No. 032-2021 of 25 June 2021 on the legal and institutional framework for public-private partnerships in Burkina Faso.
- Law No. 005-2024/ALT of 20 April 2024 on the general regulations governing public procurement (the law aims public-private partnerships and public procurement contracts).
- Act No. 020-2013 on the legal regime for public-private partnerships amended by Act No. 042-2017/AN on streamlining procedures for contracting the PPP project programme.
- Decree No. 2008-173 of 16 April 2008, amended in 2012, on the general regulations governing public contracts and public service delegations.

Burundi	– Law No. 1/19 of 19 July 2019 amending Law No. 1/14 of 27 April 2015 on the general regime for public-private partnership contracts. – Law No. 1/04 of 29 January 2018 amending Law No. 1/01 of 4 February 2008 on the Burundi Public Procurement Code (applicable to public service delegations).
Cameroon	– Law No. 2023/008 of 25 July 2023 on the general regime for public-private partnership. – Decree No. 2008/0115/PM of 24 January 2008 specifying the terms of application of Law No. 2006/012 of 29 December 2006 laying down the general rules governing partnership contracts. – Law No. 2008/009 of 16 July 2008 laying down the tax, financial and accounting rules applicable to partnership contracts. – Decree No. 2018/366 of 20 June 2018 on the Public Procurement Code abrogating the Decree No. 2004/275 of 24 September 2004 on the Public Procurement Code, which also deals with public service delegations.
Cape Verde	– Legislative Decree No. 63/2015 of 13 November 2015 (DLPPP), repealing Legislative Decree No. 46/2005 of 4 July 2005.
Central African Republic	– Law No. 19-007 of 24 June 2019 on the legal framework for PPPs in the Central African Republic.
Chad	– Ordinance No. 06/PR/2017 of 30 August 2017 on the legal regime for public-private partnerships in Chad (ordonnance n° 06/PR/2017).
Congo Brazzaville	– Law 88-2022 of 30 December 2022 on PPP contracts.
Democratic Republic of Congo	– Law No. 18/016 of 9 July 2018 on PPPs.
Ivory Coast	Ordinance No. 2019-679 of 24 July 2019 on the Public Procurement Code. – Decree No. 2009-259 (amended in 2014) on the Public Procurement Code (applicable to public-private partnerships). – Decree No. 2018-358 of 29 March 2018 determining the rules governing public-private partnership contracts abrogating the decree. – Decree No. 2018-359 of 29 March 2018 defines the remit, organisation and operation of the National Public-Private Partnership Steering Committee (CNP-PPP). – Decree No. 2012-1152 of 19 December 2012 on the remit, organisation and operation of the institutional framework for steering public-private partnerships. – Decree No. 2014-246 of 8 May 2014 amending Decree No. 2012-1152. – Decree No. 2009-259 (amended in 2014) on the Public Procurement Code (text applicable to public service delegations).
Djibouti	– Law No. 186/AN/17/7e L of 29 May 2017 on public-private partnerships. – Decree No. 2018-178/PR/MEFI implementing Law No. 186/AN/17/7ème L on Public-Private Partnerships and on the organisation and operation of the Public-Private Partnerships Department. – Decree No. 2021-192/PR/MEFI of 3 August 2021 approving the Public-Private Partnership Procedures Manual.

	– Decree No. 2018-174/PR/MEFI amending and supplementing Decree No. 2010-00083/PRE of 8 May 2010 establishing the powers, composition, organisation and operation of the National Public Procurement Commission.
	– Decree No. 2018-175/PR/MEFI implementing Law No. 186/AN/17/7th L on Public-Private Partnerships and setting up the PPP Regulatory Commission.
	– Decree No. 2018-176/PR/MEFI establishing the procedures for awarding a PPP.
Egypt	– PPP Executive Regulations of 2022 amending PPP Executive Regulations of Law No. 67 of 2010.
	– Egypt Public Private Partnership Law 2021, amending Egypt Public-Private Partnership Law No. 67, 2010.
	– Ministerial Decree No. 2735 of 2018 on the Structure and Competence of the PPP Supreme Committee.
Equatorial Guinea	– Public service delegations are governed by the 1965 text on public contracts.
Ethiopia	– Public-Private Partnership Proclamation No. 1076/2018 (Feb. 2018).
Gabon	– Ordinance No. 9/2016 of 11 February 2016 on PPPs in Gabon.
	– Decree No. 000154/PR/MPIPCI of 18 May 2018 setting out the procedures for awarding PPP contracts (Decree 154).
	– Decree No. 000155/PR/MPIPPP of 18 May 2018 on the remit, organisation and operation of the Public-Private Partnership Steering Body.
Gambia	– The National Public-Private Partnership Policy, 2015–2020 (NPPP).
Ghana	– Public-Private Partnership Act (Act 1039) of 29 December 2020.
Guinea	– Law No. 0032/2017/AN of 4 July 2017 on public-private partnerships.
	– Decree D/2021/041/PRG/SGG of 5 February 2021 implementing Law L/2017/032/AN of 4 July 2017 on public-private partnerships.
	– Decree D/2021/042 of 5 February 2021 on the institutional framework for public-private partnership projects
Kenya	
	– The Public Private Partnerships Act No. 14 of 2021 date of Assent 7th December 2021, date of commencement 23 December 20214.
Lesotho	– There is no PPP law in the country.
Liberia	– Public Procurement and Concessions Act, 2005 (PPCA).
	– There is no specific law on PPPs in Liberia.
Libya	– There is no specific law on PPPs in Libya.
Madagascar	– Law 2015-039 of 9 December 2015 on PPPs.
	– Decree No. 2017-150 implementing Law No. 2015-039 of 3 February 2016 on public-private partnerships relating to the institutional framework (JO No. 3752 of 23 May 2017).
	– Decree No. 2017-149 of 2 March 2017 implementing Law No. 2015-39 of 3 February 2016 on public-private partnerships relating to the terms of application of the provisions concerning the award of public-private t partnership contracts.
Malawi	– The Public-Private Partnership Bill, 2010 into 2013.
	– The Public-Private Partnership Policy Framework, 2011.

Mali – Law No. 2016-061 of 30 December 2016 on PPPs.

Morocco – Act No. 46-18 amending and supplementing Act No. 86-12 of 24 December 2014 on PPP contracts, promulgated by Dahir No. 1-20-04 of 6 March 2020.
– Decree No. 2-15-45 of 24 rejeb 1436 (13 May 2015) implementing Act No. 86-12 on public-private partnership contracts.
– Act No. 54-05 on delegated management of public services for local authorities, promulgated by Dahir No. 1-06-15 of 15 Moharrem 1427 (14 February 2006).

Mauritania – Law No. 2024-041 of 30 October 2024 repealing and replacing Law 2017-006 of 1 February 2017, as amended and supplemented, on public-private partnerships.

Mauritius – The Public-Private Partnership Act, 2004 (PPPA) as amended in 2008, 2016 and 2019).
– The Build Operate Transfer Projects Bill, 2016 (BOTPB) (as amended in 2017, 2019, 2020 and 2021).
– The Public-Private Partnership Policy Statement, 2003 (PPPPS).
– The Public Procurement Act (2006) and its PPP Regulations (2008) (PPA and PPPR).

Mozambique – Law 15/2011 of 10 August 2011 on public-private partnerships (LPPP).
– Decree No. 16/2012 of 4 June 2012 on public-private partnerships (DPPP).
– Decree No. 69/2013 of 20 December 2013 regulating public-private partnerships and concessions for small businesses.

Namibia – Public-Private Partnership Act, 2017, Act No. 4 of 2017.

Niger – Law No. 2018-40 of 5 June 2018 governing PPP contracts.
– Decree No. 2013-569/PRN/PM of 20 December 2013 on the Public Procurement and Public Service Delegation Code (applicable to public service delegations).

Nigeria – The National Policy on Public-Private Partnerships 2009 (N4P).
– Lagos State Public-Private Partnership Law of 24 June 2011. Other regional states also have their own PPP laws, including Ekiti and Cross River states.
– The Infrastructure Concession and Regulatory Commission Act, 2005.

Rwanda – Law No. 14/2016 of 2 May 2016 governing PPPs.
– PPP Guidelines, June 2018.

Senegal – Law No. 2021-01 of 22 February 2021 on Public-Private Partnership (PPP) contracts.
– Decree No. 2021-1443 implementing Law No. 2021-23 of 2 March 2021 on public-private partnership contracts.

Sierra Leone – The PPP Act, 2014.
– PPP Policy 2014.

South Africa – The Public Finance Management Act (No. 1, 1999) is the enabling legislation for PPPs.
– The Standardized PPP Provisions, 2004.

Sudan – Public Private Partnership Law No. 10 of 2021.

Tanzania	– The Public-Private Partnership Act (Amended), 14 July 2023. – The Public-Private Partnership Act (Amended), 12 May 2014 (as PPP Act). – The Public-Private Partnership Regulations (Amended), 27 November 2015 (as PPP Regulations). – Public Procurement Act, 2011, as amended in 2014. – National Public-Private Partnership Policy, 2009.
Togo	– Decree No. 2022-065/PR of 11 May 2022 on the procedures for awarding and executing public-private partnership contracts. – Law No. 2021-034 of 31 December 2021 on public-private partnership contracts.
Tunisia	– Decree-Law No. 2022-68 of 19 October 2022, enacting special provisions to improve the efficiency of public and private project implementation. – Presidential Decree No. 2022-451 of 6 May 2022, setting out the organisation and remit of the general public-private partnership body. – Law No. 49-2015 of 27 November 2015 on public-private partnership contracts. – Law No. 2008-23 of 1erApril 2008 on concessions. – Law No. 2021-9 of 1er March 2021, approving Head of Government. – Decree-Law No. 2020-24 of 28 May 2020, setting out specific provisions relating to the extension of concession contracts.
Uganda	– The Public-Private Partnerships Act, 2015. Public Private Partnerships Regulations 2019.
Zambia	– The Public-Private Partnership Act, 2023. N.A.B. No 18 of 2023.
Zimbabwe	– PPP Policy 2010. – Zimbabwe Investment and Development Agency Act [Chapter 14:37] (ZIDA), repealing and replacing the Ventures Act [Chapter 22:22]. – PPP Guidelines dated 2004 are under review by the Government.

Appendix 5

List of the main players in project financing in Africa

The list that follows is indicative and provides an overview of the key players involved in financing infrastructure projects on the African continent.

I. Multilateral development banks and institutions

1. African Development Bank (AfDB)
2. Asian Infrastructure Investment Bank (AIIB)
3. China Construction Bank (CCB)
4. East African Development Bank (EADB)
5. China Development Bank (CDB)
6. Central African Development Bank (BDEAC)
7. European Investment Bank (EIB)
8. Asian Development Bank (ADB)
9. Industrial and Commercial Bank of China (ICBC)
10. Islamic Development Bank (IsDB)
11. World Bank (IBRD, IDA, IFC, MIGA)
12. West African Development Bank (BOAD)
13. Green Climate Fund (GCF)
14. New Development Bank created by Brazil, Russia, India, China and South Africa (NDB)

II. Bilateral development banks and institutions

1. German Agency for International Cooperation (GIZ)
2. Belgian Development Agency (ENABEL)
3. Canadian International Development Agency (CIDA)
4. Danish International Development Agency (DANIDA)
5. Luxembourg Cooperation Agency (LUXDEV)
6. Foreign, Commonwealth and Development Office (FCDO)
7. United States Agency for International Development (USAID)
8. French Development Agency and Proparco (AFD)
9. Japan International Cooperation Agency (JICA)
10. Norwegian Agency for Development Cooperation (NORAD)

11. Swedish International Development Cooperation Agency (SIDA)
12. Swiss Agency for Development and Cooperation (SDC)
13. Austrian Development Bank (OeEB)
14. Development Bank of South Africa (DBSA)
15. Netherlands Development Bank (FMO)
16. British International Investment (BII)

III. Export credit agencies and credit guarantee institutions

1. African Export-Import Bank (AfreximBank)
2. Export-Import Bank of China (CEXIM Bank)
3. French Insurance Company for Foreign Trade (COFACE)
4. Euler Hermes
5. Export Credit Insurance Corporation of South Africa (ECIC)
6. Export Development Canada (EDC)
7. Export Import Bank of the United States (EXIM)
8. Nippon Export and Investment Insurance (NEXI)
9. Trade and Development Bank (TDB)
10. UK Export Finance (UKEF)

IV. Private sector commercial banks

1. Absa Group
2. Afriland First Bank
3. Attijariwafa Bank
4. Banque Centrale Populaire Maroc (BCP)
5. External Bank of Algeria (BEA)
6. Banque Internationale Arabe de Tunisie (BIAT)
7. BMCE Bank of Africa
8. BNP Paribas
9. Citigroup
10. Commercial Bank of Ethiopia
11. Ecobank Transnational Incorporated (ETI)
12. First Bank of Nigeria (FBN)
13. BGFIBank Group
14. Kenya Commercial Bank (KCB)
15. Mauritius Commercial Bank (MCB)
16. Nedbank
17. NSIA Banque
18. Orabank
19. Rand Merchant Bank (RMB)
20. RawBank
21. Société Tunisienne de Banque (STB)
22. Stanbic Bank
23. Standard Chartered
24. United Bank for Africa (UBA)

V. Infrastructure investment fund

1. Actis
2. Africa50
3. Africa Finance Corporation (AFC)
4. Africa Infrastructure Fund (A.P. Moller Capital)
5. African Infrastructure Investment Managers (AIIM)
6. CDC Group
7. Echosys – Afrigreen
8. Emerging Capital Partners (ECP)
9. Canada Investment Fund for Africa (CIFA)
10. African or foreign national pension funds
11. National or foreign sovereign wealth funds
12. Harith General Partner
13. Helios Investment Partners
14. InfraCo Africa
15. Meridiam
16. Old Mutual Investment Group
17. Partech
18. Quantum Global Group
19. Schwab Foundation
20. STOA
21. Transform Health Fund

Index

Note: Index terms refer to the paragraph numbers.

FSC
www.fsc.org
MIX
Papier | Fördert
gute Waldnutzung
FSC® C083411

Kolibri 360 GmbH
Ferdinand-Jühlke-Straße 7
99095 Erfurt, Deutschland
produktsicherheit@kolibri360.de